# Advanced Drama and Theatre Studies

**Second Edition**

CITY OF
LEARNING
CENTRE
SUNDERLAND COLLEGE

Jonothan Neelands
& Warwick Dobson

**HODDER**
EDUCATION
PART OF HACHETTE LIVRE UK

The editors and publishers would like to thank the following for permission to reproduce copyright material:

**Copyright text:**
pp27–29 The Prologue from *Antigone*, from 'The Thebans' translated by Timberlake Wertenbaker, Faber and Faber Ltd; pp56–58 *The Crucible*, Arthur Miller, Methuen; pp75–76, 80–85 *Mother Courage and her Children*, Bertolt Brecht, Methuen; p109 *Yerma* from Lorca – three plays translated by Gwynne Edwards and Peter Luke, Methuen; pp128–129, 133–135, 231 *A Doll's House*, Henrik Ibsen, Methuen; pp148–149 *Hedda Gabler*, Henrik Ibsen, Methuen.

**Photo credits:**
p.3 © photograph by Tass, Camera Press, London; p.5 © Donald Cooper/Photostage; p.7 l-r: © Sheffield Theatres, © Leicester Theatre Trust, © Royal Shakespeare Company; p.9 l-r: © Sheffield Theatres,© Sheffield Theatres Third Angel & Sheffield Theatres' production Parts For Machines That Do Things, Photography: Michael Thorne; p.12 l-r: © TEG Productions Ltd, © Third Angel; p.16 © Donald Cooper/Photostage; p.21 © Stockbyte/Getty Images; p.24 © Donald Cooper/Photostage; p.25 © Buddy Mays/Corbis; p.35 both © Donald Cooper/Photostage; p.41 © Michael Kim/Corbis; p.46 © Paul Almasy/Corbis; p.47 © The Illustrated London News/Mary Evans Picture Library; p.49 © Donald Cooper/Photostage; p.56 © Dennis Clark/Getty Images; p.71 © Robbie Jack/Corbis; p.78 Helene Weigel in 'Mother Courage and Her Children' by Bertolt Brecht. Deutsches Theater 1951. Photograph © Hainer Hill/Bertolt-Brecht-Archiv; p.87 © The Art Archive/Corbis; p.90 © Hulton-Deutsch Collection/Corbis p.92 (top) © Lipnitzki/Roger Viollet/Getty Images (bottom) © Bristol University Theatre Collection; p.95 © Akademie der Kunst, Berlin p.96 © Hulton-Deutsch Collection/Corbis; p.105 © by kind permission of the University of Northumbria; p.165 Bertolt Brecht and others: rehearsals for 'Katzgraben'. Deutsches Theater, Berlin 1953. Photograph © R. Berlau Hoffmann/Bertolt-Brecht-Archiv; p.167 © Nancy Kaszerman/ZUMA/Corbis; p.169 © John Haynes/Lebrecht Music & Arts; p.172 © The Grotowski Institute's Archive, Wroclaw; p.174 © David Glass Ensemble; p.178 DV8 Physical Theatre Enter Achilles, Photgraphy: Peter Jay; p.180 © Sheila Burnett/ARENAPAL/TopFoto; p.184 © Donald Cooper/Photostage; p.190 © Kalpesh Lathigra/Save The Children; p.198 © Corbis; p.233 (top) © Chris Jackson/Getty Images, (bottom) © Photos 12/Alamy; p.244 (top) © National Gallery Collection; by kind permission of the Trustees of the National Gallery, London/Corbis, (bottom) © The Frick Collection, New York; p.246 © Hekimian Julien/Corbis/Sygma

Every effort has been made to trace copyright holders of material reproduced in this book. Any rights not acknowledged here will be acknowledged in subsequent printings if notice is given to the publisher.

Although every effort has been made to ensure that website addresses are correct at time of going to press, Hodder Education cannot be held responsible for the content of any website mentioned in this book. It is sometimes possible to find a relocated web page by typing in the address of the home page for a website in the URL window of your browser.

Hachette Livre UK's policy is to use papers that are natural, renewable and recyclable products and made from wood grown in sustainable forests. The logging and manufacturing processes are expected to conform to the environmental regulations of the country of origin.

Orders: please contact Bookpoint Ltd, 130 Milton Park, Abingdon, Oxon OX14 4SB. Telephone: (44) 01235 827720. Fax: (44) 01235 400454. Lines are open 9.00–5.00, Monday to Saturday, with a 24-hour message answering service. Visit our website at www.hoddereducation.co.uk

© Jonothan Neelands and Warwick Dobson 2000
First published in 2000 by
Hodder Education,
Part of Hachette Livre UK
338 Euston Road
London NW1 3BH

This edition first published 2008.

Impression number    5  4  3  2  1
Year                 2012 2011 2010 2009 2008

Cover photo: A Kneehigh Theatre production of Tristan and Yseult © Steve Tanner
Typeset in Fairfield LH Light 12/14pt by Fakenham Photosetting, Norfolk
Printed in Italy

A catalogue record for this title is available from the British Library

ISBN: 978 0340 972 625

# Contents

We shall make lively use of all means, old and new, tried and untried, deriving from
art and deriving from other sources, in order to put living reality in the hands of
living people in such a way that it can be mastered.

(Bertolt Brecht, 1938)

# Introduction

Welcome to your advanced studies in Drama and Theatre. This book has been specially written for you. It offers a course of study which covers all the aims and objectives for the revised specifications in Drama and Theatre Studies from 2008. The book is a mix of practical and theoretical material which, taken together, will give you a thorough understanding of how drama and theatre work; it will also prepare you for success in your exams – both practical and written.

The book is organised into six sections and ten chapters, which together cover the skills and knowledge you will need to be successful in your studies and practical work.

## Overview

**Section One, The Foundations of Drama and Theatre** serves as an introduction to your subject. In Chapter 1, The Infinite Variety of Theatre, we begin with everyday and technical definitions of drama and theatre. We go on to look at the variety of theatre which is on offer today and then introduce you to the technical terms that you will need to use in your studies. In Chapter 2, The Origins of Drama and Theatre, we look at the roots of the modern art form both in fifth century Athenian culture and also in other forms and traditions of performance. These two chapters provide the foundations for the rest of the book and for your course.

**Section Two, Acting Workshops and Scene Work** gives you practical experience as an actor in two contrasting styles of acting and performance. In Chapter 3, Playing the Given Circumstances, we introduce you to the ideas and rehearsal methods developed by Konstantin Stanislavski, Michel Checkov and Lee Strasberg. These ideas are applied practically to a short scene from Arthur Miller's *The Crucible*. In Chapter 4, Finding the *Verfremdungseffekt*, we offer a contrasting workshop based on the ideas and rehearsal methods of Bertolt Brecht and apply these to scenes from his play *Mother Courage and Her Children*.

**Section Three, The Work of the Director** introduces you to directing and the twentieth century history of great directors. In Chapter 5, The Emergence of the Director, we tell the story of how directors first emerged as the new artist of the theatre in the nineteenth century and introduce you to the ideas of many of the twentieth century's most famous and important directors. In Chapter 6, From Page to Stage, we look at the director's work and the processes that lead from page to stage. This chapter includes a case study of a production of *Yerma* written by a director.

**Section Four, Textual Analysis** offers you strategies for reading plays for performance and a model for analysing play texts. In Chapter 7, Reading for Performance, we identify the strategies that are used to read plays as potential texts for performance rather than as literature; there is a wide range of practical tasks to help you. In Chapter 8, A Director's Model for Textual Analalysis, we provide you with a step-by-step process for analysing play texts from a director's point of view. Finally you will find the first of our three questionnaires – The Textual Analysis Questionnaire – which provides you with a detailed checklist of questions to help in your own analysis of a text. Like the other questionnaires it also draws your attention to the assessment criteria that will be applied to your textual analysis work.

**Section Five, Devising and Analysing Performances** equips you with clear and thorough processes for devising theatre and for the critical analysis of performances you have seen. In Chapter 9, Devising Theatre, we offer you a ten-stage framework that covers everything in the devising process from first ideas through to the evaluation of the performance. The Devising Process Questionnaire is there to help you check what you need to do at each stage and how to match the assessment criteria. In Chapter 10, Reading the Signs of Performance, we introduce you to semiotics and performance theory as a means of helping you to make your analysis and evaluation of performances that you see more thorough and effective. This chapter will also help you to check that your own performances are even more effective! The Performance Analysis Questionnaire will help you organise your responses and note-taking.

**Section Six**, **Resources** provides you with additional resources to assist in your studies and practical work. Appendix 1, the Glossary, gives you explanations and definitions for important practitioners, genres, periods, styles and other specialist terms used in the book. Appendix 2, Theatre timeline, gives you a brief history of European and non-European theatre from 600BC to 1910. This will be a useful reference which will help you see when new ideas were first introduced, what styles of theatre are associated with particular historical periods, and how the history of European theatre compares with the great non-European traditions such as Noh, Kabuki and Kathakali. Where possible web references have been included for further reading.

## How To Read and Use This Book

All names and technical words associated with drama and theatre are in **bold**. Most of these words have an entry in the Glossary/Index so you can look for more information if you need it. The sidebars in the margins of most chapters describe the content in the neighbouring paragraphs.

There are three ways in which we hope that you will find this book useful. In class you will want to use the book for the wealth of practical tasks, exercises and extracts from plays. You may also take the book home and read the theoretical and historical material in preparation for your next class, or to help you in writing assignments, or in your private study of texts. Finally, we believe that this book is an excellent foundation and resource for your future studies, or lifelong interest in theatre. Keep it as a trusted friend that you can refer back to long after your AS and A levels are finished with!

Your teacher will guide your reading of the book. It is not written so that the sections have to be read in order, although we have assumed that you will begin your studies with the first three chapters. Your teacher will know the details of your particular specifications and therefore how best to guide and sequence your reading and practical work. We hope that there will be something new for your teacher in this book as well and that you will enjoy using it together.

## Authors Health Warning!

We have tried in this book to provide you with models and frameworks that you can use in your study and practice of drama and theatre. Often these frameworks suggest categories and labels that you can use to describe the differences between play texts and performances – to distinguish between the genres of Comedy and Tragedy, for instance. Sometimes we break complex processes like devising and textual analysis into easy-to-follow stages. But be warned. The Western theatre tradition observes few rules and those that are made will be broken. Artists have resisted labels and categories and frequently blur the boundaries between style and genres. The models and frameworks we suggest are there to help you organise and make sense of your studies, but nothing is cast in stone!

## Have Fun!

Finally, we wish you every success! Work hard but also enjoy your practical work and studies. We believe that theatre is the most human of all art forms – in studying, making and appreciating theatre we discover more about ourselves, who we are and who we are becoming. Theatre and drama are living art forms, and you will find pleasure and intellectual challenges ahead and will also provide the same for your audiences. In these pages we have shared both our knowledge and also our love and enthusiasm for theatre and drama. We hope that you too will come to love and understand the subject you are about to do and study together.

# 1 The Infinite Variety of Theatre

## According to the Dictionary

We will begin by thinking about what it is that you will be studying as you read and use this book. 'Theatre' and 'drama' – what do we mean when we use these two terms? What do they cover?

When you hear the word 'theatre', what picture comes to mind?

Do you see theatre as a building?

Do you see a 'play' being performed by actors for an audience?

What about 'drama'? Is it the same thing – does it bring the same pictures to your mind?

How are the terms 'drama' and 'theatre' used both in everyday speech and within the world of 'theatre' itself? On pages 2–3 you will find some definitions from the *Oxford English Dictionary*. The tasks below will then help you to begin to define and identify what you will be doing and discovering in the next months.

### Task 1: Working with the definitions

Working from your own experiences of drama and theatre, both in school and out of it, make a list of those definitions which you would say are *accurate* and *relevant* to the study of theatre and drama.

Make an alternative list of definitions that you think are not appropriate to your course of study. For instance, is the definition of theatre as 'a scene or field of action (*the theatre of war*)' relevant? Why is the word 'theatre' used to describe such different places as a building that houses performances, a battlefield and the operating theatre in a hospital? Is it just a coincidence or is there some connection?

Some of these everyday definitions offer a view of drama and theatre as something 'showy', 'overdone' and 'affected'. Why do you think that the terms 'drama' and 'theatre' have become associated with exaggerated and emotional forms of behaviour? Is this a true reflection?

Organise yourselves into **three groups**, with each group taking responsibility for one of the following three tasks, based on three of the given definitions:

1 What is 'effective material for the stage' (**A2(b)**)? What makes 'good theatre'? Brainstorm the kinds of themes or stories which you think make *good* theatre. Choose one, and make three different **still-images** to share with the group, which illustrate different takes on the possible 'drama' of the theme or idea you have selected. If you choose 'love', for instance, the images might include:

- separation and loss;
- a single image that contains different kinds of love;
- a character torn between the love for two people;
- a more abstract picture that captures the opposites of joy and pain in love.

Share the images with the group and talk through the other suggestions that you had.

**2** What kind of events or sets of circumstances (situations) make for exciting and emotional drama (**C3**)? Brainstorm the kinds of situations and events which make for **exciting** and **emotional** drama. These situations might include: having to make a tough choice; being persecuted; mistaken identities; an act of betrayal or conflict. Events might include births, deaths, weddings; historical events; a moment of truth or point of no return; the revealing of a secret or a sudden disaster that will change lives.

Create three very short scenes to illustrate some of your ideas. The scene should do no more than introduce the actors with three or four lines of dialogue to establish what kind of situation, or event, is being represented. For example:

(*Man sits at a table with his head in his hands. Woman enters, looks at him, and begins to clear up the table in front of him:*)

| | |
|---|---|
| *Woman*: | When will we see you again, then? |
| *Man*: | I'm not sure, in a few days. (*Pause*) Perhaps. |
| *Woman*: | Can't I help? |
| *Man*: | Look, I just need some time on my own. |
| *Woman*: | On your own? |
| (*Pause*) | |
| *Man*: | I don't know who to trust any more. |

Share the scenes and the other ideas you had with the group. You might want to see what ideas people have about how to develop one of your scenes into a **plot** or storyline. What might have already happened; what might happen next?

**3** How do we turn an ordinary event, such as a meeting between two friends, into a situation that has a **dramatic quality** for an audience or for a drama workshop (**C4**)? Brainstorm the ways in which an ordinary, everyday event can be made 'dramatic'. What do we **add**, or **take away**, in order to get a dramatic effect? Your ideas might include: tension and conflict; mystery and suspense; a sense of impending doom or surprise; interesting characters; or unusual settings.

Take the meeting between friends and make three short scenes in which you will add different kinds of dramatic quality to the seemingly ordinary meeting. For example:

| | |
|---|---|
| *First Friend*: | I said I would be here to meet you. |
| *Second Friend*: | What do you want? |
| *First Friend*: | C'mon, we can still be friends, can't we? |
| *Second Friend*: | After all this time? (*Pause*) Did you really think we could just carry on as before? |
| *First Friend*: | If I'd known (*tries to touch his friend, then stops*) I would never have asked you in the first place! |

Share the three versions with the group, and ask them to identify what you have added to each to make a different kind of dramatic quality.

**Some definitions**

**A Theatre** (from the Greek *theatron* = to behold):
**1** a) a building or outdoor area for dramatic

# Technical Definitions

Now we will look more closely at how the terms 'drama' and 'theatre' are used both by those working in theatre and drama and also by those who study it and write about it. These are the specialist definitions that you will need to understand and use in your studies.

Historically, 'drama' has often been used to refer to dramatic literature and 'theatre' to refer to the performance of dramatic literature. This

performances, b) a cinema

2 a) the writing and production of plays, b) effective material for the stage (*makes good theatre*)

3 a room or hall for lectures, etc.

4 an operating theatre

5 a scene or field of action (*the theatre of war*)

6 a natural land formation in a gradually rising part-circle like ancient Greek and Roman theatres

**B Theatrical:**

1 of or for the theatre; of acting or actors

2 (of a manner, speech, gesture, or person) calculated for effect; showy, artificial, affected

**C Drama** (from the Greek *drao* = to do):

1 a play for acting on stage or for broadcasting

2 the art of writing and presenting plays

3 an exciting or emotional event, set of circumstances, etc.

4 a dramatic quality (*the drama of the situation*)

**D Dramatic:**

1 of drama or the study of drama

2 (of an event, circumstance, etc.) sudden and exciting or unexpected

3 vividly striking

4 theatrical, overdone, absurd

distinction tells us something about the particular history of Western theatre, which has developed as a 'literary' art as well as a performance art.

Since the time of the great tragedians in fifth-century Athens, the playwright has tended to dominate the development of the Western tradition of theatre. It is only in recent times that 'theatre' – the 'performance' and the 'performers' – has become a field of serious study. Even now we tend to tell the story of theatre in terms of the succession of playwrights who have shaped the development of the art form. Many students in school today still study 'drama' as part of their study of English literature rather than doing 'drama' – looking at how to produce and understand performances.

The 'play' (as a written text) remains, whereas the performance (the live experience) only exists in the moment of performance. The 'play' as literature can be read and reread as well as performed, so it provides a more permanent record for future generations. The plays of *Shakespeare* have been in print since 1623 and generations of scholars have pored over his words and discussed his importance as a 'dramatist'.

**The dominance of the playwright in the history of theatre is also a result of the historical relationship between the different producers of drama and theatre.** The first Greek playwrights were referred to as 'teachers' rather than as 'writers'. Their job was to 'teach' the chorus and actors how to perform by providing a *narrative*, speeches and directions for the actors to follow. This was the beginning of a tradition in which the playwright was established as the true 'author' of both the play and the performance; actors merely served the playwright and were of little importance. Indeed, actors were often seen as having the same social status as tinkers and beggars.

Konstantin Stanislavski

As we shall see in Chapter 7, it was only in the nineteenth century that 'directors' began to be identified as playing a part in the 'authorship' of a performance, and in modern times the director, rather than the playwright, is often seen as being the most important 'author' or *auteur* of the performance itself.

## Task 2: Who is involved?

As we have seen, the playwright has traditionally been given the highest status in Western theatre. But what about the other people involved in the creation of a performance? Theatre is unique in the sense that it is the collective achievement of a group of people who perform different kinds of roles in the production process. Once the play is written, who else gets involved? Make a list of the kinds of work or contribution that the following roles make to the creation of a theatre performance:

| Role | Contribution |
| --- | --- |
| Director<br>Actor<br>Designer<br>Stage manager<br>Choreographer<br>Lighting/Sound technician<br>Audience | |

Which of these roles do you and the rest of your group have some experience of?

Are some roles more 'vital' than others? Do you need a designer, for instance?

Which is your favourite/least favourite role? Do you prefer directing to acting, for instance?

# The Play Text and the Performance Text

The importance of the director has increasingly led to the idea that there are two kinds of text in performance: the play text and the performance text. The **play text** refers to the original play, or other written score, produced by a writer or by a devising group. The **performance text** refers to what is done with the play text by the performers in performance. Sometimes the performance text will try to represent faithfully the playwright's ideas and intentions, and sometimes a performance text will tell us more about the director's, designer's and actors' views, intentions and ideas than those of the playwright. This modern tradition of directing has been closely influenced by the rise of the status of the director in film: we speak of who directs and stars in a film rather than who wrote the screenplay. In the modern theatre the performance text may not be based on a play text at all – it may be a devised performance or an adaptation of non-dramatic literature.

**An interest in actors and what actors bring to the performance text is also a modern idea** that belongs to the same historical period as the rise of the director. Remember that acting was once considered to be a very lowly

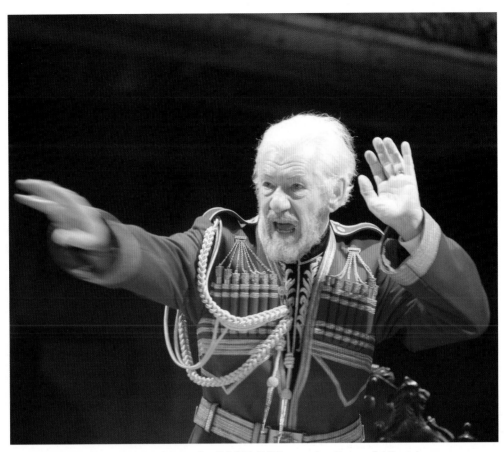

Ian McKellen in Trevor Nunn's 2007 RSC production of *King Lear*

and dubious occupation. The first actors in fifth-century Athens were called *hypocrites*, meaning 'answerers' or 'interpreters', from which we get the word 'hypocrite', used to describe someone who is false or duplicitous. In the early days of the travelling theatre companies in America, actors were buried at the crossroads with a stake in their hearts. **Molière** was the first French actor to be buried in consecrated ground in 1673, and the first actor to be knighted was Henry **Irving** in 1895. It is only since the beginning of the twentieth century that the actor has been seen as a professional artist with a similar social status to writers, painters and others. The model for **Stanislavski**'s system of actor training was based on the performances of a serf-actor (a feudal slave) called Mikhail **Shchepkin**.

In our own time, partly because of film, we are more conscious of the actor as the creator of the performance. We go to the theatre and watch films because of who the actors are as much as because of who has written or directed the piece. We also expect more of our actors in the modern age. They are not just the mouthpieces for the playwright's words, or puppets to be controlled by the director.

Actors are often referred to as 'performers', in recognition of the wide range of skills that they need in the modern theatre: singing, dancing, acrobatics and musicianship. Actor training, acting styles and increasingly **physical** forms of performance have become more and more central to our understanding and appreciation of theatre.

It is important to remember that we have, so far, been talking of the Western tradition of theatre. **There are other great performance traditions in other cultures which have not developed as 'literary' arts.** These are not based on the written score of a playwright but on genres and styles of performance. The performer, and performer training, are at the heart of these traditions and the first analyses and training manuals for performers were produced in India and Japan: the *Natyasatra* in India in the first century BC and the writings on **Noh** performance written by *Zeami* in fifteenth-century Japan. The performer-centred traditions of India (*Kuttiyattam* and *Kathakali*; of Bali (Gumbuh and Topeng); and of Japan (*Noh* and *Kabuki*) are all living traditions of theatre that place the performer rather than the playwright at the heart of theatre. In the European tradition of *Commedia dell'Arte*, the actors improvise their performances based on *stock characters* and situations and their own *lazzi*, or stage tricks, of great physical dexterity.

It is no longer customary to accept that drama refers to dramatic literature and theatre to performance. We know now that we cannot understand a play text without thinking about how it will be performed and that the performance of a play cannot be separated from a consideration of the structure and conventions of the play text. The emergence of new and distinctive forms of drama since the invention of film and TV has also led to new meanings for the term 'drama'. **It has become more usual to use the term 'drama' as a generic or umbrella term to cover all that is associated with the making, performing and responding to performance, whether it is live or recorded on film or TV.**

Drama is the big heading which includes a wide variety of subheadings, which in turn include not just dramatic literature, but drama on TV and film, dramatic events in the news and in our lives, live theatre and all that is associated with the training, preparation and working practices of those involved in the making and performing of enacted fictions. This broad definition of drama will include the dramas that you will be used to from your first years at secondary school and the kinds of exploratory drama work that you will have experienced at GSCE level and which you will continue to enjoy in your AS and A level study of the subject.

Theatre, on the other hand, is now often seen as one of the **subheadings of drama. It is used to refer to the live performance of a drama, which is shared with an audience.** In this usage, the term 'theatre' is used to make a distinction between recorded performances on film and TV and the immediate experience of live performance. It may also refer to anything to do with the preparation for a live theatre experience or performance; this would include rehearsals rather than workshops; research into character and period, and so on.

# The Role of Theatre Buildings in the Twenty-First Century

## Three theatres waiting

So far we have talked about 'theatre' as an idea and as a set of artistic practices, but of course the word 'theatre' also refers to buildings which are designed to house theatre events and performances of all kinds. **Sometimes theatres are homes for companies or *ensembles* of actors who produce** their work there. These theatres are called *producing houses*. Sometimes an *ensemble* will be hired on long-term contracts, which allows for strong working relationships to develop, so resulting in a much more fluid and interactive performance style. The ***Royal Shakespeare Company*** is an example of an *ensemble* and employs artists on two- and three-year contracts. Otherwise, producing houses may have a permanent *artistic director*, but will hire actors for a season or even for a particular show.

If there are no actors or other artists working permanently in the theatre, it is called a *receiving house*, because it will be a venue for touring work that will be shown around the country in different venues. Sometimes a *producing house* will develop work with a view also to touring it, to make the costs of production more economical.

We want to begin by looking closely at three new theatre-building projects of the twenty-first century. At the time of writing these new buildings are all in construction. **Of course, theatre can happen anywhere, but the English tradition of theatre-making which is at the heart of this book, is closely tied to the urban and building-based growth of theatre from *Shakespeare*'s time to our own.** What do the plans for these new theatres tell us about the future of the art form and its relationship to society in the twenty-first century?

Look closely at the three artists' impressions of the new buildings that will become the renovated ***Crucible*** in Sheffield, the ***Curve*** in Leicester and the new ***Royal Shakespeare Theatre*** (*RST*) at Stratford-upon-Avon. Notice how all three images stress the relationship of the building to its immediate

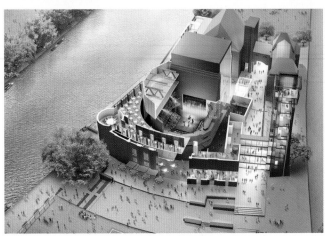

l-r: The Crucible, Sheffield; The Curve, Leicester; Royal Shakespeare Theatre, Stratford-Upon-Avon urban landscape, and how each building seeks to reach out to its public through the creation of large open spaces for the public to meet and gather. The *Crucible* image shows the open public space which includes the old *Lyceum Theatre* and adjoining bars and restaurants to the left. The new *Curve* in Leicester is turned 'inside out', so that all the working spaces of the theatre – administration, design and set-building spaces, conference rooms and even the stage itself – are all made visible to the passing public through the glass exterior walls. The *RST* image emphasises new public spaces for eating, meeting, passing through, and the aerial perspective emphasises the building as a part of the wider Stratford landscape.

At the heart of each theatre are its performance spaces. **The *Crucible* and the *RST* will both have a *thrust stage* layout and this decision reflects contemporary and future-oriented ideas about the best layout for presenting the theatre of a new century.** The *Lyceum Theatre* in Sheffield was designed by the famous theatre architect W.G.R. Sprague and is the only remaining theatre of his outside London. It has the ***proscenium*** (arch) ***stage*** layout, and balconies and boxes, which were fashionable at the time. The original *Crucible*, built as a *producing house* in 1971, was hailed as England's 'first modern theatre' and used a *thrust stage* to create an intimacy between the stage and the audience, with no audience member being more than 22 metres from the stage. The new *RST* stage is modelled on the temporary *Courtyard Theatre* at Stratford and seeks to bring a more intimate and shared audience experience. **The *RST* auditorium is also designed and lit so that the audience is made aware of itself and able to see each other even during performance.** The *Curve* is designed to be a *receiving house* and as flexible and transparent as possible for a wide range of performances, art forms and cultural traditions. There is a central stage layout which can be exposed to the public through the glass façade and either divided to create two auditoria or used as one large performance space. This emphasis in the design of the building and stage on diversity and visibility is important, as Leicester will become the first 'super-diverse' city in the UK, with no single ethnic group having a majority in the city by 2010. There is a rich tradition of Southeast Asian arts in Leicester, which the new building seeks to embrace and celebrate. The publicity for the new theatre explains that 'Leicester needed its new performing arts centre to become a landmark, symbolising the city's renaissance and reflecting its position as a centre for the cultural industries in the East Midlands. An inspirational building was needed – and a renowned international architect rose to the challenge.'

## Back to the Future

Although these are three very modern buildings which seek to capture an accessible and inclusive vision of theatre in the twenty-first century, they also reflect some important historical ideas about theatre buildings. We have already mentioned the important links between theatre and city life, and this is a relationship which (as we will see in Chapter 2), goes back to fifth-century-BC Athens. In this classical tradition, theatres have often been seen as important architectural achievements as well as housing the great arts of **theatre, dance, opera and music**. Think of the *Sydney Opera House*, for instance, designed by Jørn Utzon and first opened in 1973. This building

### Task 3: Theatre design

1 The **semiotics** (message) of the design of the three new theatres all stress public access and inclusion of a wide range of potential audiences. How else do these theatres work towards a more accessible and inclusive theatre? Look at their websites and see what else is going on in terms of:

- the use of space in each building; different performance spaces as well as other public spaces like galleries and restaurants;
- education and outreach work, including youth theatres;
- access and inclusion for disabled and other minority groups both in terms of the buildings and also plans for performance and workshops;
- programming for different audiences, including the elderly and children;
- the range of genres of performance from popular to more demanding and challenging plays.

2 Discuss how a *thrust stage* affects the relationship between performers and audiences and how this in turn would shape directorial decisions, including set design. Look at pictures of the three auditoria that make up the Sheffield Theatres: the *thrust stage* in the *Crucible*, the traditional *proscenium (arch) stage* in the old *Lyceum Theatre* and the *black box* of the *Crucible Studio*. Discuss how each of these spaces would alter and affect the style and direction of performances taking place in them. What kinds of theatre **styles** and **genres** do you think are most appropriate to each of the spaces?

Try working on a simple scene as if it was going to be performed in each of the spaces. How will it be done differently in terms of acting, design, entrances and exits and proximity to the audience?

3 What messages about theatre in the twenty-first century do these buildings represent? What role do these theatres want to play in our lives? How can theatres become more actively involved in the public life of their communities?

top: Thrust stage at the Crucible; l–r: proscenium stage at the Lyceum Theatre; the black box of the Crucible Studio was groundbreaking in terms of its construction that almost seems to defy nature, and in so doing projects an image of a city and society that sees itself as modern, risk-taking, aspirational and creative.

The *Curve* in Leicester is designed by the internationally renowned architect Rafael Vinoly, who has also designed the Brooklyn Children's Museum and the new John F. Kennedy Center for the Arts in Washington, DC. The original *Shakespeare Memorial Theatre*, which is being replaced by the *RST*, was built in 1929 and seen as a breathtaking sign of the spirit of the new twentieth century. The architect was a young woman called Elizabeth Scott and this was the first major public building in England to be designed by a woman – again, this was in keeping with the modernist spirit of the times. The original stage was a *proscenium arch*, which reflected the contemporary dominance of *realist* and *naturalist* styles of theatre-making and a more formal *fourth wall* or *representational* relationship between the performance and the audience.

The original *Crucible* was built in 1971 and was hailed as the 'first modern theatre' in England. Its earliest productions were often raw, working-class dramas, which reflected a new age of writing and performance styles associated with the cultural revolutions of the 1960s. A number of important directors began their careers at the *Crucible*, including Michael **Boyd**, now artistic director of the *RSC*; Stephen **Daldry**, perhaps best known for the film and musical *Billy Elliot*, and David **Leland**. The designer of the *Crucible* was a well-known **avant-garde** set and theatrical designer called

## Task 4: Designing a theatre

1. Using web-based resources and visits where possible, compare two theatres, one of which could be your own local theatre. We have provided these questions to guide your enquiry:

   - When was the building built?
   - Is it a *producing* or *receiving house*, or a combination of both?
   - If it is a *receiving house*, who is the artistic director and what is their career history to date?
   - What is the external and internal appearance, and what messages do these give about the role or image of the theatre?
   - What are the different public spaces and what are they most commonly used for?
   - What is programmed for each of these spaces in the next six months?
   - What is the range of art forms represented in the programming?
   - What can you find out about the production history of shows in the programme?
   - What are the different audiences that the programming is designed to appeal to?
   - What other non-peformance events go on – education, films, youth theatres, discussion groups, etc.?
   - How have recent productions been reviewed in the local/national press?

2. Looking ahead, what do you think the future of theatre should be? How can it best capture the spirit of the times and engage the full range of society in all its diversity? How should theatre buildings be designed to provide different experiences for different audiences? What should be the programming policy for a theatre of the future – what different kinds of performance work will be shown?

   Use these discussions to inform the exercise, which is to enter a competition for designing a new theatre in a city or town location of your choice. In groups, work towards presenting sketches and models of either the building or/and the auditoria to a competition panel. You should know something about the location or be prepared to research it, so that your project is both future-orientated but also working to provide for its community's local needs. In addition to your designs, you will also be asked to identify an opening performance season.

Tanya *Moiseiwitsch*. She insisted on the then radical design of the *thrust stage* and octagonal auditorium because of what she had learned from her working partnership with Sir Tyrone *Guthrie*. **The concept of the *thrust stage* was championed by *Guthrie*, who argued that a stage layout that incorporated and engaged audiences was better placed to challenge the influx of cinema and television.** *Guthrie* first experimented with the idea at the Edinburgh Festival back in 1948 and later designed the *Stratford Festival Theatre* in Stratford, Ontario in Canada, which was based on the original *Globe Theatre* in London.

It is ironic that these new theatres of the twenty-first century, which seek to reach out and engage with modern audiences in all their diversity and also to offer a shared experience of drama that is beyond film and TV, should choose one of the oldest stage layouts – that of *Shakespeare*'s own sixteenth-century theatre, the *Globe*.

## What's On?

Even if we limit the usage of 'theatre' to the live performance of drama, we must still recognise that there are many different forms of theatre available to us. Take a look at the 'what's on' section of a national newspaper such as the *Guardian* or a regional newspaper that covers a large urban area. What is advertised: *musicals*, revivals, *comedies*, thrillers, *pantomimes*? The variety of theatre that you will find is often classified, or categorised, in order to make distinctions between the different forms it takes. This classification is often made clear in the publicity for a show, so that the publicists can target the audience they think will most enjoy the performance.

What follows is a description of two different shows from the spring 2008 programme at the Sheffield Theatres. *Blonde Bombshells of 1943* is a musical adaptation of a TV film by Alan *Plater* and is programmed for the *Lyceum*, which as we have seen is a large Victorian theatre built for *pantomimes* and *music hall* with a *proscenium* (arch) *stage*. The publicity for the show reads: 'Sparkling musical comedy that goes with a swing!' *Parts for Machines That Do Things* is a devised piece by the Sheffield-based company *Third Angel*, whose work is sometimes compared to the *physical theatre* and *performance art* work of companies such as *DV8*, *Forced Entertainment* and *Frantic Assembly*. This work is programmed for the *black box* layout of the *Crucible Studio*.

There is a simple chart on pages 12–13 to help you to distinguish between these two shows or any other that you might find in the programmes for regional theatres like the Sheffield Theatres.

*Blonde Bombshells* theatre poster

*Parts for Machines That Do Things* theatre poster

| Who is producing the entertainment for whom? | | Distinction can be made between: |
|---|---|---|
| **BB1943**<br>• Professional touring, managed and developed at *West Yorkshire Playhouse*, *Hampstead Theatre*, and *Octagon*, Bolton.<br>• No well-known stars.<br>• 15-month tour in 30 large venues. | **PFMTDT**<br>• Local devising company with a national reputation.<br>• Reputation for *avant-garde* performance blurring boundaries between art/media/performance.<br>• *Crucible* has tradition for locally produced and written plays with a hard edge. | • amateur/professional<br>• local/national/touring companies<br>• adult/family/youth/children's theatre.<br>They might be further reinforced by different venues:<br>• *National Theatre* (*RNT*, *RSC*)<br>• repertory/West End<br>• civic/arts centre/community/ environmental (outdoor, museums, streets, etc.). |
| **What genre, or type, is it?** | | **Distinction can be made between:** |
| **Musical** | ***Physical Theatre*/Performance Art** | ***Musical, pantomime, mime, tragedy, comedy,** adaptation, revival, classic, **physical theatre.*** |

| How 'arty' or 'commercial' is it? | | Distinction can be made between: |
|---|---|---|
| This was originally produced as a TV film with screenplay by Alan Plater and starring Judi Dench. Musicals tend to be more commercial and appeal to a broader audience. Some may have already seen the TV version and come for that reason. | The Third Angel website reveals that the company is a partnership between two performance artists. The website is consciously intellectual and their work is designed to appeal to an audience looking for new and *avant-garde* performance styles. The audience is likely to include students of theatre and other intellectual groups and the show is unlikely to appeal to a wider audience because of its artistic conventions. | Experimental/*avant-garde*, which seeks the **cutting edge** or outer limits of what can be done in theatre; it will go against popular and accepted tastes in theatre.<br><br>Mainstream, which is produced by critically acclaimed 'serious' actors, directors and companies and is often based on the performance ideas introduced by earlier *avant-garde* movements: the *Royal Shakespeare Company* and the *Royal National Theatre,* for instance. These companies depend on government subsidies.<br><br>Commercial which often stresses its 'light' entertainment and enjoyment value; it seeks to be accessible and pleasurable to a broad audience. It also seeks to be profitable. |
| **What period or style does it represent?** | | **Distinction can be made between:** |
| The musical is advertised as being in a 1940s style, and seeks to capture the era of Big Bands and Swing which were popular at the time. The style is likely to include some melodramatic scenes, big dance routines and set piece songs. | This is a self-consciously modern piece of devised theatre which advertises itself as being experimental and blurring boundaries between genres including media, *physical theatre*, slapstick. | The periods of theatre associated with the playwright or the artistic and historical influences on the first performance (e.g. **Naturalism**, **Symbolism**, Expressionism, **Epic**, Theatre of the Absurd).<br><br>The historical period associated with the work (e.g. Classical, Medieval, Renaissance, **Restoration**, Modernist, Post-Modernist). |
| **What is the potential audience?** | | **Distinction can be made between:** |
| A broad range which might include older people who remember the Swing era, lovers of *musicals*, families, and others who are infrequent theatre goers lured by the success of the original TV film. | Artists, students, intellectuals, A level theatre students. These are all groups who are likely to have trained or been educated to understand and appreciate the experimental nature of the piece. It is unlikely to appeal to a wider audience which does not have this prior knowledge of *avant-garde* theatre. | • age group, e.g. young people<br>• cultural and social background, e.g. local, minority, social class<br>• levels and focus of education, e.g. students of theatre<br>• regular/infrequent theatre-goers<br>• tastes and preferences, e.g. conventional or experimental, musicals, text-based. |

These distinctions help us to identify the expectations that we might have of the two different performances.

If you have already decided to go to a performance, but haven't yet decided what to see, you may find yourself going through websites, looking for a play that is:

- From a particular historical **period** – Elizabethan or contemporary, for instance.
- Representative of a particular **genre** – *comedy*, *farce*, *musical* or *whodunnit*, for instance. When we choose a genre such as *comedy* we expect the performance to share certain characteristics with other examples of *comedies*. Genres change over time (new characteristics are added, and old ones discarded) so we also combine **period** and **genre** when we speak of Greek *tragedy* as opposed to Elizabethan and Jacobean *tragedy*.
- Performed or written in a particular **style** – a distinctive style of playwriting associated with a particular playwright or a group of playwrights from the same period, or a performance style such as *physical theatre*. But 'style' may also be used more loosely to refer to the most obvious characteristic of a play or performance, which might be original or might be borrowed – a performance of *Grease* that calls for a '1950s' style, for instance.

In this process of identifying similarities and differences between plays and performances, 'period' refers to a historical epoch; 'genre' refers to the general category of theatrical form and 'style' to the particular work or particular performance. Plays of a particular period may be in different genres (*Shakespeare* wrote *comedies*, *tragedies* and histories) and have quite distinctive styles (*Shakespeare's tragedies* were written in the same period as Christopher **Marlowe**'s but they have a very different style to them).

Period, genre and style can be used to distinguish works in other art forms, too. A song like Amy Winehouse's 'Back to Black' has its own distinctive style but it is also retrospective of the music of the 1960s in terms of period, a 'ballad' in terms of genre and associated with the style of the Phil Spector 'Wall of Sound' made popular by girl groups like the Shangri-Las and the Supremes. Dance music is a style which is sometimes divided into periods like '1970s disco' and is also divided into genres like 'house', 'garage', 'trance', 'hip-hop' and 'hardcore gabber'.

# Conventions are the Key!

At the heart of these categories of period, genre and style is the idea of conventions: the tricks, devices, techniques and formal elements used to communicate the performance's intentions to an audience. **Conventions in drama and theatre refer to the 'means' used to make particular kinds of 'meanings' for an audience.**

The conventions of the performance are a kind of agreement between the performers and the audience about the possibilities of dramatic representation. It is because of convention that we accept a *soliloquy*; in reality we tend not to speak our innermost secrets out loud to a large crowd – but in the theatre we accept the convention because it is a device for communicating the character's inner speech. We want to know what the character thinks so we accept the convention of the *soliloquy*.

**Task 5: What's on?**

Use the entertainment section of a national or regional newspaper, or websites. Make a grid to analyse these productions with the following headings:

| Production | Venue | Period | Audience appeal | Genre/ Style | Other features |
|---|---|---|---|---|---|
| Title: (Author:) Company: | | | | | |
| Title: (Author:) Company: | | | | | |
| Title: (Author:) Company: | | | | | |
| Title: (Author:) Company: | | | | | |
| Title: (Author:) Company: | | | | | |

As an extension activity, you could also look up any reviews of these productions to see if they give further clues as to the nature of the performances. The review might be in the same edition of the newspaper. Most national daily and weekend newspapers have a website that will give you access to the reviews section.

There is a 'convention' or agreement that the plays of *Shakespeare* can be set in other times and places. We know that the plays were written for an Elizabethan audience but we accept modern-day dress as a commentary on *Shakespeare*'s ideas, which a director thinks is relevant to understanding the play.

You may be familiar with the idea of 'conventions' from your GCSE Drama work: *tableau*, **thought-tracking**, **soundscape** and **role-on-the-wall** are common examples of the 'conventions' used in classroom drama. They are the 'means' used to represent the meanings that are explored and communicated in the drama.

# The 'Means' and 'Meanings' of Theatrical Communication

The 'conventions' of a drama may be just that – conventional, familiar and well-known means of communicating, such as the *soliloquy* – or they may be

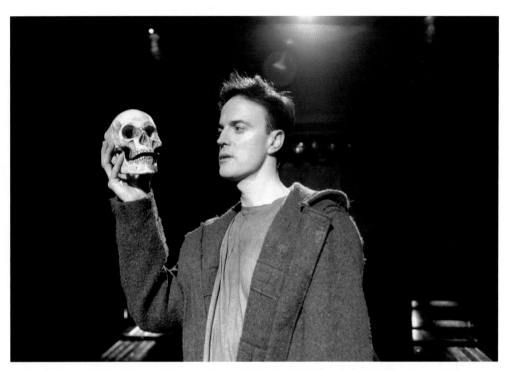

Paul Rhys as Hamlet in modern dress at the Young Vic Theatre, 1999

quite new and radical inventions by the artist who is trying to find new means of communicating.

Many of the playwrights and practitioners you will meet in your study of theatre are remembered because they introduced new conventions into drama and theatre. It is always important to remember that in their time these artists were radical and revolutionary in their practice – they changed the way that people saw and understood themselves by developing new 'means' for representing the human condition on stage.

In your studies of drama and theatre you will often be asked to recognise the 'conventions' used by a playwright or in a performance, and to suggest which period, genre or style they are associated with. At its most simple you are being asked to identify the 'means' that are used to make 'meanings' for an audience. The 'means' of masks produce different kinds of meanings from the 'means' of song, dance or narration.

Conventions may refer to the 'means' of:

- characterisation and speech
- staging
- design
- actor–audience interactions
- structuring the play text or dramatic narrative
- acting style.

When we group two or more pieces of work together and say that they are representative of a period, genre or style, we are saying that these works share **the same, or similar, conventions**.

So, we can talk about the typical conventions of a **period** such as the Jacobean theatre by looking to see what new conventions were invented

## Task 6: Thinking about conventions

Here are four popular conventions that you will be used to from your experiences of drama in school. In order to make the convention work, what do the actors need to do and what do the audience need to understand? Follow the example that is given and fill in the columns for the three other conventions. (If a convention is unfamiliar, choose another that you do know.)

| Convention | Actors | Audience |
|---|---|---|
| Role-play | Actors must improvise the words and behaviour of the roles according to the given circumstances of the situation. They cannot drop in and out of role in order to plan or discuss what's happening. | This is an unrehearsed attempt to respond to the given situation and roles. The actors are not playing fully developed characters and it is what is said and done that is important, not the quality of the acting. The audience understands that the actors are 'in role' rather than speaking as themselves. |
| Teacher-in-role | | |
| Still-images | | |
| Thought-tracking | | |

during this historical period and used by a number of artists of the time. However, the story of the theatre is not to be found in the conventional or mainstream theatre of a period but in the struggle between periods. At those times in history, some artists began to break with the conventions of their time and to invent new ones, thus laying the ground for the next period of theatre in which their new conventions will become the 'conventional' theatre of the next generation.

In the early nineteenth century, for instance, a number of playwrights reacted against the conventions of *romanticism* by abandoning verse, introducing ordinary rather than aristocratic heroic characters, and using realistic settings. By the end of the century this *realist* revolution would become the next conventional theatre and a new group of *symbolist* artists would abandon the conventions of *realism* and introduce more abstract and theatrical conventions. At the time of their first introduction, the conventions of *realism*, which we are now so used to, were considered shocking, strange and radical by audiences.

When considering the conventions of a period, then, we need to look at the 'conventional' theatre of the time and also at what was happening in the *avant-garde* theatre. The 'avant-garde' is the term used to describe the experimental, progressive and alternative theatre of a period, which seeks to break new ground and to turn against the 'conventional' – the safe, the commercial. As we have seen, the more 'conventional' *Last of the Blonde Bombshells* is programmed against the more *avant-garde Parts for Machines That Do Things* in the Sheffield Theatres spring 2008 season, and the two shows may attract very different audiences depending on what people are looking for – the conventional or the new.

We can talk about the conventions of a particular **genre** of theatre such as *tragedy* by looking at the conventions of play structure, characterisation and plot that are associated with that genre. When we speak of a genre like *tragedy*, we may also focus on how the genre has changed and developed over time because artists have introduced new conventions into the genre.

We can see, for instance, that there are differences between the conventions of the classical Greek *tragedy* and those used by *Shakespeare*. *Shakespeare* introduced comic characters and scenes into his *tragedies* and ignored the classical unities of time, place and action (see page 23). Although they come from different periods and use some different conventions, we can say that *Antigone* and *Hamlet* both belong to the genre of *tragedy* because they share a common set of conventions that have become associated with that genre. Both plays have an aristocratic main character, both have unhappy endings that result from some decision or choice taken by the main character, and the mood of both is predominantly despondent and sad.

The relationship of convention to **style** is not quite as straightforward. When style refers to a practitioner, as in **Brechtian**, we mean that a performance uses conventions first associated with *Brecht*'s work. The performance may include storytelling and song, for instance, or the structure of the play may be episodic. *Brecht* developed the genre of *epic theatre*, which has a particular set of conventions, but another practitioner may use some (but not *all*) of the conventions of *epic* in order to give a performance a *Brechtian* style. The conventions of a style can be combined with the conventions of a genre. Hence, *Macbeth* can and has been played in a number of different styles, including those of gangster and Samurai warrior films.

Style may also refer to design references to a particular historical period, as in the *Grease* example we gave earlier. A play may be given a 1960s style or a 'Victorian' style. *The Last of the Blonde Bombshells* has a 1940s style.

Style may also refer to the conventions associated with a particular performance tradition; Joan **Littlewood** and Theatre Workshop used the conventions of the Victorian music hall to give a style to her treatment of World War I in *Oh! What a Lovely War*. One aspect of Peter *Brook*'s characteristic and eclectic style is his use of conventions from Indian, Japanese and Chinese performance traditions.

When we talk of the characteristic style of a practitioner or company, we recognise that they will use certain kinds of convention regardless of the period or genre of performance that the company or practitioner is working with. *Brecht* applied the conventions of *epic* to his productions of musicals and *Shakespeare*'s plays. Companies like the *Royal Shakespeare Company* tend to have a 'house' style, which is recognisable in quite different performances. Companies like the masked group *Trestle*, the physical theatre group *Complicité* (formerly known as the *Théâtre de Complicité*) and the storytelling theatres of *Shared Experience* and *Kneehigh* have a house style; whatever the period or genre, we expect these companies to give a certain characteristic style to their work.

**Task 7: Make your own definitions**

Before moving on, you need to make sure that you are clear about the terms '**convention**', '**period**', '**genre**' and '**style**'.

- Write your own definitions based on the notes we have given you, and use them to guide you in the future. If you are unsure of your definitions, check them out with the group.

- Apply your definitions to a genre or style of music that you like. Can you find examples of period, style and genre in your collection?

# Causing a Riot!

In your own practical work you will make decisions about the conventions, or 'means', that will best express and communicate your intentions to an audience. You may well want to try and develop new 'conventions', either because you want your work to be original and different or because you are dissatisfied with the 'conventional' means of communicating in theatre. If this is the case, you are part of a long line of artists who have sought to change the theatre of their time by introducing new conventions. But, be warned – a new convention has to be accepted by the audience! If it's too far beyond what they are capable of accepting, there will be trouble. Here are some examples of artists and performances that introduced conventions that the audience was not ready for!

In 1907, Sean O'Casey's *The Playboy of the Western World* caused real riots when it was first shown at the **Abbey Theatre** in Dublin, because it was taken as an attack on the hypocrisy of Irish morality. Similarly, in 2004 there was a riot outside the *Birmingham Rep*, which forced the closure of *Behzti*, a play written by the young Sikh writer Gurpreet Kaur Bhatti, because the local Sikh community were outraged by her critique of religious hypocrisy.

In 1912, Igor Stravinsky used a new and radical twelve-tone scale in the music for *The Rite of Spring*. There was a riot on the first night, which prevented the piece being finished.

In 1922, the dancer Isadora **Duncan** finished a performance in New York by baring her breast and waving a red scarf. This also resulted in a riot!

In 1935, Antonin **Artaud** staged his version of *The Cenci* with animal movements, noises and graphic scenes of violence – once again, there was a riot!

In 1965, Bob Dylan performed a concert of folk songs at the Albert Hall in London. The first half was a conventional set played solo and acoustically. After the interval, Dylan returned in a black suit and dark glasses, carrying an electric guitar and fronting a five-piece band. Some of the audience, who had enthusiastically applauded the first half, began to shout 'Judas' at Dylan as he began his electric set.

In 2005, the Northern Irish protestant playwright Gary Mitchell was forced into exile after his home was firebombed by loyalist paramilitaries, and is still living in hiding. His *comedies* were too close to the bone for some members of his community.

In 2007, *Kneehigh* performed an adaptation of *Shakespeare's Cymbeline* as part of the *RSC's* Complete Works at the Swan Theatre. They used *mime, clowning*, pop songs and street performance techniques in their reworking of the original text. Some audience members, who were expecting a more 'conventional' performance, left in noisy disgust and demanded refunds.

# The Cooking Pot that is Theatre

**Most modern performances will consist of a mix of styles – a cocktail of conventions associated with different periods, genres and practitioners.** However radical or inventive a new work might be, it will still contain traces of earlier experiments and directions in theatre. Imagine the theatre of today to be like an old cooking pot, which is deeply crusted with all the meals that have been cooked in it over the years. When a new meal is cooked, it will be flavoured by the residues and juices left by previous meals. The same is true of a play or performance – it will reflect modern trends but will be made out of conventions that have a long history. We have already noted that *Shakespeare* wrote radically new forms of *tragedy*, but despite the 'modernness' of his plays there are still echoes of the ways in which *tragedies* were conventionally written in earlier times. *Kneehigh* are often considered as a leading *avant-garde* company, but their work includes acrobatics, *clowning*, trapeze and other street theatre and popular performance techniques that go back to the ancient Greeks.

There are few rules in theatre and such rules as do exist become the target for radical artists! **The boundaries between genres, styles and periods are always slippery and changing.** As we have seen, in any period of theatre there will be a variety of different styles and genres at work – some will be dominant and mainstream while others will be experimental and avant garde. Playwrights do not like to be restricted by the rules of genre either. *Shakespeare* introduced some conventions from comedy into his *tragedies* and **Chekhov** developed **tragi-comedy** as a new cross-breed of the genres of *tragedy* and *comedy*. Terms like 'genre' and 'period' are useful guides, but they are never rigid and fixed definitions. You will always find examples of artists 'breaking the rules' in order to offer fresh and original dramas of the human condition.

Most of this book is concerned with developments in theatre in the twentieth and twenty-first centuries. But these developments were influenced by the theatre of earlier centuries. In Appendix 2 we offer a brief history of pre-twenty-first-century periods, genres and styles. The timeline gives you an overview of major developments in Western theatre between AD 600 and 1910. You can follow the story or use the timeline to see when a new period begins and when new conventions first emerged. We have also included an account of the origins of the great non-European performance traditions, many of which have had profound influence on twenty-first-century Western practitioners. As you begin to study particular plays and practitioners, take the time to use the timeline, glossary and webliography to find out more about the other artists and developments of that period and the periods before and after.

# 2 The Origins of Drama and Theatre

How often have you seen this symbol of theatre? Perhaps you have a version yourself. Maybe someone who knew you were interested in theatre and drama bought you jewellery or a T-shirt with the symbol on. Throughout the Western world the masks of *comedy* and *tragedy* are used to refer to theatre and the performing arts. The common recognition of these signs tells us something about the story of theatre and the origins of the performances that we see now in our own time.

Tragedy and comedy masks

The masks suggest that these origins are to be found in the golden age of Athenian drama during the fifth and fourth centuries BC. It was during these times that the two classical dramatic genres of *tragedy* and *comedy* were first developed. It is sometimes said that the origins of theatre itself are to be found in the sacred rituals of ancient Athens, which later developed into the earliest forms of *comedy* and *tragedy*. This belief that *all* forms of theatre stem from sacred rites and festivals is very strong in the English theatre in particular. In fact there is little concrete archaeological evidence to suggest that drama and theatre originated in these sacred events. Nor can the early dramas of Athens be seen as the only origins of our theatre which in recent times has become more inclusive of other great cultural performance traditions and often includes elements of more recent European performance traditions – carnival, *Commedia dell'Arte*, *music hall* and *musicals*, for instance. However, it is still worth looking at the Athenian drama because it helps us to understand some general points about theatre and performance which are relevant to a wide range of cultural traditions, including the forms of theatre that we find in our own time.

## Aristotle's Theory of Tragedy

Much of what we know about the origins of *comedy* and *tragedy* have been influenced by the theories of *Aristotle* who was a fourth-century Athenian philosopher. *Aristotle* wrote on a wide range of aesthetic issues and only a small part of his work was concerned with the analysis of drama and theatre. *Aristotle* described how *comedies* and *tragedies* should be written. He did this partly by looking closely at the structure of the great plays of *Aeschylus* and *Sophocles* and partly by making his own rules. *Aristotle*'s account of *comedy* has never been fully recovered, but his writings on *tragedy* have been very influential in the development of Western theatre and drama since they were rediscovered in the fifteenth century.

*Aristotle*'s theories are still relevant today

*Aristotle* defined *tragedy* as:

> *a representation of an action that is worth serious attention, complete in itself, and of some amplitude; in language enriched by a variety of artistic devices appropriate to the several parts of the play; presented in the form of action, not narration; by means of pity and fear bringing about the purgation of such emotions*

In this short definition, *Aristotle* establishes certain features of *tragedy*, which we can still recognise in some genres and styles of today's theatre.

Many plays are based on the serious exploration of **a significant action** taken by the central character, which brings about their downfall or changes them and those around them in some profound way. Theatre, while it may often tell a story, is the **art of actions** – things happen rather than being merely described as they might be in a novel. In *Aristotle*'s analysis, actions in *tragedy* were not by chance or accident; they were made inevitable or necessary because of the characters and situations in the drama. Many plays still work on this idea of showing that characters behave as they do because of the social and psychological circumstances that they face.

*Aristotle* said that the central action should be of '*some amplitude*'. We now speak of certain kinds of action as being **dramatic** and by that we often mean '**larger than life**'. Often plays and other forms of drama depend on some big event to grab our interest and stir up the lives of the characters involved. In *Macbeth* a king is murdered. In disaster movies, some terrible natural calamity changes the course of people's lives. Sometimes we are struck by the magnitude of human choices which lead to death and destruction; sometimes by the tragedy of cataclysmic natural disasters and their effects.

Theatre seeks to move us, to make us feel strong emotions in response to the actions of the characters. For *Aristotle*, the purpose in arousing these strong emotions in the audience was to relieve or purge the same emotions in them – to allow the audience to experience strong emotions without having to suffer them as we do in everyday life. *Aristotle* called this process *catharsis*. This is a term we still use today and the dictionary defines it as 'an emotional release in drama or art'. We still enjoy *cathartic* drama – think of a film like *Titanic* and how much you enjoyed crying at the climax! As we will see in Chapter 4, in the twentieth century *Brecht* would argue against *catharsis* and suggest that the purpose of theatre was to arouse the audience's thinking so that they would consider what action to take to change the world, rather than be purged and released from their feelings and emotions.

Greek *tragedies* were based on explorations of conflict between characters, groups of people or ideas. This idea that theatre is based on the struggle between opposing sides, represented by individual characters or groups, or on a tension created by conflict of some kind, is still a common principle in Western theatre.

The idea of a theatre based on some kind of conflict is included in the terms *protagonist* and *antagonist*. The *protagonist* is the Greek term still used today to identify the main character or 'hero' in the play who initiates the main action and around whom the rest of the characters and plots revolve. The *antagonist* is the character who opposes the protagonist's objective or the main action of the play.

Many theatre words are
Greek in origin

*Epic* storytelling evolves
into *tragedy*

The unities

Many of the words that we use to speak about drama and theatre today, came into our language because they were made popular through *Aristotle's* writings: for example, theatre, drama, *tragedy*, *comedy*, poet, critic, scene, rhythm and *catharsis*.

The *tragedies* of *Aristotle's* time had their origins in the choral singing and storytelling of the great Greek myths. These performances became drama when **Thespis** turned the leader of the chorus into a character from the mythic story being told by the chorus for the first time. We still use the word *thespian* to describe an actor. **The actor wore a mask to show that he was now a character in the narrative rather than a storyteller.** At first, then, the dialogue between the main character and the chorus created the drama; the chorus would comment on, question or challenge the actions taken by the character, or *protagonist*. Later, *Aeschylus* invented a second actor, the *antagonist*, so that the conflict, or opposition of ideas, between two characters could be dramatically represented. *Sophocles* added a third actor (the *tritagonist*) and reduced the role of the chorus. This further developed the dramatic potential of *tragedy*.

Some of *Aristotle's* principles, while they survived into the eighteen and nineteenth centuries, are no longer in use. He suggested that a *tragedy* should be in five acts and of sufficient length to properly represent the 'journey' or events which 'allows the hero by a series of probable or necessary stages to pass from misfortune to happiness or from happiness to misfortune'.

*Aristotle* also suggested that there should be: **unity of time** – the events of the play should take place within a 24-hour cycle; **unity of place** – the events should all be set in the same place; and unity of action – there should be a single plot which should have a clear beginning, middle and end.

Few modern plays still observe these unities, but both eighteenth century **neo-classicism** and the *Irish theatre* of the early twentieth century revived their use. Unity of action means that there should only be one main plot or storyline in the play; even if there are sub-plots they should still be part of the main story. In the twentieth century, *Stanislavski* would adapt this idea in talking about a play's 'through-line of action'.

Within *Aristotle's* idea of unity of action there is a second point which is important. The main character is always completely exhausted by the mental, physical and emotional demands of the action or plot. This means that the character's life is finished within the time period of the play. This idea that a character's life, or career, ends when the play does is still common in modern drama. For instance, in reality, Macbeth's life would last longer than the three hours of the play. But the unity of action means that his stage life is completed within the span of the play. When there is a sense of the lives and destinies of characters concluding with the ending of the play we call it a **closed structure**.

In some modern plays, like *Waiting For Godot* or *Marat/Sade*, there is an alternative sense of the characters carrying on 'living' beyond the end of the play – we are watching an *episode* rather than a completed story. Most *soap operas* work on this principle – we imagine the lives of the characters to continue even if we are not watching. This is called an **open structure**.

The 'unities' of action, time and place together with the emphasis on the life of a single heroic character distinguishes the Athenian genre of *tragedy* from the *epic* genre of narrative. In *epic*, the story may involve a whole

23

people's history or many different characters, span across decades of time and be set in a number of places – *Homer's Illiad* and *Odyssey* are examples of *epic* and both *Shakespeare* and *Brecht*, among others, incorporated or substituted elements of the *epic* into their '*tragedies*'.

The fragments of *Aristotle's* writings on *comedy* which have survived reveal that he **considered *comedies* to be inferior to *tragedies*** because they were bawdy and frivolous, based on chance, fantasy and comic errors. While *tragedy* sought to reveal the truth of human existence, *comedy* served to make fun of and escape from the realities of life. The Greek word *komos* literally meant a drunken revel! *Tragedy* served a serious purpose whereas *comedy* was for pure entertainment. This distinction between 'serious' and 'light' forms of theatre and drama and the idea that one is more elevated and sacred than the other still persists very strongly in our discussion of today's theatre and drama. Some people look down on *comedies* and other pieces of entertainment while others prefer to be entertained rather than being asked to take everything very seriously.

*Aristophanes* was a famous writer of *comedies* like *Lysistrata* in which the women refuse to have sex with their husbands unless they give up fighting!

The *satyr play* **is the third genre of theatre with its origins in fifth century Athens**. A *satyr play* was performed after a *tragedy*. The *satyr plays* were more informal, often crude with phallic imagery. The plays satirised, or were *parodies* of, myths, legends, historical heroes and even the *tragedies* that would have been performed before them. *Satyr plays* combined songs, dances and sketches and laid the basis for the later development of both modern *farce* and *burlesque*.

**Recent studies of Athenian comedy and *satyr plays* reveal some remarkable connections with the modern theatre**. The *buffoonery* and *clowning* of the *comedy* can be seen in the development of *Commedia dell'Arte* and more recently in the work of Dario *Fo* and *Théâtre de Complicité*. The gross emotions, phallic references and the distorted and ugly facemasks of the *satyr play* would reappear in the work of a playwright

*Comedies* were often crude and considered inferior to *tragedies*

*Lysistrata* by Aristophanes, Leandra Lawrence Arcola Theatre, London, 2005

like Alfred *Jarry*, and traces of both the *satyr plays* and the Athenian *comedy* are also to be found in the ideas of Antonin *Artaud*.

**The use of savage *satires* and *parodies* reoccurs throughout the history of theatre drama** and mirrors the popular entertainment forms of carnival and the old English custom of *charivari* in which masked gangs would parade the streets mocking adulterers, profiteers, fraudsters and others in the community. The same spirit is to be found in the work of companies such as **Welfare State International**. The actors in *comedy* would also come out of character, during the *parabasis*, or interval, to comment on topical events or to make a joke or aside directly to the audience just as *Brecht*'s actors would do in the twentieth century. The *comedies* also ignored, as much modern drama does, the unities of time, space and action.

## The Athenian Influence on 'Serious' Theatre Today

Influences and comparisons in today's theatre

It was suggested at the beginning of this section that it is often assumed that our modern theatre originated in the dramas of fifth century BC Athens. Perhaps this is because there were important features of theatre of this period which closely resemble some aspects of the modern theatre. In addition to the features of *tragedy*, *comedy* and the *satyr play* that we have already considered there are some other general comparisons that can be made.

The plays were the work of playwrights and the Western tradition of theatre is, as we noticed in the first chapter of this book, based on a **literary tradition**. In other words it is remembered, principally, in terms of a long succession of playwrights and their literary works – the plays they wrote.

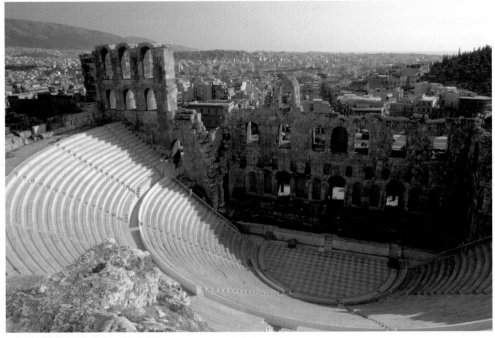

The Theatre of Dionysus, Athens, Greece

The literary tradition

The first theatre buildings

Athens became a
progressive democratic
state

Theatre contributes to
debates about society

Western theatre evolves
and changes

The **emphasis on language** in Athenian drama led to the emergence of actors whose main purpose was to 'speak' or 'deliver' their 'lines' – the words given to them by the playwright. The audience came to listen to the words rather than to watch a play. They listened attentively and quietly. Actors were judged by their ability to speak their lines appropriately rather than by their ability to physically 'characterise' their parts. Even in *Shakespeare*'s time people would talk of going to 'hear' a play rather than to 'see' a play, as we would. Many performances now are still based on the actors' skills in 'delivering' their lines to an audience that listens attentively and quietly.

The Athenian dramas began the tradition of **representing universal themes and ideas about human experience** through presenting the story of particular characters and their journeys. This idea that theatre should focus on a small group of characters and their particular story as a means of commenting on or explaining the world at large still underpins much modern drama.

The Athenian dramas took place in theatres just as many of our plays do. The creation of **theatre buildings** was the result of the development of the city as a complex political and cultural centre. Once you establish a densely populated urban area, you need to reserve spaces for worship, government and culture. This is what happened in Athens and other great cities of the time. The history of Western theatre is closely associated with the development of the great European and American cities and the theatres that have been created in them. In most modern cities you will find a 'theatre district' like the *West End* in London or *Broadway* in New York. Often playwrights, actors and directors are associated with particular theatre buildings – *Shakespeare* with the *Globe*, **Yeats** and **Synge** with the *Abbey* in Dublin, *Stanislavski* with the **Moscow Art Theatre**, Joan *Littlewood* with the *Stratford East* theatre in the East End of London. Sometimes theatres become associated with particular styles of work – the **Royal Court Theatre** in London was known as a centre for experimental work and new writing in the 1970s and 1980s.

During the fifth century BC, Athens became a progressive democratic state in which citizens of a certain rank and class were allowed to vote for a group of representatives who would then govern the city. Here lie the origins of our modern democracy. During this period, going to the theatre was seen as an important part of public life. Citizens were expected to go to the theatre just as they were expected to contribute to the public good of the city. The *Theatre of Dionysus* in Athens in its final form could house an audience of 20,000. The theatre was seen as offering citizens a mirror of the concerns and issues that faced them.

Although, like our own middle-class theatre, the Greek theatre depended on a wealthy audience of slave owners, the great Athenian leader Pericles established the theoric fund to subsidise the cost of a seat for the poor – the first government-subsidised theatre!

The idea that theatre should contribute to debates about society and the directions in which it is going is very strong in the history of Western theatre. At different times, playwrights from *Shakespeare* through to **Ibsen, Strindberg** and *Brecht* have sought to explain or challenge the times in which they lived. In order to do this, playwrights and others have often needed to introduce new conventions in order to reflect the changes that are occurring in society.

This tradition of a progressive art form that seeks new methods and new conventions for representing our private and social lives has its origins in

Athenian drama. However, in many of the world's great performance traditions, particularly those of Asia and Africa, the emphasis is on tradition and continuity – the idea is to preserve and recreate performances rather than to invent new conventions and ideas about performance. But as we have seen, in Athens during the fifth century BC there was a rapid development of drama and theatre because playwrights were encouraged to invent and develop new ways for the audience to see themselves and the swiftly changing circumstances of their lives.

# Antigone: An Example of Greek Tragedy

The plot of *Antigone*

*Antigone* (442–441 BC) was the first of a *trilogy* of plays that **Sophocles** wrote to tell the tragic story of the royal house of Thebes. At the heart of this story is the tragedy of Oedipus. Oedipus was brought up by foster-parents and set out on a journey to find his natural parents. Through a tragic series of unwitting mistakes, Oedipus kills a stranger in an angry quarrel only to discover, much later, that the stranger was in fact his father King Laius of Thebes. He also marries the widow Jocasta who bears him two sons and two daughters, only to discover that Jocasta is his natural mother. As a result of this shame Jocasta kills herself and Oedipus blinds himself and goes into exile; eventually he 'dies' in mysterious circumstances.

Oedipus passes over control of Thebes to Jocasta's brother Creon, but his sons, Polynices and Eteocles, will not accept this decision and both make rival challenges to Creon's power. Eventually, Polynices joins forces with the city of Argos, the enemies of Thebes, and invades. Despite his differences with Creon, Eteocles bravely defends Thebes against his brother's attack and both end up killing each other.

In order to deter any further treason and to bring order back to Thebes, Creon decrees that Eteocles should be buried with full honours while his brother's body must be left to rot outside the city gates. Anyone who tries to bury Polynices shall be stoned to death. The Greeks believed it to be vital for a body to be properly buried and taken to the 'underworld' below. It was the responsibility of the family to ensure that there was a proper burial ritual. The story of *Antigone* begins with the *Prologue* in which Oedipus' two daughters, Antigone and Ismene, discuss Creon's decree.

(*Thebes*)

Antigone: My own sister, dear sister, Ismene.
Tell me this: are there any evils coming from Oedipus that Zeus does not fulfil through us – the two still living?
Pain, ruin, shame
All of these
I see in your evils and mine
And now what is this proclamation the general has made to all of Thebes?
Have you heard anything? Are you aware that evils appropriate for our enemies are to be endured by our loved ones?

Ismene: I have no word, Antigone, concerning our loved ones.
Nothing sweet, nothing bitter, has come my way since we two were bereft of our two brothers – one day's double blow of a double death. And with the departure

27

of the armies from Argos last night, I do not know whether to feel more fortunate or more distressed.

*Antigone*:    I know –
and I've brought you outside the gates of the house so you alone can hear.

*Ismene*:    What is it? You're troubled – brooding over some story.

*Antigone*:    We have two brothers. Hasn't Kreon honoured one with a tomb and shamed the other?
Eteocles, they say, has been buried, with due observance of justice and custom, under the ground, to be honoured amongst the dead.
As for Polyneikes, they say it is forbidden by decree to bury him, or mourn him, but he is to be left unwept, unburied, a sweet morsel for the birds as they look down – their treasure store of tasty meat.
That is the good Kreon's proclamation to you and to me – yes, to me – and he is coming here to make this clear to those who may still not know.
And this is no small matter.
Whoever does these things anyway will be stoned in front of the people of the city. That's how it is for you as well and you will soon show whether you are well born or the bad shoot of good stock.

*Ismene*:    If these things are so, my poor sister, what can I do? Not do?

*Antigone*:    Think if you will share in the work, the act.

*Ismene*:    Share in what? What do you mean?

*Antigone*:    Will you help this hand to lift the dead?

*Ismene*:    You are thinking of burying him – and this has been forbidden?

*Antigone*:    He is my own brother, and yours too, even if you do not wish it. I will not be known as the one who betrayed him.

*Ismene*:    Such purpose – and Kreon has forbidden it.

*Antigone*:    Not for him to keep me from my own.

*Ismene*:    *Oimoi.*
Think,
sister
how our father died –
hated, in shame
shunned
uncovering himself his own guilt and striking his two eyes with his own hands.
And then the mother, wife, double name, mangling her life in that tangle of ropes.
And finally, our two brothers, in one day each miserably slaying the other, trapped in a shared fate wreaked by their own hands.
We are the two left behind. Alone. We too will die most miserably if we violate the decree and defy the power of the tyrant.
We must remember we are born women and are not meant to do battle against men.
And then that we are ruled by those who are the stronger and we must obey this

and things even more painful.
And so I beg forgiveness of those below, I am compelled: I have to obey those in power.
There is no sense in the excessive gesture.

Antigone: I won't urge you any more – no, even if you changed and wanted to do it – you would no longer be welcome.
Think as you will.
I will bury him.
And I will die well doing this.
I will lie with him I love, my friend, my kin – guilty, yes, but of a holy crime.
I believe I owe more of my time to pleasing the dead below than those here: there, I shall live for ever.
Think as you will, but you will be guilty of dishonouring the gods.

Ismene: I am not doing them a dishonour.
I cannot act against the will of the city.

Antigone: Such is your excuse.
I will go and raise a tomb for my beloved brother.

Ismene: Hard suffering, I fear for you.
Antigone: Don't fear for me; straighten out your own destiny.
(*Continues*)

# Antigone Workshop

1. Work with a partner and read through the extract together at least twice.
2. Decide with your partner what each character's *objective* might be in this scene. What does Antigone want to happen, or make happen, next? What does Ismene want to happen next?
3. Read through the extract again, but now think about the characters' objectives and how this will affect the way in which the lines are spoken and responded to by the characters. Try to make your reading of the play lifelike, in the sense that if you think that Antigone is trying to persuade Ismene or that she gets angry with her this should be reflected in the way that you speak your lines.
4. Now join together with another pair and share your ideas about the way to play the lines. Let one pair read through the extract, expressing the objectives in your voice, while the other pair improvise the physical actions of the two characters. How do they move around the stage? When are they close? When might they move away from each other? What about facial and other gestures? Work together until you feel that the actions and the words match together, then share your work with other groups.

Remember that *Aristotle* based many of his ideas about *tragedy* on the plays of *Sophocles*. Go back to *Aristotle*'s definition of *tragedy* on page 22. What do you think is the action, in this extract, that is worth serious attention? Where is the language enriched by a variety of artistic devices (imagery, metaphor)? Is the plot presented in action rather than narration? What emotions do the characters express? And what emotions do you think an audience might experience during this scene?

*Aristotle* broke down the structure of *tragedy* into six parts, and again we still use some of these terms in our discussion of today's theatre. We have described the six elements and their contemporary usage below and asked you some questions about how the six elements relate to this extract.

| Element | Questions |
|---|---|
| **1. Plot** (*mythos* from which we get the word 'myth'): this was 'the soul of tragedy' for *Aristotle* and referred to the incidents and sequence of events in the play which would include crises, conflicts, reversals of fortune, climaxes, tensions and suspense, exposition and denouement. *Aristotle* also suggested that the plot should have a beginning, middle and end. | This *Prologue* offers the 'exposition' of the play's plot. This is the essential information about characters' past lives and relationships and a foreshadowing of events to come. What events are retold? What events are foreshadowed? What conflicts and tensions are there? What crises and climax do you think there will be later in the play? |
| **2. Character** (*ethos* from which we get 'ethics'): there were four aspects of character:<br>• a character should be 'good' which often meant being of noble birth;<br>• being 'good' also meant that characters should have a moral purpose for their actions;<br>• characters should be 'typical' of the people they represent rather than odd or different;<br>• they should be 'real' not fantastical or magical and they should be 'consistent' – they should behave 'in character', as we would say – their actions should be probable, credible and plausible. | Both Antigone and Ismene are aristocrats. Many plays until the nineteenth century were about princes, kings and queens and other aristocratic heroes. What are Ismene and Antigone's moral purposes in this scene? What does each consider to be the right/wrong thing to do? In what ways are Ismene and Antigone 'typical'? What kind of person does each represent?<br><br>The idea of 'consistency' of character would become one of the principles of *Stanislavski*'s system of acting. In modern times character is more usually discussed in terms of the psychology and morality of a character and the social relations between characters. What clues are there that the characters will behave consistently for the rest of the play? |
| **3. Thought** (*dianoia*): we would now use the term 'theme', which describes the ideas of the play, or issues raised, and how the drama-world of the play relates to or illuminates the actual world in which we live. Discussion of a play's 'thought' is often concerned with an exploration of the spiritual, political or social content of a play.<br><br>This translation is by the contemporary playwright Timberlake **Wertenbaker**. Many different generations have found connections between the story of *Antigone* and their own times. During the 1940s both Jean **Anouilh** and *Brecht* adapted the play as a commentary on the decline into fascism. | What are the issues and themes that are raised in this extract? Why might these themes and issues have been of interest to a woman writing plays today and a Marxist playwright in fascist Germany? Do any of these issues have relevance for you, living today? |
| **4. Diction** (*lexis* from which we get 'lexicon' meaning a dictionary or vocabulary): this describes the literary aspects of the drama – how it is written, the language and poetry, the imagery and metaphors of speech. | Look closely at Ismene's speech beginning: *Oimoi. . .* Why has Wertenbaker laid the lines out in this way? What is intended by the line breaks? How can the intentions of the written format be played in performance? What is the effect? |

| | |
|---|---|
| **5. Music** (*melos* from which we get 'melody'): *Aristotle* didn't dwell on *melos* but a consideration of the 'acoustic' elements of a performance – what we hear in terms of music and other sounds – has become increasingly important in modern theatre. | Is there a 'melody' in the language? As you read through were you conscious of the rhythm, or sound, of the words? What music or other sound effects might you add to this scene in a modern production? |
| **6. Spectacle** (*opsis* from which we get 'optics' and 'optical'): again, *opsis* was not an important category for *Aristotle* but the visual elements of a play are now seen as being essential to the 'theatre' of a performance and both music and spectacle are of great importance in genres such as *pantomime*, *opera*, *musicals* and *physical theatre*. | The Greeks used very little in terms of scenery and other visual clues of the play's setting. The main scenery was provided by the *skene* (from which we get the word 'scene'), which was a wooden building at the back of the *orchestra* or stage. The *skene* looked like a real house and was the territory of the female characters as it was in Athenian culture. Which of Antigone's lines refers to the *skene* as a house? What other elements of setting or props might you introduce into a modern production that would be in keeping with the play's setting and themes? |

**The functions of the chorus**

The first chorus, which speaks of the same events, follows this *Prologue* but from the perspective of the citizens of Thebes who support Creon's actions. In *Sophocles' tragedies* the chorus serves a number of functions:

- they place the events of the story in a more universal theme;
- they raise anxieties, on behalf of the audience, about what is happening;
- they act as a silent and public witness to private acts;
- they speak for the citizens of Athens (the audience).

For the final exercise you are going to use a modern idea that the chorus might work visually rather than vocally – they might show through images rather than comment in words.

1. Prepare a series of *still-images* based on the content of the two sister's dialogue – events and ideas – that the chorus might present during this extract. Two pairs will provide the words and actions for the scene. The rest are the chorus who form their images at appropriate moments in the scene. Practise the timing so the images either foreshadow the events the two sisters talk about or comment, as outsiders, on the events they have already expressed their opinion about. The actors may need to freeze to allow the images to be made, and the chorus may also repeat lines as a caption or heading for their image.
2. Run the sequence together when you think the work of the chorus is satisfying some of the functions described above.

**Task 1: From Athens to today's theatre**

- What are the main similarities and differences between the fifth-century Athenian theatre culture and our own? What has changed and what has remained the same?

- How does the history of the Athenian theatre help us to understand and talk about today's theatre?

# Different Performances

In Chapter 1, The Infinite Variety of Theatre, we talked about the ways in which different kinds of plays and performances can be organised into periods, styles and genres. We can add to these by introducing three new categories for broadly distinguishing between different performances and styles. These categories are also to be found in the theatre of fifth-century Athens.

Once again we need to remind you that while it is useful to be able to talk about the differences in performance, categories and labels are always slippery and changeable! Performances are never either one category or another. But they are often more or less one category or another.

The categories are:

| | |
|---|---|
| *Realist* and *non-realist* styles and genres | Making a distinction between 'lifelike' and abstract or 'stylised' performance styles. |
| The social function of the performance | The intended purpose or effect of the performance on the audience. |
| *Presentational* and *representational* theatre | The difference between recreating another 'world' in 'another time' on stage and communicating directly to the audience 'here and now'. |

# Realist and Non-realist Styles in Theatre

*Mimesis is the origin of realism*

The various genres of *realism* in theatre, film and TV are based on the Aristotelian concept of **mimesis**, which is often taken to mean a lifelike representation of how people behave and respond to experience. *Mimesis* is the origin of *realism*, which is still the most commonly used style of theatre and is certainly the dominant style of TV and film drama.

In a *mimetic*, or *realist* style of drama we only see and hear what we would actually see and hear in life – people look as they would do, they often, though not always, use the same language that we hear in our everyday lives and they are realistically presented in their natural surroundings. The ambition of *realism* is to remove all traces of theatricality so that the drama and performance can be experienced as 'real life' rather than as a representation or construction of real life.

The opposite of the *realist* tradition in theatre can be most simply described as *non-realist*. *Non-realist* theatre, like some styles of painting, doesn't try to represent the world as we actually see and hear it. Instead, it tries to represent the invisible and imagined world of thoughts, ideas, dreams and fears through mask, dance, mime, symbolic gestures and costumes, props and set design.

Most of the great non-European performance traditions such as *Kathakali*, *Noh* and *Kabuki* are *non-realist* in style. The costume, mask and colours represent instead the spirit, the demons, the fantasy and power evoked by the character, but rather than what you can actually see when looking at a character, what you can imagine when you think, or dream, about the character.

The ambition of the *non-realist* style is well summed up by *Stanislavski* who described the problems of presenting *Maeterlinck*'s *The Blue Bird* to his actors in this way:

> *There are three main difficulties to overcome. First of all, we must express on the stage the* inexpressible. . . *Second, the sensibilities of the audience are not ready to receive and comprehend* abstract *thoughts and feelings. Third we have to* personify *sleep, a dream, a presentiment, a fairy tale. This is lace work, woven of fine threads like a cobweb, while the scenic means of modern stage technique (realism) are coarse and clumsy.*

*Non-realism* is not always as obviously symbolic and abstract as this quote suggests. **Non-realism also refers to any performance style which stresses the theatricality of the performance.** In other words, rather than seeking to persuade the audience that the events on stage are real life, the performance emphasises that it is theatre, not life. This means that the performance will stress movement, props and costumes, lighting and design and stlylised performance traditions like masks, puppets and *Commedia dell'Arte* that are obviously stylised and theatrical – only experienced and seen in the theatre rather than borrowed and copied *mimetically* from life.

Practitioners associated with this style of *non-realism* would include **Craig, Meyerhold**, *Brecht*, **Grotowski**, *Brook* and most of the great twentieth-century practitioners who sought to rebel against the *realism* of *Stanislavski*'s system. For this reason the work of these practitioners is sometimes referred to as *post-realist*. The great Russian director Vsevolod *Meyerhold*, describes this form of *non-realism* in these words in 1912:

> *The public comes to the theatre to see the art of man, but what art is there in walking about the stage as oneself? The public expects invention, playacting and skill. But what it gets is either life or a slavish imitation of life. Surely the art of man on stage consists in shedding all traces of environment, carefully choosing a mask, donning a decorative costume, and showing off one's brilliant tricks to the public – now as a dancer, now as the intrigant at some masquerade, now as the fool of old Italian comedy, now as a juggler.*

Although in this book we will use the terms *realist* and *non-realist*, you will find that there are different terms used to describe this basic difference between 'lifelike' and 'non-lifelike' or stylised theatrical forms of theatre. Sometimes the difference is expressed as '*naturalistic*' and '*non-naturalistic*'; or '*stylised*' and '*symbolic*' are used to describe *non-realist* theatre. **These terms are interchangeable; there is no general agreement about which terms to use.** But it is important to remember that *realism*, *naturalism* and *symbolism* also refer to specific genres and styles of late nineteenth-century theatre practice.

One difficulty is that when the term '*naturalism*' is used it can mean either a general 'lifelike' style of theatre or a specific genre of theatre associated with the writers Maxim *Gorky*, Leo *Tolstoy*, Gerhart *Hauptmann* and others. In some cases you will find these genres spelt with a capital letter (*Realism*) to indicate the historical genre rather than a general style (*realism*).

## Task 2: Differences between *realism* and *non-realism*

Look at the two illustrations overleaf. One is from a performance that is generally considered to be in the *realist* style, the other is *non-realist*. What are the key differences in the pictures? What do you imagine would be the different effect, or *impact*, of each production?

*Realism* is not real;
*naturalism* is not natural

It is important to remember that *realism* is a style of theatre. It presents the **illusion** of reality. It is no more real than the most abstract and stylised forms of *non-realist* theatre; *realism* will always be artificial and 'unreal' precisely because it is a **representation**, or construction, of reality on the stage rather than life as it is actually experienced and lived on the street. We are often reminded of how 'artificial' and 'unnatural' *realism* is when we see a play or drama that is based on our own experiences. Teachers, police officers and doctors probably don't think that *Grange Hill*, *The Bill* and *Casualty* are lifelike at all! And you may not find the representation of school in film and TV to be true to your own experience. As we have seen, drama is often based on 'larger than life' characters and events – everyday experience becomes dramatised for our entertainment. But we are also made conscious that however realistic the style, drama is always an **interpretation** of life *not* life itself. Theatre is always made; it is never 'natural'.

Different generations
view *realism* differently

Throughout history, theatre artists have struggled to show their audiences the world as it really is – to find the most truthful way of showing the audience who they are and who they are becoming as a society. Every generation has imagined that its theatre is more real or realistic than that of previous generations. What the Greeks took to be *realism*, or *mimesis*, would now seem quite unrealistic to us – masks, chorus, verse, etc. Many of the classic plays that you will study may seem strange and quite unreal as pictures of the human condition. But always remember that in their time these plays would have seemed to be highly realistic pictures of life to their audiences. In the same way those old black and white movies shown on Sunday afternoons may seem absurd and unreal to you, but they were realistic for the cinema audiences of 40 and 50 years ago.

## Task 3: What counts as 'realism' today?

- Which current TV or film drama would you say is the most realistic? How is the sense of *realism* created – character, plot, settings, language, camera angles?

- Choose a genre such as police dramas and compare the *realism* of today's examples of the genre with those you can remember from childhood. How have ideas of *realism* changed?

*Realism* in nineteenth-
century theatre

Different generations have different ideas about what is real in their lives and what is *realism* in theatre. In the late nineteenth century, for instance, many people believed that science alone could resolve all the unanswered questions and mysteries of life. The turn against religion and mysticism led to a way of thinking called *posiitivism*. The basis of *positivism* is that all true knowledge is scientific. Everything can be measured and classified according to scientific principles. *Empiricism* is the term used to describe the *positivist* method of inquiry.

*The Weir*, Royal Court/Duke of York's, February 1998

Nancy Crane and Stephen Dillane in *Angels in America*,
Royal National Theatre, 1993

In *empiricism* the truth can only be established if it can be proved by actual experience – in other words, the truth only exists in the material world of rational thinking and the evidence of our senses: touch, taste, sight, and hearing. *Realism* in nineteenth-century theatre, then, was based on the idea that the instantly recognisable characters, settings, language and situations on stage were 'truthful' because they were scientifically accurate descriptions of human experience and behaviour. But if we look more closely at *realism* as a style we can see through this illusion.

Most plays in the *realist* style are based on the following elements.

| | |
|---|---|
| A strong **plot** or story in a lifelike setting | **But**, we know that life is more complex than a story. Stories neatly organise experience into a beginning, middle and end. But our everyday experience is often more muddled and uncertain than this! We don't live in a story, even if stories are the main means we have of explaining our experiences to each other. A poet would argue that a poem could be just as 'truthful' a means of representing human experience as a story. The idea that characters can be explained in terms of their physical setting – the environment in which they live – is also a superficial idea of personality and behaviour. |
| Unified and consistent **characterisation** based on the idea of the 'well-rounded individual' (this is the basis of *Stanislavski*'s acting methods) | **But**, the basis of the '*realist*' character is the idea that characters should behave with a degree of consistency (in the same way) whatever the situation or setting. The purpose of rehearsal is to 'iron out' any rough edges, or inconsistencies, in the character to create the illusion of a predictable, well-rounded and unified personality. In reality of course, we know that people are not like that – they often behave 'out of character', and you know that there are many quite different 'sides' to your own personality. We also know that people change – they are never complete in the way that the *realist* character is presented. |
| A cultural and class-specific **perspective** | The 'reality' of the world that is presented in *realist* theatre is always based on how the world appears to a particular culture and class. There are exceptions, but more often than not, *realist* plays and performances seek to make a white, European, middle-class view of the world look like the only 'natural' and 'truthful' perspective. This is also the basis of *naturalism* as a genre. In *naturalist* plays the effects of environment and poor health on the morality and fortunes of the lower classes are scientifically analysed and presented for the benefit of the middle-class audience. This reflects their view of the lower classes. |

*Realist* and *non-realist* styles are often mixed

Although the origins of modern *realism* are to be found in the theatre of the ancient Greeks it is important to remember that the Greeks mixed elements of *realism* and *non-realism* in their performances, and this tradition has continued through history. *Shakespeare* wrote *realist* plays that mixed prose (*realism* in speech) with poetry (*non-realism* in speech). *Chekhov* included ideas associated with *symbolism* in his *realist* plays. *Brecht* is often considered to be a *non-realist* practitioner but he called his theatre *scientific realism* even though he often used *non-realist* settings and costumes.

In contemporary theatre we often find a mix of *realist* and *non-realist* ideas. The characters and speech may be *realist* but not the setting, or costumes or stage design. **It is often more appropriate to talk of a continuum between *realism* and *non-realism* when discussing the style of a performance**; to say that the performance was more *realist* than *non-realist*, for instance. It is also important to think about the logic behind the choice to make some elements *realist* and others *non-realist*. *Shakespeare* reserved verse for his aristocratic characters and for creating particular effects of atmosphere. *Brecht* used some *non-realist* costumes and scenery to emphasise the political messages in his plays.

**Task 4: Is *Macbeth* a *realist* or *non-realist* play?**

1   Remind yourself of the plot of the play; remember all the supernatural happenings: the witches, Hecate, the ghosts.

2   Make a line to represent the *realist/non-realist* continuum. Let each member of the group stand on the line according to where they think the play is on this continuum. Discuss your positions.

# Getting Results and Fooling Around – The Social Function of Theatre

Theatre serves different social functions

We have seen that theatre played an important role in the lives of the Athenians. It had different social functions. Sometimes, as in the *tragedies*, the social function was to both educate and create serious debate among the citizens. In *Antigone,* for instance, the conflict between the interests of the city government and the interests of family life which is represented in the conflict between the characters of Creon and Antigone was intended to both instruct and create debate among the audience of Athenian citizens. The *comedies* and *satyr plays* had a different function in entertaining and amusing the Athenians, providing pure pleasure rather than instruction.

Theatre and drama have continued since Athenian times to serve a variety of social functions, from providing a forum for debate and for promoting changes in cultural attitudes or unjust laws to the pleasurable experiences of *whodunnits, farces* and slapstick *clowning*. The social function of *Ibsen's* plays *A Doll's House* and *Hedda Gabler* was to try and change society's attitudes towards women as domestic slaves who were 'owned' like property by their husbands. The social function of his play *Ghosts* was to raise the taboo subject of venereal disease. *Brecht's* plays had a strong political social function in seeking to promote a Marxist analysis of society. His purpose was not to simply show the world as it was but to *change* it into a better world for workers and other oppressed groups. Early in his career he wrote a series of plays called *Lehrstücke* or 'learning plays'. The *Lehrstücke* offered very clear and unambiguous lessons to the audience and are an example of *didactic* theatre. The social function of *didactic* theatre is clearly educational, often political, rather than for amusement or entertainment.

Later in his career, *Brecht* would argue that for a play to be educational and instructive it should also be entertaining. Indeed, most plays and performances which have a social function to educate or promote social reform also have the secondary function of providing entertainment. **But you can still distinguish, just as the Athenians did, between plays and performances that emphasise a political or educational function and plays and performances which offer pleasure and fun** to the audience without asking them to do much thinking about the world and its problems.

We use the term 'social function' but you may also find terms like 'playwright's intention' or 'overall purpose' used in some texts. Again there is no general agreement about which term to use to describe the different functions of performances.

### Task 5: Thinking about social function

- Identify two plays or performances that you have seen which had contrasting social functions – one may have been more 'serious' and one perhaps more light-hearted and fun. Discuss with the class the differences between the performances.

- Imagine that you have been asked to lead a drama workshop for young children about road safety issues. The function of the workshop is to make the children more aware of the dangers of crossing the road. Sketch out your ideas for a workshop that combines education in this important issue with a more fun and entertaining dimension for the audience. How could your workshop be made to both teach and amuse your young audience?

# Presentational Theatre and Representational Theatre

This distinction refers to the relationship between the performance, the performers and the audience. A broad distinction can be made between performances that include, or make direct use of, the audience and what is happening to them, and performances which ignore the audience and offer an alternative 'stage reality', a different reality from that of the audience.

Performances that directly address the audience and their actual reality are termed *presentational*; they focus, and often comment on, the present, **here-and-now experience** of the audience. The effect of a *presentational* performance will be that the events on stage are happening 'here' among us, as we watch.

Performances that create a fictional 'world' that is entirely divorced from the audience and their reality are termed *representational*; they re-present a different experience which is happening somewhere else in a parallel, or virtual reality that is not the same as the actual place and time of the performance itself.

*Realism* and *naturalism* require *representational* performances

The plays and performances of the genres of *realism* and *naturalism* in the second half of the nineteenth century are purely *representational*; the 'fourth wall' of the *proscenium arch* separated the fictional world represented on the stage from the darkened and silent world of the audience in the auditorium. **In *representational* theatre there is no direct contact between the actors and the audience.** The actors are in a different world and in a different time from the audience, so there can be no contact between them. A *representational* style of theatre often depends on the use of acting styles based on the *psycho-realism* of *Stanislavski*'s system. Indeed, as we shall see later in this book, *Stanislavski* developed his system precisely in order for his actors to play in the *representational* mode – completely 'being' in character and completely unaware of the audience. (See Chapter 3 for a more detailed explanation of this acting style.)

**The plays and performances of *Brecht* on the other hand sought to directly include the audience by presenting events and characters directly to them.** The actors would comment on their characters to the audience and address the audience directly through songs and stories. *Presentational* theatre is often associated with popular forms of entertainment like *burlesque, music hall, musicals* and *stand-up comedy*; those forms of entertainment which seek to give the audience an experience rather than to represent another place and time. A *presentational* style of theatre often depends on the use of acting styles associated with *Brecht*. He developed a style of *scientific realism* in acting which mixed 'being' in character with 'showing' or presenting characters to the audience, so that his actors could both represent another world to the audience while at the same time including the audience directly in the representation. (See Chapter 4 for a more detailed explanation of this acting style.)

Again, many contemporary and historical performances mix elements of *presentation* and *representation*, just as the Greek theatre did. In *Antigone* the scene between the two sisters is *representational* in the sense that the sisters do not acknowledge the audience – they pretend 'as if' the meeting is really happening and that there is no one else watching. But the first chorus that follows on immediately from this scene does directly address its speech to the audience, as an audience of fellow citizens; it is therefore *presentational*. The chorus in Greek *tragedy* often switches from being *representational* – part of the reality of the play – to being *presentational* – directly addressing and including the audience.

In Greek *comedies*, the plays are broken into two by the *parabasis* in which the actors and chorus step out of role to directly address the audience about political and social issues, just as they would in *Brecht*'s dramas.

*Shakespeare* also mixed the *representational* and *presentational*. In *A Midsummer Night's Dream*, for instance, he mixes the representation of the world of Athens and the woods inhabited by the fairies with *presentational* sequences like the mechanical scenes which are addressed to the audience to make them laugh. The play closes with Puck's famous *presentational* address to the audience:

> If we shadows have offended
> Think, but this, and all is mended,
> That you have but slumbered here
> While these visions did appear...
> So, good night unto you all.
> Give me your hands, if we be friends
> And Robin shall restore amends.

*Epic* and other popular forms require *presentational* performances

# The Alternative Origins of Today's Theatre

In order to make and understand theatre in our time it's important to know something of the origins and structures of the Athenian forms of *tragedy* and *comedy*. But to claim that the modern theatre originates entirely in the fifth century theatre of Athens is to ignore the many other cultural traditions of performance which have influenced theatre's development in modern times. In general terms there are five other major influences which we can still recognise today even though their origins lie in the deep past of Western history.

The five influences that need to be considered alongside *comedy* and tragedy are:

- stories and storytelling
- ritual
- shamanism
- dance
- martial arts contests of skill and strength.

# Storytelling

Both stories and storytelling – the ways in which stories can be told – have had a profound influence on the development of theatre. Most of the world's great performance traditions are based on the stories and/or the storytelling styles of earlier times. We have seen that Athenian drama developed from the stories told by the great, blind *Homer* who sang his epic tales to the accompaniment of a *lyre*. The *Sanscrit* performance tradition in India was, and still is, based on episodes from the *epic* tales of the *Mahabharata* and the *Ramayana*. Similarly, the traditions of Chinese theatre and *Noh* performances are based on the playing of traditional stories. *Shakespeare* is an example of a playwright who based many of his plays on traditional stories and classical histories borrowed from *Ovid*, *Plutarch* and others.

Many plays and dramas use a *narrative* form in which there is a clear sense of a beginning, middle and end. *Narrative* is the most common way for us to share and understand experience. You tell your friends what has happened to you in the form of a *narrative*. You listen to their stories and understand something of their experiences as a result. Story, then, is the most commonly used and generally understood way of representing experiences.

There are common characteristics in both drama and story, but also some important differences.

The similarities are:

- Events are put into a **context** of time and place. Things happen at certain times in a particular place. We talk about a play's **setting**.
- We are introduced to the characters of the people involved – we find out what the people involved in the story are like from how they behave and respond to the events in the story. We talk about **characterisation**.
- There is often an appeal to our emotions; the story is told to arouse pity, fear, laughter and anger in us. We talk about the playwright or performance's **intention**. In the *Sanscrit* tradition, intention is referred to as *rasa* meaning the 'flavour'. The same story can be given different intentions or 'flavours' according to the audience.

---

*Many plays and dramas use a* narrative *form*

- The storyteller has a voice in the story that is used to give us a particular perspective on the people and events involved. The story will be told in the interests of the person telling it! The storyteller will tell the story in such a way that it persuades us that the storyteller's own view is the right one. **A play will be stamped with the playwright's own values, attitudes and experiences of the world.** When you devise a performance as a group, it will inevitably reveal something about you and the group to an audience.

- **Stories are often told to illustrate themes or ideas**, or told as particular examples of a more general **theme**. Through the particular story we are led to think about and reflect on the bigger theme. So, *Romeo and Juliet* is a particular story about the theme of young love and family disputes. We may tell stories from our own experience in order to illustrate a theme such as 'life is unkind', or 'boys always get their own way', or 'the pains of growing up'.

The differences are:

- **In drama and theatre, stories are usually, but not always, told in the** *present* – as if the events were happening here and now for the first time. In most other forms of story, including films and TV, the events are in the *past* – the story is a record of what has already happened. When a play begins it is often like being suddenly thrust into things and lives that are happening *now* on stage. We watch and listen carefully to what *is* going on and who is involved, and after a while we begin to find out what has happened before the play began and what might happen next. In the *Antigone* workshop we noticed that the play begins with two sisters meeting to discuss events. This meeting happens 'here and now' on stage as if it was actually occurring, but during this meeting the two sisters

Actors perform Yukio Mishima's Modern Noh style dramas at the Lincoln Center Festival, New York, 2005

provide the audience with information about what has already happened and also begin to foreshadow what will happen later in the play.

- When you tell a story to your friends you rely almost entirely on words. You may use some gestures and even speak like the characters in your story, but essentially it is through words that your story will be understood. **Theatre, on the other hand, uses more than words to tell its stories**. Actors physically become the people in the stories and will adapt their voices and bodies and gestures to suit the *character* of the person they are playing. They may use all sorts of costumes and props to help them. The *space* is used to tell the story; there maybe a *set* that helps us to imagine the story's setting or the space may be used to visually create the atmosphere or *mood* of the story. A play also uses *timing* to assist in the storytelling – we talk of a comedian's timing, but in a play we also talk of *rhythm* which refers to the changing *tempo* of the play; the alternation between slower and faster moments in the play. Lighting, sounds and significant objects are also used to tell the story in theatre – again, lights and sound may be used to add to the realism of the setting and/or to amplify the mood of the performance.

In theatre, then, the 'story' is presented using the *dramatic elements* of:

- time
- space
- physicality
- lights
- sounds
- objects.

Because theatre is a live performance, the way in which these elements are used will produce an *impact* or *effect* for the audience. Different performances of the same play will have a different *effect* or *impact* according to the different ways in which the elements have been used. When you are producing drama as actors, directors or designers you need to think about the impact that you want to have on your audience and how to achieve it through your use of the *dramatic elements*. When you experience drama as an audience you need to try and think about the effect that the performance has had on you and how this effect was created through the use of the *dramatic elements*.

## Task 6: Creating a performance based on a story

The exercises that follow will help you to practise some of the ideas about story that have been introduced. We begin with some simple *story-theatre* exercises based on the folk-tale of *Little Red Riding Hood*, and then move on to a short performance project based on the same folk-tale.

1   In a group, organise your memory of the story under three headings: *People*, *Places*, and *Events*. Spend a short time discussing what is in your lists – what kind of people are involved; how do you imagine them? What are the woods like, for instance?

2   Write down the eight most important events in the story in the correct sequence (beginning, middle and end) on a large sheet of paper.

**3** Now, elect one member of the group to be the storyteller. The storyteller is going to begin to tell the tale *but* in the present tense. In other words, instead of 'Little Red Riding Hood lived with her mother . . . her mother asked her to take that basket' the storyteller will say: 'Little Red Riding Hood lives with her mother . . . her mother asks her to take a basket . . . she leaves the house and she walks into the woods'.

**4** As the storyteller tells the tale, the rest of the group must act out the story as a group as it is told! No time to discuss or cast, just get on with it! Everything the storyteller speaks of must be played – flowers, baskets, smoking chimneys, everything! If you wish, you can act out scenes from the story as you go, so that when the storyteller says 'Little Red Riding Hood turns around and sees a wolf – she asks the wolf . . .' this scene could be improvised before the storyteller moves on to the next event.

**5** Now, prepare a set of ***monologues*** for different characters in the story. The idea is to think about the story from the different perspectives of the characters and then to create a monologue based on each character's version of events. Each member of your group could take responsibility for one of the following:

- Little Red Riding Hood's mother explains to her friends – some of the other mothers – what happened.

- Little Red Riding Hood explains to her school friends what happened.

- The woodcutter boasts of his bravery to the guests in the local inn.

- The wolf's wife explains what happened to her children, the wolf cubs.

**6** Perform the *monologues* to each other. When you're done you might want to *hot-seat* each character by asking them questions about their version of what happened, which must be answered in character. Finally, discuss how the story has changed for you following these exercises.

**7** In the next phase of this project you are going to work with a series of short extracts from two stories written by Angela **Carter**. The stories are *The Company of Wolves* and *The Werewolf* from *The Bloody Chamber*, which are both based on *Little Red Riding Hood*. There are four extracts, so you could share them out among the class, or try them all if you are in a small group.

- You may use all the words in the extract or only a few – but the *sense* of your extract must be fully communicated to the audience. There are two further objectives for the work. You must *vocalise* and *physicalise* your extract(s) as effectively as you can. This will mean working out how best to use the voices in the group to speak words, to repeat or echo them and also to provide any other sounds which you think appropriate. Then think about how the people in your group can be used to make shapes, gestures and movements that will provide the 'visual' dimension of your work.

- Before you begin, consider your extract alongside the headings that we used earlier:
  - events
  - context
  - characters
  - emotions/mood
  - author's perspective
  - theme.

- Then discuss the *impact* you want to have on your audience and how you will use the dramatic elements to achieve it.

- Finally, rehearse and perform, paying close attention to the audience's feedback – were they *affected* in the way that you hoped? If not, what would you now change to strengthen your performance?

> ### *From* The Bloody Chamber *by Angela Carter*
>
> **1** It is a northern country; they have cold weather, they have cold hearts. Cold, tempest; wild beasts in the forest. It is a hard life. Their houses are built of logs, dark and smoky within. There will be a crude icon of the virgin behind a guttering candle, the leg of a pig hung up to cure, a string of drying mushrooms. A bed, a stool, a table. Harsh, brief, poor lives.
>
> **2** Children do not stay young for long in this savage country. There are no toys for them to play with so they work hard and grow wise but this one, so pretty and the youngest of her family, a little late-comer, had been indulged by her mother and grandmother who'd knitted her the red shawl that, today, has the ominous if brilliant look of blood on snow.
>
> **3** The good child does as her mother bids – five miles' trudge through the forest; do not leave the path because of the bears, the wild boar, the starving wolves. Here take your father's hunting knife; you know how to use it.
>
> **4** The child had a scabby coat of sheepskin to keep out the cold, she knew the forest too well to fear it but she must always be on her guard. When she heard that freezing howl of a wolf, she dropped her gifts, seized her knife and turned on the beast.

Although stories in theatre are usually told as if they were happening rather than as reported events in the past, there are playwrights and practitioners who have been interested in using storytelling as part of the play. In this way they can combine events in the past (which are told to us by a *narrator* who may or may not be a character in the play) with events in the present (dramatised scenes from the story that occur in the present). **Bertolt *Brecht* is famous for using narrators, songs and other devices so that his plays are a combination of events from the past with events played in the present.** Contemporary practitioners who take an interest in using storytelling as part of their theatre include Mike *Alfreds* and Nancy *Meckler* who both have worked for *Shared Experience*; Brian *Friel* and other playwrights associated with the *Abbey Theatre* in Dublin; **Simon *McBurney*** and the work of *Théâtre De Complicité* and **Theatre Alibi**.

# Ritual

Since the beginnings of time, rituals have been used as communal events that celebrate or confirm the shared beliefs, customs and taboos of a community. Rituals usually require that all who are present must participate in, or believe in, the ritual. Taking part in a ritual is like saying 'this is what we believe in, this is the group that I belong to and by taking part I am showing the world that I agree to live by this group's rules and beliefs'. The rituals of a society may include examples such as: the Catholic Mass, funerals, calls to prayer, circumcision and bar mitzvah, Diwali, Eid and Ramadan rites, weddings, coronations, investitures, school prize-giving ceremonies, protest marches, chanting at football matches, trick or treat and other Halloween rituals.

Rituals may be no more than the customs and courtesies of everyday life – the way that we greet each other or show politeness to each other. But the purpose of rituals may also be to transform or change something or someone,

The purpose of rituals may be to transform or change something or someone forever. Through various symbolic acts, through the participation and belief of those who are present, it is imagined that some lasting change can be made. In the Catholic Mass, for instance, the bread and wine become transformed into the body and blood of Christ. In the wedding ceremony, a spinster or bachelor becomes a bride or groom – a wife or a husband. In many societies there are rituals, or rites of passage, which transform boys and girls into men and women, The ritual is a way of showing that from now on this person has joined the world of adults and left childhood behind.

Rituals share common features with theatre. They are both social rather than private events, they both use symbols and symbolic gestures, and they both comment on and explain the culture they belong to. In the twentieth century, many theatre practitioners have been drawn to the idea of ritual and ritual performances because of their transformational power and the sense of community associated with ritual. **Imagine how attractive the idea is that through your play or performance you could change or transform people forever!** Theatre artists have also been interested in harnessing the spirituality and sense of shared experience in rituals that celebrate or mark the changing seasons or rhythms in the natural world – rituals to mark winter, harvest, births and deaths. *Meyerhold, Grotowski, Artaud,* **Barba**, *Brook* and **Wilson** are among well-known twentieth-century practitioners who have included ritual ideas and forms in their work. There is also a long tradition of playwrights who have focused on the negative effect of our everyday rituals, which they have sought to reveal as oppressive, reactionary, or false. Such authors would include *Ibsen, Chekhov, Synge,* **Beckett**, **Pinter** and others.

A ritualistic performance will seek to appeal to the audience's sense of the spiritual and may use the elements of fire, water, earth and air in highly symbolic ways. The audience in ritual theatre will be treated more as a congregation or as a community than as a paying audience of individuals.

# Shamanism

The shaman transforms into a spirit – the spirit takes on the physical form of the shaman

The shaman is a special kind of priest who officiates in healing rituals. Sometimes the shaman is referred to as a 'witch-doctor', 'sorcerer' or 'medicine man'. The shaman enters into a trance by taking hallucinogenic drugs or by fasting and meditating. It is believed that powerful spirits take hold of the shaman while he/she is in the trance – in other words the shaman transforms into a spirit – the spirit takes on the physical form of the shaman. There are two important connections with theatre here. First, the shaman brings the invisible world of sprits and demons into the actual world, which is also the ambition of some forms of *non-realist* and *symbolic* theatre. Second, the shaman, from the audience's point of view, transforms into another character for the duration of the trance. This idea of the shaman transforming into another being is very like the *Stanislavskian* and *Grotowskian* styles of *representational* acting which seek to convince the audience that the actor has *become* the character.

In many Western cultures people are suspicious of the idea of spirits, demons or ghosts – anything that can't be seen or heard or touched or proved to exist, but that hasn't stopped theatre practitioners from trying to physically and visually represent both the visible world and the invisible worlds of dreams, nightmares and fantasies. Artists who have sought to combine these worlds in their work would include *Ibsen* in *Peer Gynt*, **Strindberg**, Antonin *Artaud*, and Eugenio *Barba*.

A witch-doctor in Bulawayo, Zimbabwe

The transformation of the shaman into another spirit-being is closely related to those forms of acting in which the actor is skilful enough to create the illusion that she or he has literally become or turned into the character he or she is portraying. Practitioners associated with the 'shaman' model of acting would include Eugenio *Barba*, Jerzy *Grotowski* and Peter *Brook*.

# Dance

From the earliest of times people in many cultures have been both entertained by dance and also have used it for ritual and communal activity. When you go 'clubbing' with your friends on a Saturday night you are participating in an ancient tradition! The fifth-century Greeks combined dance and drama in the performances of the *tragedies*, *comedies* and *satyr plays*, and in other cultures the imitation of animals, the introduction of masks and the *miming* of human behaviours in dances blurred distinctions between what we would now call dance, drama and storytelling.

**The idea that dance and drama are two different art forms is particular to Western culture.** In many non-European performance traditions there is a mix of drama, dance, songs and music, which together make a single performance style.

The idea that dance and drama are different art forms is also relatively modern. The earliest ideas about dance as an art form in its own right emerged in Italy in the fifteenth century, and in 1661 the rules and principles of *ballet*, which are still in use today, were developed by the

The performers of the *Commedia dell'Arte* were highly-skilled dancers

Académie Royale de Danse in Paris. In the *Renaissance* period of theatre, no distinction was made between actors and dancers, and indeed performers were expected to be skilled actors, dancers and acrobats. The performers of the *Commedia dell'Arte* were highly-skilled dancers and much of the pleasure of a performance came from the acrobatic dance routines. *Molière* is best known now as an actor and playwright, but in his own time he was also famous as a *mime* artist and dancer. We do not know as much about the training of actors in the past as we do about the playwrights, but it can be assumed that professional performers have always been trained in dance as well as in acting.

In the chapter on directing (see Chapter 5), we shall see that many of the great directors of the twentieth century have been drawn again to dance and *mime* as key elements in theatrical performance. The focus on developing the actor's use of *movement* to convey meaning is based on the tradition of *Commedia dell'Arte* actor training.

**The influence of dance in twentieth-century theatre**

Dancers and *mime* artists have had a considerable influence on the development of *non-realist* theatre styles. At the turn of the twentieth century there was an extraordinary dancer called Isadora *Duncan* whose free use of movement and the body shocked audiences. She rejected the formalism of the *ballet* and sought to create the dancer of the future who would 'dance the freedom of women'. She was also responsible for introducing her lover Gordon *Craig* to *Stanislavski*.

*Craig* saw dance and movement as being the essential language of the stage and proposed removing *realist* actors entirely and replacing them with *uber-marionettes* or dancing puppets. As a result of these theories and *Craig*'s contact with the *Moscow Art Theatre (MAT)*, Vsevolod *Meyerhold* developed his *non-realist* acting style of *bio-mechanics*, based on the principle that movement rather than words conveyed the 'reality' of behaviour. *Meyerhold*'s actors trained in *Commedia dell'Arte* techniques, acrobatics, fencing and throwing the discus in order to develop a highly balletic acting style.

The work of other great dancers like Mary **Wigman** and Pina **Bausch** is often referred to as dance theatre because their work blurs and crosses the

Isadora Duncan and her School of Greek Dancing, 1908

boundaries between the two art forms. Between 1914 and 1942, *Wigman* performed her own solo dances but she also choreographed for the stage. She said:

> *I feel that the dance is a language which is inherent, but slumbering in every one of us. It is possible for every human to experience the dance as an expression in his own body and in his own way.*

Contemporary dance performances by Pina *Bausch* and the *Wuppertal Dance Theatre* often attract a theatre audience and are reviewed as theatre. *Bausch* represents 'characters' and 'settings' in her work through attention to the detail of gestures and body movements. She seeks to discover 'not how people move but what moves them'. Her sets are often highly realist or covered in natural materials like earth, flowers and water.

In recent times, *non-realist* directors (*Artaud*, *Grotowski* and *Brook*, for example), have continued the tradition of highlighting the physical movement and gestures of the actor as the core of performance. The Italian director Dario *Fo* has reclaimed the skills and techniques of the *Commedia dell'Arte* in his energetic and stylised physical performances of *Mistero Buffo*. Many modern *physical theatre* practitioners like *Théâtre de Complicité* and *DV8* combine elements of the *Commedia dell'Arte* style with ideas from the great twentieth-century *mime* teachers Etienne **Decroux** and Jacques **Lecoq**.

# Martial Arts/Contests of Skill and Strength

In many cultures, exhibitions and contests of martial arts and other physical skills are a popular form of entertainment and are closely related to theatre and drama. We have already noted that Athenian drama developed the idea of a conflict or tension between characters, groups or ideas, and that most plays have some sort of contest at their core. The Athenians had a lively sporting culture as well as an interest in the theatre – our modern Olympic games have their origin in this same period of history.

In some forms of Chinese, West African and Latin American theatre, the skills, grace and dexterity of a martial art are included as part of the performance style. In the modern Western tradition of theatre actors are often now expected to have the same physical capabilities as athletes. The increasing influence of *physical theatre* and the tendency towards blurring drama and dance in theatre has led to a much more acrobatic style of acting that requires a strong physique and great stamina. Some contemporary Western performers will use exercises taken from *t'ai chi*, *kung fu*, *aikido* and other systems of physical training based on the martial arts.

In earlier times, audiences would enjoy both theatre and the spectacles and excitement of physical contests and displays of skill. The *Globe* and *Rose* theatres of *Shakespeare*'s time, for example, staged wrestling matches and bear-baiting contests alongside plays. In the unlicensed theatres of the eighteenth century, extracts from plays would be performed as part of a mixed evening of entertainment that would also include jugglers and acrobats and tests of strength. This tradition was kept alive in the nineteenth and early twentieth century by *music hall* and **vaudeville** performances.

*The Street of Crocodiles*, Théâtre de Complicité, Royal National Theatre, 1992

### Task 7: The Keeper of the Keys exercise

In this exercise you are going to use the old children's game of 'Keeper of the Keys' to explore the similarities and differences between games, contests and theatre.

1 To play the original game, set a chair in the middle of a large circle of spectators. A volunteer is placed on the chair and blindfolded. A large set of keys, or other object that will jangle, is placed under the 'keeper's' chair. The 'keeper' is given a stick or rolled sheet of paper to help 'protect' the keys. Ask for silence and then ask for a second volunteer who will try and creep forward and 'steal' the keys without being hit by the 'keeper'!

2 Try playing the game a few times, then pause for reflection. What is the difference between a game such as this in which there are only two 'players' and an audience as opposed to games in which everyone participates? What holds our interest as the audience? What emotions do we experience as we watch?

The game has a clear link to sporting events, which also involve two or more players in a contest which has an unknown result – part of our interest in watching is to see who will win. In this game, as in many other forms of entertainment, there are two sides competing against each other and there is a clear sense of what will be lost and gained from victory.

3 Now play the game again but this time the two players should try and 'show' the audience that there is some sort of contest going on in which both players have a 'stake' – they both need to win. How does the contest change now that it is being 'acted'? In other words, now that the players are trying to show what it would be like to be the 'hunter' and the 'keeper'. Are we still interested as an audience? Is there anything added to what we experience as we watch?

4 Now play the game for the third time but this time without the blindfold! You could either work in pairs to choreograph your movements and consider how to make the 'game' interesting for the audience, or improvise in front of the group. You should still leave the outcome of the game to be worked out between the players as the 'game' develops. What is the interest for the audience now? What are we watching? Is this now a drama?

The model for much theatre and drama, which is based on the idea of conflict, can be found in games and contests, but drama does more than present us with a simple trial of skill and strength. **In drama, we are conscious that we are watching a *'representation'* of a contest – a story about a contest rather than the contest itself.** We are interested in the characters, their motives, backgrounds, strengths and weaknesses. Sometimes the 'contest' at the heart of the drama might make us laugh at the vanity or foolishness of the competing characters; sometimes we are moved to tears or anger by the tragedy or futility of the contest. The simple game model of drama is sometimes a useful way of checking that your own devised performances or scenes will be interesting to follow. Try using these questions about your own work:

- *Who are the players?*
- *What is the nature of the contest between them?*
- *What is at stake for the players – what will be won and lost?*
- *What will interest the audience in this contest (why should they be 'bothered' by what goes on)?*
- *How will the contest be played out (the scenes or events of the drama)?*

# 3 Playing the Given Circumstances

## Outline

In this chapter we are going to look at, and practise, *realist* styles of acting. *Realism* is still the most popular acting style in film and TV and we will begin, in Part 1, by considering the core concept of **given circumstances** and how the actor identifies and plays them.

We will focus on the ideas of two of the greatest practitioners of the *realist* style of acting: Konstantin *Stanislavski* and Lee **Strasberg**. Both developed specific approaches to *realist* acting which focused on building a complex psychological understanding of character – *Stanislavski*'s system and *Strasberg*'s *method*. The work of both these directors and theatre teachers is complex and we will only be introducing ourselves to the basic techniques associated with their work. We will return to the ideas of *Stanislavski* in particular in our more advanced work on directing in Chapter 6 and on textual analysis in Chapter 8.

Part 2 is a workshop in *realist* acting based on a scene from Arthur *Miller*'s *The Crucible* in which we will explore how to play a scene in the *realist* style and practically explore some of the ideas presented in Part 1.

## Part 1  What are the Given Circumstances?

The 'given circumstances' is the term that *Stanislavski* gave to the essential information about characters' past lives and relationships, the circumstances and incidents which are revealed by the playwright, particularly near the beginning of the play in the *exposition* but also as the play develops. In most *realist* styles of drama it is understood that the characters behave in ways that are 'true' to their given circumstances. In other words, what characters do and say and how they react to others is a consequence of their past lives and relationships. The 'given circumstances' determine how a character will react to each new event in the plot of the play. When you look at a scene from a *realist* play, the problem is to know how the words and directions given by the playwright should be 'played' rather than merely read through. The 'given circumstances' tell you how the lines and other directions should be delivered.

*Stanislavski* tried to present characters who behaved 'consistently'. **He tried to make his characters credible for an audience by ensuring that every action and reaction was part of a consistent pattern of behaviour –** the character would respond to new events in ways which were consistent with how they responded to similar events in the past. This method of working required his actors to undertake deep research into the psychology of character – searching the text for clues, thinking about the character's past, imagining the character in a variety of different situations. The effect of this style of direction is to produce characters that are predictable, unified and constant.

The American director Lee *Strasberg* developed his method from *Stanislavski's* work, but with a difference. *Strasberg* believed that characters often experienced a conflict between their own inner feelings and sense of truth and the behaviour that is socially or culturally expected of them. In *Strasberg's* style of direction, characters may sometimes behave unpredictably, or have sudden outbursts of strong emotions which may seem 'out of character' but which help an audience to understand the inner turmoil (or 'inner circumstances' as *Stanislavski* called it) of a character's life. In both forms of *realist* acting, close attention to the 'given circumstances' is essential in the preparation and rehearsal of character. The actor is expected to play the 'given circumstances' for the audience – in other words, the actor must find ways to physically express as much of the information in the 'given circumstances' as possible.

## Identifying the Given Circumstances

The simplest way of identifying the 'given circumstances' of a scene is to record:

* Who is present?
* When is it happening?
* Where is it happening?
* What is happening?
* What has happened/What might happen next?

Making notes in response to these questions will help you to identify the basics of the 'given circumstances' of a scene (see opposite). This simple list also tells us something about the depth and complexity of the work that actors and directors need to do in order to create a performance that is really consistent with the 'given circumstances' of the play.

Making a list of the given circumstances is only the beginning for the actor and director. In order to play the given circumstances, both use all the available elements of drama to physically create the scene for the audience. Timing, use of space, objects, sounds and lighting can all be used to help in this creation. For the actor, the body will be the principle means of conveying the given circumstances for the audience. The actor will 'physically' experience the circumstances – physically respond to the place, for example. This often means doing a lot of 'sensory' work in rehearsal. The actor who plays *King Lear* on the verge of madness alone with the fool on the storm-swept moors might need to try (and physically through the senses) answer the following questions:

* What does the moor look like? What and how far can you see?
* What would the cold and wet feel like?
* What does it smell of?
* What can you hear?
* Is there a wind blowing, is it raining, how does the rain feel when it touches you?
* Does a madman experience the moor in the same way as a sane man?
* If you fall to the ground, how would it feel – soft/hard, wet, brambly?
* How easy/difficult is it to walk across the moor – would you stumble or need to jump over holes and dips?

The director and designers may assist in the creation of the illusion of a storm-swept moor by using design, objects and sound and lighting effects, but in the end **it is the actor who must convince us that he is experiencing**

| Who is present? | How a character behaves in a scene will depend on who else is present. The status, age, dramatic importance and previous shared experiences of the characters will all influence how each actor plays their character in the scene. In thinking about how to play the scene you must consider how to play with the other actors so that the relationships between characters are made clear for an audience. Sometimes, the actors must also think about other characters in the play who are not present but whose influence will be strongly felt by those involved in the scene. |
|---|---|
| When is it happening? | The 'when' of a scene is also complex. What **period** of time is the scene/play set? People behaved and thought differently in different historical periods. The actors may need to research the customs and manners of a particular period in order to play the character in the context of their, rather than our, time.<br><br>'When' also refers to the place of the scene in the play. In playing the scene the actors must remind the audience of what has already happened and also lay the ground for what will come later on in the play. A play 'unfolds' and actors must take care to let their characters develop as it does. How an actor plays a particular scene will therefore depend on the place of the scene in the overall structure of the play or the stage in the character's development. 'When' will also refer to the **actual time** of the scene – a morning scene may have a different feel to an evening scene. The scene may be leisurely and relaxed or it may have a sense of urgency and pace. |
| Where is it happening? | **The place that the scene is set in will also have an important influence on how the actors play it.** Is it a public place, requiring formal behaviour, or is it an intimate and private place that will allow actors to reveal their true feelings and thoughts? The physical characteristics of the scene must also be considered – is it outdoors/indoors, is it cold/warm, and is it threatening/claustrophobic? Does this place have a particular significance for a character or characters? Have they been there before? Are they likely to have memories that might influence them now? |
| What is happening? | At a simple level, what is happening refers to the most obvious level of 'doing' in the scene. A family dinner, for instance, or a meeting. But in most *realist* plays we also expect there to be a *sub-text* which refers to what is happening underneath the surface. The family dinner might also be a power struggle between two characters. The meeting might be an opportunity to reveal a character's true motives. **The actors have to play both the surface and the sub-text.** This often means working out what each character's motives are – why do they do what they do. This in turn may lead to thinking about what a character's objective is for the scene – what is this character trying to make happen in the scene? |
| What has happened/What might happen next? | A scene is always written as if it is happening 'here and now' rather than as a record of some past event. The actors need to create the illusion that the scene is actually taking place now. But in most forms of *realism*, the 'here and now' is different from the 'here and now' of everyday life. **The scene will also reveal what has happened and suggest for the audience what will happen later on in the play.**<br><br>When a play begins, the audience seems to be suddenly involved in what is happening to the characters on stage, but the playwright will need to give information that will help the audience understand the 'given circumstances' – the history and other significant factors which will help the audience understand what they are seeing and create an interest in what might happen next. In other words, what will be the consequences of what we are seeing now? **The problem for the actors is how to play the scene as an immediate 'here and now' experience while also expressing what has happened prior to the play's beginning and hinting at what is to come.** |

the physical reality of the scene. For each of the 'What' questions above, the actor needs to experiment and play with the sensory details – it is not an intellectual exercise in making lists of relevant information; it is about discovering how a character experiences the touch, sound, sight and smells of a scene. What *Stanislavski* wanted was for his actors to physically and mentally *live through* the characters and the situations in a play; to behave *'as if'* they had become the characters and were actually living their lives.

## Exercises

Both *Stanislavski* and *Strasberg* created exercises to help actors develop their physical and sensory experience of the 'given circumstances' of their character. Actors in rehearsal still commonly use some of, or variations on, these exercises.

|  | **STANISLAVSKI'S SYSTEM** |
|---|---|
| Magic if | This is based on the human ability to imagine what it would be like to be in a different situation, to walk in someone else's shoes – if *I* were King Lear on the moor what would *I* do, what would it be like, how would *I* feel? In the **system** the actor builds a character on his or her own self – she or he finds themselves in the character and finds the character in themselves! |
| Emotion memory | The actor and director identify the **dominant emotion** that the character will experience in the scene. The actor then tries to remember a time in their own life when they felt that emotion – of great sadness, of loss, of uncontrollable rage, of joy. The actor then tries to recall the experience in as much detail as they possibly can; they keep on concentrating until they can re-experience the emotion as if it was happening now. |
| Units and objectives | Each actor plots the major experiences and turning points in the character's development across the whole play. These are the milestones that establish the character's **through-line of action** – the path this character will travel, changing and evolving as the play develops. Discussion then leads to each actor defining the **super-objective** for his or her character – what is at stake for this character (the motivation) and what the character is trying to make happen in the play. |
| | Once the super-objective is established the actor then looks at each scene of the play, or smaller **units** within a scene of the play, and decides on the character's objective for that scene or unit. The objective for each scene or unit must be named. For example, I want to convince X or I want Y to trust me. Finally, the actor compares the objectives for each scene with the super-objective and through-line of action in order to make sure that the super-objective will be realised through the objectives for each scene. In other words, if the objectives for each scene are taken together, do they add up to the super-objective? |
| Circle and/or object of attention | These exercises are designed to help actors to overcome their self-consciousness of the audience and to prevent them from self-consciously playing the characters. They are intended to produce performances that are 'natural'; the actors lose themselves behind the mask of the character. |
| | In the first exercise, the actors work in a blacked-out studio – a small space is lit around the actors who focus on every detail of the space. As the actors improvise or play the scene their attention remains entirely focused on the lit space rather than on the darkness and audience beyond. Gradually, the space is increased and the actors take in more and more detail until they become 'unconscious' of what lies in the darkness beyond. |
| | In the object exercise, the actor focuses entirely on a significant object or prop while improvising or playing the scene. The actor gives total concentration to how the character would touch and feel the object, how they would gaze at it and what thoughts and feelings the object might arouse for the character. |

| Communion | The above exercises are intended to help actors create what *Stanislavski* called 'communion', which describes the total attention that the actor must give to something or someone other than the audience. For *Stanislavski*, there were five types of communion that actors might focus on to help their concentration:<br><br>**1** With oneself as in a *soliloquy* between the character's heart and mind.<br>**2** With another 'soul', meaning another actor.<br>**3** With a real object.<br>**4** With an imaginary object (the dagger in *Macbeth* for instance).<br>**5** With a crowd or chorus. |
|---|---|
| **Method of physical actions (MPA)** | The *system* often resulted in actors spending a great deal of time working on the text at an intellectual level – making notes and identifying objectives and the given circumstances from their reading of the text prior to rehearsals. At the end of his career *Stanislavski* invented the MPA to encourage the actors to begin with physical work on the character. The actor would be asked to perform a simple stage direction like entering a room. As the actor tries to execute this action they are forced to consider the given circumstances – why am I entering the room? How would I enter the room? What's my objective for doing so? As the actor continues to work on the action they begin to work out the physical and psychological life of the character. The MPA led to the breaking down of each scene into three or four key actions, each of which was given a name or motive – for example, I open the door to attract X's attention. |
| | **STRASBERG'S METHOD** |
| **Sense memory** | *Strasberg*'s exercise is similar to 'emotion memory' but with a greater emphasis on the actors' abilities to forcibly express strong and painful emotions. The actors recall an experience that was a powerfully strong emotional event for them. They build up all their sensory memories of the event – how it felt, how it smelt and looked. They talk about the experience of how they felt physically and any other sensory information they can recall, until they are able to trigger the emotion in themselves. The idea was to keep working on a range of powerful memories in this way so that the actor could have a set of emotions that they could trigger when needed – pain, loss, tears, laughter, etc. |
| **Singing the words** | *Strasberg* believed that the text and the words were often blocks to the actor's characterisation, so he developed a series of exercises to help. These included playing the scene but using 'gibberish' language so that the actors would focus on the details of action and the expression of emotion. Actors might also be asked to speak their lines, or recite a poem or *monologue* while performing a number of completely different activities suggested by the class – having a shower or shopping in the supermarket, for example. |
| **The scene** | *Strasberg* placed great emphasis on improvisation as a means of helping actors to discover and play the inner depth of their characters. 'The scene' is a semi-prepared improvisation involving one or more of the characters in a usually very ordinary or domestic scene. The idea was for the actors to be given time on stage in front of an audience to 'become' the character – to explore how the character would sit and how they would respond to the detail of the stage and the other characters. This exercise helps actors to 'naturally' become the character on stage. |

# Part 2 The Crucible Workshop

## Identifying the Given Circumstances

*The Crucible*, by the American playwright Arthur **Miller**, is set in the village of Salem in the State of Massachusetts, USA, in 1692. The plot of the play is based on the historical facts of a witch-hunt of the time that resulted in many innocent people being hung for witchcraft. At first the accusers were a group of adolescent girls, but many people became accusers in order to settle old scores or to try and gain more land and property. The play was written in 1953 when many Americans felt that the House Un-American Activities Committee under Senator Joseph McCarthy was imprisoning and ruining innocent people on trumped-up charges of being communists. The scene that follows is taken from the opening of the second of the play's four acts. It involves John and Elizabeth Proctor – a husband and wife who farm near to the village of Salem.

*(The common-room of Proctor's house, eight days later)*
*At the right is a door opening on the fields outside. A fireplace is at the left, and behind it a stairway leading upstairs. It is the low, dark, and rather long living room of the time. As the curtain rises, the room is empty. From above, ELIZABETH is heard softly singing to the children. Presently the door opens and JOHN PROCTOR enters, carrying his gun. He glances about the room as he comes towards the fireplace, then halts for an instant as he hears her singing. He continues on to the fireplace, leans the gun against the wall as he swings a pot out of the fire and smells it. Then he lifts out the ladle and tastes. He is not quite pleased. He reaches to a cupboard, takes a pinch of salt, and drops it into the pot. As he is tasting again, her footsteps are heard on the stair. He swings the pot into the fireplace and goes to a basin and washes his hands and face. ELIZABETH enters.*

Liam Neeson and Laura Linney in *The Crucible*, Virginia Theater, New York, 2002

There is a tradition in *realist* playwriting of using detailed stage directions to provide the details of setting and action for actors to follow. Like *Chekhov*, *Ibsen*, **Shaw** and others, *Miller* prefaces the scene with these directions. They are meaningful signs of the 'given circumstances' of the scene that follows. Begin by working practically, using the MPA technique with these directions.

## Task 1: Working the stage directions

Begin with a copy of the directions and mark any words, actions or descriptive details that you think will prove to be significant to the scene that follows. Does the description of the room as being 'low' and 'dark' matter? Is it important that we hear Elizabeth singing off-stage? Once you have marked your directions discuss your ideas with your friends and discuss how the marked sections might become significant in the scene that follows. Now, prepare a list of questions about the directions that might include: Why is Proctor 'not quite pleased'? Why does he add salt to the pot? Why does he wash his hands afterwards? Keep this list for future reference.

You will need to work in a group of three for this task. Two of you will act the characters of Elizabeth and John while the third reads the stage directions. You can alternate these roles as you go through the task.

1  Arrange the space with objects and furniture to represent the room, the staircase and the room above where Elizabeth is singing to her children. The actors go through the actions exactly as the reader of the directions describes them. Try this a couple of times until you are familiar with the sequence.

2  Now go back to your annotated copies of the directions and the list of questions and consider them again. How can the actors draw attention to the highlighted words? Are the questions any clearer now? Begin the sequence again but this time the actors must try to draw attention to the significant details. You might also try playing the sequence until one of the characters reaches a question, at which point he or she stops and asks: 'Why am I doing this?' Anyone present can make suggestions to the actor before they carry on: 'Because you don't like her cooking'; 'Because you haven't heard your wife singing before'; etc.

3  Play the sequence again but this time the reader will add directions on pace and timing: QUICKLY enters; SLOWLY walks to the fireplace; swings a pot out of the fire and PAUSES; HURRIES to the basin; Elizabeth enters VERY SLOWLY.

Discuss and make notes on the dramatic potential of this sequence – why should it hold an audience's interest? What potential tensions or 'sub-texts' are there?

This is the dialogue that follows.

|   |   |   |
|---|---|---|
| 1 | *Elizabeth*: | What keeps you so late? It's almost dark. |
| 2 | *Proctor*: | I were planting far out to the forest edge. |
| 3 | *Elizabeth*: | Oh, you're done then. |
| 4 | *Proctor*: | Aye, the farm is seeded. The boys asleep? |
| 5 | *Elizabeth*: | They will be soon. (*And she goes to the fireplace, proceeds to ladle up stew in a dish*) |
| 6 | *Proctor*: | Pray now for a fair summer. |
| 7 | *Elizabeth*: | Aye. |
| 8 | *Proctor*: | Are you well today? |
| 9 | *Elizabeth*: | I am. (*She brings the plate to the table, and indicating the food*) It is a rabbit. |
| 10 | *Proctor*: | (*going to the table*) Oh, is it! In Jonathan's trap? |
| 11 | *Elizabeth*: | No, she walked into the house this afternoon; I found her sittin' in the corner like she come to visit. |

| 12 | Proctor: | Oh, that's a good sign walkin' in. |
| 13 | Elizabeth: | Pray God. It hurt my heart to strip her, poor rabbit. (*She sits and watches him taste it*) |
| 14 | Proctor: | It's well seasoned. |
| 15 | Elizabeth: | (*blushing with pleasure*) I took great care. She's tender? |
| 16 | Proctor: | Aye. (*He eats, she watches him*) I think we'll see green fields soon. It's warm as blood beneath the clods. |
| 17 | Elizabeth: | That's well. |
| 18 | | (*Proctor eats then looks up*) |
| 19 | Proctor: | If the crop is good I'll buy George Jacob's heifer. How would that please you? |
| 20 | Elizabeth: | Aye, it would. |
| 21 | Proctor: | (*with a grin*) I mean to please you, Elizabeth. |
| 22 | Elizabeth: | (*it is hard to say*) I know it, John. |
| 23 | | (*He gets up, goes to her, kisses her. She receives it. With a certain disappointment, he returns to the table*) |
| 24 | Proctor: | (*as gently as he can*) Cider? |
| 25 | Elizabeth: | (*with a sense of reprimanding herself for having forgot*) Aye! (*She gets up and goes and pours a glass for him. He now arches his back*) |
| 26 | Proctor: | This farm's a continent when you go foot by foot droppin' seeds in it. |
| 27 | Elizabeth: | (*coming with the cider*) It must be. |
| 28 | Proctor: | (*drinks a long draught, then, putting the glass down*) You ought to bring some flowers in the house. |
| 29 | Elizabeth: | Oh, I forgot! I will tomorrow. |
| 30 | Proctor: | It's winter in here yet. On Sunday let you come with me, and we'll walk the farm together; I never see such a load of flowers on the earth. (*With good feeling he goes and looks up at the sky through the open doorway*) Lilacs have a purple smell. Lilac is the smell of nightfall, I think. Massachusetts is a beauty in the spring! |
| 31 | Elizabeth: | Aye it is. |

(*There is a pause. She is watching him from the table as he stands there absorbing the night. It is as though she would speak but cannot. Instead, now, she takes up the basin. Her back is turned to him. He turns to her and watches her. A sense of their separation rises*)

## Task 2: Identifying the given circumstances

Read through the scene, take time to discuss with the others how the scene clarifies or changes the ideas and questions that came from the previous task. Now begin to fill out the given circumstances of the scene based on the information you have. Wherever possible you should provide line references to support your views. Leave yourself room to add to the given circumstances later in the workshop.

| Who is present? | There are only two characters present but what can you tell about the characters from this scene? Are there any clues about their relationship? Look at the words spoken and the directions to help you. |
| --- | --- |

| When is it happening? | Are there any clues about the historical period of the scene – in the language perhaps, or in the status relationship between man and wife? Is it important that the scene is set in the evening? How does the time of day affect the pace of the scene – does it seem rushed or leisurely to you? |
|---|---|
| Where is it happening? | Again the setting is obvious, but what is the relationship between the setting and the feel of the scene? Could the same scene have occurred in a public or outside setting? Does the language and mood of the scene fit the setting? Does the description of the room contribute to the mood of the scene? |
| What is happening? | On the surface the scene is of a man returning from the fields and being given his supper by his wife, but what else is going on in this scene? What is the 'sub-text'? Make a note of any lines that you think provide a clue to what is going on beneath the surface (e.g. 23, 21 and 22). Try to build a theory or idea about what is happening beneath the surface of the meal. |
| What has happened/ What might happen next? | Does the playwright provide any clues in this scene as to what has happened previously or what might be going to happen later in the play? Again, pick out the lines that you think provide the clues and try and imagine what has happened/will happen. |

Look through your notes and compare with others where there are points of difference. Look together at the text. Words, actions and directions in *realist* drama are often ambiguous – i.e. they can be understood in more than one way. Now read on! Below, the given circumstances of the scene have been fleshed out by adding details from the rest of the play. Read through this new information and think about how it changes the given circumstances that the two actors would need to respond to in order to play the scene.

**John Proctor** is a key character in the play. When we first meet him, *Miller* describes him thus:

> Proctor was a farmer in his middle thirties ... powerful of body, even-tempered and not easily led ... there is evidence to suggest that he had a sharp and biting way with hypocrites ... a man in his prime ... with a quiet confidence and an unexpressed, hidden force.

In the first act of the play it seems as though the rest of Salem has gone mad – everyone seems willing to believe the girls and their wild accusations of witchcraft, except John Proctor. He suspects that the girls are lying to cover up their own mischief. They had been discovered dancing naked in the woods by **Thomas Putnam**, the father of one of the girls. Such an activity, in a Puritan society, would have led to a severe whipping for the girls. So, they invent the charges of witchcraft. Proctor is a well-respected leader in the community. He has the power to stop the witch-hunt, and people will listen to him. But he does nothing. Why?

*Miller* also says of Proctor:

> the steady manner he displays does not spring from an untroubled soul. He is a sinner, a sinner not only against the moral fashion of the time, but against his own vision of decent conduct.

What troubles his soul? He has had a sexual relationship with **Abigail Williams**, who is the leader of the girls; she is described by *Miller* as:

Abigail Williams, seventeen, enters – a strikingly beautiful girl, an orphan, with an endless capacity for dissembling.

Abigail worked for the Proctors as a maid until Elizabeth suspected that her husband was having an affair with her. She then threw Abigail out onto the streets. Proctor has tried to end his relationship with Abigail. He says to her:

I will cut off my hand before I'll ever reach for you again.

But Abigail still has strong feelings for Proctor and believes he still 'loves' her (and maybe he does!). Her reason for dancing in the woods was to cast a charm on Elizabeth to kill her and get her out of the way.

So, the problem for Proctor is that in order to reveal the truth he must publicly declare himself to be a lecher – a middle-aged man who seduced a 17-year-old girl employed as his servant – and so destroy his reputation in the community. It is possible to read the play and feel some sympathy for Proctor's dilemma while blaming Abigail for leading him on. Abigail is responsible for the accusations of witchcraft and she will go on to accuse both Elizabeth and John with tragic results. But, it should be remembered that Abigail is young and vulnerable. She is an orphan with no father of her own and seeing her own parents die traumatised her:

I saw Indians smash my dear parents' heads on the pillow next to mine.

**Elizabeth Proctor** is not introduced in detail. We have to pick up on the clues in the text. It appears that John had his affair while his wife was ill from childbirth. In other words, he wasn't enjoying a sexual relationship with her at the time. But is this a good enough excuse for the affair? There are frequent references to Elizabeth being cold towards John. For example:

She is a cold, snivelling woman. (Abigail to Proctor)

Oh. Elizabeth, your justice would freeze beer. (John to Elizabeth)

Even Elizabeth herself seems to excuse John because of her own temperament:

It needs a cold wife to prompt lechery.

And in the scene we are studying, John seems to refer to Elizabeth's coldness again when he says:

It's winter in here yet. (line 30)

In Act 1 there is a sexually charged and very intimate, private scene between John and Abigail in which she reveals that the charges of witchcraft are a cover-up. The next time we see Proctor is in the scene that we are studying. So he carries any feelings Abigail may have aroused from the first scene into this one. His wife may also strongly suspect that he is still seeing Abigail. She certainly hasn't forgotten what he has done. In this sense there are really *three* characters present. Abigail haunts the scene.

Remember how the scene begins. John enters and *secretly* adds salt to the pot and keeps this secret from Elizabeth. This is a very important action, because it exactly describes the present relationship between John and Elizabeth. He is keeping secrets from her and he has added to the pot/plot without her knowledge.

As the scene begins, Elizabeth knows the dilemma that John is in, and when he enters she expects him to tell her the news from Salem but he does not, nor does she ask. Why?

### Task 3: Working with the new information

Discuss with the class your reactions to this new information; what are your feelings towards the three characters and their dilemma? Now, read through the scene again and make notes on how the scene changes because of what we now know.

1 Work on a *still-image* that will show the rest of the class what you think the relationships are now between Abigail, John and Elizabeth. How can you mould the actors to show their dilemmas, passions, fears and insecurities?

2 Go back to your list of given circumstances and add this new information. Finally, highlight the given circumstances that you think are essential to the scene - how much of the information given should the actors' concentrate on expressing in the scene?

So far, we have made an intellectual analysis of the scene. Now we must think about the emotional levels that will need to be played. It's one thing to understand the scene; quite another to be able to play it as if it was actually occurring to flesh and blood characters.

## Playing the Given Circumstances

We now understand a great deal about the scene, but the biggest problem is still to come – how must the scene be played so that the performance itself will express our understanding of the play to an audience. In theatre there is only what we see and hear on the stage – all that you might want to say about the scene (the characters, the ideas you have) must now be translated into a living performance for an audience. The tasks in this section will work best if you can work in a group of three; two of you will be cast as John and Elizabeth and the third will work as the director. **The two actors now need to learn the lines! And the director needs to review all the material so far produced.**

### Task 4: Dominant emotions

1 You will have begun to feel for John and Elizabeth and their given circumstances. Perhaps you pity Elizabeth as a woman betrayed by her husband, or feel pity for John, because his passions have destroyed his relationship with the wife he loves. But what of the characters themselves? What emotions do they experience during this scene? How would you react to your wife/husband if you were in this situation? Use the grid below to brainstorm the possible feelings experienced by each character during the scene.

|  | **John feels** | **Elizabeth feels** |
|---|---|---|
| Before |  |  |
| During |  |  |
| After |  |  |

2   Are there any key moments in the scene where you think a definite **change of emotion** takes place for either character? Mark these lines.

3   Without raising any painful memories for yourself, can you think of a time when you also experienced any of these emotions? Guilt, perhaps, or fear of losing someone? Think about that time; try and recall your sense memories – what was said, the sights, smells, tactile sensations and the taste it left in your mouth. How close can you get to the emotions of John and Elizabeth in this scene?

4   Finally, decide on the **dominant emotion** for each character in this scene. In other words, John may feel frustrated, sorry, frightened and ashamed but the strongest emotion might be guilt. Now work with three others – two of you will read the scene carefully and slowly while the other two silently play John and Elizabeth. Both pairs, the readers and the actors, should try to express the dominant emotions as the scene progresses. Discuss your experience.

## Task 5: Reflections on the scene

1   Look again at the closing stage directions:

*(There is a pause. She is watching him from the table as he stands there absorbing the night. It is as though she would speak but cannot. Instead, now, she takes up the basin. Her back is turned to him. He turns to her and watches her. A sense of their separation rises)*

2   Arrange two actors to represent John and Elizabeth at the end of the scene, and use the rest of the class to make two *still-images*: the first will appear behind John as Elizabeth watches him in the doorway, the second will appear behind Elizabeth when John turns and watches her at the basin. The directions include the words: 'she would speak but cannot'. In your work, Elizabeth might now speak her thoughts as she watches John and her image. Then let John speak as he watches her. You could end by repeating the image you made earlier of Abigail, John and Elizabeth. Present your work as a dramatic sequence in which we see the actors watching each other in turn and the images of what each sees forming on stage.

## Task 6: Structure of Language

We are going to pause and go back to look at how the text is written. In the previous section we began to generate our own ideas, as performers, about the characters and the situation they are in and to make connections with our own experience. The performance of a play such as *The Crucible* will be a meeting between the ideas and intentions of the performers and those of the playwright. We have already noticed that it is common in *realist* plays for the playwright to give very detailed directions to the players and director. *Miller* has *written* the play to be performed and the given circumstances provided through the words and directions are the principal means by which *Miller* tells actors how to perform his written play text. **As a writer, *Miller* uses all the conventions of writing to help guide the actors.**

1   Look again at the scene and notice how punctuation is used. What is *Miller* telling the actors to do with his use of commas in lines 21 and 22? Why are they there? What effect do they have? Look at when *Miller* uses exclamation marks – why? With what effect? It is not enough to learn the lines in this scene, you must learn the punctuation as well!

*Miller's* punctuation and the length of each character's line also help us to understand the **pace** and timing of the scene. Read the scene again. But this time pay very careful attention to the punctuation and line length: if there is a full stop, exaggerate the pause; if there are no marks, exaggerate the pace.

Can you sense a rhythm of fast, slow exchanges or moments? Make notes about the pacing of the scene to remind you of where the rhythm is.

## Task 7: Scene objectives

In order to play the scene effectively it is important to work out what the objectives for each character might be. You will remember that there are two levels of objective in the *Stanislavskian system* of acting: the super-objective and scene/unit objectives. Below are suggestions for the super-objectives of John and Elizabeth. Now suggest what the **objective** will be for each character in this scene. The objective is always expressed as an action; something the character wants to try and make happen.

| If the super-objective is. . . | John: I want to use my good reputation to stop the madness in this village and I want to forget my mistake and make my wife love me again.<br><br>Elizabeth: I want my marriage back but I must make him face up to what he has done instead of trying to bury his head in the sand. |
|---|---|
| Then the scene objective is. . . | John:<br><br><br><br><br>Elizabeth: |

## Task 8: Strategies, obstacles and tactics

Having decided on the objective for each character in the scene, you now need to decide how the character will try and achieve their objective. This means identifying a *strategy*. **The strategy is the means of achieving the objective.** If your objective for Elizabeth is to make John feel relaxed enough to open up to her, by what strategy will she do this? By trying to please him perhaps, or trying to make him laugh and forget his troubles, or getting him to show some affection? If you decide on a different objective – to make him feel guilt for his betrayal, for example – you will obviously suggest different strategies.

In order for a strategy to work, we often need to adopt different *tactics*. Imagine a game of football: the objective for each team is to win, but they may adopt different strategies for doing so – playing defensively or attacking, for instance. But as the game develops, each team might need to use a range of tactics to achieve their objective. If a player is injured or sent off, if the opposing team's strategy is more successful, a team might need to adopt a new tactic. **In drama, there are two principle tactics that are used by**

**characters: threats and lures** (sticks and carrots). Look at the scene again. Can you identify the tactics? Isn't John using a lure in lines 14 and 21? And threat, or reprimand, in lines 28 and 30?

One reason for a character to change tactics is because another character creates an *obstacle* that must be overcome in order for the character to achieve their objective. Earlier in the play, one imagines that John was trying to achieve his super-objective by avoiding any contact with Abigail and staying at home with Elizabeth, hoping that time would heal the wounds. But the witch-hunt becomes an obstacle and he has to change his tactics. In this scene, line 23 seems to suggest that Elizabeth's lack of enthusiasm for John's kiss is an obstacle to his tactic of showing her physical affection. In the same way John, drawing attention to the lack of flowers and cider, seems to be an obstacle to be overcome for Elizabeth.

Let us now review the whole scene in terms of objectives, strategies, tactics and obstacles.

|  | John | Elizabeth |
|---|---|---|
| Objective |  |  |
| Strategy |  |  |
| Obstacle | 1<br><br>2<br><br>3 | 1<br><br>2<br><br>3 |
| Tactic | 1<br><br>2<br><br>3 | 1<br><br>2<br><br>3 |

 Try rehearsing the scene a few times and experimenting with the information you have collected. With the help of the director, try and work out how best to express the objectives and strategies and when tactics change. You should aim for a dynamic piece that feels as if it is driving forward – a keen sense of both characters developing their own strategy as they respond to each other.

**Task 9: From scene to scene**

If you have copies of *The Crucible* go back to the scene between John Proctor and Abigail towards the end of Act 1. Use the strategies that we have introduced to work on the scene. Run the two scenes together. Then answer these questions:

**1** How will the actor playing Proctor in the second scene be affected by the experience of the first scene. How will the first scene effect how the second scene is played?

**2** Let Elizabeth sit in on the first scene, witnessing how her husband behaves. Let Abigail sit in on the second scene, witnessing her 'lover' with his wife. *Hot-seat* both characters immediately after each scene.

**3** Now play the second scene again. How has the acting of the scene changed as a result of these further rehearsals?

Finally, if you want to find out more about *The Crucible* and the work of Arthur *Miller* try visiting: http://www.levity.com/corduroy/millera.htm

# **4** Finding the *Verfremdungseffekt*

## Outline

Having looked at *realist* styles of acting and *representational* theatre in the previous workshop, we now turn our attention to the *non-realist* acting style and *presentational* theatre which *Brecht* developed as part of his theory of *epic* theatre. Like *Stanislavski* and *Strasberg*, *Brecht* was both a practitioner (he wrote and directed plays) and a theatre teacher. We know of *Brecht*'s ideas about theatre from his theoretical writings. We also know about the detail of his own productions because he kept a *modelbook* for all of his major plays. The *modelbook* is the play text with illustrations and explanatory notes, made during *Brecht*'s own rehearsals. These notes and photographs interpreted the play's characters, settings and actions for the actors and designers and were intended to be used by others who wished to perform his plays. They are, if you like, an interesting example of the kind of working diary you will be expected to keep of your own practical work!

In **Part 1**, we will consider the two fundamentals of *Brechtian* theory: the *epic* and the *Verfremdungseffekt*. It is important to remember that, although *Brecht* had tremendous respect for *Stanislavski*'s work, his theories were developed largely in reaction against *Stanislavski*'s 'theatre of empathy'. We will see how *Brecht*'s political convictions led him in a very different direction. **Part 2** is a workshop designed to help us understand the complex workings of the *Verfremdungseffekt* in practice.

## Mother Courage and Her Children

In our work we will be exploring a scene from *Brecht*'s famous play *Mother Courage and Her Children*, which was completed in 1939. It is set in Europe during the Thirty Years' War (1618–1648) and tells the story of a woman who makes her living by trailing around the battlefields with her canteen wagon, buying and selling whatever goods she can lay her hands on. At the beginning of the play she is accompanied by her two sons, Eilif and Swiss Cheese, and her dumb daughter, Kattrin. The play tells the story of how Mother Courage eventually loses all of her three children to the war. As the Sergeant prophetically says to her at the end of the first scene:

> *Like the war to nourish you?*
> *Have to feed it something too.*

*Brecht* was a committed Marxist and he intended his theatre to be **dialectical**, because *dialectics* lies at the heart of Karl Marx's philosophical thinking and revolutionary politics. Broadly speaking, *dialectics* refers to the clash of **opposites**, and the **contradictions** which are bound to arise when opposites come into conflict.

Mother Courage herself embodies a clash of opposing ideals – a *dialectic*: she is a walking contradiction. She needs the war in order for her business enterprise to thrive, but, at the same time, she fears it for the threat it presents to the safety of her children. **She is caught in the contradiction between being a merchant and being a mother.** So, essentially, the play is about the contradictory claims of business and motherhood; and about the inevitable loss that the mother suffers as she tries to negotiate these contradictory demands.

### Task 1: The mother-merchant

In the *modelbook* for *Mother Courage*, *Brecht* describes Mother Courage's situation thus:

> She longs for the war but at the same time fears it. She wants to join in but as a peaceable businesswoman, not in a warlike way. She wants to maintain her family during the war and by means of it. She wants to serve the army and also to keep out of its clutches.

In each of these sentences *Brecht* expresses the contradictions in Mother Courage's character. The basic contradiction of course is between her role as a mother and her ambition as a merchant. *Brecht* uses the exceptional circumstances of war as a means of forcing the contradictions in her character to the surface; to dramatically confront and reveal the contradictions through the brutal events of war.

Make *still-images*, based on each of the sentences, which explore and represent clearly the contradictions in Mother Courage's character. An image that shows the two faces of mother and merchant for instance.

Discuss what kind of scenes or situations might force the contradictions to the surface. What might happen as she tries to serve the army which will also put her in their 'clutches'? What might happen as she tries to make money for her family from the war which would also threaten her family? *Remember* that she loses all of her children to the war, one by one, as the story develops.

# Part 1  The Fundamentals of Epic Theatre

## Circumstances are Changeable, not Given

We have seen how *Stanislavski*'s concept of the 'given circumstances' is one of the cornerstones of *realist* acting; but this was precisely the point at which *Brecht* believed that it was necessary to part company with *Stanislavski*'s methods. For *Stanislavski*, it is the given circumstances that ensure consistency of characterisation, and determine how a character will behave; for *Brecht*, circumstances which are 'given' are, ultimately, inescapable. To state the case even more forcefully: the 'given' circumstances imprison the character in fairly fixed patterns of behaviour, and suggest that the world is beyond her or his control.

*Stanislavski*'s brand of *realism* is a theatre of empathy which produces a number of effects on the spectators:

- it seeks to draw them into the stage illusion and not to question the picture of life on the stage;
- it encourages them to share and empathise with the experiences of the characters;
- it provokes a degree of emotional involvement and emotional release (*catharsis*);
- it implicates and entangles them in the stage action – it presents the stage world as being 'natural' and unchangeable.

According to *Brecht*, this kind of theatre produces a passive, accepting, uncritical attitude in the audience. They are drawn into a world which seems natural, inevitable and unalterable. Their tolerance of this world prevents them from seeing the circumstances they encounter there as being subject to question and criticism. The last thing *Brecht* wanted was a tolerant, suggestible, empathic spectator; he needed an active, enquiring, thinking audience.

**It was *Brecht*'s studies in Marxism, and his revolutionary politics, that led him to imagine a new kind of spectator.** Traditionally, the theatre audience (under *Stanislavski*'s spell), was content to accept the world depicted on the stage as a true picture of the world as it really is; something which simply has to be accepted as 'natural'. *Brecht* wanted a theatre that would show that, in any set of circumstances, a number of different options exist for the characters; and the job of the spectator was to judge the validity of the characters' selected course of action. **Stanislavski's theatre tended to create submission in the spectator; *Brecht* wanted to create dissent.** In political terms, submission produces acquiescence, deference and conformity to the status quo; dissent produces defiance, protest and a desire for change.

The two elements in *Stanislavski*'s theatre that elicit submission in the spectator are: **identification and cause and effect**. Because the spectator is encouraged to identify with the plight of the characters, he or she begins to see them as victims of circumstance; helpless individuals, with no real power to shape their own destinies. This sense of helplessness is reinforced by the logic of 'the through-line of actions' in an endless chain of cause and effect, whereby action A will inevitably cause action B, and the effect of action B will be to cause action C.

For *Brecht*, it was these two elements in *Stanislavski*'s system that produced its politically 'conservative' nature. Consequently, he had to develop techniques that would counteract these politically reactionary tendencies which he had identified in *Stanislavski*'s work. **The overriding principle in *Brecht*'s theatre is a commitment to fundamental social change**; and, consequently, he set out to develop a theatre which presents the world and human nature as knowable and alterable. As we shall see, it is the device of the *Verfremdungseffekt*, and the *epic* form that provide him with the tools for achieving this end.

*Brecht* wore his politics on his sleeve. He directly addressed his audience and challenged them to look at what happens in the world of human affairs not as being 'natural', like the weather or the changing of the seasons, but as being man-made, socially unjust and therefore changeable. Many of his ideas both about politics and a new 'anti-realist' theatre are contained within this *prologue* to his *Lehrstuck*, or 'learning play', *The Exception and the Rule*. Notice the *presentational* style of performance. The players directly address the audience; they present themselves and their story, rather than beginning by creating the illusion of another place and time.

> We are about to tell you
> The story of a journey. An exploiter
> And two of the exploited are the travellers.
> Examine carefully the behaviour of these people:
> Find it surprising though not unusual
> Inexplicable though normal
> Incomprehensible though it is the rule.

*Consider even the most insignificant, seemingly simple*
*Action with distrust. Ask yourselves whether it is necessary*
*Especially if it is usual.*
*We ask you expressly to discover*
*That what happens all the time is not natural*
*For to say that something is natural*
*In such times of bloody confusion*
*Of ordained disorder, of systematic arbitrariness*
*Of inhuman humanity is to*
*Regard it as unchangeable.*

---

### Task 2: Playing with contradictions

- What clues are there in the *prologue* that there will be differences between *Brecht's* style of theatre and the *realist* style we have explored in the previous workshop?

- What can you tell about *Brecht's* politics, or world view, from this *prologue*?

- Who might the 'exploiter' and the 'exploited' be in this story – a master and slaves; a ruthless guide and innocent travellers? What events do you expect to happen during the journey? How will *Brecht* use these characters and what happens to them as a means of teaching his political view? Remember that *Brecht* used *dialectics* – contradictions and opposites – to show how the powerful try to make their exploitation of the powerless look 'natural' and 'unchangeable'.

 **1** The prologue is spoken by the players; the actors in the story that follows. Work in two groups. The first group will try to find the most effective way of speaking the lines. How will you allocate the words to different voices so that the intentions of the words are clearly emphasised for the audience? Meanwhile, the second group will work on a series of images to illustrate the words. These images will show the 'exploiter' and the 'exploited' and some of the events or changes in their relationship as the journey unfolds.

**2** When both groups are ready, find the most effective way of combining both groups' work into a dramatic sequence.

## The Verfremdungseffekt and the Epic

For *Brecht*, the *Verfremdungseffekt* is the antidote to identification and empathy; it is designed to cultivate in the audience a more clinical, detached and objective form of socially critical spectatorship. When reading about *Brecht* and his work, you will often find this term translated as 'alienation effect', which is inaccurate; we prefer the more literal translation, '**strange-making effect**' (either of the words 'estrangement' or 'defamiliarisation' would be more in keeping with the spirit of the German term).

*Brecht* did not invent this concept himself. It was first used by the *romantic* poet, William *Wordsworth*, as long ago as 1802. And, in the early years of the twentieth century, Victor Shklovsky, the Russian formalist, wrote about defamiliarisation in *realist* novels. The *Verfremdungseffekt* **forces the spectator to look at ordinary, familiar, everyday things in a striking, peculiar or unexpected way**; its aim is to encourage the audience to step back from its habitual, obvious ways of seeing, in order that they might see the world afresh.

The second concept essential in helping the audience to view the play in a thinking, rather than a feeling, way is *Brecht*'s idea of the *epic*. The *epic* form was first identified by *Aristotle* in his *Poetics*. In an *epic narrative*, the separate story elements are broken up in such a way that the different events are recounted outside of the traditional time sequences that we find in other poetic forms; in other words, '**epic time' is not linear, sequential, chronological time**.

This form suggested itself to *Brecht* because of the way in which it disrupts the chain of cause and effect which is indispensable in *Stanislavski*'s theatre of empathy. *Brecht* believed that the 'through-line of action' fostered in the spectator the illusion that the play's final outcome was always inevitable; that things could never have turned out otherwise. *Brecht*'s solution to this problem was to dislocate the 'through-line of action' by ensuring that each scene in the play was self-contained and free-standing. This technique places demands on the spectator that he or she should make his or her own connections between different episodes. An '**episode' is a scene, complete in itself, which is set in a single location and deals with one particular event**. In the gaps between such episodic scenes, *Brecht* wanted the spectators to exercise their judgement and arrive at their own conclusions about the events they had just witnessed.

The *Verfremdungseffekt* and the use of the *epic* then work together to counteract the essential *Stanislavskian* features of identification and causality. The important question for us to consider in this workshop is: how, in practice, are they able to do this?

In order to give a full answer to this question, it is necessary to consider three crucial aspects of *Brechtian* theatre:

- its style of presentation
- the structural devices which *Brecht* used in his playwriting
- the function of the actor.

## Style of Presentation

Everything about a *Brechtian* production is designed to remind the audience that it is sitting in a theatre, watching a series of fictional events unfold in the form of a play. In stark contrast to the theatre of empathy, it is **anti-illusionistic** and it is *presentational*.

For *Brecht*'s own production of *Mother Courage*, the first thing the audience noticed was the bare, grey stage, backed by a pale cyclorama. On the floor was a large circular revolve (or turntable) representing Courage's world. Each scene took place inside the circle, and the travelling was represented by a wagon moving around the revolving circumference. The wagon was made to look as authentic as possible, being constructed of materials that were consistent with the seventeenth-century setting. The goods that hung from the wagon changed from scene to scene, reflecting Courage's changing fortunes. The costumes were realistic without being historically authentic; *Brecht* expressly ruled out any 'folksy' tendency or excessive concern with historical accuracy. **Scenery and props were mostly authentic, but the most important thing was that they should be *usable*.** They were also minimal: a stool for a scene in which someone was required to sit down; a roof for Kattrin to climb on in the scene where she warns the villagers of Halle of the imminent attack.

*Brecht* **used bright, white light for every scene**, irrespective of whether it was a spring afternoon in Sweden or the dead of night in Saxony; and the lanterns, hanging from a metal grid, were plainly visible. Also visible to the audience was a four-piece orchestra in one of the side boxes, although some of Paul Dessau's music was played on a backstage record player. All of this was intended as a constant reminder to the spectators that they were attending a theatrical presentation.

The famous *Brechtian* half-curtain ran the whole length of the stage on a wire. The curtain was drawn whenever there was a scene change. As the stage hands set up the next scene, a sign dropped in from above. Crude letters scrawled on a frame, made up of what looked like metallic branches, indicated the location: 'SAXONY'; and other summary details were projected onto the half-curtain:

> *January 1936. The emperor's troops are threatening the Protestant town of Halle. The stone begins to speak. Mother Courage loses her daughter and trudges on alone. The war is a long way from being over.*

The important thing to note here is that the scene summary tells the audience exactly what is about to happen. *Brecht* did not want the spectators wondering '**what** happens next?' There should be no surprises in the action which was about to unfold; knowing that Courage loses Kattrin in the forthcoming scene allows the audience to focus on **how** things happened.

By using signs and projected captions, *Brecht* is effectively **labelling** the events about to be portrayed. He draws attention to them and implies that they call for an explanation. *Brecht* likened these disruptions to a **footnote** in a piece of text; something that breaks the reader's stream of thought and forces her or him to pause for further consideration.

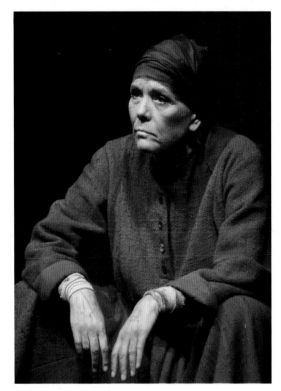

Diana Rigg in a National Theatre production of *Mother Courage and Her Children*, 1995

| The *epic* structure | As we have already noted, the use of the *epic* form itself is essentially a structural device for disrupting the flow of action. In *Brecht*'s own words:<br><br>**the individual episodes have to be knotted together in such a way that the knots are easily noticed. The episodes must not succeed each other indistinguishably but must give us a chance to interpose our judgement.**<br><br>This kind of strategic interruption in the flow of the *narrative* subverts the sequence of cause and effect and, more importantly, it also helps unmask the nature and the momentum of the **social forces** that are at work on the **individual** characters. |
| --- | --- |
| *Types* that are socially real, not characters that are psychologically real | Whereas *Stanislavski*'s theatre of empathy focuses on the individual and her or his psychological make-up, *Brecht*'s attention is firmly directed towards the **historical** and **social pressures** that make the individuals what they are. Whereas *Stanislavski* was concerned to develop highly individual characters who were unique in their psychology and other characteristics, *Brecht* presented universal **types** of character. Mother Courage represents all poor working-class mothers struggling to make ends meet in times of war – she is not a particular woman with a name, but a mother who shares the same characterisitcs as other mothers of her social class and historical circumstances. Whereas in *Stanislavski*'s theatre we are fascinated by **who** the character is, in *Brecht*'s theatre we are shown **what** a character does, and through their actions we come to understand history and the class system at work. |
| **Narrators, music and singers** | Aspects of the *Verfremdungseffekt* can also assist in this process of disruption. We have already mentioned *Brecht*'s use of music in *Mother Courage*. He is highly specific about how actors should perform the songs in his plays. He recommends that the actor should not 'drop into' song (in the manner of the Hollywood musical); rather, he or she should clearly mark it off from the surrounding lines of dialogue.<br><br>In *Mother Courage*, **the songs serve a variety of purposes**: both Yvette's 'Song of Fraternisation' and Courage's 'Song of the Great Capitulation' tell us about each character's past, but they also provide a biting comment on the harshness of seventeenth century life. The 'Song of the Girl and the Soldier' acts as a warning, whereas the 'Song of Solomon' neatly summarises one of the play's major themes – that the rewards of virtue are meagre in corrupt times; there's no use trying to be an angel when you live in hell!<br><br>*Brecht* did not use a storyteller or narrator in *Mother Courage*, although it was a device which he sometimes employed – for example, in *The Caucasian Chalk Circle*. In *Brechtian* theatre, song and storyteller function in much the same way. As with the songs, the storyteller addresses the audience directly. In so doing, she or he can comment on the action, alert us to any important details we should be paying particular attention to, and offer us a different viewpoint from those that the characters hold. Alternatively, he or she can pose questions for us to consider. |

## Structural Devices

As with the overall presentational style, many of the structural devices that *Brecht* used in his writing were also calculated to ensure that **the audience remained critically alert during the performance.**

# The Function of the Actor

However, by far the most important means of achieving the *Verfremdungseffekt* is to be found in the work of the actor. In the rest of this workshop we will explore and understand the techniques that *Brecht* used in order to develop the style of acting best fitted for his *epic* theatre.

As we have already emphasised, because *Brecht* does not want the audience to empathise with the characters, in performance the actor must avoid any measure of identification between the actor and her or his character. This is a contrast with *Stanislavski* who sought to create in his actors a very strong and personal identification with the character; finding the 'I' in the character.

**Brecht, on the other hand, insisted that a definite distance has to be created between the actor and the role.** This means that the actor, instead of identifying with the role to create the fully rounded character, should demonstrate the role instead. In *Brecht's* theatre, representation gives way to presentation.

This separation between actor and role is most vividly illustrated in the way the actor Charles **Laughton** played the part of Galileo in *Brecht's* play, *Life of Galileo*. *Laughton*, the actor, is present on stage smoking a cigar; each time he is required to take on the role of Galileo, he sets the cigar down in order to show us some aspect of Galileo's behaviour. By means of this simple device, the smoking of the cigar comes to be associated with the actor, and the absence of the cigar tells us we are watching the character, Galileo.

Demonstrating the role is only one aspect of the *Brechtian* actor's job; the other is finding a way to let the audience see exactly what attitude the actor has to the role he or she is playing. In order to provide his actors with a model of how this should be done, *Brecht* used the example of a street scene in which an eyewitness explains to passers-by how an accident occurred.

In 'The Street Scene', the eyewitness *demonstrates* the sequence of events surrounding the accident, and *shows* how the driver and the victim behaved. The eyewitness does not get carried away in describing the detail of the incident; she or he does not 'become' any of the people involved; and he or she does not attempt to create the illusion in the passers-by that they are watching the real accident. Instead, she or he relates the detail of the incident in a detached manner; impersonates, or even caricatures, the people involved; and probably offers an opinion as to the rights and wrongs of the accident, and who was to blame.

In summary then, *Brecht* wanted his actors to:

- use their natural abilities as storytellers and mimics;
- appear, in performance, as themselves, impersonating the characters as they speak the playwright's lines;
- stand outside of the character;
- adopt a definite, objective, critical attitude towards the role they are playing;
- invite the audience to make their own critical judgements, which may or may not be consistent with the actor's own attitude and evaluation.

**Task 3: Telling and showing a story**

1   Think of an incident that actually happened to you in the last few weeks: it could be something amusing that happened at school; some argument that took place at home; or something unusual that happened to you and your friends on a night out.

2   Take a few minutes to remember the detail of what happened and then give as full an account of the incident as you can to your partner, using gestures, voices and actions to fully illustrate what happened. Make sure they know who was involved, what the sequence of events was, and what you thought about the incident.

3   As your partner describes their incident, watch carefully how they tell the story, paying particular attention to how the people involved are presented. What did you notice?

4   Now join together with another pair and take it in turns to show and tell the story that your partners told with all the mannerisms and gestures they used in the original retelling. *But* also exaggerate your partner's gestures and way of telling the story so that you are now showing your partner showing the story! As an actor, these exaggerations show us that you are commenting on the 'character' (your partner) who tells the story as well as showing the story itself.

# Rehearsal Techniques

In his work with actors, *Brecht did* make use of some of *Stanislavski's* techniques. In the early stages of rehearsal, *Brecht* knew it was important for his actors to go through a stage of identification with the character before they could go beyond it. Once the actor had gone through the stage of identification, they were ready to try to see the character from the outside, from the point of view of society, and to generate a critical attitude towards that character.

In order to help his actors achieve this *Verfremdungseffekt* (simultaneously being and not being the character), *Brecht* developed a number of rehearsal techniques. These techniques created for the actors the sense of detachment from the characters that is essential to the *Verfremdungseffekt* in *Brechtian* acting.

Whereas *Stanislavski's* starting point was the given circumstances, *Brecht's* was the social relevance of the events depicted in the drama. Actors were encouraged to analyse their lines by asking four questions:

- Who is the sentence of use to?
- Who does it claim to be of use to?
- What does it call for?
- What practical action corresponds to it?

These questions are designed to help the actors understand the relationship of the fictional world of the play to the real world in which they live.

**Like *Stanislavski*, *Brecht* also divided his scenes up into units.** But whereas for the *Stanislavskian* actor the units are primarily designed to help determine the character's motivation and objective in the scene, for *Brecht*, each unit sketches in the basic actions and the relationships between all the characters.

We will be using the following extract from *Mother Courage* to describe four exercises that *Brecht* used to help his actors find the appropriate acting style.

## Task 4: Comparison with *Stanislavski*'s given circumstances

**1** How are the questions on page 74 *different* from the questions used to identify the given circumstances in *Stanislavskian* theatre? Go back to these questions on page 52 and compare the kinds of information that the two sets of questions throw up.

**2** In the light of your work on *The Crucible* scene, apply *Brecht*'s questions to the following lines from the scene we studied and discuss how this new information might change the way that the lines would be played in a *Brechtian* style:

| 1 | *Elizabeth*: | What keeps you so late? It's almost dark. |
| 22 | *Elizabeth*: | (*it is hard to say*) I know it, John. |

For example:

| 8 | *Proctor*: | Are you well today? |

The sentence is of use to Proctor who is trying to make things right with Elizabeth. The sentence claims to be of use to Elizabeth – it shows that Proctor cares. The sentence calls for Elizabeth to reciprocate with a kindness towards Proctor. Proctor tries to please Elizabeth with a kiss which 'she receives'.

It is a 'unit' taken from Scene 5, in which The Chaplain wants to help a peasant family who have lost their farm in the war. Although Kattrin is keen to help rescue the injured family, Mother Courage is reluctant to let them use linen shirts as bandages.

| A peasant: | (*brought in by the chaplain*) My arm's gone. |
| The Chaplain: | Where's that linen? |
| Mother Courage: | I can't give nowt. What with expenses, taxes, loan interest and bribes. (*Making guttural noises, Kattrin raises a plank and threatens her mother with it.*) You gone plain crazy? Put that plank away or I'll paste you one, you cow. I'm giving nowt, don't want to, got to think of meself. (*The Chaplain lifts her off the steps and sets her on the ground, then starts pulling out shirts and tearing them into strips.*) My officers' shirts! Half a florin apiece! I'm ruined! (*From the house comes the cry of a child in pain.*) |
| The peasant: | The baby's in there still! (*Kattrin dashes in.*) |

### Rehearsal Exercise 1: Speaking the Stage Directions

In a group of four, read through the above extract enough times for it to become familiar (remember that, although Kattrin is unable to speak, her actions form a vital part of the scene). Play the sequence through three or four times to get a sense of the dynamic of the incident. Now read the following version of the same extract:

| A peasant: | The peasant entered with the Chaplain, and seeing the two women, told them that his arm was hurt. |
| The Chaplain: | The chaplain made an urgent enquiry about linen. |
| Mother Courage: | Mother Courage dismissed his enquiry, saying that her expenses made it impossible for her to give linen away. |
| Kattrin: | As Kattrin made rasping noises in her throat, she picked up a plank of wood and held it over her mother in a threatening manner. |
| Mother Courage: | Mother Courage enquired whether her daughter had taken leave of her |

|  |  |
|---|---|
|  | senses. She told Kattrin to put the plank of wood down, adding a few threats of her own. She repeated that she could not afford to give her linen away. |
| *The Chaplain*: | The Chaplain lifted Mother Courage from the steps of the wagon and placed her firmly on the ground. He then pulled four linen shirts from the wagon and began to tear them into strips. |
| *Mother Courage*: | Mother Courage protested and lamented the loss of two florins, saying that the Chaplain's actions had ruined her. |
| *The peasant*: | The peasant heard the sound of a child's cry from inside the house. He remembered that the baby was still inside. |
| *Kattrin*: | Kattrin rushed into the house in search of the baby. |

Try to play this version of the scene. You will notice that the characters now speak the stage directions aloud and that the content of the speeches have been included in these directions.

When you play the scene you still play to the other characters, so use a change of voice for words or phrases that are directly addressed to other characters. For instance, the first line might be: 'The peasant entered with the Chaplain, and seeing the two women, told them that (*different voice*) HIS ARM WAS HURT'.

Rehearse the sequence until you have a version that you are happy with. With the other members of your group, discuss the effect of playing the scene in this way, and compare it with your original version. What was the impact of speaking the stage directions aloud on the physical action of the extract?

### Rehearsal Exercise 2: Paraphrasing the Text

This time, play *Brecht*'s original scene but paraphrase the text. Try paraphrasing it in a number of different ways: you could turn *Brecht*'s everyday language into *Shakespearean* verse (e.g. 'Methinks I have no sensation in my arm'); try the scene using different dialects (e.g. Cockney, Birmingham, Geordie), or accents (e.g. American, Australian); strip the dialogue down to its absolute essentials (e.g. **reduce each sentence to a single word**).

When you have experimented with the sequence, find a way to play the extract that really brings out the **differences in social background** between the characters.

### Rehearsal Exercise 3: Making the Present Historical

Return to *Brecht*'s original text, but try to put the lines into the **past tense** (e.g. *A peasant*: My arm *was* gone; *The Chaplain*: Where was that linen? etc.). Because Kattrin doesn't speak any lines, make sure that she speaks her own stage directions at the appropriate time (the other three should only speak the dialogue). Don't worry if this sounds strange (you're playing with a 'strange-making effect', remember). In this version, the characters are looking back on events that happened in the past. Discuss how playing the scene in the past tense changes it. What is the effect of playing it in this way?

### Rehearsal Exercise 4: Working in the Third Person

Play the sequence one last time. Retain the **past tense**, but also put each speech into the **third person** (e.g. *A Peasant*: His arm was gone; etc.). Once again, discuss how this effects the scene.

**Task 5: Reflecting on the rehearsal techniques**

- What is the effect of these excercises for you as an actor? In what ways have they helped you to both **identify** and **not identify** with the characters?

- Remember your experiences in rehearsing the scene from *The Crucible*. How are these two approaches to acting different?

- From an actor's point of view, what is the difference between rehearsing in a *realist* style in which you are 'being' the character and rehearsing in a *Brechtian* style in which you are 'showing' the character?

These four exercises were designed to help actors *avoid* identification with their roles, encouraging them instead to *stand outside* of themselves, producing the critical objectivity that is so vital to *Brechtian* theatre. Having already done the *playing the given circumstances* workshop you should already be developing a sense of the different demands that *Brecht* placed on his actors. We will shortly have the opportunity to push our explorations a little further, but first we need to consider one final, crucial distinction between *realist* forms of acting and *Brechtian* acting.

## Contradiction, Changeability and the Gestus

We have seen how **consistency** in characterisation is a vital part of *Stanislavski*'s approach. For *Brecht*, the opposite is true: he wanted the audience to see the many different, often **contradictory**, sides of a character.

If you were to chart Mother Courage's different moods throughout *Brecht*'s play, you would find her, by turns: confident; thoughtful; flirtatious; doubting and sceptical; amused; preoccupied; conceited and full of herself; egotistical; shy; devastated and desolate. Her changes of mood happen quite suddenly (a factor that calls for great versatility in the actor, of course).

At the end of Scene 1, having seen her eldest son recruited against her wishes, she is dismayed, but at the beginning of the second scene we see the shrewd businesswoman bargaining (and flirting) with the Cook. Each scene shows a different side of Courage, and we are forcibly struck by her changeable moods. Being a Marxist, **change**, of course, is a key word for *Brecht*: Mother Courage changes; her wagon changes from scene to scene; circumstances can change; and, above all, **the world can change**.

So, the changeable and contradictory natures of *Brecht*'s characters is a vital ingredient in *epic theatre*. **But, we see contradiction not only in the changing sides and moods of the characters, but also in the smallest physical gestures.** Hans Curjel watched *Brecht* at work on his 1948 production of *Antigone*. He was struck by *Brecht*'s attention to the smallest physical detail:

> *The directorial method was based on investigation and varied experimentation that could extend to the smallest gestures – eyes, fingers . . . Brecht worked like a sculptor on and with the actor.*

Contradiction then, is also to be found in the actors' gestures, and, in order to formalise this concept, *Brecht* invented the word *gestus*. It is based on the German word for gesture ('*Geste*'), but is somewhat confusingly defined, even by *Brecht* himself. We can, we think, narrow *gestus* down to two essential components. The first is that it must contain a **contradiction**.

In *Brecht's* 1950 production of *Der Hofmeister* (*The Private Tutor*), the character Lauffer, in an attempt to secure work, tries to ingratiate himself with the Mayor. He respectfully approaches the Mayor, who is in conversation with someone else, and bows in a most exaggerated fashion. The Mayor sees Lauffer, but chooses to ignore him; so Lauffer repeats the same exaggerated bow three more times. On the final bow, exasperated with the Mayor's indifference, he mutters under his breath, 'Go to the devil, louts!' The contradiction lies in between the respectful bow and the impertinent insult: the physical gesture says one thing, which is contradicted by the words which are spoken.

The second component of *gestus* is that the physical action also stands for a **social relationship**. Lauffer's exaggerated bow to the Mayor emphasises the difference in social status between the two characters.

*Brecht's* 1949 production of *Mother Courage* contains probably the most famous and celebrated *gestus* in the whole history of *Brechtian* theatre. Courage was played by Helene **Weigel** (*Brecht's* wife). In Scene 3, when Courage hears the volley of shots that signals the execution of her son, Swiss Cheese, *Weigel's* response was the **Silent Scream**.

*Weigel's* Courage is seated on a stool with her hands in her lap. She grabs the coarse material of her skirt and leans forward with a straight back. At the same time, she thrusts her head back and opens her mouth as if to scream. But no sound comes out.

Helene Weigel's Silent Scream in *Mother Courage and Her Children*, Berlin, 1951

A member of the audience later described the scream in these words:

> *A harsh and terrifying, indescribable sound issued from her mouth. But in fact, there was no sound. Nothing. It was the sound of absolute silence. A silence which screamed and screamed throughout the theatre, making the audience bow their heads as if they had been hit by a blast of wind.*

The **contradiction** is contained in the idea of a scream that is silent; and the physical action indicates that Courage's **social position**, as a helpless mother unable to save her son, means that she is powerless to prevent the soldiers from carrying out the execution. She silently refuses to recognise her son, but she cannot refuse to recognise *and* express her horror at what happens – so the scream is silent.

It is also interesting to note that *Weigel* played with the positioning of the silent scream in the scene. There are accounts of performances in which she used the scream at the end of the scene when her son's body is brought on stage by the soldiers and she silently shakes her head, twice refusing to acknowledge the dead boy as her own. As the soldiers take off the body, *Weigel* turns away and does the silent scream.

This shows us that as a *Brechtian* actor, *Weigel* could both identify with the character by expressing the pain and horror felt by Mother Courage and also be detached enough from the character to use such a powerful *gestus* as a staging device which could be 'turned on' at different places in the scene's development.

**Task 6: *Gestus* in *The Crucible***

The idea of *gestus* was used by other playwrights, even in the *realist* tradition. Remember in the scene from *The Crucible* when Proctor secretly adds salt to the cooking pot?

- What does this action tell us about the social relations between Proctor and Elizabeth and how does it comment on what Proctor has been up to prior to this action?

- In what sense is this action contradictory? In other words, does it go against the grain of Proctor's other actions and words in this scene?

Having grasped the fundamentals of Brecht's *epic theatre*, and the major implications for the *Brechtian* actor, we move on explore how the *Verfremdungseffekt* can be made to work in practice.

# Part 2 The Mother Courage Workshop

The best-known scene in *Mother Courage and her Children* is Scene 11, sometimes called the 'drumming scene', in which Kattrin saves the townspeople of Halle but loses her own life in the process. Before proceeding to the workshop, you might like to familiarise yourself with the whole scene. We gave you the location and caption for the scene on page 71. The dialogue is spread out over the next few pages.

To complete the workshop, you will need to form groups of at least eight, corresponding to the eight characters in the scene (Kattrin, The Peasant,

The Peasant's Wife, The Young Peasant, The Ensign, First Soldier, Second Soldier, Third Soldier).

You will also need to construct a makeshift set to work on, and find some essential props. You will definitely need the following: stage right, the roof of the peasants' house, sturdy enough to bear Kattrin's weight; a ladder to reach the roof, which Kattrin can then pull up; a drum and two beaters; a chopping block, in front of the roof, and something to chop with; pikes for the soldiers; a piece of wood; a musket. *Brecht* would, of course, insist on props that have been 'lovingly made', but serviceable rehearsal props will suffice for our purposes.

## Task 7: Marking off the fixed points

*The cart is standing, much the worse for wear, alongside a peasant's house with a huge thatched roof, backing on a wall of rock. It is night.*

*An ensign and three soldiers in heavy armour step out of the wood.*

| | |
|---|---|
| *The Ensign:* | I want no noise now. Anyone shouts, shove your pike into him. |
| *First Soldier:* | Have to knock them up, though, if we're to find a guide. |
| *The Ensign:* | Knocking sounds natural. Could be a cow bumping the stable wall. (*The Soldiers knock on the door of the house. The peasant's wife opens it. They stop her mouth. Two soldiers go in.*) |
| *Man's voice:* | (*within*) What is it? (*The soldiers bring out the peasant and his son.*) |
| *The Ensign:* | (*pointing at the cart, where Kattrin's head has appeared*) There's another one. (*A soldier drags her out.*) Anyone else live here beside you lot? |
| *The peasants:* | This is our son. And she's dumb. Her mother's gone into town to buy stuff. For their business, 'cause so many people's getting out and selling things cheap. They're just passing through. Canteen folk. |
| *The Ensign:* | I'm warning you, keep quiet, or if there's the least noise you get a pike across your nut. Now I want someone to come with us and show us the path to the town. (*Points to the young peasant.*) Here, you. |
| *The Young Peasant:* | I don't know no path. |
| *Second Soldier:* | (*grinning*) He don't know no path. |
| *Young Peasant:* | I ain't helping Catholics. |
| *The Ensign:* | (*to the second soldier*) Stick your pike in his ribs. |
| *The Young Peasant:* | (*forced to his knees, with the pike threatening him*) I won't do it, not to save my life. |
| *First Soldier:* | I know what'll change his mind. (*Goes towards the stable.*) Two cows and an ox. Listen, you: if you're not reasonable I'll chop up your cattle. |
| *The Young Peasant:* | No, not that! |
| *The Peasant's Wife:* | (*weeps*) Please spare our cattle, captain, it'd be starving us to death. |
| *The Ensign:* | They're dead if he goes on being obstinate. |
| *First Soldier:* | I'm taking the ox first. |
| *The Young Peasant:* | (*to his father*) Have I got to? (*The wife nods.*) Right. |
| *The Peasant's Wife:* | And thank you kindly, captain, for sparing us, for ever and ever, Amen. (*The peasant stops his wife from further expressions of gratitude.*) |
| *First Soldier:* | I knew the ox was what they minded about most, was I right? (*Guided by the young peasant, the ensign and his men continue on their way.*) |

In this short extract, under orders from The Ensign, the three Soldiers round-up The Peasant, his Wife, their Son and Kattrin, who has been sleeping in the wagon.

1 Play the scene through, from the beginning up until the stage direction *A soldier drags her out*. At this point freeze the action. Pay particular attention to the physical and spatial relationships between the military characters and their captives. Spend a few moments sculpting this image, so that the attitudes of the captives are reflected in their physical positions and relationships to the soldiers. At this point, we know that the son is in a defiant mood, but what of The Peasant and his Wife? What do you think Kattrin's attitude is at this moment?

2 When you are happy with your 'sculpture', use it as the starting point for the next short extract, which runs from The Ensign's line, 'Anyone else live here beside you lot?' to the First Soldier's, 'I'm taking the ox first'. Once again, freeze the action on this line. How defiant is the son now? What is the attitude of the father and mother? Has Kattrin's attitude changed? Once again, sculpt the image so that these new attitudes are made clear in the physicality of the captives.

Immediately afterwards, the mother indicates to the son that he should follow The Ensign's order to show the soldiers the way to the town. When the son agrees, The Peasant's Wife says: 'And thank you kindly, captain, for sparing us, for ever and ever, Amen'. She is immediately stopped from any further expressions of gratitude by her husband, and almost immediately the soldiers leave.

3 Remember our comments on *Brecht*'s concept of *gestus*. It is a *physical action* that stands for a *social relation*, which also contains a *contradiction*. Together, help the actor playing The Peasant's Wife to find an appropriate *gestus* to accompany her line (the action needs to stand in contradiction to the expression of thanks). When you are satisfied with The Peasant's Wife's *gestus*, try to find an appropriate physical action for The Peasant, The Young Peasant and Kattrin to perform as the woman delivers her line.

For this short extract, you now have three **fixed points**: the initial attitude of the captives; the attitude when the son is in the greatest danger; and the mother's expression of gratitude.

4 Rehearse the extract, and try to find a way of marking off these fixed points from the surrounding dialogue (perhaps by using a momentary freeze, or some kind of sound cue). Discuss what the effect of marking off these fixed points is. *Brecht* used the analogy of a **knot** to indicate points at which the flow of action is disrupted. How does this 'marking off' help distinguish the 'knots' between the different parts of the episode?

## Task 8: Using *Brecht*'s idea for a scene

Following the departure of the son with the soldiers, the peasants are left wondering what is about to happen. This is the quietest passage in the whole scene, and one which directors tend to gloss over. *Brecht*, of course, did not make this mistake; and we are going to use one of the techniques that *Brecht* himself used when rehearsing his own 1949 production of the play.

| | |
|---|---|
| *The Peasant*: | What are they up to, I'd like to know. Nowt good. |
| *The Peasant's Wife*: | Perhaps they're just scouting. What you doing? |
| *The Peasant*: | (*putting a ladder against the roof and climbing up it*) Seeing if they're on their own. (*from the top*) Something moving in the wood. Can see something down by the quarry. And there are men in armour in the clearing. And a gun. That's at least a regiment. God's mercy on the town and everyone in it! |
| *The Peasant's Wife*: | Any lights in the town? |
| *The Peasant*: | No. They'll all be asleep. (*Climbs down*.) If those people get in they'll butcher the lot. |
| *The Peasant's Wife*: | Sentries're bound to spot them first. |

| The Peasant: | Sentry in the tower up on the hill must have been killed, or he'd have blown his bugle. |
| The Peasant's Wife: | If only there were more of us. |
| The Peasant: | Just you and me and that cripple. |
| The Peasant's Wife: | Nowt we can do, you'd say... |
| The Peasant: | Nowt. |
| The Peasant's Wife: | Can't possibly run down there in the blackness. |
| The Peasant: | Whole hillside's crawling with 'em. We could give a signal. |
| The Peasant's Wife: | What, and have them butcher us too? |
| The Peasant: | You're right, nowt we can do. |
| The Peasant's Wife: | (*to Kattrin*) Pray, poor creature, pray! |

**1** To begin with, play the exchange between The Peasant and his Wife as *Brecht* wrote it.

**2** Replay the scene, but this time the actor playing The Peasant should add the words, '... said the man' following each of his speeches; and, similarly, the actor playing The Peasant's Wife should add the words '... said the woman'. Try this out a few times.

- What is the effect of adding these words each time a character speaks?

**3** *Brecht*'s reason for doing this, he said, was to make the actors emphasise the peasants' failings, to show how they reassure each other that there really is nothing that they can do. Play the scene once more, with *Brecht*'s intention firmly in mind.

As the peasants wonder what is happening, the stage directions give us no sense of what Kattrin is doing. Go back to the third fixed point in Task 7, where the captives' different physical actions accompany The Peasant's Wife's expression of gratitude. This time, just work with the peasant, his wife and Kattrin.

**4** Begin the scene with the words, 'What are they up to...' Play the scene with the peasants using 'said the man/woman', but this time leave a pause in between the spoken lines. In this pause, the actor playing Kattrin is going to use **action narration**. She simply speaks aloud any action that Kattrin performs, even if there is apparently no action. It might go something like this:

| The Peasant: | What are they up to, I'd like to know. Nowt good, said the man. |
| Kattrin: | Kattrin remains motionless. |
| The Peasant's Wife: | Perhaps they're just scouting. What you doing, asked the woman. |
| Kattrin: | She looks at the wife, and then at the peasant. |
| The Peasant: | (*putting a ladder against the roof*) etc. |

Note that it is only *actions* that are narrated. **In this technique, you should always avoid telling us what the character is thinking or feeling. We are only interested in the action**. By using 'action narration' you can build up a sense of what Kattrin is doing as The Peasant and his Wife discuss the situation.

- What does the action narration exercise tell you about Kattrin's response to the events at the peasants' farmhouse?

## Task 9: The drumming scene

We will be looking at the drumming sequence in two parts: the first is a very short section, just after Kattrin begins, where the only other characters present are The Peasant and his Wife. The longer, second part is when the soldiers return.

In the first part, the Peasant's Wife has been praying. During the course of her prayer, she mentions her brother-in-law and his four children. We have already seen, in the extract from Scene 5 that we worked on earlier, that Kattrin is prepared to endanger herself in order to rescue a baby; so, once she realises that children are at risk in the town, she steals away to the wagon, takes a drum and climbs onto the roof of the house to warn the townspeople.

| | |
|---|---|
| The Peasant's Wife: | Forget not the children, what are in danger, the littlest ones especially, the old folk what can't move, and every living creature. |
| The Peasant: | And forgive us our trespasses as we forgive them that trespass against us. Amen. (*Sitting on the roof, Kattrin begins to beat the drum which she has pulled out from under her apron.*) |
| The Peasant's Wife: | Jesus Christ, what's she doing? |
| The Peasant: | She's out of her mind. |
| The Peasant's Wife: | Quick, get her down. (*The peasant hurries to the ladder, but Kattrin pulls it up onto the roof.*) |
| The Peasant's Wife: | She'll do us in. |
| The Peasant: | Stop drumming at once, you cripple! |
| The Peasant's Wife: | Bringing the Catholics down on us! |
| The Peasant: | (*looking for stones to throw*) I'll stone you. |
| The Peasant's Wife: | Where's your feelings? Where's your heart? We're done for if they come down on us. Slit our throats, they will. (*Kattrin stares into the distance towards the town and carries on drumming.*) |
| The Peasant's Wife: | (*to her husband*) I told you we shouldn't have allowed those vagabonds on to farm. What do they care if our cows are taken? |

1 Kattrin should begin drumming immediately after the word, 'Amen' is spoken. Allocate the parts to three members of your group. Play the first, short sequence with the drumming continuing throughout the dialogue between The Peasant and his Wife. Find out, from the other five members of your group, how the scene works when you play it this way. What are the problems that need to be addressed?

In rehearsal, *Brecht* knew that this whole sequence demanded clarity and precision; and it is important to avoid creating a scene that is just plain messy, noisy and chaotic. **Careful orchestration is required to get the clarity that *Brecht* wanted.** Clearly, the drumming cannot continue throughout the dialogue, because a stage direction tells us that Kattrin pauses to pull the ladder up onto the roof to prevent the peasant from climbing up to stop her; but, other than this, there are no further indications as to how the drumming is to be orchestrated.

2 Use the **action narration** technique again, so that you can work out the detail of the action sequence that takes place as The Peasant and his Wife try to work out how they can stop Kattrin. In this version, Kattrin should *describe* what she is doing. At the same time she should make the *action* of drumming, but not actually strike the drum-skin. Try this as a starting point:

| | |
|---|---|
| The Peasant's Wife: | She gets up from her knees, looks at Kattrin, looks at her husband, and says, 'Jesus Christ, what's she doing?'. |
| Kattrin: | She looks at the peasant woman and keeps on drumming. |
| The Peasant: | He looks at the roof, and says, 'She's out of her mind'. |
| Kattrin: | She looks at the peasant and continues drumming, *etc.* |

Make sure that you create enough space for Kattrin to narrate her actions after every spoken line. We know she has to stop drumming to pull up the ladder, but does she stop at any other point in this sequence?

3 As you begin to develop a more detailed sense of what the three characters are *actually doing* throughout this sequence, you can work your way back to playing the scene as *Brecht* wrote it. When you

83

have arrived at a version in which the drumming and the spoken dialogue are effectively orchestrated, ask the members of your group who have been watching to describe their feelings towards Kattrin as she tries to warn the people of Halle. The key question for them to address is: **as a spectator to these events, are you able to maintain the kind of critical detachment and distance that** *Brecht* **wanted from his audience?**

### Task 10: Sympathy or detachment?

| | |
|---|---|
| *The Ensign:* | (*runs in with his soldiers and the young peasant*) I'll cut you to ribbons, all of you! |
| *The Peasant's Wife:* | Please, sir it's not our fault, we couldn't help it. It was her sneaked up there. A foreigner. |
| *The Ensign:* | Where's the ladder? |
| *The Peasant:* | There. |
| *The Ensign:* | (*calls up*) I order you, throw that drum down.<br>(*Kattrin goes on drumming.*) |
| *The Ensign:* | You're all in this together. It'll be the end of you. |
| *The Peasant:* | They been cutting pine trees in that wood. How about if we got one of the trunks and poked her off… |
| *First soldier:* | (*to The Ensign*) Permission to make a suggestion, sir! (*He whispers something into The Ensign's ear.*) Listen, we got a suggestion could help you. Get down off there and come into town with us right away. Show us which your mother is and we'll see she ain't harmed.<br>(*Kattrin goes on drumming.*) |
| *The Ensign:* | (*pushes him roughly aside*) She doesn't trust you; with a mug like yours it's not surprising. (*Calls up.*) Suppose I gave you my word? I can give my word of honour as an officer.<br>(*Kattrin drums harder.*) |
| *The Ensign:* | Is nothing sacred to her? |
| *The Young Peasant:* | There's more than her mother involved, sir. |
| *First Soldier:* | This can't go on much longer. They're bound to hear in the town. |
| *The Ensign:* | We'll have somehow to make a noise that's louder than her drumming. What can we make a noise with? |
| *First Soldier:* | Thought we weren't s'posed to make no noise. |
| *The Ensign:* | A harmless one, you fool. A peaceful one. |
| *The Peasant:* | I could chop wood with my axe. |
| *The Ensign:* | Good: you chop. (*The peasant fetches his axe and attacks a tree-trunk.*) Chop harder! Harder! You're chopping for your life. (*Kattrin has been listening, drumming less loudly the while. She now looks widely round, and goes on drumming.*) |
| *The Ensign:* | Not loud enough. (*To the first soldier*): You chop too. |
| *The Peasant:* | Only got the one axe. (*Stops chopping.*) |
| *The Ensign:* | We'll have to set the farm on fire. Smoke her out, that's it. |
| *The Peasant:* | It wouldn't help, captain. If the townspeople see a fire here they'll know what's up.<br>(*Kattrin has again been listening as she drums. At this point she laughs.*) |
| *The Ensign:* | Look at her laughing at us. I'm not having that. I'll shoot her down, and damn the consequences. Fetch the harquebus.<br>(*Three soldiers hurry off. Kattrin goes on drumming.*) |

| | |
|---|---|
| *The Peasant's Wife:* | I got it, captain. That's their cart. If we smash it up she'll stop. Cart's all they got. |
| *The Ensign:* | (*to The Young Peasant*) Smash it up. (*Calls up.*) We're going to smash up your cart if you don't stop drumming. (*The Young Peasant gives the cart a few feeble blows.*) |
| *The Peasant's Wife:* | Stop it, you animal! (*Desperately looking towards the cart, Kattrin emits pitiful noises. But she goes on drumming.*) |
| *The Ensign:* | Where are those clodhoppers with the harquebus? |
| *First Soldier:* | Can't have heard nowt in town yet, else we'd be hearing their guns. |
| *The Ensign:* | (*calls up*) They can't hear you at all. And now we're going to shoot you down. For the last time: throw down that drum! |
| *The Young Peasant:* | (*suddenly flings away his plank*) Go on druming! Or they'll all be killed! Go on, go on. . . (*The soldier knocks him down and beats him with his pike. Kattrin starts to to cry, but she goes on drumming.*) |
| *The Peasant's Wife:* | Don't strike his back! For God's sake, you're beating him to death! (*The soldiers hurry in with the arquebus.*) |
| *Second Soldier:* | Colonel's frothing at the mouth, sir. We're all for court-martial. |
| *The Ensign:* | Set it up! Set it up! (*Calls up while the gun is being erected.*) For the very last time: stop drumming! (*Kattrin, in tears, drums as loud as she can.*) Fire! (*The soldiers fire. Kattrin gives a few more drumbeats and then slowly crumples.*) |

 **1** Use the methods we employed in the previous task to help you orchestrate the climax to the drumming scene. You will find that this section is much more complicated, simply because now you have *eight* characters to worry about, instead of three.

**2** When you have worked out the mechanics of this section, try to find a way of performing the scene which helps the audience maintain the critical distance and detachment that we talked about in our reflections on Task 9.

● Do you think it is possible to minimise the emotional impact of the scene, and prevent the audience from empathising with Kattrin? If so, how?

### Task 11: Contradictory emotions

Look at the last two lines of the spoken dialogue.

| | |
|---|---|
| *The Ensign*: | That's the end of that. |
| | (*But Kattrin's drumbeats are taken up by the town's cannon. In the distance can be heard a confused noise of tocsins and gunfire.*) |
| *The First Soldier*: | She's made it. |

After the drumming stops, The Ensign enjoys a moment of triumph, but his pleasure is short-lived as we hear the town's cannons firing in the distance. When we talked about the importance of contradiction in *Brecht*'s plays, we noted the many different sides of Mother Courage's character, and how her mood changed quite markedly from scene to scene. Here, The Ensign's mood changes from triumph to dismay in the blink of an eye.

- Play the second section of the drumming scene once more. But continue the scene right to the end. As Kattrin crumples following the musket shot, show each character's immediate reaction to The Ensign's line, 'That's the end of that'. Hold the reactions, frozen, for a few seconds. At the sound of a single drumbeat (representing the town's cannon) each character should show, in a *five-second slow motion* sequence, how the reaction to The Ensign's words changes as the cannon-fire registers. Make sure that the reaction is expressed *physically* (you may even want to *exaggerate* the physical reaction to heighten the effect). The end of the slow motion sequence should be marked by The Soldier's line, 'She's made it'.

- What do you notice about the changes that are registered in this five-second period? How would you describe the change in each of the characters' reactions? Whose reaction changes the most? Whose is the least perceptible? What do these changes indicate about the various characters?

# 5 The Emergence of the Director

## Playwright as Director

We have already noted how the director only came to prominence in the last quarter of the nineteenth century. We have also seen how, in the classical theatre of fifth century Athens, the entire production of the play was under the supervision of the playwright, who was commonly referred to as a 'teacher'. *Aeschylus*, in particular, was noted for his brilliance in instructing the performers in their intricate dance movements, in their speaking of his poetry and in the orchestration of what, today, we might call the *mise en scène*.

For centuries to come, **the playwright continued to assume major responsibility for the mounting of his plays**. Hamlet's advice to the travelling troupe of players who arrive to perform at the castle of Elsinore is often taken to be evidence of *Shakespeare*'s own directorial approach; and we know that, in the great French theatre of the seventeenth century, *Molière* was especially noted for the precision of his instructions to actors. But the playwright who, perhaps, came closest to the modern idea of the director was *Goethe*, supervisor of the productions at the *Weimar Court Theatre*. *Goethe*'s rehearsals were meticulously planned and rigorously organised; so much so that he, reputedly, used a baton at rehearsals and conducted his actors in much the same way as the conductor of an orchestra controls the musicians.

Johann Wolfgang von Goethe

When we use the term 'rehearsal' in relation to the above theatre practices, we are using it very loosely. **The kind of carefully planned, meticulously detailed rehearsal process that we are used to in today's theatre is a relatively recent phenomenon.** Historically, the preparation period for mounting a play was usually very short, and, therefore, there was little time for exploration, experimentation and discussion. It was literally a case of entering, speaking the lines and making an exit. With the coming of the actor-manager, rehearsal practices slowly began to change.

## Actor as Director

In the late eighteenth century, the balance of power began to change in the English theatre. Up until that point, the playwright had always been the central figure in the production process. But, with the emergence of a number of dazzlingly talented performers, the 'star' actor (who was often also the manager of the theatre) began to replace the playwright in importance. David *Garrick*, who took over the Theatre Royal in *Drury Lane*, was the first great actor-manager. He devoted rather more time to rehearsals than was customary, and paid much greater attention to the casting of minor roles. Following in *Garrick*'s footsteps came John Philip *Kemble* and Charles *Macready* – both of whom insisted on rehearsals being a testing ground for dramatic ideas, rather than just a mechanical run-through of lines. Charles *Kean* became known as the 'Prince of Managers' not only because his productions were thoroughly researched to achieve historical accuracy in settings and costume, but also because of his beautifully orchestrated stage pictures.

## The Modern Director

The *Meininger*: the first disciplined *ensemble*

Although the early years of the nineteenth century saw massive changes in the whole process of theatrical production, it was not until 1874 that the modern idea of the director really began to take shape. It was on 1 May of 1874 that George II, Duke of Saxe-*Meiningen*, brought his then unknown company to perform in Berlin. What was striking about the work of the company was the **complete integration of every aspect of the production into a coherent, unified and harmonious performance**. The disciplined acting, painstakingly choreographed crowd scenes, a continuous and fluid flow of action, historically accurate sets and costumes, and meticulous attention to detail all contributed to the triumphant success of the company's first appearance in Berlin.

Here, for the first time in European theatre history, the audience was able to witness a true ensemble, with every actor submitting to the iron discipline of the company, tirelessly striving to serve the needs of the play and working flat-out for each other. The artistic vision for each new production came from the Duke himself, assisted, no doubt, by his actress wife, Ellen Franz; but Ludwig *Chronegk*, employed as stage manager, was the disciplinarian who drilled the actors to achieve the highest possible standards of performance.

Following the success of the *Meiningen* company's work, the new director came to be seen as the key figure in the process of production. The roles of both playwright and actor began to be seen in a new perspective. In the hands of some directors, the playwright's words became a pretext for daring, new interpretations, although others were intent on creating faithful reproductions of the writer's intentions. The demands of performance became much more strenuous as different directorial approaches required greater discipline, dedication and versatility in actors.

The work of the *Meiningen* company inspired the great directors André **Antoine** (in France), Otto **Brahm** (in Germany) and Konstantin *Stanislavski* (in Russia).

# Behind the Fourth Wall:
# The Great Realist Directors

*Antoine*: The first *realist* director

*Antoine* founded the **Théâtre Libre** in Paris in 1887. The disciplined approach of the *Meiningen* company became one of the hallmarks of *Antoine*'s theatre, but he had a broader vision. His aim was to create an experimental, scientific, theatre 'laboratory' in which the ideas of the *naturalist* writer, Émile **Zola**, could be put into practice. In keeping with *Zola*'s theories, *Antoine* **set out to create the realistic environments that shaped the life and actions of the characters**. This meant reproducing the exact physical details of everyday life (he even transported the furniture from his own home to the theatre in order to create the setting for *Zola*'s play, *Jacques Damour*). Having created his environment in minute detail, *Antoine* would then decide which of the four walls he would remove, in order to provide the audience with the best view of the dramatic events that would unfold there.

In Germany, Otto *Brahm* followed in *Antoine*'s footsteps, founding his **Freie Bühne**. **Brahm understood the importance of creating detailed and realistic stage settings** but left this aspect of the work to his two assistants, preferring, instead, to concentrate his own attentions on the development of new plays, and on detailed rehearsals with actors.

*Antoine*'s preoccupation with the creation of the visual setting was an important feature of *Stanislavski*'s early work. **He would begin his preparations by producing extremely detailed production notes, which were then transposed to the stage during the process of rehearsal.** *Stanislavski* originally modelled himself on *Chronegk*, who he had seen at work during the *Meiningen* company's visit to Moscow in 1890. But *Stanislavski* soon became dissatisfied with this autocratic style of directing, with its emphasis on reproducing the details of external reality. Consequently, he turned his attentions to developing a style of acting whose aim was to produce a sense of inner (or *psychological*) reality.

*Stanislavski* and psychological *realism*

The *realist* dramas of Anton *Chekhov*, which had become a cornerstone of the work of the *Moscow Art Theatre* (founded by *Stanislavski* and *Nemirovich-Danchenko* in 1898), **demanded more true-to-life character portrayals**. *Stanislavski*, therefore, set himself the task of researching and codifying the principles of the acting style which has come to be known as *psycho-realism*. *Stanislavski* thus came to share *Brahm*'s concern with the richness of the rehearsal process, and his research led him to develop valuable rehearsal techniques (some of which are used in the acting workshop on playing the given circumstances see page 52).

*Antoine*, *Brahm* and *Stanislavski* may be seen, therefore, as the foremost *realist* directors at the turn of the nineteenth century; the artists who attempted to put the theatrical flesh on the bones of *Zola's naturalistic theories*. But another important theatrical movement was also under way during these years. Based on the work of Richard **Wagner** (the nineteenth-century composer of *operas*), directors like Edward Gordon *Craig*, Jacques **Copeau** and Vsevolod *Meyerhold* were pushing theatrical boundaries in other directions.

## The Quest For the 'Idea of a Theatre': Early Non-realist Directors

*Wagner* had attacked the decaying theatre of his own time, saying that it was no longer capable of expressing humanity's noblest aspirations and deepest spirituality. The ancient Greeks provided *Wagner* with his template. He set out to develop the idea of a **total theatre**, rooted in the old Northern European mythologies, which would bring together into a coherent work all of the elements of theatre: action, poetry, music, movement, design and visual spectacle. *Wagner* gave the name, *Gesamtkunstwerk* (or total art work) to what he believed would be 'the art of the future'.

Richard Wagner

**_Craig_'s theatre of visions**

In 1905, Edward Gordon _Craig_ (son of the great actress, Ellen **_Terry_**) published _The Art of the Theatre_. _Craig_'s book was a manifesto for the new 'art of the future'. In it, he argued that the demands of the new theatre required a new kind of '**theatre artist**' (or director) – a visionary, who would be capable of bringing together the diverse elements identified by _Wagner_ into one harmonious whole. In keeping with _Wagner_'s theories, _Craig_ **wanted to create 'a theatre of visions'** rather than 'a theatre of sermons'; an art form that would say less, yet show more. _Craig_'s own approach to directing was very much a hit-and-miss affair. He admitted that, in preparing his productions, he worked in an illogical manner, preferring to work by intuition rather than by analysis. Consequently, as a director, it would probably be true to say that _Craig_ himself achieved little. Yet, as a serious thinker about the possibilities and potentialities of theatre, _Craig_ remains a major figure in twentieth-century European theatre history.

**_Copeau_ sees the director as a specialist in interpretation**

In many ways, it was Jacques _Copeau_ who embodied most fully in his practice the qualities _Craig_ envisaged in his 'theatre artist'. _Copeau_ created the **_Vieux-Colombier_** in 1913, in order to bring together an ensemble of young, dedicated performers whose one ambition was to serve the art of the theatre. In his own directorial work, _Copeau_ **sought to clarify the nature of the relationship between playwright and director – who, he argued, were involved in two distinct stages of the same intellectual operation.** He acknowledged that the great playwrights of the past (_Aeschylus_, _Shakespeare_, _Molière_) had been able to successfully combine both functions. But he claimed that modern playwrights needed the expertise of the director as a specialist in interpretation. Unlike many of his contemporaries, _Copeau_ was especially concerned to produce interpretations which kept faith with the playwright's original text. He was also concerned with developing a more intimate performer–audience relationship. And, in order to do this, he designed a small platform stage with a permanent architectural background, appropriate for the staging of any play.

Copeau's stage at the Vieux-Colombier

Meyerhold and
constructivism; the
mechanical stage

*Copeau* and Vsevolod *Meyerhold* were both engaged in a search for what *Copeau* called 'the idea of a theatre': the unchanging, essential heart of theatre, capable of capturing the universal life of the human spirit.

*Meyerhold*, one of the original members of the *Moscow Art Theatre*, had worked extensively with *Stanislavski*, who saw *Meyerhold* as his natural heir and successor. Having performed in the early *Moscow Art Theatre* productions, *Meyerhold* became dissatisfied with the limitations of *realist* theatre and branched out. He worked with both Vera **Komissarzhevskaya**'s company in St Petersburg and as director of the new Studio Theatre of *Moscow Art Theatre*. *Meyerhold*, in his search for a new theatre, conducted a number of daring theatrical experiments, many of which were considered to be failures. He mounted a *symbolist* production of *Ibsen*'s *realist* play, *Hedda Gabler*, and championed the theatrical work of the *symbolist* poet, Aleksandr **Blok**. He researched earlier popular forms of theatre, including 'the grotesque' and *Commedia dell'Arte*; and eventually arrived at a new concept which he called *constructivism*.

In keeping with the scientific and technological spirit of the times, *Meyerhold* wanted to develop 'a machine' upon which actors could perform. He designed and developed a flexible construction consisting of platforms, walkways, ramps and steps which could, theoretically, be used for the staging of any play. And, in order that his performers could exploit the full potential of this 'machine', he devised a system of movement exercises which he called *biomechanics*. Each day's rehearsal began with the *biomechanical* exercises, which were designed to foster flexibility and versatility, giving the actor perfect control over his bodily movements.

Meyerhold's 'Machine for acting'

As a director, *Meyerhold* did not favour the meticulous pre-planning of *Antoine* or the early *Stanislavski*. He preferred to arrive at rehearsals with a sense of what he wanted to explore, and was quite prepared to rework the scene the following day incorporating ideas that had arisen during his experiments. He viewed each rehearsal as a preliminary sketch, reworking scenes over and over again until he arrived at a version that would find its way into the final product. *Meyerhold*'s approach led to startling new productions of plays, which featured prominently in the repertoires of many European theatres and were already well known to theatre-going audiences. One Russian commentator suggested that his production of *The Government Inspector* owed very little to the original text written by Nikolai *Gogol*, and should be re-christened *Meyerhold's Mental Associations Apropos The Government Inspector*.

**Meyerhold's revolt against the restrictions of *realism* led him to strike out in a multitude of new and daring theatrical directions.** His boldness eventually brought him into dispute with Soviet officialdom and, despite his own vigorous defence of his work, he was imprisoned and finally executed by the KGB during one of Stalin's purges in 1942. As a result of his artistic rehabilitation in 1956, scholars have been able to painstakingly reconstruct *Meyerhold*'s whole theatrical career, and it is now quite clear that many of the new and innovative developments in late twentieth-century performance practice (including *Brecht*'s *epic* theatre, Peter *Brook*'s *A Midsummer Night's Dream* and the whole contemporary physical theatre movement) owe a considerable debt to *Meyerhold*'s adventurous and audacious experiments.

*Meyerhold's* experiments lead to the firing squad

## Measures of Control: Reinhardt and Vakhtangov

*Reinhardt* develops a highly detailed and technical theatre

Max *Reinhardt* was renowned for the dazzling diversity of his many productions. Unlike *Copeau* and *Meyerhold*, who, in their individual quests for an 'essential idea of theatre', eventually designed all-purpose, permanent 'platform stage environments' on which to mount their productions, *Reinhardt* was of the view that such a quest was futile. The richness of the world's drama could never be reduced to a single essence; each different theatrical form demanded its own unique approach, and the job of the director consisted in realising the specific atmosphere and ambiance of the play. Each new directorial challenge provided him with the opportunity to create a new world, with its own light and shadow, its own beauty and ugliness, its own heaven and hell.

**Reinhardt's overall approach was characterised by a determination to fully exploit all of the resources that theatre has to offer.** His brilliant theatrical effects were produced as a result of carefully mobilising and orchestrating all of the elements at his disposal: the text of the play; the dramatic action; the performers' skills; mass movement; music; light; costume; stage setting; and environment (for his production of *The Miracle*, he turned the theatre into a Gothic cathedral). Such effects could never have been achieved without the thorough preparation that was *Reinhardt*'s trademark. He arrived at the first rehearsal with his blueprint, and proceeded to mould every aspect of the production according to the master plan he had drawn up in his study. According to one of his actors, in the early stages of rehearsal *Reinhardt* treated actors as though they were puppets, controlling their every movement and intonation until their performances began to conform to the interpretation he had conceived in his mind's eye. Unlike *Copeau*, whose respect for the playwright's text was legendary, *Reinhardt* saw the play as a pretext for his own bold interpretations.

*Reinhardt*'s controlling directorial style stands in marked contrast to the approach of Eugene **Vakhtangov**, another of *Stanislavski*'s protégés from the *Moscow Art Theatre*. Although both sought to achieve a highly vigorous theatricality in their productions, the means by which they pursued their aims were quite different. *Vakhtangov*, working in the immediate aftermath of the October Revolution in Russia, built **a theatre collective whose working style was intended to be in keeping with the new socialist ideals**. *Vakhtangov* saw himself as an efficient, theatre craftsman rather than an autocratic, controlling director. He reputedly never lectured his performers, preferring instead to participate fully and actively in the creative work of rehearsals.

Unfortunately, *Vakhtangov* never lived to see his own ideals realised. But, following his death in 1922, his successor, Boris **Zakhava** translated these ideals into a working practice. The decision about which plays were to be produced was left in the hands of the collective; each play was then assigned to one of the company's directors.

The director was first required to submit, for formal approval, his production plans. At a meeting of the collective, and (if possible) the playwright, the plans were considered (and perhaps revised and modified in the light of discussion) before the director was permitted to go into production. But, even at this point, the director did not assume complete control. The first rehearsals consisted of a series of detailed discussions with the actors on how the different roles were to be interpreted. Ideas submitted by other company members were incorporated into the director's production plans and rehearsals proceeded in consultation with the whole company.

*Vakhtangov*'s collective style of direction

# Political Directors

The Workers Theatre of *Piscator*

During the 1920s, Erwin **Piscator** joined *Reinharbdt* in the front rank of German theatre directors. His early work consisted of small-scale touring productions of *agit-prop* (short for 'agitational-propaganda') plays, which were intended to instruct the workers in the key political issues of the day. He also toured 'Living Newspapers', which were, quite simply, enacted news stories for workers who were unable to read the real, printed newspapers. These touring productions would be performed at factory gates, workers' canteens and meeting halls, and, literally, on street corners.

In 1924, *Piscator* took over as director of the *Volksbühne* in Berlin. Here, *Piscator* developed larger-scale documentaries dealing with pressing, current social and political issues. **Piscator's use of new stage devices and technology was one of the most striking features of his new, documentary style**. The stage action was enhanced and supplemented by the use of charts, maps, placards, large-scale written slogans, conveyor belts, slides, film and newsreel inserts. Dismissed from his post at the *Volksbühne*

**Task 1:** Discuss the different directorial approaches of *Reinhardt* and *Vakhtangov*

Drawing on your own experiences of being directed, consider the advantages and disadvantages of the two directing styles and record them on a chart similar to that shown below.

| *REINHARDT'S* APPROACH | | *VAKHTANGOV'S* APPROACH | |
|---|---|---|---|
| Advantages | Disadvantages | Advantages | Disadvantages |
| | | | |
| | | | |
| | | | |
| | | | |
| | | | |
| | | | |
| | | | |

Piscator's Living Newspaper Performances, 1927

in 1927, *Piscator* moved to his own theatre where he adapted the Czech novel, *The Good Soldier Schweik*, which tells the woeful, wartime adventures of an ordinary soldier. This production, using filmed cartoons of drawings by the famous artist George Grosz, gave *Piscator* his greatest popular success.

One of *Piscator*'s collaborators on the adaptation of the novel was the playwright-poet-director, Bertolt *Brecht*, shortly to become a major figure in twentieth-century theatre history.

**Brecht took ideas from** *Brecht* **took ideas from his early work with** *Piscator* **and transformed** **his early work with** **them into a fully developed set of theories**. Some theatre theorists were *Piscator* **and transformed** unable to put their ideas into practice (Edward Gordon *Craig* as we have **them** seen; and Antonin *Artaud*, the writer who conceived the idea of the 'Theatre of Cruelty'), but *Brecht* was a practical man of the theatre and his theoretical ideas were tried and tested in the rehearsal room, and in the legendary productions of his own plays. *Brecht* would often say 'The proof is in the pudding!'

As we know from the acting workshop on finding the *Verfremdungseffekt*, *Brecht*'s politics led him to react sharply against *Stanislavski*'s approach. As far as *Brecht* was concerned, the *feeling* connection, essential in *Stanislavski*'s theatre of empathy, impaired the spectator's ability to view the play in a detached, objective, *thinking* manner. Empathy is the enemy of thought because it produces an inability in the spectator to make considered judgements about those circumstances and conditions that have contributed to the problems and dilemmas that the characters face. It also encourages the spectator to accept that these circumstances are beyond the control of the characters in the play, something that simply had to be put up with.

Bertolt Brecht

We have seen that *Brecht*'s studies in Marxism led him to think differently. The point of *Brecht*'s theatre was not to offer his spectators a view of the world which seemed given (as in the 'given circumstances') and unchangeable, but rather to present them with the possibility that circumstances *could* be changed by the actions of the characters. *Brecht* adopted the words of Karl Marx as his guiding principle in his work: '**it is not just a matter of interpreting the world, the point is to change it**'. *Brecht*'s purpose in making theatre, then, was openly political. His revolutionary outlook demanded that the spectators should open their eyes, see the extent of the inequity and injustice in the world and understand that there was an urgent need to change it.

**Brecht develops the *epic* and the *Verfremdungseffekt***

*Brecht*'s theatre, therefore, was designed to cultivate in the audience a more clinical, detached and objective form of spectatorship, and we have already outlined the two concepts that are vitally important in achieving this end. The first is the concept of the *Verfremdungseffekt*, which forces the spectator to look at ordinary, familiar, everyday things in a new light. The second is the *epic* which dislocates the 'through-line of action' by ensuring that each scene in the play is self-contained.

In accounts of modern European theatre, the theories of *Stanislavski* and *Brecht* are almost always presented as being antagonistic to each other. But this is only partly true. The political distance between the two men meant that each was working towards different political (and, ultimately, theatrical) ends. But *Brecht* wrote a series of *Notes on Stanislavski*, and in these notes made it clear that **Stanislavski's ideas about empathy were vital to his own theories**.

**Stanislavski's influence on Brecht**

*Brecht* was in no doubt that, in his own theatre, the illusions fostered by the realist theatre of *Stanislavski* had to be broken; but he also understood that an illusion had first to be created before it could be broken. He therefore devised a three-stage rehearsal programme (significantly entitled '*Building a Character* – also the title of the second of *Stanislavski*'s books on acting) for his actors. In the first stage of the process, the actor must become intimately acquainted with the character that is to be played. The second stage is that of empathy (in *Stanislavski*'s terms, becoming one with the character). The final stage is where the actor, now being thoroughly familiar with the role, is able to *stand outside* of it and offer the audience a more detached, critical insight into the character being played.

## The Late Twentieth-century Directors

**Grotowski's theatre set out to probe the question: 'How should one live?'**

Jerzy *Grotowski*'s theatre set out to probe the question: 'how should one live?' His productions were designed to offer the audience some insight into this problem. In order to do this, he expected his actors to confront this same question through the process of rehearsal, and in performance. His aim required a thorough investigation into the nature and process of acting. His early work was undertaken in his 'Theatre of the Thirteen Rows' which was established in 1959 in a small Polish town.

*Grotowski* believed that authenticity, in life as in the theatre, was essential. **To live and perform authentically meant peeling away what he called the 'life mask' – that set of social roles that we assume in our everyday encounters with others.** This process of stripping away allows the performer to come face to face with that inner core of being that is the **true self**. Rehearsals are designed in such a way that each actor undertakes a creative exploration of the self.

But *Grotowski* recognised that it is impossible to view the self directly. He understood that in order to become thoroughly acquainted with the self, an other was required. This is because, in everyday life, we measure ourselves alongside other people. For example, we understand our own weaknesses by recognising the strengths in others, and vice versa. In *Grotowski*'s early work, the character in the play provided this 'other': as the actor struggles to find a connection between her or his own qualities and characteristics and those of the character, the performer inevitably learns something about him- or herself.

We have already seen how in *Brecht*'s rehearsal programme, the *Stanislavskian* stage of empathy was vital. Similarly, the first stage of *Grotowski*'s rehearsal process requires the actor to become one with the character. However, as with *Brecht*, *Grotowski* soon parts company with *Stanislavski*. Whereas the *Stanislavskian* actor uses parts of the self to bring the character (or 'other') into being, the *Grotowskian* actor uses the 'other' (or character) to bring about a greater understanding of self. *Grotowski* believed that the world's great plays open doors for the actor (and the spectator) to achieve greater self-knowledge.

At the end of the 1960s, *Grotowski*'s thinking began to change. 'The Theatre of the Thirteen Rows' became an 'Institute of Research into Acting Method – Laboratory Theatre'. The shift in *Grotowski*'s thinking can perhaps be best summarised as follows: '**I am myself when I do not think about myself**'. Since *Grotowski* believed that 'thinking' did not help in the search for self, he sought the means of self-discovery in 'action'. For the actor, this means immersing her- or himself in action and in 'existence'. Therefore, *Grotowski* removes the character and **places the actor in the situation of the character**. In other words, the actors play their characters by playing themselves. At this point, *Grotowski* declares that acting has been abandoned.

The repercussions of this renunciation of acting were tremendous. We should remember that *Grotowski*'s aim, throughout, was to help both actor and spectator in their search for their authentic selves. The demands that *Grotowski* placed on his actors in the *Laboratory Theatre* were enormous, but the technical virtuosity and powerful intensity of the performers was often met by incomprehension in the audience. One critic wrote that he learned nothing about human suffering from watching the actors suffer. During this period, *Grotowski* set his actors increasingly difficult physical challenges until they eventually become impossible. For example, actors were asked to punch holes in the wall using only their voices! But, here again, the physical skill and technical wizardry had the effect of alienating the audience, forcing them to confront their own limitations in the face of extraordinary expertise.

*Grotowski* realised that the mesmerising physical abilities of his actors did not permit the act of self-revelation that was his ultimate goal; all that was revealed in performance was the actors' skills. *Grotowski*'s solution to this problem was to veer towards the opposite extreme, and in so doing he developed the concept of the **via negativa** ('the negative way'). *Grotowski* continued to set his actors difficult challenges, but his aim changed: instead of asking themselves 'How do I do this?', the performers were required to discover what obstacles prevented them from meeting the challenge. In

*Grotowski* believed that the world's great plays open doors for the actors to achieve greater self-knowledge

Gradually *Grotowski*'s company became preoccupied with self-exploration and less concerned with public performance other words, they had to know what *not* to do. Gradually *Grotowski*'s company became more and more preoccupied with self-exploration through intensive workshop sessions, and less and less concerned with public performance.

But it soon became obvious that the company's introversion and isolation could not last for long. In his early writings, *Grotowski* had emphasised that theatre was defined by the nature of the encounter which took place between actor and spectator, adding that everything else was supplementary. Several of *Grotowski*'s productions attempted to draw the spectators into the dramatic action: *The Ancestors,* for example; and Kordian, in which the audience were threatened with a cane if they did not join in the singing! Later, **the spectators were given roles**, but in keeping with their passive status as audience members. In *Dr Faustus,* the spectators were asked to act as the central character's 'witnesses'.

*Grotowski* abandons performance for rituals

Frustrated at his inability to find a satisfying and productive kind of encounter between actor and spectator, *Grotowski* abandoned the idea of theatre altogether and embraced, in its place, the notion of meeting. From this point, his encounters with the public took the form of communal events in which the 'guests' were invited to participate in creative activities (improvisations, movement exercises and music-making) alongside the performers. In this creative contact **the social masks were intended to fall away as guests and performers embarked together on individual and shared journeys of self-discovery**. Theatre historians have tried to explain *Grotowski*'s change of direction as an attempt to rediscover, through these events, forms of authentic human contact which have been lost in the course of civilisation's development.

Peter *Brook*: gathering the fragments of theatre

We have seen how a number of the early *non-realist* directors were in search of an essential 'idea of a theatre' (*Craig, Copeau, Meyerhold*). Towards the end of the twentieth century, Peter *Brook* took up this challenge. In his book, *The Shifting Point, Brook* observes that 'nowhere in the world is there a complete theatre but only fragments of a theatre'. One could argue that *Brook*'s long career has been dedicated to bringing these fragments together into one complete whole: from his ground-breaking production of *Romeo and Juliet* in 1947, through the 1960s' attempts to bring *Artaud*'s **'Theatre of Cruelty'** to life, the flamboyant *Meyerhold*-inspired production of *A Midsummer Night's Dream*, the journey through Africa with *Conference of the Birds*, to the magnificent achievement of *Le Mahabharata*.

*Brook* develops his minimalist and poetic style of theatre

In terms of the rich diversity of his theatre work, *Brook* can perhaps best be compared to Max *Reinhardt*. But *Brook*'s contribution to twentieth-century theatre goes far beyond *Reinhardt*'s. **Having thoroughly absorbed the influences of Stanislavski and Brecht into his early work, Brook went on to find close affinities with Grotowski's approach**. For *Brook*, acting was never a process of 'building'. Rather, it was a question of removing the blocks and obstacles that stand in the way of creating the role. Once these obstacles are removed, the character is able to 'penetrate' the actor. The production process itself required the removal of everything that was inessential. *Brook* records that in his preparations for the 1962 production of *King Lear* he systematically eliminated scenery, costume and music, and, finally, colour. Nineteen years later, in his production of *Carmen*, his watchword was still simplicity.

*Brook* develops an interest in intercultural performances

In 1968, *Brook* was invited to Paris to run a workshop with actors from a variety of different countries and cultural backgrounds. Two years later, he moved to Paris where he set up the *Centre International de Recherche Théâtrales* ('International Centre for Theatre Research'), and soon afterwards the *Centre International de Création Théâtrales* ('International Centre for Theatre Creation'). He gathered together a group of performers from all over the world with the intention of fully researching the potential resources of the actor, and putting the results of this research to the test in performance.

As part of his work with the *Centre International*, *Brook* embarked on the most ambitious project of his career. Accompanied by his performers, he set out to journey through Africa with a series of improvisations based on Farid Ud-din Attar's fable, *The Conference of the Birds*. *Brook*'s purpose in undertaking this work was broadly similar to *Grotowski*'s: the company was involved in a search for authenticity, wholeness and the self. And, as with *Grotowski*'s approach, much of the work had a real physical intensity, with rehearsals sometimes continuing for up to 19 hours.

Work on the fable continued throughout the journey, and performances were offered to different tribes along the way. As we noted above, one of *Brook*'s abiding concerns has been with simplicity and clarity. He was therefore anxious to perform to audiences who shared no common assumptions with his company. This meant that the company could not rely on the established conventions of Western theatre. Any barrier that stood in the way of communicating the meaning of the work had to be stripped away. This was *Brook*'s own version of *Grotowski*'s 'via negativa'.

But perhaps *Brook*'s greatest achievement is his mammoth, nine-hour long production of the Indian *epic*, *Le Mahabharata*. Fifteen times longer than the Bible, *Le Mahabharata* consists of an intricate web of mythology, history, philosophy and politics. *Brook* spent nine years researching his material with Jean-Claude **Carrière**, who was responsible for producing the final text. Many would argue that this production represents *Brook*'s most concerted attempt to bring together the 'fragments of a theatre' into the *complete theatre* that has been the dream of so many theatre artists from *Wagner* onwards.

## The importance of *Le Mahabharata*

The most striking feature of *Le Mahabharata* is not just the consummate interweaving of the many different stories contained in the *epic*, but the brilliant fusion of the various theatrical forms into one complex but coherent whole. **Brook's production seems to move effortlessly between many different and diverse theatrical traditions**: simple storytelling sits comfortably side by side with *epic* scenes of combat; gods, demons and plain mortals present themselves simultaneously to the audience; realistic scenes blend harmoniously with highly-stylised *mime* sequences; and character transformations occur smoothly and seamlessly. The author figure who appears in the production is called Vyasha, which derives from a Sanskrit word meaning 'to fit together'. Vyasha seems to serve as a symbol of *Brook's* achievement in this work.

**Brook's work is often described as eclectic, drawing as it does on so many diverse influences and sources.** For some critics, he is more of an emulator than an innovator; someone who, lacking real originality, absorbs and recycles the ideas and techniques of others. A magpie, opportunistically and indiscriminately picking up bits and pieces from here, there and everywhere.

These same critics point to the lack of stylistic consistency in *Brook*'s work over the years – but this was never his aim. Instead, he was looking to develop performances that moved fluidly between different conventions – a modern production style, comparable with the works of *Shakespeare*, which moves deftly from *tragedy* to *comedy*, in which a clown can be companion to a king. To maintain that *Brook* is inventive but not innovative, one has to play down the immense significance of works like *Le Mahabharata*. Historians and critics will, no doubt, continue to debate and differ over the scope of *Brook*'s achievement; only history will reveal whether or not his contribution to theatre practice has enduring substance.

**The influence of *Artaud*'s ideas**

We have attempted to identify and describe those directors who have, in some measure, either changed the course of twentieth-century theatre production, or pushed back the boundaries of performance practice. Such an undertaking has to be selective, and we have had to leave out some important figures. Perhaps the most striking omission is Antonin *Artaud*. We justify this on the grounds that, although *Artaud* was undoubtedly a visionary in terms of his thinking on the power and potential of theatre, his work as a practising director fell far short of the groundbreaking ideas that he put forward in his theoretical writings. Undoubtedly there are a multitude of reasons why this may have been the case: an inability to persuade the French theatre establishment to take him seriously; a failure to secure the necessary financial backing for his daring and scandalous experiments; psychological illness; or maybe he was just too many years ahead of his time. Whatever the truth, **it was left to *Grotowski* and *Brook* to partially realise *Artaud*'s vision**.

Others who are absent from our survey include Harley *Granville Barker*, David *Belasco*, Elia *Kazan*, Joan *Littlewood* and Eugenio *Barba*.

---

**Task 2: What do we learn from the great directors?**

The work of the great directors that we have described continues to affect the theatre of today. When you see plays or produce plays yourself you will find the influence of their ideas at work.

- Write a paragraph on each of the directors in this chapter, which contains the key ideas associated with each. We have included some further research opportunities in the Webliography in the Resources section (Section Six). Keep these brief notes to refer to when you are producing or analysing performances.

---

# Conclusion

For every major twentieth-century director who has broken new ground, there are thousands who have been quietly absorbed in the everyday business of bringing new plays to the stage, and breathing new life into the tried and tested texts of the past. Unspectacular though this work seems in comparison to the exciting innovation described above, it is the bread-and-butter work of the theatre director; and it is to this that we turn in the next chapter.

In this chapter we have provided you with a brief history of the emergence of the director as the new artist of the theatre. You will find further references to many of these artists scattered throughout the book.

**Use the Index to find out more**

You could build a practitioner file for directors who interest you by looking up all the references in the Index and then compiling a report on your chosen practitioner. You could add to this file by researching your chosen practitioner using the Webliography in Section Six. Or just type a name into your search engine and see what you find!

# 6 From Page to Stage

## The Work of the Director

We have already noted that *Stanislavski* was co-founder of the *Moscow Art Theatre* with *Vladimir Nemirovich-Danchenko*. The two colleagues enjoyed a long and productive professional relationship. *Nemirovich-Danchenko* is often remembered as *Stanislavski's* 'literary adviser', the man who brought the plays of *Chekhov* to the company. But this is only part of the story. *Nemirovich-Danchenko* was a practising director of some stature and, in point of fact, for the *Moscow Art Theatre's* original production of *The Seagull* he directed more of the rehearsals than *Stanislavski* himself. The two men were credited as 'joint directors' for most of the company's productions.

So it is worth pausing for a moment to consider how their collaboration worked in practice. *Nemirovich-Danchenko's* reputation as a 'literary man' is well deserved; his detailed study of the text provided the basis for the whole production. After this painstaking textual work, the two men would meet for long discussions during which *Nemirovich-Danchenko* would provide a basic interpretation of the work. *Stanislavski* took notes as his colleague spoke. These notes would then form the basis of the *mise en scène* that *Stanislavski* developed prior to beginning rehearsal. During the period of preparation, *Nemirovich-Danchenko* would try to ensure that *Stanislavski's* flair for theatricality and stage effects did not overwhelm or obscure the basic interpretation that had been agreed upon.

In one sense we can think of *Nemirovich-Danchenko* as 'reining in' some of *Stanislavski's* more extravagant flights of fancy. He was not always completely successful in this, since we know that *Chekhov* became increasingly irritated by the excessive number of special effects that *Stanislavski* insisted on adding to his plays.

## Functions of the Director

The division of labour that *Stanislavski* and *Nemirovich-Danchenko* had agreed upon is instructive for us as we try to tease out the role of the director in the process of production. Essentially, the director's role can be reduced to two **essential functions**: the first is to evolve a **vision** of the play which is consistent with the *interpretation*; the second, once this is successfully accomplished, is to help the designer, the actors and the technical team **bring the interpretation to life on the stage**.

We will begin by considering the first of these functions – the vision or *conception*. Later on, we will look in more detail at how the director works with actors in order to *realise* the interpretation.

In this chapter our primary focus is on the directing of text-based plays. However, we will not be concerned here with the kind of detailed analysis that engaged *Nemirovich-Danchenko* in the first stages of the *Moscow Art Theatre* process. Chapter 8 covers this ground. A good deal of contemporary theatre work is not text-based, and the whole area of devising for theatre is considered in Chapter 9.

# Conception

Peter *Brook*, in *The Shifting Point*, talks about how he begins his work as a director. He begins, 'with a deep, formless hunch which is like a smell, a color, a shadow'. In other words, his first feeling about the play is a vague one; something, perhaps, which he is unable to put his finger on, but which nevertheless drives him to give shape and form to his 'hunch'. Something in the play text catches his imagination. This is the feeling that *Nemirovich-Danchenko* must have experienced when he first read *The Seagull*.

Whatever it is about the play that has caught the director's attention, the starting point provided by the play text will be returned to, time and time again, in order that the director can gain a clearer sense of what it is about the play that has caught their eye. In the early stages of detailed textual work, the director will focus on what it is that the playwright is trying to say – the meanings which are embedded in the work.

**Some directors, *Nemirovich-Danchenko* and *Copeau* among them, see themselves as playwright's directors, who look deep into the heart of the text in an attempt to keep faith with what they believe to be the author's intentions.** When working on a play, they try to empty themselves of any preconceptions they might have (perhaps from an earlier reading, or from having seen previous productions) in order that the play can speak to them afresh. The archetypal 'playwright's director' likes to be invisible, so that it seems as if the play speaks directly to the audience without them having any real sense that the play has been directed at all. Generally speaking, it would be true to say that the 'playwright's director' allows their own interpretation of what the playwright intended to shape the conception. This would roughly correspond to *Nemirovich-Danchenko's* first stage of preparation.

As this work proceeds, a more fully formed idea about the play begins to develop as the director gains greater insight into the world of the play and a fuller understanding of the lives of the characters who inhabit that world. Slowly, a vision takes shape and thoughts turn to 'the look of the play'. At this point in the working methods of the *Moscow Art Theatre, Stanislavski*, under *Nemirovich-Danchenko's* guidance, would develop his *mise en scène*.

For the 'playwright's director', this vision will represent a fairly faithful attempt to make clear to the audience the playwright's intended meanings. **Other kinds of directors (*Craig* and *Meyerhold*, for example) may be somewhat more adventurous in their interpretations. Their concern is not so much with fidelity to the playwright's intentions, but rather with shedding new light on a classical or well-established text.** Where this is the case, the director will read and reread the play in an attempt to clarify whether their interpretation can really be supported by the playwright's text (if not, it's back to the drawing board). Having confirmed the viability of the new interpretation, the director will proceed.

The vision developed by this kind of director, which may involve a more or less radical departure from the original intentions of the playwright, can result in a complete transformation in how the audience views the play – a completely new 'perspective' that illuminates the text in previously unimagined ways. Sometimes, the interpretation is so far removed from the playwright's original version that it's possible to argue that the director has, in a very real sense, 'rewritten' the play: they become, alongside the playwright, its 'co-author'. **This kind of director is often referred to as an *auteur*** (*auteur* being the French word for 'author').

Interpretations of the classics

New interpretations of old, established or classical plays can come about in a number of different ways. Perhaps some of the most common are as follows:

- A realignment in the angle of vision, when a play is interpreted from the viewpoint of a particular character. In *Shakespeare*'s day, the character of Shylock in *The Merchant of Venice* was presented very unflatteringly as a stereotypical Jew, until the great nineteenth-century actor-manager, Henry *Irving* offered a much more sympathetic depiction.
- A new pattern is perceived in the structure of a play. In his book, *Shakespeare Our Contemporary*, the Polish critic Jan **Kott** offers a new interpretation of *King Lear* based on *Shakespeare*'s previously unnoticed repetition of negatives: 'no'; 'never'; 'nothing'; etc. – a pattern which, *Kott* claims, points to Lear's increasingly nihilistic view of the world.
- A new form is found for the presentation of a play. Peter *Brook*'s conception for his *A Midsummer Night's Dream* took shape after he and Sally Jacobs, the designer, saw a performance by a troupe of Chinese acrobats.
- A play takes on new significance because its themes speak powerfully of contemporary social and political events. At a time when civil wars are raging throughout the world, *Shakespeare*'s *Coriolanus*, or *Titus Andronicus*, or *Timon of Athens* seem to offer pertinent commentaries on events that are regularly reported in the news media.

---

### Task 1: New interpretation of a classic play

Think back over the classic plays you have studied, or been involved in. Can you see how one of them might be **reinterpreted**? Perhaps you can imagine reconfiguring the play in order to present it from the point of view of one of the characters; or perceive a new pattern in the play's imagery; or, find a new form for presenting the play; or see new significance in the play because of recent events you have seen reported in the news.

- Draw up a one-page outline of your new interpretation, offering some justifications for your original approach. Remember, you don't have to make it work in practice, so be as bold and ambitious as you like!

---

Exceptions to the rule

Although we have suggested that, at the conceptual stage, there are two broad types of director (the **playwright's director** and the *auteur*), we should not think of these as the only two possibilities. Neither type really exists in a pure form. It's entirely possible, for example, that a 'playwright's director' will, at times, find it necessary to become an *auteur* in order to make a particularly difficult scene work. Elia *Kazan*, the great American director, is almost always described as a 'playwright's director', but found it necessary to revise a good deal of Tennessee **Williams**' most famous play, *A Streetcar Named Desire*, and even redrafted two of the scenes completely. On the other hand, if the *auteur* were to totally 're-write' the play, then clearly it would cease to be the original author's work at all. This is what happened with Robert **Lepage**'s version of *Shakespeare*'s *Hamlet* – so much so that it was renamed *Elsinore*. Between the two pure types then, there are many combinations of each.

The play must have an appeal for the director

Whether the director is an *auteur* or a playwright's director, something in the play must have caught their attention: it may be a desire to offer a new

A production of *Yerma* by University of Northumbria students

perspective on the play as a result of their having seen a new pattern of meanings (which may have emerged for any one, or a combination, of the reasons stated above); it may be a wish to clarify the meanings in the play; or it may be that the director has come across a new play which they feel *must* be brought before an audience.

**We believe that it is useful to see the role of the director as standing between the playwright and the spectator**, illuminating and clarifying the writer's text for the play's potential audience.

Below we have included a description of how a new interpretation of *Lorca*'s *Yerma* evolved.

## Conceiving *Yerma*: A Case Study

We have recently directed a student production of Federico García *Lorca*'s play, *Yerma*. In this section there are a number of exploratory tasks that we used in the early stages of our rehearsal process. In order to carry out the tasks it will be necessary for you to read and be familiar with *Lorca*'s play.

We had read some of *Lorca*'s other plays a while ago, and, as we recall, they left us fairly cold. Then, a colleague mounted a production of *Lorca*'s little-known play, *The Billy-Club Puppets*. We read the play, and subsequently we decided to re-visit his major works. It was *Yerma* that made the biggest impression on us. At the time we weren't sure why; but there was no mistaking the power of the play.

*Yerma*: the plot

The story is a simple one. The central character, Yerma, longs for a child but is unable to conceive. As her repeated attempts to become pregnant fail, she becomes more and more frustrated, and, as her frustration turns to bitterness, her relationship with her husband, Juan, comes under increasing strain. Her prayers remain unanswered, and a pagan woman offers her the solution to her predicament. The pagan woman reveals to Yerma that the fault lies not with her, but with her husband; and she offers Yerma her youngest son as a lover. Yerma's sense of religious duty and honour prevent her from acceding to this, and, in the final scene, following another bitter quarrel with her husband, she kills him.

105

**Great plays are great because they have the power to disturb.** As the weeks following our reading of *Yerma* passed, we became aware of a sense of disturbance. We tried to work out what it was about the play that was creating this feeling. Yerma's anguish? A husband and wife tearing themselves apart because of circumstances over which they have no control? A woman increasingly alienated from the community in which she has grown up? But no. Compelling though these different possibilities are, we knew that they did not *fully* account for our disturbance. The question remained.

The director's 'hunch' begins to form

Some months later, we were visiting a university in Norway with a colleague. We were thinking about a workshop we were due to lead with some undergraduate students. Out of the blue, he suggested using a short piece of text from *Yerma*: the speech by the pagan woman in which she gives a brief flavour of the life she has led (the speech is on page 109). After some introductory work, we invited the students to develop a series of scenes from the pagan woman's life based on the (somewhat sketchy) information contained in the speech. The scenes they produced were full of life, exuberance and humour. What struck us, on reflection, was the contrast between the experiences of the pagan woman as they were depicted in these improvisations and the sombre, troubled, oppressive life of Yerma herself. At the heart of *Lorca*'s play, it seemed to us, was a clash of two apparently incompatible worlds; and it was this that began to interest us.

Ideas based on the historical context

A few weeks before our visit to Norway we had seen a film, *Libertarias*, which examines the important role played by women in the early days of the Spanish Civil War. We were struck by the women's intensely passionate desire to see a new future for Spain, once the forces of fascism had been defeated. Their hopes and aspirations were given added poignancy following their betrayal by the men alongside whom they had been fighting. *Yerma* was written in 1934, two years before this savage civil war in which *Lorca* himself would become a victim of the fascists both for his politics and for his alleged homosexuality.

As we continued to think about *Lorca*'s play in its historical context, **Yerma's desperate desire for a child seemed to mirror the hopes of the women for the future of Spain.** It is often said that children represent hope for the future, and, as our formless hunch started to take shape, we began to see Yerma's unborn child as a symbol of the spark of revolution which was extinguished by the victory of General Franco's fascists in Spain. The treachery of the former male comrades of the women seemed to be akin to the sense of betrayal felt by Yerma when her husband dismisses her concerns, and tells her that their life together is better without children.

Ideas from other artistic interpretations of the historical context

*Libertarias* triggered a memory of *Land and Freedom*, another film (by Ken Loach) which dealt with the Spanish Civil War. The scene that kept coming back to us was one in which a priest is executed by the revolutionaries for revealing to the fascists the names of members of left-wing organisations.

The collaboration between the Church and Franco's forces is well documented in histories of the period, and it was this discovery that brought us back, full circle, to **the clash between the two worlds which are present in *Lorca*'s play**: the suffocating world of Yerma's village, dominated by the reactionary forces of Church, convention and tradition; and the earthy, natural world of the pagan woman and her free-spirited, liberated outlook, unfettered by the bonds of custom.

Gradually, over a period of several months we came to understand what it was that had drawn us back to the play time and time again: the clashing forces of reaction and revolution, and the ways in which these powerful forces were symbolically present in Yerma's dilemma.

The director returns to the text to explore his or her interpretation

On returning to *Lorca*'s play, we had to convince ourselves that the text would support the interpretation that was beginning to take shape in our minds. We wanted to begin by exploring the relationships between the three central characters. As you read the play, you undoubtedly became aware of the triangle of relationships between Yerma, Juan and Victor, which lies at the heart of the play.

## Task 2: A triangle

1   Identify the scenes where any combination of Yerma, Juan and Victor appear together. In your group, reread them carefully.

2   When you have done this, make a *still-image* that captures the true essence of Yerma's relationship with both men **at the beginning of the play.**

3   Find the line of dialogue which you think most clearly expresses Yerma's feelings for each of the men. One member of the group should speak the line of dialogue aloud as the others recreate the image, so that you can see the effect of placing the line alongside the visual picture.

Towards the end of the second act, Victor reveals that he is leaving the village to be with his father, and comes to say goodbye to Yerma and to Juan.

4   Look again at this scene, and then repeat the same exercise (first the image, and then the accompanying line of dialogue). But this time show Yerma's feelings towards both men **at the moment of Victor's departure.**

5   Create a very simple movement sequence in which your first image from the beginning of the play changes into the second.

6   Talk about what these two images reveal about how Yerma's feelings have changed in the years that pass between Act 1 and Act 2.

Imagining Yerma's world

It was important for us to be sure that the atmosphere of Yerma's village was indeed as stifling and oppressive as we had remembered it. What struck us most forcefully was the scene by the river, in which a group of village washerwomen gossip as they wash their laundry. Their focus of attention is, of course, Yerma and her increasingly unconventional behaviour (for example, walking barefoot through the streets at night when she should be at home). The gossip, slyly malicious at the beginning of the scene, becomes positively menacing towards the end, as the early, naturalistic chatter gives way to an insistent and sinister chant, in which the more poetic lines are relentlessly hammered out to the work rhythm of the women. **One gets the sense of a puritanical and vengeful community sitting in judgement on an innocent victim of circumstance.**

## Task 3: Yerma's World

In this task, we will be trying to develop a sense of the village community in which Yerma lives.

1   To begin with, look again at the first scene of the play. Reread the section where Maria, a friend of Yerma, brings the news that she is pregnant.

**2 Using improvisation**, rather than the script itself, try to find out how Maria breaks the news, and how Yerma receives it.

**3 Try the scene a number of different ways**, giving different people the chance to try out the roles.

- Discuss with your group which version seems to best capture the tone of *Lorca*'s scene. How does Maria tell Yerma, and what are Yerma's *true* feelings when she hears Maria's news?

In the next exploration, we will be experimenting with different stylistic conventions. Look again at the washerwomen's scene. **From the point of view of style**, what do you notice about it? The scene falls into two parts: the first, realistic; the second, more poetic and stylised.

**4** In groups, try to create a version of the scene in which these two different styles are as sharply differentiated as you can make them. Discuss what effect the different styles have on the washerwomen's gossip.

**5** Look again at the opening exchange between Yerma and Juan in the very first scene. Create a new piece of text, where you punctuate this scene with the washerwomen's gossip; and then perform it.

- Discuss the effect that is produced by juxtaposing the intimate conversation that takes place within the privacy of Yerma and Juan's home with the public condemnation and disapproval of the village washerwomen.

To add to Yerma's misery, Juan finally moves his two sisters into the house so that they can keep a close watch on his wayward wife; she literally becomes a prisoner in her own home.

## Task 4: Someone to watch over you

Think about the image of Juan's two sisters 'watching over' Yerma. They actually say very little, but look again at Act 2, Scene 2; despite their silence, they represent a very powerful presence. This task is designed to analyse the role of the sisters.

**1** Visit the library to see if you can find a book containing the religious paintings of El Greco (a Greek-born artist who subsequently lived and worked in late sixteenth- and early seventeenth-century Spain). Look for images of angels in El Greco's paintings and study them. You can find some good examples at this website address: http://spanishculture.miningco.com/culture/cultureeurope/spanishculture/gi/dynamic/offsite.htm?site=http://members.aol.com/kerujo/greco/index.htm

**2** Look at the opening image of the play where, in the early light of dawn, Yerma sits in a chair dozing and dreaming. In your group, see if you can create an image, *based on the paintings*, of two angels, compassionately and protectively watching over Yerma as she sleeps.

**3** When you have an image that you are satisfied with, very slowly and gradually transform these heavenly angels into jailers, but try to retain the essential quality of the El Greco images.

- Does your transformation make it possible for you to see the sisters as guardians and jailers at the same time?

- Does one seem more appropriate than the other, and if so, why?

Interpreting the symbolism of the pagan woman

If Juan, his sisters and the village women embody the forces of reaction in the play, we felt that the revolutionary impulse was to be found in the philosophy of the pagan woman. Once again, we had to be sure that we could find justification in the play for this feeling, and so we began to analyse the character of the pagan woman.

Thoroughly sceptical of the Church and its teachings, she puts her faith in the world of nature. She tells her that it is no good offering up prayers to a non-existent god; rather, that she should understand that Juan's family has never been particularly fertile (his two sisters remain childless and his male relatives are 'made of spit'), whereas her own family has a long history of producing strong and healthy children.

The answer for Yerma lies in renouncing the stuffy, bigoted and repressive world represented by the village and embracing the pagan woman's way of life. In the last scene of the play, it seems that Yerma's religious convictions make it impossible for her to follow the advice of the pagan woman. But, having apparently rejected it, she then kills her husband (her oppressor) and the play ends with Yerma poised between the censure of the villagers and the escape route which has been offered to her.

## Task 5: The Pagan World

Reread the pagan woman's speech in Act 1, scene 2.

*Yerma:* I am Enrique the Shepherd's daughter.

*Pagan Woman:* Enrique the Shepherd! I knew him. Good people. Get up sweat. Eat a few loaves of bread and die. No time for larking about. I could have married an uncle of yours, but there you are . . . (*Laughs*) . . . I've chucked my skirts over my head in my time. Oh, yes, I've cut myself a good slice of the cake in my day, I can tell you. Many is the time in the night I've run to the door thinking I've heard the sound of guitars at the Fiesta, but it was only the wind. (*Laughs*) You may laugh but I've had two husbands and fourteen sons, five of whom died, and yet I'm not sad and I'd like to live a good while longer yet. But it's like I always say, look at the fig trees how long they last! And the houses! It's only us blessed women who go to rot.

1 Try to imagine what her younger life was like. Develop five short scenes which depict this past.

2 Condense each scene into a *still-image*. Give each a title that begins with the words 'The pagan woman learns. . .' (e.g. 'The pagan woman learns the pleasure of sex').

The pagan woman must be roughly the same age as Yerma's mother, the wife of Enrique the Shepherd. Although Yerma's mother never appears in the play, try to imagine what *her* life would have been like as a girl and a young woman (presumably she was brought up in the same village as Yerma, and it is probably fair to assume that the lives of the mother and the daughter would not be vastly dissimilar).

3 Return to the scene titles for the pagan woman *still-images* and try to come up with a new title that suggests the opposite of what the pagan woman had learned. When you have these five new titles, use them as a starting point for an equivalent scene describing the life of Yerma's mother (e.g. 'Yerma's mother learns that sex is sinful. . .').

4 Finally, play the five scenes describing the life of the pagan woman one after the other, and, straight away, play the five scenes showing the experience of Yerma's mother. What differences do you perceive between the lives of the two women?

**From conception to realisation**

By returning to *Lorca*'s play, rereading it with great care, and subjecting it to some rigorous textual analysis, we finally persuaded ourselves that our initial conception was viable and that our developing interpretation did not involve distorting the play beyond all recognition. Once the director has satisfied themselves that the conception is viable, they begin to work with the designer to develop the visual aspects of the production. **A good designer is able to highlight aspects of the director's conception by ensuring that visual motifs reinforce the themes which are foregrounded in the director's interpretation.**

At this point, the stage of conception gives way to the **stage of realisation**, where the director begins to work with their actors in order to explore, develop and give final form to the initial conception.

# Realisation

**Realisation = exploration + rehearsal**

We can think of the process of realising a play as having two important aspects to it: an **exploratory** aspect and a **rehearsal** aspect. Some of the major directors we have already encountered were able to enjoy the luxury of prolonged exploration before embarking upon the rehearsal period leading up to the final production (Peter *Brook*'s production of the *Marat/Sade* began life as an exploratory workshop on madness). It is our belief that 'exploration' has a vital role to play in the process of realisation.

**Improvisation is an essential rehearsal aid**

Joan *Littlewood*, in her long career as director of *Theatre Workshop* and Stratford East's *Theatre Royal*, used **improvisation** as an essential rehearsal aid to:

- **improvise scenes that are implicit in the text**, but which the playwright 'forgot' to write (e.g. Macbeth hiring the assassins who are to kill Duncan);
- **find a parallel situation** that is closer to the actors' experience than the one in the play;
- **use contemporary language** to grasp the meaning and tone of classical verse.

**Such exploratory improvisations help the actors gain a fuller understanding of context and background**, the full weight and significance of individual scenes and the richness of the poetic language. Improvisation, of course, is not the only rehearsal aid. There are a wide range of conventions and exploratory techniques available to the creative director that not only serve to open up the world of the play for closer analysis and inspection, but also allow for a more thorough investigation into character and the network of relationships within the play. Most directors would, we think, agree that the more mechanical aspects of rehearsal will be considerably enriched by carefully considered, creative and imaginative explorations.

There does come a point, however, when the explorations have to stop. The demands of the schedule will require that decisions are made and certain aspects of the production are firmed-up and fixed. Now, the focus of the director's work begins to change. The more open, exploratory atmosphere of the early stages of realisation gives way to a period of consolidation in which the director's editorial and technical functions take over.

**From exploration to rehearsal**

At this point the director guides the actors to be more selective in what they are doing. In helping them decide what essentials must be preserved in their performances, the director eliminates any elements which serve to clutter and obscure. At the very end, the technical demands of the production become the main preoccupation. This is a time when the director ensures that all the technical elements (lighting, sound, scene changes, etc.) combine to create a clear, flowing, stylistically coherent whole which will hold the attention of the audience.

Unfortunately, however, for most professional directors, the combination of financial constraints and scheduling logistics means that productions have to be rehearsed and ready for performance within a period of four (sometimes three) weeks. Many directors would argue that their impossibly tight rehearsal schedules leave precious little time for the kind of enriching explorations that would fill out their actors' understandings of the play. It is inevitable that these pressures will affect how a production is realised and, although many directors seek to combine the process of creative exploration with the business of rehearsal, there is little doubt that many present-day productions come to the stage if not under-rehearsed then certainly inadequately 'filled out'.

Over the years, the pattern of the modern rehearsal process has become fairly firmly established. Typically, this is how it might look:

**The modern rehearsal process**

- On the first day, at the **read-through** of the play, the director and the designer will unveil their plans for the production. The actors and the production team will discover what the director's conception is, and how the designer has translated that conception into visual terms.
- Next, the director will work through the scenes of the play, giving the actors their **blocking** (this is the term that refers to the patterns of the actors' movements on stage). Some directors like to set these patterns before the rehearsal process begins, while others prefer to work out the movements as they go from scene to scene.
- As rehearsals proceed, the director will find ways to help the actors explore **characterisation**, and the network of **relationships** within the play.
- The overall **style** of the play will need to be firmly established and refined in order that all the actors achieve some measure of consistency in their playing.
- As the whole play begins to come together, the director will give increasing attention to the **pacing** of the play, the **contrasts** between different elements in the production, and the building of **tension** in those scenes where matters come to a head.
- Once this preliminary work has been done, the whole production team will want to see a complete run-through, from beginning to end, to make sure that the play hangs together as a **coherent whole**.
- The **technical rehearsal** is next, where all of the technical production elements are worked through in meticulous detail (smooth scene changes, lighting and sound cues, ensuring that any costume changes can be done in the time available, etc.).
- Then come the **dress rehearsals** in which actual performance conditions are replicated (sometimes 'dress rehearsals' may be public, or be described as 'previews').
- **First performance** (when the critics will be invited!).

These, then, are the vital components of the rehearsal process. Given that all of this has to be accomplished in a relatively short space of time it is easy to see why some directors feel that there is little time for wider exploration of the play's context, themes or characters. We would hold to the view that a broader exploration of key thematic, textual and character elements can actually save time because a carefully considered and well-structured exploration can have the effect of increasing the actors' understanding of the play and its meanings.

**Task 6: Do you enjoy rehearsals?**

How close is our model of the rehearsal process to your own experience of performing in plays? Which is your favourite/least favourite stage in the process?

- Based on your own experiences, write a list of dos and don'ts for actors and directors for each of the stages of the rehearsal process. How practical is your list? Pass it to another group or student and see whether they would follow your advice!

# Realising *Yerma*

In directing *Yerma*, the early exploratory work was invaluable in helping the actors really come to terms with the conception already outlined. As a company we now embarked on the four-part exploration of the text that is outlined in the textual analysis questionnaire which follows Chapter 8. The four parts are:

1  an examination of the **triangle of relationships** at the heart of the play;
2  building **Yerma's world** (this also involved some attempts to experiment with different stylistic conventions);
3  building the contrasting **world of the pagan woman**;
4  examining the **role and function of Juan's sisters**.

What are Yerma's feelings for Victor? What is Victor's function in the play?

On a first reading of *Yerma*, the easy assumption is that Juan is the villain of the piece. But the other important central character is Victor. We know that Victor has known Yerma since childhood, and it appears that Juan and Victor, who are both shepherds, have also developed a close friendship. In her conversation with the pagan woman it becomes clear that Yerma has enormous affection for Victor and that, as her relationship with Juan deteriorates, her thoughts turn increasingly to the happy times she spent with Victor when she was a young girl. Although there are moments of real tenderness between Yerma and Victor in the brief scenes when they are alone together, *Lorca* gives no hint that anything improper has happened in their shared past; or, indeed, that anything is about to happen. Nevertheless, *Lorca* leaves us in no doubt that there is a certain 'chemistry' between them. However, the extent to which Juan is aware of his wife's feelings for Victor is never made wholly explicit.

In Task 2 you created two *still-images* that showed how Yerma felt towards Juan and Victor at two different points in the play. In watching the transition from the first image to the second, we were able to develop a clearer insight into how Yerma's feelings had changed during the years that elapse between the first two acts; and how the triangle of relationships at the core of the play have become much more intricate.

Given our interpretation, clearly the process of building Yerma's world, and a sense of the community in which she lives, was critically important. We attempted to do this by stages. First of all, we experimented with how Yerma's friend, Maria, breaks the news that she is pregnant. You tried out this improvisation for yourself as part of Task 3. In our work, Maria's excitement only served to highlight Yerma's own predicament, but we found that she, nevertheless, managed to put on a brave face and was genuinely happy for her friend. After trying the scene in a number of different ways it became clear to us that the most effective tone for the encounter was one of enthusiastic, girlish delight: Maria's authentic, bubbly exhilaration clashing somewhat with Yerma's slightly more forced enthusiasm.

**This exercise served two important purposes for us: first, it highlighted the fact that, at the beginning of the play, Yerma is still able to retain some of her youthful optimism** (which stands in stark contrast to her increasing sense of disillusion and despair as the play progresses); and second, **it clearly demonstrated the significance which the community attaches to the impending birth of a child** (and, equally, the extent to which Yerma feels her own failure to meet the community's expectations).

Our next exploration focused on the washerwomen's scene. As well as providing an opportunity to experiment with different stylistic conventions, this work proved to be crucial in building up the sense of oppression felt by Yerma as the full implications of her and Juan's inability to produce a child begin to dawn on her.

We have already mentioned the importance of the washerwomen's scene in developing our original conception into a workable proposition, and we decided that this was the scene that was integral to creating the whole atmosphere of moral censure surrounding Yerma. As you already know from your own practical work, the scene falls into two parts: the first, realistic; the second, poetic and stylised. We worked up a version of the scene in which the *realism* of the early part gave way to an elaborate choral recital, accompanied by appropriate work rhythms. We were forcibly struck by how the insistent, relentless rhythms of the second part created a truly menacing effect. **For us, this was an important exercise in terms of finding a suitable performance style for the 'chorus scenes' that *Lorca* has woven into the fabric of the play.**

When this was done, we returned to the opening scene of the play in which we first begin to sense the rift that exists between Yerma and Juan. We then played this scene side by side with the washerwomen's scene, as you did in Task 3. The effect of this juxtaposition between an intimate conversation taking place within the privacy of the marital home and the widespread public condemnation and disapproval, was startling. So compelling was this orchestration and rearrangement of *Lorca*'s original narrative, that it eventually found its way into the opening sequence of the production.

The repressive world of Yerma's village stands in stark contrast to the world of the pagan woman, and we felt that it was important to find a concrete way for us to understand what it means to live in each of these worlds. We began with the exercise our colleague had introduced to us in Norway, creating six scenes from the pagan woman's past. Each scene was then given a title that began with the words, 'The pagan woman learns...' (e.g. 'The pagan woman learns the joys of love'). Subsequently, we contrasted the life of the pagan woman with the experience of Yerma's mother, as you did in Task 5 (e.g. 'Yerma's mother learns that love means sacrifice'). **By contrasting the life of the pagan woman with the experience of Yerma's mother, we were able to develop a real sense of the two worlds that coexist in the play.**

During the second act we discover that Juan has brought his two sisters to the house so that they can keep watch over his wayward wife. The double image of the sisters as, simultaneously, angels and jailers began to take root in our thinking. Like you, we created images, based on the religious paintings of El Greco, of angels compassionately and protectively watching over Yerma as she slept. These angels were then slowly transformed into vigilant jailers. **The effect was a subtle but powerful one, and convinced us that we could productively work with this 'double image' of the sisters as both guardians and jailers.**

Having completed these series of explorations, the student company was now in a position to begin working with a slightly adapted version of *Lorca's* text. It is important to make the point that most of the textual modifications and adaptations were made as a result of these preliminary explorations.

The student actors were now ready to bring the understandings gained in their exploratory work to the rehearsal process itself. The explorations continued, but nowhere near as intensively, as we moved towards the production dates.

The next important consideration for the director is to decide how they will create the conditions in which the play's characters can most effectively be brought to life, so that they are able to fully inhabit the world of the play. Different directors have different ways of working with actors, and, in the final part of this chapter, we turn our attention to the different directorial approaches.

However, before reading the next section, we would like you to take a few minutes to consider the workshops and rehearsals that you have been involved in.

### Task 7: The highs and lows of rehearsal

- Think back over the times when you have been involved in group work, or in rehearsal, and try to remember those occasions when you felt that you had done your most creative work. Try to recall the *conditions* in which this creative work occurred. What were your own feelings? What was it about the group, or the rehearsal, that made the work so satisfying? What was the atmosphere like? Was there a leader/director? If so, how did they help/hinder?

1 Write a paragraph recalling as clearly as you can the conditions in which this work took place.

- Similarly, try to recall a time when you were frustrated by the whole rehearsal or group process. Once again, try to identify the conditions that produced this feeling. *Exactly* what was it that produced this frustration in you? What was the atmosphere like? Did the other group/cast members share your frustration? Were their reasons the same as, or different from, your own?

2 Write a second paragraph in which you identify some of the reasons why this work was so difficult for you.

Having completed Task 7, your own past experiences of rehearsal, and of group work, should already be indicating to you the kinds of working conditions that you find most conducive to achieving your best and most creative work. Some actors respond well to a strong directorial lead, while others might find it too inhibiting, or intrusive, or stifling.

On the other hand, certain types of actor find that they do their best work with a more open, relaxed director, while others find this approach too free and easy, wishy-washy and lacking in leadership. This is why certain actors seem to do their best work with particular directors. Your reflections in Tasks 6 and 7 should already be indicating to you the directorial approach that suits you best; but additionally, it is also telling you something about the kind of actor you are.

## Working with Actors

In a famous article, Tyrone *Guthrie*, one of the early directors at Stratford-on-Avon's ***Shakespeare Memorial Theatre*** (in the days before the Stratford operation came to be called the *Royal Shakespeare Company*), wrote that the separate work of the director, designer and actor should 'grow together . . . and be the result of a productive exchange of ideas'.

**Actors need to feel a sense of ownership**

If you have already completed a GCSE drama course, this idea will not be totally alien to you. In creating group and class dramas, you will have discovered that it is important for everyone involved to feel that they have had the opportunity to contribute their own ideas to the creative process. If individuals know that their ideas are accepted and valued, they inevitably feel **a sense of ownership** of what is being created. Professional actors are not so very different. As the first night approaches, the director has to 'let go' of the work they have created; at this point, they have to put their faith in the performers who will go out, night after night, to realise their conception in front of an audience.

The actors' confidence in their ability to do so will be increased in direct proportion to the sense of ownership they feel of the production that they are a part of. The director, therefore, has a vested interest in ensuring that the actors are in tune with the interpretation that they have created together.

**No two directors are alike in their work**

The early autocrats (*Chronegk*, for example) would not necessarily have subscribed to *Guthrie*'s view, but few present-day directors would, we suspect, quarrel with it. However, while broad professional agreement probably exists on this ideal, the variety of methods employed to achieve its end can appear to be somewhat bewildering. Any actor will tell you that no two directors are alike, and it is sometimes said that for every different director working in the theatre there is a different approach.

It remains the case that no systematic codification of the art of directing has been firmly established. There are a number of reasons why this is so. First, as we have seen, the director, as a key figure in the making of theatre, only emerged towards the end of the last century. The 'job description' took shape gradually and progressively. Documented practice tends to be inconsistent in terms of outlining particular, detailed approaches. Second, theatre is a collaborative art, and the director's job is to coordinate the various contributions into a coherent, unified, whole; but, here again, the nature of the collaborative endeavour varies enormously from production to production. Finally, the process of conception and realisation takes place over a relatively long period, sometimes over many years (nine, as we have seen, in the case of *Brook*'s *Le Mahabharata*). This means that **initial ideas** become modified as a result of changing circumstances, scheduling logistics and production deadlines.

All of these reasons, therefore, make it very difficult to separate out the essentials of the director's art when it comes to examining rehearsal-room practice. In the next section, we offer descriptions of five different types of director, and some analysis of the working methods associated with each type. In reading through this typology, you might like to bear in mind your own reflections on the approach that has helped you create your best work.

## The Five Types of Director

**1. The instructional director**

The instructional director has its origins in the Greek playwright/ director (or *didaskalos*) who, as we have seen, was referred to as a 'teacher'. Instructional directors tend to be very well organised. Their conception (which they may, or may not, share with their acting company) is thoroughly worked out in advance of their arrival in the rehearsal room, and their efforts are all directed towards realising the strong vision that they have developed during the period of preparation.

The early stages of rehearsal tend to be dominated by 'blocking' the actors' entrances, movements and exits, and by composing the visual elements of the stage picture. Control is established from the read-through, and many aspects of the final production are fixed very early in the rehearsal process. Instructional directors do a lot of one-to-one work with actors, often providing extremely detailed character sketches, and they also tend to be avid note-givers. Ludwig *Chronegk* and the early *Stanislavski* would offer good examples of this type of director.

It is immediately obvious that this type of director is going to provide strong leadership and, in addition, can forge a real sense of unity in the acting company, as a clear sense of direction is evident to everyone from the outset. As a result of thorough preparation and pre-planning, this type of director is also likely to produce results in a very short space of time – a distinct advantage in these days of strict financial control and tight rehearsal schedules.

**The disadvantage of this kind of approach is that actors can begin to feel that they are little more than puppets in the hands of the puppet-master.** Because the artistic vision is so well developed in advance of rehearsals, they may feel that there is minimal opportunity for them to make any kind of significant or meaningful input to the production. Consequently, they may be reluctant to offer suggestions for fear of obscuring or distorting the director's conception. The rehearsal process also tends to move very quickly, leaving actors with little time to experiment, or try things out, or become comfortable with the director's instructions. We have already noted how important it is that actors feel of a sense of ownership in their work, but the imposition of the strong vision and fast-moving rehearsal process of the instructional director can work against this.

**2. The coaching director**

**Coaching directors usually tend to be 'actor's directors'. Rather than imposing their vision onto the acting company (in the manner of the 'instructional director') they work *with* the actors in order to realise it.** The coaching director may still have a strong conception, but their means of realising it are more subtle than those of the instructional director. They tend to leave more room for the actors to make their own understandings and find their own ways with the interpretation.

The essence of the coaching director's work is simultaneously to draw out the character from the actor, and to lure the actor ever closer to the character. Coaching directors usually have a strong interest in, and understanding of, the process of acting and are therefore able to give actors very practical help and advice in the rehearsal room. For this reason, they tend to be very popular with performers. Like the instructional director, the coaching director may also spend a lot of time on one-to-one work with actors, but unlike the instructional director this will be a two-way process in which the emphasis will be on dialogue and interdependence. The later *Stanislavski*, *Brecht* and Elia *Kazan* would be good examples of coaching directors.

We have seen how the approach of the instructional director can sometimes work against the actors feeling much of a sense of ownership, but the coaching director's methods will often produce the opposite effect. Because they feel they have been 'nursed' through the rehearsal process, actors tend to develop a real sense of enthusiasm and commitment to the production because they have been made to feel an integral part of it. The benefits of this level of dedication can often be seen in strong performances and a high-quality production.

As with any other directorial method, there are pitfalls as well as advantages. It is essential that the coaching director has a genuine, technical understanding of the process of acting. They have to know what works for actors in rehearsal. If they falter in this, actors can quickly become frustrated and disillusioned, and the whole process can grind to a halt. The coaching director generally tends to work fairly slowly anyway, setting things fairly late (simply as a consequence of their desire to give the actor plenty of time and space), and this can be another source of frustration for performers. **All in all, this can be a high-risk approach, unless the director is assured in their handling of the whole rehearsal process; and instinctively attuned to the needs of the actors.**

## 3. The input director

Adrian **Noble**, one of the major *Royal Shakespeare Company* directors of the last decade, begins with a strong conception of the play he is directing, but believes in allowing his actors tremendous freedom within the framework he has created, placing great faith in the 'inspiration' of actors. **Provided that the actors' contributions to the rehearsal process do not massively distort the conception, the input director tends to be very receptive and responsive to their ideas.**

The characteristics of this type of director are: an inside-out knowledge of the play and its possibilities; a commitment to dialogue with actors and a willingness to listen; and adaptability and flexibility within the confines of the overall vision. Like the coaching director, the input director also tends to be popular with actors, especially those who enjoy the creative freedom that this type of director offers. In addition to Adrian *Noble*, Eugene *Vakhtangov* would be an example of the input director.

Because the input director has such a thorough knowledge of the play being produced, they tend to inspire confidence in the acting company. This confidence is, of course, vital because the kind of exploratory, 'inspirational' work that is encouraged by the input director requires an environment and atmosphere in which actors feel that they can work without inhibitions, and where they can take risks. The receptivity of this type of director is also

117

beneficial in creating a feeling of 'ensemble' in the acting company – a willingness to work for each other to best serve the needs of the play.

**One of the major drawbacks of this working method is that it can, if the director is not alive to the problem, quickly become a very intellectual process.** Because so much time is spent listening to ideas, discussing their possibilities and evaluating their merits, the rehearsal can deteriorate into a 'talking shop'. It is inevitably the case that, if a director is open to suggestions, many more ideas will be generated than can actually be used in the production.

The input director therefore needs a range of strategies for sorting, sifting and testing the ideas that arise during rehearsal, and also needs to be able to justify why some suggestions are taken on board while others are rejected. Actors who feel that their ideas are constantly being neglected can become alienated by this working method.

## 4. The critical director

**Like the input director, the critical director relies a great deal on the contributions of their actors. They will encourage experimentation in the rehearsal room, will evaluate its effects and then decide whether or not the results are worth holding onto.**

In many respects, the critical director is the opposite of the coaching director; intervening less, but usually offering comments and observations after having seen rehearsal in action. They will often leave actors to their own devices, allowing plenty of time and space for them to make discoveries and come to their own understandings (the very opposite of the stop/start directorial approach), but will usually make extensive notes which will then be fed back to the actors.

Because of this non-interventionist style, the critical director will often get to the run-through stage very early in the rehearsal process. Despite the fact that Max *Reinhardt* came to the rehearsal room with a highly developed and thoroughly prepared conception, his rehearsal methods were very much those of the critical director. He saw his role as being a receptive, concentrated, critical sounding-board for the performers: in Tyrone *Guthrie*'s famous phrase, 'an audience of one'.

Actors' attitudes to the critical director will vary according to the kind of performer they are. **Actors who enjoy creative freedom appreciate the amount of leeway that they are given, while others feel that the lack of intervention can leave them somewhat adrift and lacking in leadership.**

## 5. The empirical director

Deborah *Warner*, who formed *Kick Theatre Company*, reflecting on her first *Royal Shakespeare Company* production *Titus Andronicus*, said, 'I think a director's role is to create the right environment and then step out of it for as long as possible and hope the actors will feel confident and brave enough to try to experiment'.

**Experiment and discovery would be the watchwords of the empirical director.** Sometimes, the empirical approach is thrust onto a director because of circumstances. Michael *Bogdanov*, co-founder (with Michael Pennington) of the **English Shakespeare Company** in 1986, describes how, in his attempts to direct seven plays in a 13-week period, he was forced to set different groups of actors tasks which they had to complete without any sustained help. He likened this approach to playing 20 games of chess at the same time. *Bogdanov* claimed that, by discovering the plays *together* in this way, everyone has a stake in the productions.

It goes without saying that empirical directors must place great faith and trust in their actors. This belief in the creative abilities of the performers makes the empirical director very much the opposite of his instructional counterpart, who keeps a very tight rein on the actors. As with the critical director, the process leaves lots of room for the actors to make their own discoveries and this approach, which often generates fresh thinking about (and original insights into) the text, can result in highly creative and inventive productions.

Ironically, given Michael *Bogdanov*'s adoption of this approach to solve the problem of directing a number of productions at the same time, the empirical director's process can be very slow-moving, simply because the acting company's discoveries have to be evaluated before being moulded into the overall directorial conception. **Final production decisions are often taken very late on in the rehearsal process, and actors who like to fix aspects of their performance gradually during the course of rehearsal sometimes find this approach stressful.**

We have now considered the difference between a playwright's director and an *auteur*, and we have identified **five** different types of approach that directors use when working with actors. We have already cautioned against thinking that the playwright's director and the *auteur* exist in a pure form, and we should also bear in mind that any *typology* of directorial approaches is only useful as a model that helps us understand the variety of methods open to any director. It would be an oversimplification to say that *Reinhardt always* used the critical approach. In his directing, there is a *tendency* towards this particular method, but a detailed study of his notebooks would indicate that he also made use of other approaches. Richard *Eyre*, artistic director of the **Royal National Theatre**, does not apply any particular method across the board; he observes that each play generates its own working process, and his approach will vary with the demands of the production in hand.

To close our examination of the director, you might like to complete one final task.

### Task 8: Categorising directors

Copy the grid below and, working with a partner, try to assign particular directors to each of the empty boxes in the '**Playwright's director**' and '*Auteur*' columns. For example, Max *Reinhardt* would sit quite comfortably alongside the critical director category in the '*Auteur*' column. Use your reading of this chapter and any additional research you have done, to place some of the better-known directors on the grid. It would also be useful to give reasons for the choices you have made.

|  | Playwright's director | Auteur |
|---|---|---|
| Instructional director |  |  |
| Coaching director |  |  |
| Input director |  |  |
| Critical director |  |  |
| Empirical director |  |  |

# 7 Reading for Performance

## Reading Texts

Reading different kinds of literary text is part of our everyday schoolwork. We have all studied poetry, short stories, novels and plays, and sometimes our tendency is to read each of these different kinds of text in much the same manner. But it is important to understand that each of these literary **genres** is quite distinctive, and each benefits from being read in a quite particular way. So, we want to spend a little time considering how we approach the reading of poems, novels and plays.

**Task 1: Reading strategies exercise**

**1** Think about your own ways of reading literary texts. Make three columns on a sheet of paper like this:

| Poetry | Stories and novels | Plays |
| --- | --- | --- |
|  |  |  |
|  |  |  |
|  |  |  |
|  |  |  |
|  |  |  |
|  |  |  |
|  |  |  |

**2** Under each heading, make a list of the things you think about and look for when you are reading each of these three types of text. Compare your own lists with those of others in the class.

In the first part of this chapter we will be examining these different genres. We want to look, first of all, at what is distinctive about each one; but, more importantly for our purposes, we will want to see **how the various strategies we use in reading poetry and fiction can help us when it comes to analysing dramatic texts.**

# Reading Poetry

A **lyric** (probably the most popular category of poem, which includes sonnets, odes and haikus) is a short, highly-condensed poem which usually expresses the poet's innermost feelings. So, the reader has to pay particular attention to the **mood** which the poet is trying to create by means of the **rhythm** of the verse, the **tone** which the sound of the words helps create, and the visual **images** which are used to reinforce the emotional quality and content.

**Narrative** poems (including ballads and *epics*) tend to be much longer, and more extended, because they tell a story which can be wide-ranging in terms of the timescale, the number of characters involved, and the various different locations in which the action takes place. So, close attention should be paid to how **time** is used and manipulated by the poet, the pattern of **relationships** between the different **characters**, and the ways in which the movement of the verse helps the reader follow the twists and turns of the **plot**.

Almost all modern plays are written in prose, but there is a strong tradition of **dramatic poetry** in European drama. Classical Greek and Roman drama, the medieval mysteries and moralities, Elizabethan and Jacobean drama in England and the plays of the classic French, Spanish and German dramatists (*Racine, Corneille, Lope De Vega, Calderón, Schiller,* Goethe) were mostly written in verse. But, even where these playwrights use prose, they still employ more heightened forms of language than we are used to encountering in modern plays. In a sense, the dramatic poetry of *Marlowe* and *Shakespeare* combines both narrative and lyric sub-genres. The *narrative* elements in these plays are obvious enough: *The Merchant of Venice*, for example, tells the story of a financial bond struck between the merchant, Antonio, and the Jew, Shylock. The dramatic action involves 19 named characters, and extends over a period of three months, alternating between two locations – Venice and Belmont. But it is also important to note that within the narrative structure of these verse plays, we will also find lyric elements.

## Task 2: Reading verse in a play

**1** Read the following extract from *Shakespeare's* tragedy, *King Lear.* The lines are taken from Act 3, scene 2, which takes place on a wild and windswept heath, during a temporary lull in a violent storm.

The context of the extract is as follows. At the beginning of the play, the king has announced his intention to divide up his kingdom between his three daughters, Goneril, Regan and Cordelia. But first, the daughters are required to say how much they love him. Goneril and Regan play along with their father, professing their boundless love for him. But when it comes to Cordelia's turn, she refuses to follow the extravagant example of her two sisters, saying that she loves her father as a daughter's duty demands, 'nor more, nor less'. Upset by his youngest daughter's refusal to indulge him, Lear disowns and disinherits her. He divides the kingdom between Goneril and Regan. Before long, the sisters begin to show their true colours. Once they have secured their portion of the realm, they turn their father and his servants away, and he is left to wander the countryside - a deflated, disappointed and defeated old man.

| | |
|---|---|
| *Lear:* | Blow, winds, and crack your cheeks! Rage! blow! |
| | You cataracts and hurricanoes, spout |
| | Till you have drench'd our steeples, drown'd the cocks! |
| | You sulphurous and thought-executing fires, |
| | Vaunt-couriers of oak-cleaving thunderbolts, |

Singe my white head! And thou, all-shaking thunder,
Strike flat the thick rotundity o' the world,
Crack nature's moulds, all germens spill at once
That make ingrateful man! . . .
. . . Rumble thy bellyful! Spit, fire! Spout, rain!
Nor rain, wind, thunder, fire are my daughters.
I tax not you, you elements, with unkindness;
I never gave you kingdom, call'd you children.
You owe me no subscription; then, let fall
Your horrible pleasure. Here I stand, your slave.
A poor, infirm, weak, and despis'd old man.
But yet I call you servile ministers,
That will with two pernicious daughters join'd
Your high-engender'd battles 'gainst a head
So old and white as this. O! O! 'tis foul.

We noted earlier that lyric poems express emotion. We are going to approach this piece of dramatic text in much the same manner as we might analyse a lyric poem.

- Examine Lear's speech and describe the feelings he is experiencing as he stands on the heath. What is the prevailing tone and mood that *Shakespeare* creates? Next, look carefully at the rhythm of the verse, noting particularly the punctuation, and how the lines are broken up. What clues to Lear's state of mind does the movement of the verse provide?

2  Make a list of the images that *Shakespeare* uses in this speech. Try to say how these images reinforce the emotional quality of the speech.

3  Take a little time to prepare a rehearsed reading of the speech, trying to capture as accurately as you can Lear's mood and state of mind. Paying particular attention to the rhythm of the verse, and pointing up the images which *Shakespeare* uses will help you enhance the dramatic quality of the lines. This task could take the form of a prepared *monologue*, or you could work on the speech in a group to produce a choral reading, in which you use the different voices to heighten the effect of the lines, rhythms and images.

The plays of the great Elizabethan and Jacobean dramatists (not to mention the French, Spanish and German classical playwrights) often appear to be extremely difficult when we first encounter them. But if we remember to apply some of the strategies we use in our reading of poetry, the prospect of tackling a full-scale verse drama becomes a little less daunting.

# Reading Novels

Both plays and novels have a plot

Reading novels (and short stories) requires a somewhat different approach to that of reading poetry. As in *narrative* poetry, the *plot* or storyline is probably the most important element in drawing-in the reader – we are keen to know 'what happens next'. If the plot is compelling, our interest is maintained and we continue to engage with the novel's themes as the *narrative* unfolds. Most of us, as we read, visualise the pictures which the action conjures up in our mind's eye and we try to link them together in an unbroken line, almost as if we have a movie running inside our heads as we read.

In common with novels and short stories, most (but not all) plays have a plot: a sequence of events carefully arranged to emphasise relationships between the different incidents that make up the storyline.

**The *well-made play***

We have already seen that critical discussion about plot originates with *Aristotle* in the fourth century BC. However, in the nineteenth century, French dramatists developed a comic form, which was based on a formula initially recommended by *Aristotle*. This formula enabled writers like Eugène **Scribe** and Victorien **Sardou** to produce a type of play which came to be known as *la pièce bien faite* (or the **well-made play**). There are five stages in this kind of play:

1 **exposition**, where we are introduced to the characters and the situation in which they find themselves (which often refers to events that took place before the play begins);
2 **conflict**, where a central problem is introduced which the *protagonist* must deal with;
3 **complication**, where the problems and difficulties become much more complex;
4 **climax**, where the tension builds towards a crisis which must be dealt with;
5 **denouement**, where the complications in the plot are finally resolved.

This formula was widely used in the late nineteenth century, and is still used in some plays, novels and many Hollywood movies today.

---

**Task 3: Recognising a '*well-made play*'**

- Can anyone in your group think of a play or film that seems to follows the structure of the *well-made play*? Listen to the suggestion and then use the list above to analyse the structure of the play or film to see if it really does fit the pattern.

---

Although the plot is the engine which drives us to finish the story, the careful reader of fiction will also pay attention to a number of other factors, such as:

- characterisation
- structure
- function of the narrator.

**Analysis of character**

Analysis of character plays an important part in the reading of both novels and plays. We can begin by identifying three **character types**: the *stock character*; the **flat**, or **two-dimensional** character; and the **rounded** character.

**Stock characters are stereotypes**

*Stock characters* are stereotypes, which are familiar and easily recognisable to us, simply because we have encountered them many times before. Examples might include the country bumpkin, the damsel in distress, the old miser, the wicked stepmother, the absent-minded professor, and so on. A number of theatrical styles rely on the use of *stock characters*. Perhaps the best known are *Commedia dell'Arte* and Victorian *melodrama*. In *Commedia dell'Arte*, the plot usually revolves around some kind of intrigue practised by lovers (Pierrot and Columbine), or servants, clowns and villains (Pulcinella, Harlequin and Scaramouche), against the rich father (Pantaloon). Many of the *stock Commedia dell'Arte characters* survived in other dramatic forms, like *farce* and *pantomime*. The *stock characters* of *melodrama*, an extremely popular form throughout the first half of the nineteenth century, usually include the black-cloaked villain, the pure, innocent, naive maiden, and the hero who invariably manages to save the maiden from the evil clutches of the villain.

**The flat, or two-dimensional character**

**The flat, or two-dimensional character is a staple of the nineteenth-century *well-made play*.** Such characters are usually simple, straightforward and fairly predictable. They lack psychological depth and, perhaps most importantly, they almost always manage to stay the same in spite of the tide of events that engulfs them.

**The rounded character is more fully developed**

**By contrast, the more rounded character that we usually encounter in the *realist* plays of the twentieth century** (and the plays of *Shakespeare* and the classical European writers), **is much more fully developed and dynamic, with a complex psychological make-up** that changes in response to the dramatic circumstances in which they find themselves. It is not uncommon to find both flat and rounded characters in the same play. In the hands of a skilled playwright, the former tend to be found in the minor roles, while the more complex characters are usually the major players.

**Structure**

When we read fiction, we might find ourselves thinking about how the novel is structured: is there one main plot (supported and illuminated by sub-plots), or are a number of storylines woven together? How do the various storylines connect with each other? In the end, do the different *narratives* in the novel come together to make sense to the reader, or are there loose ends which the reader has to tie up for themselves?

**Plots and sub-plots**

According to *Aristotle*'s recommendations, the plot of a play should consist of one unified action. The French classical playwrights followed *Aristotle*'s prescription to the letter: *Racine*'s *Phèdre* consists of a single action with no distracting sub-plot to divert our attention away from the plight of the central character. On the other hand, *Shakespeare* showed a healthy disregard for *Aristotle*'s advice, often choosing to augment his main plot with one or more sub-plots which are designed to shed light on the play's central action. In *King Lear*, for example, the sub-plot involving the Duke of Gloucester's relationships with his two sons is designed to provide a commentary on Lear's relationships with his daughters.

Although many playwrights do layer-in a sub-plot to support the main action, **as a general rule dramatic texts do not seek to juggle a number of different narratives in the way that some modern novels do. The main line of action is usually readily apparent.**

**Narration**

In reading a novel, we might ask the question: who is telling this story, and with what intention? And this could lead us to consider the function of the narrator: what is their relationship to the events being recounted? Are they disinterested and impartial, or do they have an axe to grind? Are they a reliable storyteller, or should we take what they have to say with a pinch of salt?

**Whose story is it?**

In fiction, the narrator functions as a guide who directs our attention to significant matters in the story. By doing this, the narrator often *manipulates* our view of events so that we see things from their *particular perspective*. Most plays do not rely on a narrator to guide us through the plot (although plays written in the *Brechtian* style will sometimes use a 'storyteller' or a 'singer' to comment on the action). Each of the characters provides us with a new perspective on the dramatic action, and this enables us to view the events from a number of different points of view. Inevitably, we will be more sympathetically inclined towards some viewpoints rather than others, but the good playwright always provides us with an *all-sided* perspective on the events they want us to consider.

When we read fiction, ultimately we will want to make our own assessment of what the novel amounts to – what its major themes and preoccupations are. The same is true when reading a play. **We are concerned to find out what connections we can make between the world of the fiction (whether it is a novel, or a dramatic fiction) and our own experience**.

It should be clear from the above that many of the strategies we employ when reading fiction are also useful in analysing play texts – the two genres share much in common. Therefore, it is perhaps not at all surprising that, over the last 20 years, there has been an explosion in the number of novels that have been adapted for the stage (Charles Dickens' *Nicholas Nickleby*, Jane Austen's *Pride and Prejudice* and Victor *Hugo*'s *Les Misérables*, to name just three of the more successful adaptations).

Having considered some of the different reading strategies for poetry and fiction, many of which can be applied to the reading of dramatic texts, it is now time to turn our attention to the reading of plays.

# Reading Plays

Plays are written to be performed

The reading of a play poses some problems that we do not encounter in the reading of other literary genres. This is because, with very few exceptions, plays are written to be performed, and in reading the play text we need to keep this very firmly in mind. If we read a play simply with the intention of finding out 'what happens next' (as we sometimes do with a novel, or short story), our focus will almost certainly be on the spoken dialogue, since this is the principal means by which the playwright advances the storyline. (Some modern plays, of course, have no plot to speak of – e.g. Samuel *Beckett*'s *Not I* – and reading them on the basis of a 'what happens next' approach will quickly become an exercise in frustration.) **In concentrating on the dialogue alone, we are likely to miss other important details that the playwright wishes to convey to us**. It is important, therefore, to look beyond the spoken words and stage directions as we read a play text. In this section, we examine three additional elements:

1 the **visual**
2 the **action**
3 the **sub-textual**.

*Mise en scène*

When considering the visual elements of a play it is important at this point to introduce the French term, *mise en scène*. This term refers to the staging, or visual arrangement, of the entire dramatic production. Included under this heading would be: setting and scenery, costume, lighting, properties, the movement of the actors and any other visual elements (e.g. slide projections, film clips, videotaped inserts).

Some playwrights are highly specific about the visual picture they wish to create. Henrik *Ibsen*, in *A Doll's House*, after telling us that the action takes place in a small Norwegian town in 1879, calls for a tasteful, well-furnished room and goes on to detail the precise location of the doors leading into and out of the room, and the windows; he specifies the exact positioning of the piano, a round table, armchairs, sofa, a rocking chair, a small bookcase, a stove lined with porcelain tiles; moreover, he tells us that the floor is carpeted, that there are engravings on the wall, that the books in the bookcase are leatherbound, and that a fire burns in the stove (see Chapter 10, page 237 for an exercise based on this description). By contrast, Sarah *Kane*, at the beginning of *Phaedra's Love*, simply tells us that the action takes place in a royal palace.

**The world of play**

**The playwright's descriptions of the physical environment in which the dramatic events unfold provide important clues about the fictional world which the characters inhabit. They help us to form a picture of the world of the play**.

In *A Doll's House*, *Ibsen*'s stage directions conjure up a very clear picture of a comfortable family home (see page 231). And, because his description of the Helmers' sitting-room immediately reminds us of the kind of actual room which we are used to seeing all the time, we can be fairly sure that the world of the play is going to be *true to life* – an accurate representation of the reality around us. Once we read the first lines of dialogue, our original impressions are reinforced as we begin to settle into a familiar, recognisable, domestic world (even though it is a nineteenth-century domestic world). The consistency of the setting (and costume, which the writer, by specifying the exact year in which the play is set, suggests should be in keeping with the historical period), the behaviour of the characters and the *realistic* dialogue is reassuring for the reader who can straight away see a correspondence between the world of the play and their own experience.

But this measure of consistency between the various dramatic elements is not always present at the beginning of a play. In *Phaedra's Love*, a man called Hippolytus inhabits Sarah *Kane*'s royal palace. Hippolytus is a figure from classical tragedy, so we could be forgiven for thinking that this play is going to be set in ancient Greece. But such expectations are immediately confounded as we read that Hippolytus is sitting in a darkened room, watching television. We then learn that he is eating a hamburger! Clearly, the world of this play is a confusing mixture of dramatic elements, some of which suggest that the play is set in the present day, while others hint at a remote, historical past. It quickly becomes apparent that there is work to be done in making sense of these sharply conflicting dramatic elements. The world of Sarah *Kane*'s play is nowhere near as easily recognisable as the domestic world of *A Doll's House*.

**The world of the play can be *represented* or *presented***

Crudely speaking, we can say that in *Ibsen*'s *realist* play, the world of the Helmers is **represented** (it is an accurate *representation* of the world as we know it), whereas the world of Phaedra and Hippolytus is **presented** to us in somewhat unfamiliar, *non-realist* terms. We noticed this difference in the acting workshops. The world of *The Crucible* is *represented* to us, while the world of *Mother Courage* is *presented*.

Often, as in *Ibsen*'s *realist plays*, the playwright largely provides the world of the play. In such cases, the visual clues in the text enable the reader to piece together a coherent view of the world of the play. But, sometimes, the confusing assortment of clues provided in the text requires readers to make certain decisions about the visual quality of the play for themselves (e.g. will the royal palace in *Phaedra's Love* suggest ancient Greece as a conscious contrast to the contemporary figure of Hippolytus watching television, or will the palace be consistent with our contemporary view of how a modern prince lives?). In this case, the reader will, to a certain extent, be **constructing** the world of the play.

In addition to the visual clues, which help in constructing the *mise en scène*, the text also gives the attentive reader a sense of the play's **dramatic action**.

**Sometimes this action is made explicit in the stage directions provided by the playwright.** At the beginning of *A Doll's House*, we are told that, after tipping the porter who has carried the Christmas tree, Nora closes the door and that she laughs happily as she takes her coat off. After taking out a bag of macaroons from her pocket and eating a few, she walks towards the door of her husband's study and listens.

When the text includes this kind of explicit direction it makes it relatively easy for the reader to visualise the action of the scene; **but sometimes important actions are implicit within the dialogue and these can be easily missed.** In the first scene between Nora and her husband, after Torvald has gently rebuked his wife for spending too much money on Christmas presents, *Ibsen* tells us in an explicit stage direction that Nora walks away towards the stove, and that her husband follows her. As he does so, Torvald says, 'My little songbird mustn't droop her wings. What's this? Is my little squirrel sulking?'. These lines contain an important note for the actor playing Nora. Even though *Ibsen* has not specified the manner in which Nora walks away in an explicit stage direction, this line of dialogue makes it clear that she is somewhat deflated by her husband's rebuke, and tells us precisely how she moves across the stage.

The more general behaviour of a character can also often be inferred from the dialogue. The opening scene of Sarah *Kane*'s *Phaedra's Love* contains fairly detailed stage directions for the actor playing Hippolytus – so the reader has no trouble in visualising the dramatic action. But, at the beginning of the second scene, a doctor tells Phaedra that Hippolytus is depressed, and this piece of information, of course, will help the actor decide precisely how the actions in the opening scene are to be carried out.

Both of these examples highlight the importance of checking and rechecking the detail, which the playwright provides for us. **Constant reference back to earlier passages is essential if we are to build up a complete picture of the play's given circumstances, the characters and the developing action.**

It is much easier for a novelist to help the reader follow the action of the narrative, and indicate exactly how the characters behave (and what their innermost thoughts and feelings are), by means of descriptive passages. But reading a play text requires more of the reader. Action and behaviour often have to be inferred from scanty textual evidence. But, as we have discovered, important clues are to be found in the explicit stage directions provided by the playwright, and in the dialogue spoken by the characters themselves.

In addition to the words spoken in the play text, a good play will also have a *sub-text*. Perhaps the most important part of the playwright's text is the spoken dialogue, and it is perhaps best to think of the *sub-text* as the *unspoken* words of the characters.

This idea can be best explained if we think about our own behaviour in ordinary social situations. We can probably all remember times when what we said did not correspond with what we were thinking or feeling.

---

**The text also gives the attentive reader a sense of the play's dramatic action**

**Explicit and implicit actions**

**Clues in the dialogue**

**A good play will also have a *sub-text***

Sometimes, we may have decided that what we are thinking is better left unsaid, perhaps because it would cause offence. So, instead of speaking out, we remain silent. The thoughts or feelings remain inside us (as a *sub-text*) but they are not spoken.

At other times, we may say something which is quite different to what we are thinking. If someone is upset, for instance, we may say 'the right thing' in the circumstances ('There was nothing you could do about it') when we really think that they were to blame in the first place ('Well, it was all your own fault'). 'There was nothing you could do about it' is the *text*, whereas 'Well, it was all your own fault' is the *sub-text*.

We can perhaps also think of times when we didn't quite say what we meant to say – somehow 'It all came out wrong'. This can happen when we find it difficult to tell someone exactly how we are feeling (feeling = *sub-text*); but the words that come out (text) don't properly express what we were trying to say. And sometimes, of course, words simply fail us. The 'text' may be a shrug of the shoulders while the *sub-text* is 'I'm not telling'.

As in real social life, so too in theatre. The actual words the characters speak may or may not truly reflect their actual thoughts and feelings: what is *not said* may be more important than what is spoken out loud.

It has often been said that the plays of Anton *Chekhov*, the great Russian playwright, are *all sub-text*, and what is actually spoken by the characters is simply intended to mask their real hopes and disappointments. What the reader must judge is whether the given dialogue is a genuine expression of the character's thoughts or feelings, or whether the words are veiling a deeper, unspoken emotional *sub-text*.

---

As in real social life, so too in theatre

---

## Task 4: Finding the *sub-text*

1  At the beginning of *A Doll's House*, Nora receives a visitor. It turns out to be an old school friend, Christine Linde, who she has not seen for many years. It transpires that Mrs Linde has been living in a town many miles away from where she and Nora grew up together. After the initial pleasantries, the following exchange of dialogue takes place. When you have read the passage below, consider the questions that follow. They will help you to distinguish between those lines which are sincerely meant, and those which hide a *sub-text*. (Each sentence is numbered, and the question numbers correspond to the sentences, which have the same number.

| | |
|---|---|
| *Nora*: | (1) All that way in winter? (2) How brave of you. |
| *Mrs Linde*: | (3) I arrived by the steamer this morning. |
| *Nora*: | (4) Yes, of course, to enjoy yourself over Christmas. (5) Oh, how splendid. (6) We'll have to celebrate. (7) But take off your coat. You're not cold, are you? (*Nora helps her off with it.*) (8) There! Now, let's sit down here by the stove and be comfortable. (9) No, you take the armchair. (10) I'll sit here in the rocking chair. (11) (*Clasps Mrs Linde's hands.*) Yes, now you look like your old self. (12) Just at first I – you've got a little paler, Christine. And perhaps a bit thinner. |
| *Mrs Linde*: | (13) And older, Nora. Much, much older. |
| *Nora*: | (14) Yes, perhaps a little older. Just a tiny bit. (15) Not much. (*Checks herself suddenly and says earnestly.*) (16) Oh, but how thoughtless of me to sit here and chatter away like this! (17) Dear, sweet Christine, can you forgive me? |
| *Mrs Linde*: | (18) What do you mean, Nora? |
| *Nora*: | (19) Poor Christine, you've become a widow. |
| *Mrs Linde*: | (20) Yes. Three years ago. |

| | |
|---|---|
| *Nora*: | (21) I know, I know – I read it in the papers. (22) Oh, Christine, I meant to write to you so often, honestly. (23) But I always put it off, and something else always cropped up. |
| *Mrs Linde*: | (24) I understand, Nora dear. |

**2 Questions to consider:**

(1) Is this a genuine request for information, or just small talk? Does it disguise Nora's surprise, or disapproval?

(2) Does Nora mean 'brave' or in the *sub-text*, might she mean 'foolish'?

(3) Does this seem straightforward? Is Mrs Linde simply replying to Nora's first question, or is there more to it? An urgency, perhaps ('I couldn't wait until Christmas was over')?

(4) Does Nora *really* believe that this is a social visit, with no other motive? Or is there a *sub-textual* 'fishing' for more information?

(5) Is this expression genuine, or what social convention demands?

(6) Does she mean this?

(7) Is this a real show of concern, or has she just remembered her social obligations?

(8) Is Nora really anxious about Mrs Linde's comfort and well-being? Or is she 'softening her up' in order to get the full story of the past nine years out of her?

(9) A straightforward request? An order? Or is the *sub-text*, 'You really must stay for a while'?

(10) A simple statement of intent, or does the careful physical arrangement of the two women indicate some hidden *sub-textual* intention on Nora's part? If so, what?

(11) Does she mean this, or is she trying to lower Mrs Linde's defences?

(12) A straightforward observation, or a coaxing?

(13) A simple statement of fact, or a defensive manoeuvre?

(14) 'A little older', or, 'My God, you really have aged'?

(15) An honest response, or a dismissive response? Probably depending on the answer to question (14).

(16) Has she really been thoughtless? Or has she been working her way around to this subject?

(17) Is she really feeling guilty?

(18) Is this genuine naivety, or does she really know what Nora has just remembered and is simply forcing her hand?

(19) Remembering or fishing ('Tell me what happened')?

(20) Providing information, or making Nora feel more guilty?

(21) Did she read it in the papers, or was there talk and gossip?

(22) Did she mean to write, or has she just remembered that writing would have been the right thing to do?

(23) Is Nora really so busy that she couldn't find a minute to write?

(24) Does she understand, or has she seen through Nora's lie?

Of course, the *sub-textual* dimension to this whole exchange will depend upon the way that the relationship between Nora and Mrs Linde is being set up for the remainder of the play. The key question might be: are they genuinely trying to re-establish the terms of a former relationship? In which case much of the text might be taken at face value. Or is there a sense in which each of the women sees the other as being of some possible use to them in the future? In which case the *sub-text* would take on much greater significance. A director working on the text with a view to performance would need to pose these questions as part of the preparations for rehearsal. The answer will depend upon the interpretation the director wants to offer of *Ibsen*'s text.

**Reading as a director**

A director, of course, is a very particular kind of reader, but the ordinary reader of a dramatic text should approach the play with the same kind of attention as the director does when envisaging a production of the play. In reading the text, the director will be trying to build up a visual picture of the world they will create on the stage, and this will involve them having an eye for the action and *sub-textual* elements outlined above. All of these concerns help in constructing the world of the play which is contained within the text. (We will consider the director's whole approach in Chapter 8.)

Different texts = different reading strategies

Different kinds of text, then, require different **reading strategies** and we have suggested that in any reading of a dramatic text **visual**, **action** and *sub-textual* elements should *all* be taken into account. This is a useful way to begin thinking about how to read a play, but theatre professionals, of course, need to have a much more comprehensive method of analysing dramatic text. In the final part of this chapter, we suggest how you might go about making a thorough textual analysis of a play that you are either studying or working on. But first, we need to briefly consider the terms 'meaning' and 'interpretation', since any careful reading of a play is an attempt to distil meaning from the text, and any production of a play requires an act of interpretation by the director, designer, actors and technicians.

## Meaning and Interpretation

Making connections to our own experience

As we try to make sense of a literary text, we try to establish some sense of connection between the events, experiences and feelings we read about and our own life experience. We have probably all read a poem, or a story, or a play, which seems to 'speak' directly to us because it somehow manages to express exactly how we were feeling at a particular moment in our lives. What this implies is that there is a strong connection between life as it is expressed artistically and life as it is lived. When we make this kind of connection, we are perceiving meaning in the text because the experience described there is similar to something that has happened to us.

**Any work of art (not just literary works) carries meaning, but because our life experiences differ, the meanings that are perceived in the work of art will vary from person to person.** As we revisit a work of art, we sometimes begin to see a larger pattern of meaning emerge. When this happens, the larger pattern begins to come together to form an **interpretation**. This is a vitally important concept in theatrical terms, because each production of a play represents the director's interpretation of the playwright's work. Once the director's work reaches the stage, the audience is then invited to make its own (secondary) interpretation of the (primary) interpretation offered by the director. It is this complex layering of interpretation on interpretation that creates a space in which multiple meanings can emerge from the performance.

In the next section, we try to tease out some further distinctions between the terms 'meaning' and 'interpretation'.

## The Meaning not the Message

You will often hear people talking (and writing) about a play's 'message'. We prefer *not* to think in terms of 'messages' because the word 'message' implies something clear, explicit and unambiguous. For example, 'I'll come to your house at seven o'clock this evening' is a straightforward message that, provided we heard it right, is impossible to mistake. To suggest that a play has a clear message implies that, once it has been seen, the audience will all be able to agree on what the 'message' was. But theatre, in common with all other art forms, doesn't quite work in this way.

Theatre consists of a system of signs and symbols, and these signs and symbols do not have *fixed* meanings. You will find a more detailed analysis of how the sign systems of theatre are used to make meanings in Chapter 10.

In *A Doll's House*, Helmer asks Nora to dance the tarantella at a fancy dress party. At the end of the second act, Nora rehearses the dance as her husband, Dr Rank and Mrs Linde look on; and, in the final act, Helmer describes Nora's performance to Mrs Linde. Clearly, the dancing of the tarantella carries symbolic meaning, but what are we meant to make of the dance?

For some observers, the dance is a symbol of Nora's rebellion, and in support of this they point to the fact that in the rehearsal at the end of Act 2, Nora refuses to listen to her husband as he tries to offer her advice about the dance steps. Furthermore, since she dances immediately before finally turning her back on her home, husband and children, the dance acts as a kind of springboard for her liberation. For others, the dance is a symbol of Nora's entrapment – she dances at the request of Helmer, and, as soon as the dance is over, he insists that she leave the party.

The picture is confused even further once we understand a little more about the origins of the tarantella. In southern Italy, where the dance originated, it functions as a kind of *catharsis* – crudely, a way of 'letting off steam', getting certain emotions out of the system. Its original purpose was to allow women a temporary escape from marriage and motherhood into a liberated, lawless world of uninhibited movement. At the dance's conclusion, the woman returns to her responsibilities and duties as a wife and mother, purified and cleansed of any feelings of resentment, restraint and rebelliousness.

That the dance operates symbolically within the play is not open to doubt, but the *precise meaning* we attribute to the dancing of the tarantella will depend on how we *interpret* it within the broader context of the play; and, as we now understand, the **meanings may vary** from one observer to another.

As we have already suggested, the whole question of meaning and interpretation, and their interrelationship, is complicated, but it is important to try to disentangle what the two words designate and how they are connected.

When a playwright begins to write a play, they will have some sense of what they want the play to be about. By this, we mean much more than simply the story they want to tell. The story, if there is one, operates as a pretext, or particular example, for a bigger idea or a broader *theme*.

At one level, the story in *Chekhov's* play, *Three Sisters*, is about three women who yearn to escape from their rural backwater to the excitement of the big city. But, at a deeper level, it could be argued that the play is about the passing of an old, outdated social order. It is at this deeper level that we begin to sense something of the play's meaning. Usually, a playwright will set out with an intention to tackle some idea, or theme, that is important to, and significant for, them. They may want to explore a psychological conflict within an individual, a moral or ethical contradiction within a community, a

---

**Theatre consists of a system of signs and symbols**

**Signs and actions can be interpreted differently**

**The story operates as a pretext for a bigger idea or a broader theme**

pressing contemporary social issue, an unresolved historical question or a complicated philosophical or political argument.

In the process of writing, the playwright is undertaking an *investigation*, or *exploration*, of the subject matter; and the finished play will be shaped and formed to convey the playwright's overall perspective on the idea, or theme they have chosen. However, because the idea being explored is undoubtedly complex and contradictory, this perspective is unlikely to be firm, fixed and absolute. During the course of their exploration, the playwright will undoubtedly have discovered that different people hold different points of view about the subject matter under investigation. As we noted earlier in this chapter, these diverse points of view will usually be represented in the different outlooks of the various characters that appear in the play. At one level, therefore, the playwright's job can be seen as *orchestrating* these differing viewpoints.

**Different characters offer different perspectives**

Each particular viewpoint, embodied in one of the characters, offers the audience a different *angle of vision*, or perspective, on the subject matter that the playwright set out to explore. In *A Doll's House*, each of the characters offers a different angle of vision on the question of the role of women in late nineteenth-century Norwegian society. For example, Mrs Linde believes that a woman can find fulfilment only in looking after and caring for her husband, whereas Nora comes to understand that only by standing on her own two feet will she be able to find the self-respect and sense of human dignity that have been denied to her as Torvald's doll-wife.

Simply put, in this play, your angle of vision on the role of women in society depends on where you are standing. Mrs Linde's more traditional view is reinforced by the experience of having been prevented from giving whole-hearted support to her husband, because of the demands placed on her by a helpless, bedridden mother and two younger brothers. On the other hand, Nora's determination to seek a measure of independence is driven by the need to escape the stifling atmosphere of Torvald's unbending self-righteousness. In listening to the words of Mrs Linde and of Nora we become aware of the *shifting viewpoints* in *Ibsen*'s play.

Of course, it is often the case that the playwright's own perspective coincides, more or less, with the particular viewpoint of one of the characters. The unsympathetic manner in which *Ibsen* has drawn the character of Torvald gives us a strong indication that his own position was much closer to Nora's than to her husband's.

But it is also interesting to speculate on what *Ibsen*'s attitude to Mrs Linde might have been. In offering to give herself to Krogstad, she makes him 'the happiest man in the whole wide world'; and we may feel some sense of pleasure because these two people, who were once in love, have found each other again and are embarking on a relationship rekindled by a new sense of hope and optimism.

### Task 5: Playing the playwright's intentions

In this task we are going to explore a key scene between Mrs Linde and Krogstad, to see if we can pinpoint *Ibsen*'s attitude towards Mrs Linde.

1 In pairs, read the following scene between Krogstad and Mrs Linde which is taken from the beginning of Act 3 of *A Doll's House*.

1.   *Mrs Linde:*   (*whispers*) Come in. There's no one here.
2.   *Krogstad:*   (*in the doorway*) I found a note from you at my lodgings. What does this mean?
3.   *Mrs Linde:*   I must speak with you.
4.   *Krogstad:*   Oh? And must our conversation take place in this house?
5.   *Mrs Linde:*   We couldn't meet at my place; my room has no separate entrance. Come in. We're quite alone. The maid's asleep, and the Helmers are at the dance upstairs.
6.   *Krogstad:*   (*comes into the room*) Well, well! So the Helmers are dancing this evening? Are they indeed?
7.   *Mrs Linde:*   Yes, why not?
8.   *Krogstad:*   True enough. Why not?
9.   *Mrs Linde:*   Well, Krogstad. You and I must have a talk together.
10.   *Krogstad:*   Have we two anything further to discuss?
11.   *Mrs Linde:*   We have a great deal to discuss.
12.   *Krogstad:*   I wasn't aware of it.
13.   *Mrs Linde:*   That's because you've never really understood me.
14.   *Krogstad:*   Was there anything to understand? It's the old story, isn't it – a woman chucking a man because something better turns up?
15.   *Mrs Linde:*   Do you really think I'm so utterly heartless? You think it was easy for me to give you up?
16.   *Krogstad:*   Wasn't it?
17.   *Mrs Linde:*   Oh, Nils, did you really believe that?
18.   *Krogstad:*   Then why did you write to me the way you did?
19.   *Mrs Linde:*   I had to. Since I had to break with you, I thought it my duty to destroy all the feelings you had for me.
20.   *Krogstad:*   (*clenches his fists*) So that was it. And you did this for money!
21.   *Mrs Linde:*   You mustn't forget I had a helpless mother to take care of, and two little brothers. We couldn't wait for you, Nils. It would have been so long before you'd have had enough to support us.
22.   *Krogstad:*   Maybe. But you had no right to cast me off for someone else.
23.   *Mrs Linde:*   Perhaps not. I've often asked myself that.
24.   *Krogstad:*   (*more quietly*) When I lost you, it was just as though all solid ground had been swept from under my feet. Look at me. Now I'm a shipwrecked man, clinging to a spar.
25.   *Mrs Linde:*   Help may be near at hand.
26.   *Krogstad:*   It was near. But then you came, and stood between it and me.
27.   *Mrs Linde:*   I didn't know, Nils. No one told me till today that this job I'd found was yours.
28.   *Krogstad:*   I believe you, since you say so. But now you know, won't you give it up?
29.   *Mrs Linde:*   No – because it wouldn't help you even if I did.
30.   *Krogstad:*   Wouldn't it? I'd do it all the same.
31.   *Mrs Linde:*   I've learned to look at things practically. Life and poverty have taught me that.
32.   *Krogstad:*   And life has taught me to distrust fine words.
33.   *Mrs Linde:*   Then it has taught you a useful lesson. But surely you still believe in actions?
34.   *Krogstad:*   What do you mean?
35.   *Mrs Linde:*   You said you were like a shipwrecked man clinging to a spar.
36.   *Krogstad:*   I have good reason to say it.
37.   *Mrs Linde:*   I'm in the same position as you. No one to care about, no one to care for.
38.   *Krogstad:*   You made your own choice.
39.   *Mrs Linde:*   I had no choice – then.
40.   *Krogstad:*   Well?
41.   *Mrs Linde:*   Nils, suppose we two shipwrecked souls could join hands?
42.   *Krogstad:*   What are you saying?

| | | |
|---|---|---|
| 43. | *Mrs Linde*: | Castaways have a better chance of survival together than on their own. |
| 44. | *Krogstad*: | Christine! |
| 45. | *Mrs Linde*: | Why do you suppose I came to this town? |
| 46. | *Krogstad*: | You mean – you came because of me? |
| 47. | *Mrs Linde*: | I must work if I'm to find life worth living. I've always worked, for as long as I can remember. It's been the greatest joy of my life – my only joy. But now I'm alone in the world, and I feel so dreadfully lost and empty. There's no joy in working just for oneself. Oh, Nils, give me something – someone – to work for. |
| 48. | *Krogstad*: | I don't believe all that. You're just being hysterical and romantic. You want to find an excuse for self-sacrifice. |
| 49. | *Mrs Linde*: | Have you ever known me to be hysterical? |
| 50. | *Krogstad*: | You mean you really – ? Is it possible? Tell me – you know all about my past? |
| 51. | *Mrs Linde*: | Yes. |
| 52. | *Krogstad*: | And you know what people think of me here? |
| 53. | *Mrs Linde*: | You said just now that with me you might have become a different person. |
| 54. | *Krogstad*: | I know I could have. |
| 55. | *Mrs Linde*: | Couldn't it still happen? |
| 56. | *Krogstad*: | Christine – do you really mean this? Yes – you do – I see it in your face. Have you really the courage – ? |
| 57. | *Mrs Linde*: | I need someone to be a mother to; and your children need a mother. And you and I need each other. I believe in you, Nils. I am afraid of nothing – with you. |
| 58. | *Krogstad*: | (*clasps her hands*) Thank you, Christine – thank you! Now I shall make the world believe in me as you do! Oh – but I'd forgotten – |
| 59. | *Mrs Linde*: | (*listens*) Ssh! The tarantella! Go quickly, go! |
| 60. | *Krogstad*: | Why? What is it? |
| 61. | *Mrs Linde*: | You hear that dance? As soon as it's finished, they'll be coming down. |
| 62. | *Krogstad*: | All right, I'll go. It's no good, Christine. I'd forgotten – you don't know what I've just done to the Helmers. |
| 63. | *Mrs Linde*: | Yes, Nils. I know. |
| 64. | *Krogstad*: | And yet you'd still have the courage to – ? |
| 65. | *Mrs Linde*: | I know what despair can drive a man like you to. |
| 66. | *Krogstad*: | Oh, if only I could undo this! |
| 67. | *Mrs Linde*: | You can. Your letter is still lying in the box. |
| 68. | *Krogstad*: | Are you sure? |
| 69. | *Mrs Linde*: | Quite sure. But – |
| 70. | *Krogstad*: | (*looks searchingly at her*) Is that why you're doing this? You want to save your friend at any price? Tell me the truth. Is that the reason? |
| 71. | *Mrs Linde*: | Nils, a woman who has sold herself once for the sake of others doesn't make the same mistake again. |
| 72. | *Krogstad*: | I shall demand my letter back. |
| 73. | *Mrs Linde*: | No, no. |
| 74. | *Krogstad*: | Of course I shall. I shall stay here till Helmer comes down. I'll tell him he must give me back my letter – I'll say it was only to do with my dismissal, and that I don't want him to read it – |
| 75. | *Mrs Linde*: | No, Nils, you mustn't ask for the letter back. |
| 76. | *Krogstad*: | But – tell me – wasn't that the real reason you asked me to come here? |
| 77. | *Mrs Linde*: | Yes – at first, when I was frightened. But a day has passed since then, and in that time I've seen incredible things happen in this house. Helmer must know the truth. This unhappy secret of Nora's must be revealed. They must come to a full understanding. There must be an end of all these shiftings and evasions. |
| 78. | *Krogstad*: | Very well. If you're prepared to risk it. But one thing I can do – and at once – |

79. *Mrs Linde:* (*listens*) Hurry! Go, go! The dance is over. We aren't safe here another moment.
80. *Krogstad:* I'll wait for you downstairs.
81. *Mrs Linde:* Yes, do. You can see me home.
82. *Krogstad:* I've never been so happy in my life before!

**2** Decide with your partner how you think *Ibsen* intended this scene to be played. Should it be played with real sincerity? Or do you detect any note of expediency, suspicion or cynicism in either or both of the characters?

**3** Mark those lines which you think contain a *sub-text*.

**4** Give a reading of the extract to the rest of the group – can they detect your ideas about *Ibsen's* intentions for the scene? Can you detect theirs?

While it is probably true to say that *Ibsen* is obviously unsympathetic towards Torvald's viewpoint, his view of Mrs Linde is, perhaps, more difficult to discern. If she is truly sincere in wanting to offer Krogstad the happiness she once denied him, then perhaps *Ibsen* intended her, along with Nora, to be an object of admiration. If her behaviour is at all calculating or opportunist, then perhaps he intended her to be an object of pity or scorn. **The important lesson here is to understand that it is not always wise to imagine that one particular character speaks for the playwright**; good writers, recognising the complex and contradictory nature of their subject matter, will usually offer a number of angles of vision in order that the play presents the audience with some sense of just how complicated the issue is.

*The playwright has conscious and unconscious intentions*

We have seen in Chapter 2 how Western theatre forms often developed out of a desire to explain, or challenge, the prevailing social conditions. Hence, the playwright's primary intention is to **communicate** her or his view of these conditions to a potential audience. These views are embedded in the play's meanings, but because, as we have seen, theatre consists of a system of signs and symbols which are always ambiguous, the audience may see more layers of meaning in the play than the playwright intended. If this happens, and we see some meaning that was never intended, it does not necessarily mean that we have 'got it wrong'. **The writer sets out with *conscious intentions* to communicate meanings; but any art-making is also susceptible to the artist's *unconscious mind*.**

Sometimes, unbeknown to the artist, the unconscious mind will layer in deeper levels of meaning than those which are consciously intended. Often, these unconscious meanings will only surface when the work of art is placed before a reader or spectator. The 'reader' sees beyond the artist's conscious intentions to the unconscious mind, which has also been at work in the making of the artwork. When the poet has completed a poem, it appears printed on the page, ready for the reader; similarly, when the sculptor's work is finished, it is offered for public view at an exhibition. In theatre, the process is more complicated. The playwright's work is never put before an audience until the written word has been transformed into the living, dynamic performance we see on the stage. And before the play reaches the stage, it must, of course, undergo a period of preparation and rehearsal.

*The director must interpret the playwright's intentions*

**Preparing a play for public performance is the job of the director.** The director's role is considered in full in Chapter 6, but it is worth making a few observations here about the *interpretative* function that the director fulfils. As you saw in Chapter 6, some directors see their job as being to interpret

135

the playwright's intentions and create a production that is faithful to the original conception (in so far as this can be known). Others view their interpretative function more creatively, and see the playwright's work as a pretext for a bolder and more adventurous production. But, whatever the case, it is useful for us to view the director as the **primary interpreter** of the playwright's work.

# Interpretation

We have already seen how the ambiguity of an artwork can give rise to different readings or interpretations. This is not to suggest that any old interpretation will do. For example, over the years, there have been a number of interesting interpretations of *King Lear*, but any interpretation designed with the intention of transforming *Shakespeare*'s text into a comedy would, in the normal run of events, be rejected as unworkable and invalid.

*Interpretations need to be logical and reasoned*

Generally speaking then, interpretations will be valid within certain limits. A playwright's text will stand a variety of directors' interpretations, but an interpretation could only be considered valid if the director was able to provide a **reasoned justification** for it, and if the interpretation can be **supported by the text** itself.

As you develop more confidence in your own analytic skills, you will be able to offer your own original interpretations of the plays you read. But always remember that you need to argue your case patiently, rationally and carefully. You will have more chance of persuading others that your interpretation is valid if a body of supporting evidence backs it up.

The great classic plays achieve their eminence because they have something fundamental to say about the human condition. Because they touch on universal areas of experience, they are plays that we can return to time and time again. Each time we revisit them, we see something new. They teach us a little more about what it means to be human.

*The classic plays are the ones that are open to the greatest number of interpretations*

This is probably why the classic plays are the ones that are open to the greatest number of interpretations. And it is probably why, in the twentieth century, we are used to seeing new and bolder interpretations of the classics. It is not uncommon to see productions of *Shakespeare*'s plays set in eighteenth-century period costume, or in Edwardian times, or in modern dress.

If a director decides to set, say, *The Tempest* in modern dress, then this is because his or her interpretation suggests that the themes of the play are relevant to contemporary society, as well as to the fictional and magical world of Prospero's island. Some might argue that to set *The Tempest* in modern dress is pushing the limits of interpretation. In support of their position, they might point to the fact that Prospero's magic is not believable within a twentieth-century context, or that the fantastical spirit figure of Ariel and the savage slave Caliban are out of place in a contemporary setting. **The bolder the director's vision, the more likely it is to provoke discussion and argument about the validity of the interpretation.**

*Rehearsals begin from the director's interpretation*

At the beginning of the rehearsal period, the director has to justify the validity of her or his interpretation to the actors who will have to make it work in performance. Assuming that the director is successful in this, the actors (who also have a creative and interpretative function to fulfil) will be keen to bring their own ideas to the process.

An essential part of the director's job is to find out which of his or her ideas are feasible, and which do not work. The director will be keen to harness the creativity and inventiveness of the actors in order to test out those ideas in practice. For example, the actor cast as Ariel in the modern dress version of *The Tempest* will have to discover (with the director's help) how the spirit can be played in such a way that it is compatible with the contemporary setting. As a result of the actors' input, the director's original conception will perhaps need to be modified as the production begins to take shape.

**The acid test of the director's interpretation**

The acid test of the director's interpretation comes on the first night when the production opens. This is why the work of the playwright, director and actor is not complete until it has been publicly performed. Indeed, the word **'performance'** is derived from the Old French verb *parfournir*, which means 'to complete', where 'completion' refers to the act of communication (with an audience).

Different spectators come to the theatre with diverse expectations. Some will come to our imaginary modern-dress production of *The Tempest* never having read or seen the play before; one or two may come having seen every British production of the play in the last 40 years. The former will undoubtedly have some expectations of a *Shakespeare* play, and may be pleasantly surprised to find that the modern setting helps them grasp part of the play's meaning. They may not be unduly bothered by the fact that the production is pushing the limits of interpretation. The latter might have seen Trevor **Nunn**'s *Royal Shakespeare Company* 'white magic' production, and believe that this is the definitive *Tempest*. They may therefore feel that the contemporary setting makes a nonsense of *Shakespeare*'s play. The likelihood is that these spectators will reject the new interpretation as invalid because it is at odds with the range of possibilities they are prepared to accept as a result of their intimate acquaintance with the play.

Our first group of spectators may be happy to accept the director's new interpretation because it seems to make perfect sense. They perceive in the play the pattern of meanings that the director's interpretation has attempted to bring out, and are also able to see a significance beyond what the director intended. Their **secondary interpretation** builds on the primary interpretation and the playwright's original conception.

As a result of being exposed to the play in performance, spectators may begin to form their own interpretations of the work they have been watching. The play as written, and the performance as staged, are bound together in an **interdependent relationship** (the play needs the production just as much as the production needs the play). The director's 'reading' (even if it is a daring new interpretation) will inevitably shed light on the playwright's original conception. What the individual spectator takes away from the encounter with the play may be a vague sense of the play's rich fabric of meaning, or it may be a profound understanding of the director's insight into the intentions of the playwright.

We have now considered some of the ways in which plays and other literary texts can be read. In the next chapter we will set out a model for making a full-scale analysis of a dramatic text.

# 8 A Director's Model for Textual Analysis

## Outline

The German director Max *Reinhardt*, was famous for working out the minute detail of a new production in advance of the first rehearsal. Inevitably, this involved hours and hours of painstaking preparation and careful planning in his study. *Reinhardt* produced a *Regiebuch* (a producer's plan) for each of his productions. His plans contained: detailed breakdowns of each scene; descriptions of the positions and expressions the actors were to adopt in composing the *mise en scène*; paraphrases of the text; detailed scenic directions; and other helpful hints for the actors.

Not all directors are as methodical as *Reinhardt*, preferring instead to experiment with ideas and solve problems as they arise during the rehearsal process. But **every director who embarks on a new production of a play**, irrespective of their preferred rehearsal methods, **will have undertaken a thorough analysis of the play text prior to meeting the designer, actors and production team**. Different directors have their own particular methods of analysis, so there is no generally accepted way to proceed. Although the model we offer here is not the only way of undertaking an analysis, it does represent a comprehensive way of breaking down a play text into its constituent parts.

Directors, of course, are not the only theatre professionals who engage in this kind of detailed analysis. Set, costume, lighting and sound designers all have specific responsibilities in the production process, but each one needs to approach their own work with a thorough understanding of the whole play. The actor(s) who is to perform in the play also needs to subject the text to detailed study so that they understand how their part fits into the larger scheme of things. Some theatres employ a *dramaturge*, whose job it is to act as a literary adviser to the artistic director and/or the theatre management – the *dramaturge*, too, makes use of analytic skills in order to assess the suitability of plays for performance.

In addition to the professionals, of course, students taking A level and undergraduate theatre studies, performing arts and drama courses also need to be equipped with the tools of analysis!

**We suggest that this chapter should be read in parallel with your study of a full-length set text.** At the end of the chapter you will find a textual analysis questionnaire, which you can use to help you organise your study of the text. As we go through the chapter we will suggest when to apply the questionnaire to your study of the set text. In this chapter we will explain the headings that we suggest you use for organising your analysis of the set text and give you examples drawn from different periods, styles and genres. You can read our advice and apply it by using the questionnaire.

We recommend looking at a play under five main headings:

1 the **given circumstances**
2 the play's **language**
3 the **dramatic action**
4 the **characters**
5 the playwright's **intention**, or **ruling idea**.

Each of these main headings is then broken down into a number of sub-headings. Because the model seeks to cover all of the major aspects of a play's structure, as well as its content, it may well be the case that some of the sub-headings are not appropriate for *all* plays. For example, under the sub-heading 'Environmental facts' in the 'Given circumstances' section, the model suggests that the economic, political, social and religious environments should be taken into account. Clearly, when analysing *Brecht*'s play, *Galileo*, the religious background will be of enormous significance, but this is unlikely to be the case in an analysis of *Brecht's Resistible Rise of Arturo Ui*.

**Our model is intended to be used by directors for the pre-rehearsal analysis of the text.** It focuses on what the director needs to be aware of and think about so that they can begin work with the actors and designers. We have based our model on the work of the American teacher Frances Hodge in *Play Directing: Analysis, Communication and Style*.

# The Given Circumstances

As we now know, this term is borrowed from the work of *Stanislavski*, and we are already familiar with it from the acting workshop on *The Crucible*. It refers to the **essential information** about the past histories of the characters, their relationships, and the background against which these histories and relationships are set. For the purposes of analysis we can subdivide the given circumstances into three separate but complementary parts: the environmental facts and background; the previous action, or important events, that precede the opening of the play; and the principal polar attitudes (the *protagonist/antagonist*) that produce the tension and conflict in the play.

# Environmental Facts and Background

Geographical location

As we have already noted, some playwrights are explicit about the location of their plays – for example, Sarah *Kane*'s play, *Blasted*, takes place in an expensive hotel room in Leeds. The spacious, expensive, interior setting of *Blasted* suggests luxury, comfort and warmth, and these conditions will have a particular effect on the characters' behaviour (which would be different if they were in a cheap boarding house). At the end of the second scene there is a huge explosion, and, at the beginning of Scene 3, we learn that a mortar bomb has ripped away one of the walls. The intrusion of the brutal external world into the luxury of the expensive hotel significantly changes the way the characters behave.

*Ibsen* tells us that *An Enemy of the People* takes place in a coastal town in southern Norway. The geographical location of the play will give some indication as to the likely weather conditions, but other clues are to be found in the text. Mayor Stockmann enters his living room wearing an overcoat, so we would be justified in assuming that the weather outside is cold. Cold weather affects people differently to warm weather, so we could generally expect the behaviour of *Ibsen*'s Scandinavian characters to be rather different from the behaviour of *Lorca*'s Mediterranean characters in the hot, dusty setting of *Yerma*.

**Where the location is not specified in the stage directions, or cannot be deduced from textual clues, it is usually safe to assume that the behaviour of the characters is not significantly affected by location or climate.**

## Date and time

Occasionally, a playwright will be quite specific about the **year** in which a play, or a scene from the play, is set. This is usually the case when the play deals with documented historical events: *Brecht*'s *Galileo* takes place in the final years of Galielo's life, in the 1630s and 1640s, and, logically, Peter *Weiss*' play, the *Marat/Sade*, has to be set during the years in which the Marquis de Sade was incarcerated in the asylum at Charenton. If a playwright tells you that their play is set 'today', or 'in the present', it poses something of a problem. Does the author want the play to be set in the year that it was written, or are they telling us that it should be updated to coincide with the new date of production? If we assume the latter we have to be convinced that the play will work in a modern setting.

**On balance, it is probably safest to assume that the setting should approximately coincide with the year that the play was written.**

In some plays, it is the **season** which is important, rather than the year. The action of *A Doll's House* takes place over the Christmas holiday period. *Ibsen* has chosen his season with particular care. In the West, Christmas is traditionally a time of year when families come together to celebrate, and the fact that Nora abandons her family at precisely this time is calculated to increase the sense of shock the audience should feel at the end of the play. *Strindberg*'s *Miss Julie* takes place on midsummer's eve, and in his Author's Preface the playwright tells us that the festive and magical atmosphere of the midsummer celebrations is an important factor in *Miss Julie*, allowing her to be seduced by the servant, Jean.

**Where the season is specified, it is usually worth asking: what is the dramatic effect of setting the play (or scene) at this particular time of year?**

Sometimes the playwright will indicate that the action takes place at a particular **time of day**. The two acts of Samuel *Beckett*'s *Waiting for Godot* take place in the evening. Estragon and Vladimir return to the same place each evening to wait for the mysterious figure of Godot, who never arrives. Because the second act has the same kind of circularity as the first, Beckett perhaps wants us to infer that they spend all of their evenings waiting, day after day. Evening precedes nightfall, and nightfall is often symbolically associated with death. If Godot represents death, then evening becomes significant because night (death) beckons; evening becomes a kind of 'chamber' in which the two men wait for death. **The significance of a particular time of day is always worth considering.**

## Timescale

In performance, plays usually last anything between an hour and a half and three hours. But the **timescale** which is covered in that short space of time varies enormously from play to play. At one extreme, the time it takes for a play to run in performance may coincide exactly with the amount of time it would take for those events to unfold in reality. For example, the running time of the *Marat/Sade* corresponds with the amount of time it would take for the events depicted there to actually happen.

At the other extreme, some plays span many years; David **Hare**'s play, *Plenty*, covers three decades. And, in between, there are an infinite number of possibilities: from the four or five hours covered by *Shakespeare*'s *Comedy of Errors*, through the few days over the Christmas holiday in *A Doll's House*, and the months it takes for Jimmy Porter and Alison to lose their unborn child in John **Osborne**'s *Look Back in Anger*, to the years *Brecht* needs to chronicle the rise to power of *Arturo Ui*.

**Economic environment**

**In any textual analysis, it is usually worth considering how the economic environment significantly impacts on the lives of the characters.** All of the classical Greek and Roman *tragedies*, as well as many of the plays of the Elizabethan and Jacobean playwrights, deal with the lives of kings, princes and other high-born nobility, for whom money is rarely a factor. But in some plays, the economic environment has a very significant effect in determining the destinies of the characters. Many of *Shakespeare*'s plays include 'lower-class' characters (for example, in *Henry IV, Pt.1*, Falstaff and his companions plan robberies in the tavern), and several seventeenth-century *comedies* concern themselves with the whole economic spectrum. In Ben **Jonson**'s *Bartholomew Fair* we see how the poorer characters try to earn a living by playing on the weaknesses, foibles and follies of the well-to-do. In a more modern context, many of Noël **Coward**'s plays depict the somewhat decadent lifestyles of the 'upper classes', while at the other extreme, Jim **Cartwright**'s *Road* shows his various characters grappling with the consequences of terrible poverty. In Arthur *Miller*'s *Death of a Salesman*, it is Willie Loman's sense of professional failure and his inability to adequately provide for his family that leads ultimately to his suicide.

**Social environment**

**Often the social and economic environments are intimately connected,** and it is sometimes difficult to separate the two, simply because our social position (or class) is so closely tied in with our economic status. As we have suggested above, *Shakespeare* and many of his contemporaries were acutely aware of the class differences to be found in Elizabethan and Jacobean England and many of their plays reflect this social diversity. The social environment also provided a significant backdrop to the nineteenth-century drama, where class differences often determined the destinies of the characters. As the title of Tom **Robertson**'s play suggests, *Caste* describes the obstacles that the wealthy George d'Alroy has to overcome before he can marry the woman he loves – the 'lower-class' actress, Esther. In analysing the characters who appear in a play, attention should always be paid to relative social status and background: try to work out which characters have the most social 'prestige', and which tend to be dismissed on account of their 'inferior' social status. In *Ibsen*'s *Hedda Gabler*, for example, Hedda's social standing as the daughter of the renowned General Gabler sets her head and shoulders above the profligate and dissolute Eilert Loevborg.

**Political environment**

The various 'political theatre' movements of the twentieth century have provided us with a number of plays in which the political background is by far the most significant factor in shaping the dramatic events. Trevor **Griffiths**' play, *The Party*, offers a sustained analysis of the various factional groupings on the political left, and the plays of the Chilean playwright, Ariel **Dorfman** are mostly set against the backdrop of General Pinochet's ruthless, fascist regime.

Shakespeare wrote a number of plays in which political events are portrayed. Most obvious, perhaps, is *Coriolanus*, but in any textual analysis it would be unwise to ignore the political landscape of *Richard III*, or *Antony and Cleopatra*. In plays like this, the importance of the political environment is very obvious, but in many other plays the influence exerted by the political background is more subtle, but no less significant. The stuffy, political conservativism of late nineteenth-century Scandinavia is an important, but understated, feature of *Ibsen*'s work; and *Chekhov* was politically attuned to the changes which were about to happen in Russia at the turn of the nineteenth century.

**The important lesson here is not to dismiss the political landscape simply because it does not present itself as immediately obvious. Clues can often be found by researching the significant real-world social and political events that coincided with the writing of the play.**

Religious environment

As with the political environment, the significance of the religious environment will be more or less evident from play to play, and in some historical dramas the religious and the political are closely connected. The religious background of Greek tragedy cannot be ignored: it is not uncommon for gods, or goddesses, to make an appearance, and we are constantly made aware, often by means of the chorus, of how the gods are at work, determining the destinies of the principal characters. Similarly, the religious environment of the medieval mystery and morality plays is difficult to ignore.

**As the power of religious conviction and the strength of religious belief has declined somewhat in the twentieth century, the significance of the religious environment is less prominent in many modern plays.** *Lorca* is a notable exception. His major works are set against the backdrop of Spanish Catholicism, and the behaviour of his characters is profoundly affected by the religious expectations of the rural peasantry. In T.S. *Eliot*'s *Murder in the Cathedral*, a complex relationship exists between the religious background and the political situation surrounding Henry VIII's decision to divorce Catherine of Aragon. Substantial research would be necessary in order to get a firm grasp of these historical events.

Arthur *Miller*'s *The Crucible* provides an even more complicated example of the relationship between religious and political factors. The repressive puritanism of seventeenth-century New England permeates the play, so a thorough analysis would require detailed research into the historical background of puritanism. But as we have already seen in the acting workshop on playing the given circumstances, *Miller* wrote the play intending to draw parallels between the proceedings of the House Committee on Un-American Activities. Research into the background surrounding the political witch-hunt of the 1950s would also be required to gain a full understanding of *Miller*'s play. Generally speaking, however, the religious influences working on the characters in contemporary plays are harder to discern and evaluate.

**Careful character analysis will sometimes reveal how religious beliefs shape behaviour, but clues can be hard to find.**

## Previous Action

In classically constructed plays, the exposition usually comes in Act 1

We have already introduced the term *exposition*, which refers in part to the events that took place before the action of the play begins. In classically constructed plays, the *exposition* usually comes in Act 1 and furnishes the audience with the necessary background for them to make sense of what is about to happen.

An obvious illustration of how a playwright immediately sketches in 'the story so far' is to be found in *Shakespeare's Comedy of Errors*. Here, the complete background to the play is revealed in the first 140 lines. The merchant from Syracuse, Egeon, under threat of execution, explains to the Duke of Ephesus how he came to be in the city. Essentially, he is looking for his twin sons. He explains that, on a sea voyage, he and his wife were separated during a fearful storm. Egeon is rescued, and ends up with one of the twins in Syracuse. He knows that his wife and the other twin were also rescued, but has no idea what became of them subsequently. He reports how his son became curious about his twin brother, and set out on a journey to find him. When his son fails to return, Egeon himself sets out on a journey to discover his whereabouts, and as part of these travels, he arrives in Ephesus, ignorant of the law which forbids any Syracusan merchant to set foot in the city. It quickly becomes clear that, unbeknown to Egeon, the son he is searching for has also just arrived in Ephesus where, unbeknown to both of them, the lost twin has been living for most of his life. Thus the scene is set for the series of 'errors' that are referred to in the play's title.

It is not always the case, however, that the complete background is revealed at the very beginning of a play. Sometimes, essential information referring to previous action is scattered throughout. In *Ibsen's Hedda Gabler*, the full details of Hedda's past relationship with Eilert Loevborg are only revealed gradually, and the complete picture has to be pieced together, bit by bit. 'Scattered exposition' is very much a feature of *Chekhov's* plays.

**Each scene of a play, therefore, has to be read very carefully for any clues that might indicate what has happened in the past lives of the characters.** The amount of information available varies from writer to writer, and from play to play. Usually, *Ibsen* is kind to the reader, providing plenty of detailed background for his major characters, whereas in Harold *Pinter's* early plays (for example, *The Birthday Party* and *The Caretaker*), he is notoriously vague about the background and past histories of his characters.

As you read, keep a note of any background information that the playwright provides in relation to:

- the **past histories of the characters** (e.g. Hedda's relationship with Loevborg);
- **significant events that took place before the play begins** (e.g. details of Hedda and Tesman's honeymoon).

Sometimes it may appear, as you read, that a detail is incidental or too insignificant to be noteworthy; but remember that it is rare for a major playwright to include detail which is irrelevant to the action of the play.

Sometimes, essential information referring to previous action is scattered throughout the play

# Protagonist/Antagonist

Identify the opposing attitudes held by the principal characters in the play

Plays are full of: enemies who oppose each other in battle (e.g. *Richard III*); adversaries who argue over a burning issue (e.g. who has the right to bring up the child in *Brecht's Caucasian Chalk Circle*); families which tear themselves apart (e.g. *Death of a Salesman*); husbands and wives who constantly bicker and argue (e.g. Edward **Albee**'s *Who's Afraid of Virginia Woolf?*); lovers betrayed (e.g. *Troilus and Cressida*); and friends who part company (e.g. Prince Hal and Falstaff in *Henry IV*, Pt. 2). At the heart of almost all plays is a tension which arises from a conflict in beliefs, values and attitudes. The sharpest expression of this conflict is usually to be found in the attitudes held by the *protagonist* and the *antagonist*. So, it makes sense to look for and identify the opposing attitudes held by the principal characters in the play.

In *Shakespeare*'s *Henry IV*, Pt. 1, the principal conflicting attitudes are to be found in Prince Hal and Hotspur. The comparison between them is drawn by the king in the very first scene of the play: he despairs of the prince, his son, saying that 'riot and dishonour stain the brow of my young Harry', while he views Hotspur as 'sweet fortune's minion and her pride'. However, the king is deceived by appearances, and it is quickly confirmed for the audience that Prince Hal and Hotspur are indeed 'opposites', but not in the way the king imagines. In the second scene, the prince tells us that his behaviour is carefully calculated, and, throughout the play we become aware of his true 'kingly' qualities: his courage and heroism, his modesty, his generosity and his versatility. By contrast, the king's view of Hotspur is also quickly dispelled, as we learn that he is hot-headed, boastful, arrogant and self-obsessed.

The *true* attitudes and qualities of the two characters are revealed during the course of the play, so that our first impressions (heavily influenced by the king's comparison) are gradually modified as we find out more about them. When we attempt to identify this conflict in the early stages of the play, we should always bear in mind that our view of these attitudes is liable to change as we make further discoveries about the characters; and the attitudes, at the end of the play, may have changed quite radically in response to the events that we have witnessed. We should, therefore, attempt to chart how these original conflicting attitudes change as the action of the play progresses. In a modern play like *Look Back in Anger*, Jimmy Porter, the central character, is outspoken, abrasive and explosive; but at the end of the play, after learning about his wife's miscarriage, he is altogether different.

---

### Task 1: Identify the given circumstances

Turn to the textual analysis questionnaire and complete Section 1, The given circumstances for your set text. There are questions and prompts to help you. In order to complete this section you will need to read the whole play at least once.

---

# Language

Language reveals character

It is usually the case that the play text consists mostly of dialogue. Hence, in any textual analysis we will do well to **pay particular attention to the spoken word**. The language used by each of the characters will usually have its own distinctive idiom, and careful study of the dialogue will tell us a great deal about the following.

| Social class: does the character's language reveal their social status? | Compare, for example, the way Henry Higgins and Eliza Doolittle speak in Shaw's *Pygmalion*. |
| --- | --- |
| The character's image of self: what does the character say about him/herself? | Examine, for example, the self-important tones of Malvolio in Shakespeare's *Twelfth Night*, and Othello's address to the Senators in Act 1, Scene 3 of *Othello* (see page 146). |
| The character's view of others: how does the character talk to others and what is said about other characters? | Look, for example, at the contemptuous way in which Caius Marcius speaks to the citizens of Rome in the opening scene of Shakespeare's *Coriolanus*. |

It is useful to examine the language in a play under four headings:

- the characters' choice of words, or **vocabulary**;
- how the characters' phrases and sentences are put together (the **structure** of the language);
- how **imagery** is used; and
- any **peculiarities** in a character's speech.

Vocabulary

The actual words used by a character often convey a great deal of information about them. If we look carefully at the restricted vocabularies of the characters in Edward **Bond**'s *Saved*, we immediately become aware of their working-class environment, and their somewhat limited educational backgrounds. In Arnold **Wesker**'s *Roots*, we are quickly struck by the contrast between Beattie's more self-conscious, 'elevated' language (influenced, as it is, by her 'intellectual' boyfriend, Ronnie) and her mother's much more direct, down-to-earth choice of vocabulary. The university-educated Jimmy Porter in *Look Back in Anger* metaphorically batters all those around him with his carefully-chosen, intimidating barrage of sophisticated insults (at one point he refers to his wife as 'The Lady Pusillanimous').

Generally speaking, in looking at a character's choice of vocabulary, we might consider some or all of the following questions:

- Does the character use slang, everyday speech, or a more formal (or 'posh') vocabulary?
- Does the character use monosyllables?
- Does the character speak plainly and to the point, or does he or she 'beat about the bush'?
- Do words 'come easy', or does the character struggle to put thoughts and feelings into words?
- Is the character easy or awkward in conversation with others?
- Does the character speak to everyone in the same way, or does the character adjust his or her vocabulary according to who he or she is speaking to?
- What does the vocabulary tell us about the character's general level of education?

- Does the character use specialist vocabulary or jargon, and if so what does this tell us about him or her?
- Does the character use words to abuse and intimidate others, or to 'show off', or to 'put others down'?

## Structure

Taken together, the answers to these questions can provide some real insight into the background and psychology of a character.

The way in which the vocabulary is strung together into phrases and sentences makes up the structure of a character's speech. Vocabulary and structure work very much in tandem, and we would normally expect someone who has a good command of language to also be fluent when it comes to putting the words together. The structure of Jimmy Porter's speeches varies enormously; he is equally at home with the punchy, one-line put-down and the more extended and elaborate sardonic diatribe. By contrast, the characters in *Saved* tend to speak in short, simple and direct sentences. Many of the questions we listed in the 'vocabulary' section would also apply to the structural aspects of a character's language.

### Task 2: Stucture of language exercise

Look at the following speech. These are Othello's words, spoken to the Venetian Senate, in reply to Brabantio's accusation that his daughter, Desdemona, has been bewitched, and stolen away, by Othello.

1 *Othello*: Most potent, grave, and reverend signiors,
2 My very noble and approv'd good masters,
3 That I gave ta'en away this old man's daughter,
4 It is most true; true, I have married her:
5 The very head and front of my offending
6 Hath this extent, no more. Rude am I in my speech,
7 And little bless'd with the soft phrase of peace;
8 For since these arms of mine hath seven years pith,
9 Till now some nine moons wasted, they have us'd
10 Their dearest action in the tented field;
11 And little of this great world can I speak,
12 More than pertains to feats of broil and battle;
13 And therefore little shall I grace my cause
14 In speaking for myself. Yet, by your gracious patience,
15 I will a round unvarnish'd tale deliver
16 Of my whole course of love; what drugs, what charms,
17 What conjuration, and what mighty magic,
18 For such proceeding I am charg'd withal,
19 I won his daughter.

In line 6, Othello says that he is 'rude' (i.e. 'rough' or 'crude') in his speech. Let's see if we agree with him. To begin with, look at the structure of the 19-line speech:

1 How many sentences are there?

2 Look at each of these sentences in turn: what do you notice about them?

3 Take the sentences in turn and try to determine what Othello's *intention* is in each. Put yourself in the position of one of the Venetian Senators: from these few lines, what impression do you form of him? Are you inclined to believe Brabantio's accusations, or Othello's account of events? Why?

This brief examination of Othello's words should illustrate that there is a great deal to be learned about him simply from the way in which his sentences are structured. So careful attention to the structural aspects of a character's speeches will almost always repay study.

**Structural features of the dialogue can also provide us with important clues about the rhythm and pace of a scene.** Always look at the relative lengths of the speeches: where the lines are short (and aren't broken by 'pauses' or 'silences') we can usually assume that the scene should be played at a reasonable pace; longer speeches usually indicate that a more leisurely pace is appropriate. If one of the characters has longer speeches than anyone else, it is a fairly strong indication that this character dominates the scene, and controls the pace at which it should be played.

**Imagery**

In studying *Shakespeare*'s plays in English courses, we have probably all learned about how **the pattern of imagery in the play provides important clues to the meaning.** In *The Merchant of Venice*, in keeping with the background of commerce and trade, we are struck by the number of references to gold, silver and other precious metals and stones. The blood imagery in *Macbeth* is appropriate in a play which deals with a ruthlessly ambitious couple who will, literally, stop at nothing to gain the throne. But it is not only *Shakespeare*, and the other Elizabethans and Jacobeans, who use imagery to such telling effect in their work. Based on the pattern of images he perceived in *Ibsen*'s play, the celebrated Russian director, Vsevolod *Meyerhold* set out to create a cold, regal, autumnal *Hedda Gabler*. The animal imagery in *Look Back in Anger* (bears and squirrels) offers a telling commentary on the relationship between Jimmy and Alison.

So, the lesson is clear: **pay careful attention to the patterns of images that playwrights weave into their plays, and try to assess what clues the imagery provides to some of the deeper layers of meaning.**

**Peculiarities of speech**

Occasionally, you will find characters who have quite distinctive and peculiar speech patterns. Probably the most famous of all is Mrs Malaprop in **Sheridan**'s eighteenth century play, *The Rivals*, who persistently confuses one word for another. She refers to another character in the play as 'the very **pineapple** of politeness', when she really means to say 'the very **pinnacle** of politeness'. Although this kind of mistake is now widely known as a 'malapropism', it was not invented by *Sheridan*. In *Shakespeare*'s play, *Much Ado About Nothing*, the constable, Dogberry, is prone to making the same kind of mistake.

Where a character is given this kind of peculiarity, we should try to judge what the effect is likely to be on the audience. Clearly, the effect of Mrs Malaprop's mistakes is to make the audience laugh by making her an object of ridicule. Often the effect of an exaggerated peculiarity is to irritate; and when an audience becomes irritated by a peculiarity of speech, then, by extension, they are also likely to quickly become irritated by the character. But some peculiarities of speech can have the opposite effect of endearing the character to the audience. As a conscious opposite to Jimmy Porter in *Look Back in Anger*, *Osborne* gives his friend Cliff a slightly old-fashioned, 'folksy' Welsh idiom when he tries to protect Alison from Jimmy's verbal onslaughts. This gentle, consoling tone makes him a character for whom we have enormous sympathy. Sarah *Kane* tells us that Cate, in *Blasted*, speaks with a stutter when she is under stress; hence the playwright wants us to know that this character is prone to feelings of anxiety.

**Dialects and marked accents, either regional or foreign, can also be described as peculiarities.** In *Roots*, *Wesker* makes it very clear in his writing that Beattie's mother, Mrs Bryant, should have a broad Norfolk accent, the effect of which is to reinforce her narrow-minded parochialism, but also to provide a contrast to Beattie who consciously 'parrots' Ronnie's ideas in an effort to sound more refined and worldly than she really is. Where a dialect, or accent, is indicated in a play text it is usually for a specific purpose, and we should try to work out why it is important for us to see this character as different. (Where the playwright indicates that all of the characters speak the same dialect, it is usually because she or he wishes to reinforce the importance of the regional setting.)

## Task 3: *Hedda Gabler* exercise

We are going to look at a passage from *Ibsen's Hedda Gabler*, and subject the language of Hedda and her husband, George Tesman, to some detailed scrutiny. (You do not need to know the play in order to complete this exercise.)

This is the section where we first meet Hedda. She and her husband have just returned from their honeymoon. Hearing that the newly-weds have arrived home, Juliana, Tesman's maiden aunt, has called to pay her respects. Prior to the section we are interested in, there has, first of all, been a short conversation between Tesman's aunt and Bertha, the maid; and then a brief exchange between Tesman and his aunt.

| | |
|---|---|
| Miss Tesman: | (*goes to greet her*) Good morning, Hedda dear! Good morning! |
| Hedda: | (*holds out her hand*) Good morning, dear Miss Tesman. What an early hour to call. So kind of you. |
| Miss Tesman: | (*seems somewhat embarrassed*) And has the young bride slept well in her new home? |
| Hedda: | Oh – thank you, yes. Passably well. |
| Tesman: | (*laughs*) Passably? I say. Hedda, that's good! When I jumped out of bed, you were sleeping like a top. |
| Hedda: | Yes. Fortunately. One has to accustom oneself to anything new, Miss Tesman. It takes time. (*Looks left.*) Oh, that maid's left the french windows open. This room's flooded with sun. |
| Miss Tesman: | (*goes towards the windows*) Oh – let me close them. |
| Hedda: | No, no, don't do that. Tesman dear, draw the curtains. This light's blinding me. |
| Tesman: | (*at the windows*) Yes, yes, dear. There, Hedda, now you've got shade and fresh air. |
| Hedda: | This room needs fresh air. All these flowers – ! But my dear Miss Tesman, won't you take a seat? |
| Miss Tesman: | No, really not, thank you. I just wanted to make sure you have everything you need. I must see about getting back home. My poor dear sister will be waiting for me. |
| Tesman: | Be sure to give her my love, won't you? Tell her I'll run over and see her later today. |
| Miss Tesman: | Oh yes, I'll tell her that. Oh, George – (*Fumbles in the pocket of her skirt.*) I almost forgot. I've brought something for you. |
| Tesman: | What's that, Auntie Juju? What? |
| Miss Tesman: | (*pulls out a flat package, wrapped in newspaper and gives it to him*) Open and see, dear boy. |
| Tesman: | (*opens the package*) Good heavens! Auntie Juju, you've kept them! Hedda, this is really very touching. What? |
| Hedda: | (*by the what-nots, on the right*) What is it, Tesman? |
| Tesman: | My old shoes! My slippers, Hedda! |
| Hedda: | Oh, them. I remember you kept talking about them on our honeymoon. |
| Tesman: | Yes, I missed them dreadfully. (*Goes over to her.*) Here, Hedda, take a look. |

| | |
|---|---|
| Hedda: | (*goes away towards the stove*) Thanks, I won't bother. |
| Tesman: | (*follows her*) Fancy, Hedda, Auntie Rena's embroidered them for me. Despite her being so ill. Oh, you can't imagine what memories they have for me. |
| Hedda: | (*by the table*) Not for me. |
| Miss Tesman: | No, Hedda's right there, George. |
| Tesman: | Yes, but I thought since she's one of the family now – |
| Hedda: | (*interrupts*) Tesman, we really can't go on keeping this maid. |
| Miss Tesman: | Not keep Bertha? |
| Tesman: | What makes you say that, dear? What? |
| Hedda: | (*points*) Look at that! She's left her old hat lying on the chair. |
| Tesman: | (*appalled, drops his slippers on the floor*) But, Hedda – ! |
| Hedda: | Suppose someone came in and saw it? |
| Tesman: | But, Hedda – that's Auntie Juju's hat. |
| Hedda: | Oh? |
| Miss Tesman: | (*picks up the hat*) Indeed it's mine. And it doesn't happen to be old, Hedda dear. |
| Hedda: | I didn't look at it very closely, Miss Tesman. |
| Miss Tesman: | (*tying on the hat*) As a matter of fact, it's the first time I've worn it. As the good Lord is my witness. |
| Tesman: | It's very pretty, too. Really smart. |
| Miss Tesman: | Oh, I'm afraid it's nothing much really. (*Looks round.*) My parasol. Ah, there it is. (*Takes it.*) This is mine, too. (*Murmurs.*) Not Bertha's. |
| Tesman: | A new hat and a new parasol! I say, Hedda, fancy that! |
| Hedda: | Very pretty and charming. |
| Tesman: | Yes, isn't it? What? But Auntie Juju, take a good look at Hedda before you go. Isn't she pretty and charming? |
| Miss Tesman: | Dear boy, there's nothing new in that. Hedda's been a beauty ever since the day she was born. (*Nods and goes right.*) |
| Tesman: | (*follows her*) Yes, but have you noticed how strong and healthy she's looking? And how she's filled out since we went away? |
| Miss Tesman: | (*stops and turns*) Filled out? |
| Hedda: | (*walks across the room*) Oh, can't we forget it. |
| Tesman: | Yes, Auntie Juju – you can't see it so clearly with that dress on. But I've good reason to know – |
| Hedda: | (*by the french windows, impatiently*) You haven't good reason to know anything. |
| Tesman: | It must have been the mountain air up there in the Tyrol – |
| Hedda: | (*curtly, interrupts him*) I'm exactly the same as when I went away. |
| Tesman: | You keep on saying so. But you're not. I'm right, aren't I, Auntie Juju? |
| Miss Tesman: | (*has folded her hands and is gazing at her*) She's beautiful – beautiful. Hedda is beautiful. (*Goes over to Hedda, takes her head between her hands, draws it down and kisses her hair.*) God bless and keep you, Hedda Tesman. For George's sake. |
| Hedda: | (*frees herself politely*) Oh – let me go, please. |
| Miss Tesman: | (*quietly, emotionally*) I shall come and see you both every day. |
| Tesman: | Yes, Auntie Juju, please do. What? |
| Miss Tesman: | Good-bye! Good-bye! |

- Look carefully at the language of Hedda and Tesman (since Miss Tesman is a minor character in the play, we will leave her out of our deliberations). You will need to read through the extract a number of times. When you have done so, fill in the chart below:

| LANGUAGE | | |
| --- | --- | --- |
| Category | Hedda | Tesman |
| Vocabulary | | |
| Structure | | |
| Imagery | | |
| Peculiarities of speech | | |

**Task 4: Identify language features**

- Turn to the textual analysis questionnaire (pages 159–161) and complete Section 2: Language – for your set text.

## Dramatic Action

In the first part of the model, we focused attention on the essential information relating to the environmental facts and background, including the past histories of the characters and the significant events which took place before the play begins. In this section we shall be concentrating on the *action* of the play itself. In the acting workshop on playing the given circumstances, you started to explore, from the **actor's point of view**, the significant action of a short scene from *The Crucible* between John Proctor and his wife, Elizabeth (see pages 57–8). Since you are, by now, very familiar with this scene, we will continue to work with it; but this time we will undertake a broader analysis under three headings: breaking the scene down into **units**; giving descriptive **titles** to the units; and finding a way to express the **sub-text** of each speech.

*Break the scenes into units*

*Stanislavski* recommended that, in order to understand the shape, rhythm and true significance of a play, each scene should be divided into its constituent parts; and he called each of these parts a 'unit' of meaning. (If you read some American accounts of the process of directing, you will often find that these units of meaning are referred to as 'beats'.) According to *Stanislavski*, each unit of meaning, or sequence of thought, can be logically marked off from the other parts of the scene as being relatively self-contained.

If we look again at the beginning of the scene between Proctor and Elizabeth, we might identify the first unit as beginning with Elizabeth's line,

'What keeps you so late?' and ending with Proctor's words, 'Aye, the farm is seeded'. In this section, the two characters are, on the surface, simply establishing the reasons for Proctor arriving home later than Elizabeth anticipated. At the simplest level, the unit deals with the demands of running the farm. The next part of Proctor's speech, 'The boys asleep?' represents a change in the line of thought; attention switches from issues relating to farm work to concerns about the family. Where do you think this next unit ends?

### Task 5: Breaking a scene into units

Go through the rest of the scene with a partner. Divide it up into units and number them. Make sure that there is a logic to the way in which you have broken down the scene (in a way, the next task is a test of the logic you have brought to bear on your work). This will involve you and your partner agreeing that your breakdown makes good sense. Remember, though, that this is not rocket science. There are no definitive right and wrong answers; breaking down the dialogue in this manner is simply a way of seeing the mechanics of how the playwright has put the scene together. Different directors would probably break up the scene in different ways; the important thing is that you can give logical reasons for your own analysis.

**Give each unit a descriptive title**

The next stage in analysing the dramatic action is to go back over the units, giving each one a title. **Titles should be descriptive:** this ensures that the title really captures the essence of the unit. Vague or ambiguous titles can be unhelpful and, sometimes, misleading. Sometimes the title can be found in the dialogue itself. If we take the first unit of the scene between Proctor and his wife, we have already noted that it deals with the practical aspects of running the farm. We could borrow the title from words taken from Proctor's last line, 'Seeding the Farm'. Alternatively, we might choose to give it the title, 'A Farmer's Work'. The act of finding a descriptive title for the unit will usually tell us if we have been successful in isolating a single unit of meaning; if two very different, competing, titles suggest themselves, it probably makes sense to go back and look at the unit to make sure that it does not include two or more separate sequences of thought.

### Task 6: Naming the units

- With your partner, look at your breakdown of the Elizabeth/Proctor scene, and give each unit a descriptive title. Once again, try to make sure that you are both in agreement over the titles you select.

**Note how the *sub-text* should be played**

In the previous chapter we distinguished between text and *sub-text*, and in Task 4 of that chapter you examined a short sequence from *A Doll's House* with a view to exploring the possible *sub-textual* elements in the exchange between Nora and Mrs Linde (see page 128). It might be useful, briefly, to turn back to that exercise and remind yourself of the kinds of questions that we posed as a way of discovering what the *sub-text* might be.

In the analysis of the scene from *The Crucible*, in the acting workshop, you looked at the speeches in order to try and assess whether the spoken text disguises a deeper *sub-text*. Remember that the scene opens with a question from Elizabeth, 'What keeps you so late?' If we take the line at face value, it appears that this is a straightforward enough question; but, once we know that Elizabeth is aware of the fact that her husband has had an affair with a much younger woman, then the question assumes much greater significance. We may think that there is an accusation lurking just below the surface. The words 'It's almost dark', seem to reinforce this impression.

In order to really pin down what lies beneath the surface, we could choose a suitable verb to express the *sub-text* for Elizabeth's opening speech. We might decide that the appropriate verb is 'accuses'. But, if we go a little further, we may think that Proctor's lateness suggests to his wife that he is still continuing the affair, in which case we might choose the verb 'fears' to most accurately convey Elizabeth's *sub-text*.

---

### Task 7: Adding the *sub-text* verbs

- With your partner, go through the scene one last time. Look at each speech in turn, and try to assign the verb that best expresses the *sub-text* for each of the speeches. **Write the verb beside the speech, in the left-hand margin**; this way the verb acts almost as a note to the actor who speaks the line.

---

### Task 8: Identify the dramatic action

- Turn to the textual analysis questionnaire (pages 159–161) and complete Section 3: Dramatic action – for your set text or selected scenes from the set text.

---

# Characters

We have already noted the important part that character analysis plays in the study of both novels and plays, and we have examined the different kinds of character types that are to be found in literary texts. In the acting workshop on *The Crucible*, we saw how defining objectives provides the character's through-line of action, and leads to the determination of an overall **super-objective**; a statement of what the character is trying to achieve and what is at stake if he or she fails. But, in a full-scale analysis, we can go further.

Super-objective = wants vs. will + moral stance

In order to build up a rounded-out picture of the major characters and their significance within the play, each super-objective can be broken down and studied under a number of sub-headings. We do this by trying to decide what the character's principal **want** is. We can then make some judgement about the strength of the character's **will** in trying to get what they 'want'. Finally, it is useful to assess the character's **moral stance** in relation to these 'wants' (for example, will the character stop at nothing, or are there limits to what they will do in order to achieve their ends?).

We might also find it useful to develop a sense of the **physical appearance** of the character. Having done all of this, our final task in our analysis of character is to draw up a summary list of adjectives that provide us with a full description of the character's qualities and attributes.

He/she wants to. . .

Broadly speaking, **the character's overriding 'want' is contained within the super-objective**. In *Shakespeare*'s most famous play, Hamlet's want is straightforward enough: to revenge his father's death. As the action of the play develops, we discover that a number of obstacles stand in the way of him achieving this end. We, therefore, have to examine each scene in which Hamlet appears in order to establish the want that is specific to that scene (for example, in Act 1, Scene 5, Hamlet wants confirmation from the ghost that the new king, Claudius, was responsible for the death of his father).

A careful reading will reveal that the **tension in a play results from the fact that the various characters have different (and sometimes competing) wants**, and one of the purposes of this kind of character analysis is to try to understand, first of all, how these varying wants bring the characters into conflict (the strongest wants are usually manifest in the competing objectives of the *protagonist* and *antagonist*). As the play draws to its end, we may realise that some of these wants are irreconcilable; Nora wants to escape from the stifling clutches of her husband, while Torvald wants Nora to remain his doll-wife. Clearly, in these circumstances, something has to give – her want prevails and she walks away from her family and her home.

**Sometimes, the tension in a play is resolved by the characters reaching a point where their diverse wants have to be negotiated and modified.** At the end of *Look Back in Anger*, Jimmy and Alison manage a kind of reconciliation after her miscarriage. Each scene then, has to be carefully examined in order that all of the specific wants are clearly understood. And how these subsidiary wants relate to the principal want is the super-objective that motivates and drives the character through the play.

But will he/she?

**The next consideration is to judge the intensity of the characters' 'will' in achieving their wants.** In making this judgement it is important to pay attention to the actions of the characters, rather than to their stated **intentions**; to what the characters actually *do*, not to what they *say* they will do.

As we read *Hamlet*, we may begin to question the central character's strength of will. He talks a great deal about his intention to kill Claudius in revenge for his father's death, but his actions betray hesitation, indecision and, at times, paralysis. It is not until the very end of the play that we glimpse Hamlet's real determination and strength of will. By contrast, in *King Lear*, the king's youngest daughter, Cordelia, wants to have no part in her father's 'test of love', preferring instead to retain her dignity by speaking plainly and truthfully of her real feelings. She shows an unshakable determination and strength of will (some would say, remarkable foolishness) in her refusal to indulge her father's wishes; and, as a consequence, she is disowned, disinherited and effectively banished. At the heart of *Ibsen*'s *Hedda Gabler* there is a fatal test of will between Hedda and Eilert Loevborg, the consequence of which is a double suicide.

Sometimes, strong-willed characters are presented as being full of integrity and wholly admirable (Portia in *Merchant of Venice*, for example; and Grusha in *Brecht's Caucasian Chalk Circle*). But, equally, the kind of iron-willed determination shown by characters like Cordelia and Hedda produces tragic consequences. Many plays show us characters engaged in a struggle to overcome their indecision, faint-heartedness and lack of courage, and, here again, the outcomes can vary. In *Chekhov*'s play, *The Three Sisters*, each is destined never to fulfil her dreams of escaping to Moscow, whereas in *Strindberg's Miss Julie*, the central character marches from the kitchen to her tragic fate. And, finally, there are those characters who are simply lacking altogether in will: Trigorin, in *Chekhov's The Seagull*, tells Arkadina that he has no will of his own. Consequently, his dominant characteristic is his passivity.

In any thorough analysis, **it is important to try to establish the nature of the relationship between each character's principal want and the strength of will that drives them to achieve it**. However, a moral element often enters into this equation, and this element can present the character with a substantial barrier in getting what they want. We now turn our attentions to this third element in character analysis.

In our everyday lives, most people tend to live by a set of moral standards. Individually we may be more, or less, conscious of these standards and the way they shape our behaviour, and these moral standards anchor our behaviour in a strong sense of what is right and what is wrong. For some people, religious belief underpins their sense of morality, while for others it is a particular political conviction that provides them with their moral orientation. For the majority, perhaps, **our moral outlook comes from a combination of factors: parents, upbringing, education, experience, etc**. Most of us understand that you can't always have what you want: we may desperately want an expensive item of clothing but know we can't afford it; usually, our moral sense of what is right and wrong prevents us from walking into the shop and stealing it.

In general terms, then, we may say that **our moral stance acts as a kind of check, or curb, on our wants**. Some plays revolve around this conflict between want (and the will to pursue it) and moral stance. Macbeth, in his desire to be king, understands perfectly well that murder is morally wrong, but, driven by a sense of destiny (the prophecies of the witches) and his wife's ruthless ambition, he kills Duncan and spends the rest of the play wrestling with the consequences of his amoral action. Some characters seem to have no moral qualms about their actions: in *Othello*, Iago sets out to take his revenge on Othello and his lieutenant, Cassio, in the most cool and calculating manner; and Jacobean *revenge tragedy* is littered with similar Machiavellian types, who set aside all moral considerations in their desire for revenge.

**The conflict between want/will and moral stance is often to be found at the heart of a play**. In John *Ford*'s *'Tis Pity She's a Whore*, Giovanni and his sister, Annabella, driven by overwhelming desire, defy the moral taboos surrounding incest and become lovers. In *Brecht*'s *Good Person of Setzuan*, the good-hearted Shen-Te has to transform herself into the morally corrupt Shui-Ta simply in order to survive. In both of these cases, morality is cast aside, and we witness the triumph of want.

This is not always the case – morality can also win the day. In *Shakespeare*'s *Measure for Measure*, Isabella's moral stance, backed up by an iron will, is implacable. Her icy resolve to spurn the advances of Angelo almost brings about her brother's death. In *Ibsen*'s play, *The Wild Duck*, the character of Gregers Werle, driven by his own moral crusade, is responsible for a chain of events that brings tragedy to the Ekdal family.

These examples illustrate how **the interrelations between want, will and moral stance offer playwrights a rich seam to work**. A complete analysis has to take account of all three elements in coming to terms with the complexities of the main characters.

A playwright's text will occasionally determine a character's physical appearance. In *Shakespeare*'s play, Othello is described as a 'Moor', and this tells us that he is black. It would make no sense to ignore this fact, and play Othello as a Caucasian, because, by doing so, a good deal of the text would then be ridiculous. In point of fact, the whole plot revolves around Othello's 'blackness'. In this play, at least, there is no room for doubt: Othello has to be black. (Of course, this has not stopped most of the 'star' actors throughout history 'blacking-up' in order to take on the role, but in the last few years this tendency has almost become obsolete.)

The case of Othello is extremely clear-cut, but textual requirements often provide strong hints about a character's physical appearance: in *Twelfth Night*, Viola's physical appearance is such that she has to be able to pass for a boy when she disguises herself as Cesario; and in *Romeo and Juliet* the lovers are quite definitely teenagers, so it makes sense to cast actors who look fairly young (once again, the history of theatre is full of 'star' actors coming to these roles in middle-age, and Peter *Brook*'s 1948 production, in which he cast young actors as the lovers, was considered ground-breaking).

It is not uncommon for a playwright to give a fairly detailed description of a character. *Ibsen* tells us not only that Hedda Gabler is 29 years old, and distinguished, with an aristocratic face and figure, but also that she has a pale complexion, steel-grey eyes and auburn hair.

Textual evidence will also give strong hints about physical appearance. *Lorca* never describes the physical characteristics of Yerma and Juan in a stage direction, but we can assume that Yerma is strikingly attractive, since the text tells us that she is capable of turning heads in the street, and we know that Juan is pale and thin, as a result of a conversation he has with Yerma in the very first scene. *Lorca* clearly wants to convey a real physical contrast between the two.

When the playwright gives clues as to the physical appearance of the characters, it is always important to think about what these details add to our general understanding of them.

**Who shall we cast?**

Sometimes, as we read a text, we will begin to form a picture in our mind's eye of the character whose words we are reading. And, while there may not be any definite clues available to us in the text, our intuition may suggest to us how a particular character might look. An interesting exercise is to try to think of a famous stage, screen or TV actor who you could imagine playing the part.

**Summary adjectives: what makes him/her tick?**

The final task in building up a rounded picture of the character is to review our findings in relation to want, will, moral stance and physical appearance, and to draw up a list of adjectives which give as full a description as possible.

---

### Task 9: Identify characters

- Turn to the textual analysis questionnaire (pages 159–161) and complete Section 4: Characters – for no more that three of the characters in your set text.

---

**Variations in characterisation**

The headings we have used above are intended to help you arrive at as comprehensive a character analysis as possible. However, within the limits imposed by the character's overall consistency, complex characters do tend to vary from scene to scene. A good playwright will show us the many different sides and moods of the characters, and we should **examine each scene carefully in order to try to chart the different moods and intensities of the characters**.

In *The Seagull*, the difference between Konstantin and Trigorin in Act 1 is striking. When we first meet Konstantin he is in a state of tremendous excitement at the prospect of Nina performing the play he has written. His intense excitement shows itself in restlessness, high energy and extreme agitation. In reality, this emotional state would be accompanied by certain bodily sensations: an inability to be still; a faster heart rate; perspiration; and 'butterflies' in the stomach. The contrast with Trigorin, the other writer, is remarkable: he enters unobtrusively, in a group of six which includes Arkadina, and does not speak until the performance is over. Trigorin's mood is relaxed, almost to the point of boredom, so that his bodily sensations will be almost the exact opposite of Konstantin's.

If we then compare Konstantin's mood in Act 4, we find it is very different. He has become disillusioned with his career as a writer and has lost Nina, who ran away and became involved in an affair with Trigorin. After his final encounter with Nina, we see Konstantin standing grim-faced and motionless. He then proceeds deliberately to destroy all of his manuscripts prior to committing suicide. His bodily sensations, following Nina's final departure, will be very different from those which attended his sense of anticipation at the play's beginning: absolute stillness; the 'butterflies' replaced by a knot in the stomach; an overall feeling of tension in the muscles.

In attempting to assess the mood of a character at the beginning of a scene it is important to bear in mind the general characteristics that your overall analysis has revealed. In real life, most people behave with a certain degree of consistency from situation to situation, but within the limits of this consistency we can also be contradictory and unpredictable. We should **pay particular attention whenever a character's behaviour departs significantly from what we have come to expect** (for example, Nora's unexpected departure). **This normally indicates a vital turning-point in the play's action.**

## The Playwright's Intention

We are already familiar, from Chapter 2, with the idea that plays can be viewed as having a social function, and this function can range from the didactic plays of *Brecht*'s earlier years to the pure entertainment value of the Whitehall farce. Playwrights, of course, are acutely aware of the social function their work is designed to fulfil. An important consideration, therefore, in analysing the playwright's intention, or ruling idea, is to assess the play's intended **social function**: What is the play designed to do? And to whom? Looking carefully at the play's form, genre and style will help us work out the answers to these two questions.

We can then move on to examine the content and action of the play under four headings:

- the **title**;
- any **philosophical statements** *drawn* from the text itself;
- an overall **synopsis** (or summary) of the play's action; and
- the particular **significance of individual scenes** within the play's overall structure.

The title gives clues

An important clue to the playwright's intention is often to be found in the title. Some titles are purely literal (for example, *The Three Sisters* is a play, as you would expect, about three sisters): if a playwright names his play after one of the characters, we can be reasonably certain that the play's principal focus will be on that character (for example, *Miss Julie*).

But titles can also be more metaphorical. *Chekhov* did not name his play *Nina*; instead he gave it the title *The Seagull*. On a number of occasions, during the course of the play, Nina refers to herself as a seagull. This metaphor works on several different levels. At the simplest level, Nina sees herself as a seagull soaring away to escape from the confines of her limited, provincial existence (she longs to become an actress). In Act 2, Konstantin enters with a dead seagull, and sets it on a bench. It is possible to see the dead bird as a symbol for the doomed relationship between Nina and Konstantin, but the writer, Trigorin, on seeing the dead bird, makes the association with a girl (Nina?), and immediately begins to formulate a story: a man comes along, sees her, and – just for the fun of it – destroys her, like the seagull lying on the bench. This outline, of course, foreshadows the story of the affair between Nina and Trigorin which happens in the two years that pass between Acts 3 and 4. The symbol of the seagull in *Chekhov's* play is so multi-layered that it gives an important insight into the playwright's intentions in writing the play.

**Playwrights will occasionally choose a title which is intriguing, mysterious, or enigmatic.** It is interesting to speculate on the significance of titles like *Strindberg's The Ghost Sonata*; *Beckett's Endgame*; Edward *Bond's Saved*; David *Hare's Plenty*; C.P. *Taylor's Bandits*; and Mark **Ravenhill's** *Shopping and F***ing*.

**Philosophical statements**

A careful textual analysis will often reveal a line of dialogue that seems to encapsulate the playwright's intention, or the play's major theme. It is often useful to go back over a play to see if such a line presents itself.

In *The Seagull*, Masha, one of the more minor characters, replies when asked why she always wears black that she is in mourning for her life. *Chekhov's* play deals with the various characters' inabilities to find the happiness that they seek. Masha is in love with Konstantin, but she understands that her affections will never be returned because Konstantin is obsessed with Nina. Consequently, she is doomed to unhappiness, and is, therefore, in mourning for the life she can never have as Konstantin's wife. Gradually, as the play unfolds, we discover that all of the main characters are in much the same situation: each longs for a sense of emotional fulfilment which is never forthcoming. In this sense, we could view all of them as being 'in mourning for their lives'.

**A careful reading should always yield at least one quotation that helps crystallise the playwright's intention:** in *The Merchant of Venice*, we could argue that the famous phrase 'the quality of mercy' adequately captures *Shakespeare's* ruling idea; the line 'I don't believe in miracles any more' neatly sums up Nora's journey of self-discovery in *A Doll's House*; and, in *Waiting for Godot*, the oft-repeated line 'Nothing to be done' seems apposite in relation to the lives of Estragon and Vlaidmir.

**Synopsis**

Having considered the significance of the title of the play and after pinning down the playwright's intention, or ruling idea, the next step is to draw up a full synopsis of the action of the play. This helps us see how the playwright's overall intentions are realised, and how the ruling idea develops as the play progresses towards its conclusion. As we make our synopsis, we begin to get a much firmer sense of the play's shape and structure. We should begin to see the main plot in sharper relief, and we should also perceive what the relationships are between the main action of the play and any sub-plots.

The significance of
individual scenes

Each scene must be examined in order to establish its precise **function** and **purpose** within the overall structure of the play. Generally speaking, in a *realist* text where the narrative is linear, we will find that each of the scenes develops organically from those that have gone before. Although there may be varying lengths of time between the events depicted in the play, it is usually possible to discern a sense of continuity and a logical relationship between the scenes. In more *episodic* plays, written in the manner of *Brecht*, we may have to work harder to discover how the scenes work together to create a coherent whole.

---

### Task 10: Identify writer's intentions

- Turn to the textual analysis questionnaire (pages 159-161) and complete Section 5: Writer's intentions - for your set text.

---

# Conclusion in Seclusion

The practice of analysing texts usually suggests a solitary individual, deep in concentrated thought, studiously poring over books and papers. And this is certainly the image that springs to mind when we imagine *Stanislavski*, in the summer of 1898, closeted for six weeks in a tower overlooking the grain fields of his brother's farm, analysing *The Seagull*, and preparing his *mise en scène* for the forthcoming *Moscow Art Theatre* production. And certainly, the model we have offered in the preceding pages requires, for the most part, just such a quiet, desk-bound approach.

However, we should also bear in mind that analysis can also be an active as well as a passive process. Some directors, who are able to enjoy the luxury of a series of exploratory workshops prior to the beginning of the rehearsal period proper, engage in a practical analysis of the text in order to deepen the acting company's understandings of the play they are working on. In Chapter 6 there was a study of a student production of *Lorca*'s play, *Yerma*. The case study consists of a number of practical activities which formed the early stages of the rehearsal process.

After reading this chapter and the case study on *Yerma* in Chapter 6, you now have **two ways of analysing a play text: the first, a detailed model for desk work; the second, a practical workshop method.** Each can be used to great effect on its own and both can, of course, be used in tandem. This kind of detailed analysis is essential preliminary work for anyone who is preparing to direct a play, and a more detailed discussion of the work of the director can be found in Chapters 5 and 6.

# Textual Analysis Questionnaire

The textual analysis questionnaire is designed to help you make a detailed analysis of a play text from a director's point of view. It is the level of analysis which a director needs to apply prior to rehearsals so that they can offer an interpretation of the play and ideas about the *mise en scène* to the actors and designers. The previous pages give a detailed breakdown of each of the sections in the questionnaire and offer illustrations from a wide range of plays as examples for you to follow, or as the basis for comparisons between different kinds of plays.

| | | |
|---|---|---|
| **The given circumstances** | | **Environmental Facts and Background** |
| | Geographical location | Where is the play set?<br>What is significant about the locations used in the play? |
| | Date and time | Are there any specific references to time of day, season, year?<br>How will the time or season effect the characters? |
| | Timescale | How much time passes during the play?<br>How will the 'passage of time' be played/represented? |
| | Economic environment | What is the economic environment of the characters?<br>How are they affected by their economic environment? |
| | Social environment | Is the social and economic environment the same?<br>What differences are there in the social environment of the characters?<br>How will this affect how characters interact? |
| | Political environment | Are there any references to political events?<br>What was the political environment of the writer?<br>How will the political context be played/represented? |
| | Religious environment | Are any of the characters influenced by their own religious beliefs, or by the beliefs of others?<br>What effect does religion have on the way characters behave? |
| | | **Previous Action** |
| | Past histories of characters | What clues are there to the biographies of the main characters?<br>How will the characters' future actions be affected by their biographies? |
| | Events prior to play | Are there references to key events prior to the play?<br>Do any of the characters carry scars or memories from these events?<br>How will the characters be affected by these events? |
| | | *Protagonist/Antagonist* |
| | *Protagonist*'s attitude and how it changes | Which character is the *protagonist* – who initiates the play's central action?<br>What is their attitude?<br>How does it develop or change during the play? |
| | *Antagonist*'s attitude and how it changes | Which character is the *antagonist* – who opposes the *protagonist*'s objectives?<br>What is their attitude?<br>How does it develop or change during the play? |

| | | |
|---|---|---|
| **Language** | Vocabulary | How formal/informal is each character's language?<br>Are there any clues to levels of education or background in the words used by characters?<br>Do any of the characters use language to bully, or to impress, or to promote themselves to others?<br>Do words come easily or are they struggled over?<br>What does the vocabulary used tell us about the personalities of the characters? How do you imagine them based on the words they use? |
| | Structure | How are speeches structured? Are they elaborate and long or short phrases, for instance?<br>What does the structure of each character's speech tell us about the character and their relationship to others?<br>Does the structure change according to who the character is talking to?<br>Are there any clues to the pace and rhythm of the scenes in the structure of the speeches? |
| | Imagery | Are there any patterns in the imagery used?<br>Are these patterns scattered across the play or restricted to certain characters?<br>Does the imagery relate to setting? Ideas? Mood? Atmosphere? Character traits?<br>How can the imagery be pointed out so that an audience is aware of its pattern?<br>How will the design of the play reflect the imagery? |
| **Dramatic action** | Peculiarities of speech | Do any of the characters have accents, dialects, speech problems?<br>If so what does this *add* to the character? |
| | Scene units | How many identifiable 'units' are there in each scene?<br>What is the logic of your choice of unit breaks?<br>How should each unit be played? |
| | Labelling the units | What word or phrase best describes the action, or objectives, in each unit?<br>Do the unit titles accurately summarise the scenes? |
| | Playing the *sub-text* | What is the *sub-text* of action in each scene? What is *really* going on?<br>Which verbs accurately describe for the actors how the speeches should be played so that the *sub-text* becomes visible to an audience? |

| | | |
|---|---|---|
| **Characters** | Wants | What are the super-objectives of the main character/s?<br>What do the main characters *want* to happen in the scenes they appear in?<br>Are there conflicts or tensions between what different characters want?<br>Do the main characters wants significantly change or create contradictions during the play? |
| | Will | Is there a difference between what characters say they will do and what they *actually* do?<br>What is the intensity or strength of the main characters' resolve or determination? Do they really want their super-objectives to be realised? |
| | Moral stance | How do culture, morality and upbringing shape the main characters' behaviours?<br>How does the main characters' moral stance encourage, justify or constrain the fulfilment of their wants? |
| | Physical appearance | Are there direct references to the physical appearance of characters?<br>Are there any other clues or inferences about physical appearance?<br>Are there any implications for casting?<br>What significant connections are there between how a character looks and how they behave? |
| | Summary adjectives | Which sets of adjectives best describe the characters?<br>How will these adjectives be played? What are the design and costume implications? |
| | Variations in characterisation | Are there any significant changes or variations in the way that characters behave in different scenes?<br>Are there any inconsistencies in how characters react to situations or other characters?<br>How will the 'inconsistencies' be either smoothed out or exaggerated in the playing of the characters? |
| **The playwright's intention** | Title | What is the significance of the title?<br>Is the title metaphoric or literal?<br>What sub-title or alternative title might be given to clarify the writer's own title? |
| | Philosophical statements | Are there any key lines or speeches which seem to encapsulate the writer's view or which summarise and capture the ideas or mood of the play?<br>Where are these lines positioned in the play and who speaks them? Is there anything significant in this? |
| | Synopsis | What is the main plot of the play and how does it develop?<br>What sub-plots are there and how do they relate to the main plot?<br>How are the writer's ideas developed over the play?<br>How can the shape of the play be best described and represented? As a story? As episodes? As a journey? As a diagram or map? |
| | Significance of individual scenes | What is the function and purpose of each scene within the overall structure of the play?<br>Which scenes are the most important and which the least?<br>What is the logic of the relationship between scenes? Is it cause and effect? *Brechtian* knots? Contrasts in mood, atmosphere, location? |

# 9 Devising Theatre

## Devising: A Brief Overview

So far, we have been focusing most of our attention on text-based theatre: works written by playwrights; interpreted, rehearsed and orchestrated by directors; performed by actors; and presented in a building specifically designed for the performance of plays. When most people think about theatre, this is the kind of event that comes to mind.

However, there is another kind of theatre that is at least as old as the **plays** of fifth-century Athens. And, although its development is less well documented in theatre histories, it has continued in an unbroken tradition right up to the present day. This kind of theatre is usually known as **devised theatre**. In the later part of this chapter, we are going to suggest a way of creating your own work that is not dependent on a pre-existing text. Devised theatre emerges as a result of a **collaborative** process of exploration arising from concerns and ideas **collectively** generated by a group of devisers.

You will already be aware that any theatre venture demands commitment, discipline and teamwork; devising your own plays is no different. This is by no means an 'easy option'. On the contrary, it demands:

- resourcefulness, motivation and commitment;
- ability to tolerate ambiguity and uncertainty;
- spontaneity and willingness to be 'playful' in exploring ideas;
- high levels of imagination and creativity;
- readiness to negotiate, compromise and collaborate;
- determination (and the stamina) to see the project through.

Although the methods suggested in this chapter represent tried-and-tested approaches, it is important to bear in mind that there is no 'magic formula' that can guarantee a successful devising process. The recommendations contained in this chapter will, we hope, minimise the risk of failure; but much will depend on the abilities of the individual devisers to respect the ideas and opinions of others, and on their creativity in generating, exploring, sifting and shaping the material into a compelling theatrical experience. And, as is the case with most kinds of theatre practice, it is important that the devisers find their own approach to the whole process of devising.

Having sounded a warning note, it is also important to remember that much of this work will not be quite as unfamiliar as it might at first sound. Much of your drama work in school thus far has been based on devising of one sort or another. Being asked to make a *still-image*, to develop a scene, to create a soundscape, to thought-track a character, are all examples of devising. The work you created was based on your own ideas and imaginative resources. This previous experience of devising, albeit on a somewhat smaller scale, will stand you in good stead as you embark on a full-scale devising project; and, returning to the positive, always bear in mind that the process of creating your own work from scratch can be a hugely exciting, exhilarating and fulfilling experience!

**Task 1: What is different about devising?**

- Draw up a list of the differences you would expect to find between creating a performance based on an existing play text, and making a devised performance.

- In what ways would you expect the challenges and problems to be different?

# The Development of Devised Theatre

As we have already mentioned, the history of devised theatre goes back at least as far as the Greek classical period. Alongside the *tragedies*, *comedies* and *satyr plays* which we learned about in Chapter 2, we know that an alternative *mime* tradition existed. *Mimes* (or **mimus**) are known to have been performed from as early as the fifth century. Little is known about them, but it is likely that the original *mimes* were improvised comic representations of everyday life, animated by *buffoonery* and *clowning*. There is a good case for arguing that the original Greek *mimes* were the first examples of devised theatre in the Western tradition.

During the Roman period, the *mimes* continued to be popular; they consisted of short, improvised scenes that depicted current events as well as stories of love and adultery. The performers devised their scenarios using *stock characters* and a basic vocabulary of gesture. The *Atellan farce* (named after the town of Atella, where it is said to have originated) was another early type of devised dramatic entertainment. Originally improvisational, the *Atellan farce* relied on everyday situations, masked characters and slapstick.

It is a tribute to the popularity of these kinds of entertainment that the tradition of the *mimus* and the *Atellan farce* continued throughout Europe. Both traditions were absorbed into the *Commedia dell'Arte*, a form of devised theatre that began in Italy in the fifteenth century. *Commedia* performances invariably took place outside and were free to watch (the *Commedia* troupes survived by inviting their audiences to make donations). The troupes usually consisted of ten people (seven men and three women) and, like the *Atellan farce*, their performances relied on *stock character* types, masks, farcical action, and scenes full of acrobatics, *clowning* and *buffoonery*. The scenarios were short and simple, and provided ample opportunity for the performer to improvise, *mime* and *clown*. An important aid to improvisation was the *Commedia* actor's use of *lazzi*. These are pre-set comic routines, often repeated with variations. The skilful use of *lazzi* and other physical and visual gags have provided inspiration for a wide range of contemporary performers – from the political *satires* of Dario *Fo*, through the *stand-up comedy* routines of someone like Peter Kay, to characters in television situation comedies like Kramer in *Seinfeld* (watch, particularly, his entrances to Jerry's apartment, which, almost invariably, elicit enthusiastic audience applause).

*Commedia dell'Arte* remained popular through to the eighteenth century, but many of today's *physical theatre* companies are indebted to the traditions of *Commedia*.

Within the twenty-first century, there is little doubt that devised works have become an important phenomenon in contemporary European and North American theatre. There are a number of reasons why there has been increased interest in this kind of collective and collaborative endeavour, four of which are set out below.

# A Changing Theatrical Landscape

In the British theatre of the post-war period, experimentation and innovation were rare. British drama schools did little more than equip student actors with the basic technical skills of voice, stage movement and building a character that would enable them to survive in a repertory system, with its punishing schedule of production where one scripted play followed another, each rehearsed from scratch in a two-week period. By contrast, devised theatre allows for the coming together of diverse performance skills in the search for new forms of performance – different combinations of actors, dancers, actor/teachers, performance artists, directors, writers and designers have produced inventive and exciting works that have the effect of breathing new life into theatre practice.

As we discovered in Chapter 5, during the eighteenth and nineteenth centuries the English theatre was dominated by the great actor-managers, from David *Garrick* to Henry *Irving*. With the emergence of the modern director, European theatre practice gradually moved away from the 'star system' towards the creation of acting *ensembles* (for example, the *Moscow Art Theatre Studio*, under *Meyerhold*'s direction in Russia; *Brecht*'s **Berliner Ensemble** in East Germany; and *Grotowski*'s **Theatre Laboratory** in Poland). In the early twentieth century, the director still retained his or her pre-eminence, orchestrating the work of the actors and creating the *mise en scène*. We have already noted, in Chapter 6, an important distinction between what we called the playwright's director (who faithfully attempts to present the play text in accordance with the author's intentions) and the *auteur* (who re-interprets, and often modifies, the original play in such a way that it creates a performance text which is as much the work of the *auteur* director and the performers as it is of the playwright).

# The Impact of Ensemble

Devising reflects the change in status for directors and performers

The twentieth century witnessed a considerable change in the relationship between writers and other producers of theatre. The director as *auteur* gradually began to rival the playwright and, within many of the *ensemble* companies, the creative status of the actor began to change from passive, interpretive instrument to more active, creative participant in the production process. This change was made possible, in large measure, because many of the *ensemble* companies we have mentioned were funded by government and cultural agencies, and were consequently freed from the demands of commercialism. (*Brecht's Berliner Ensemble* was particularly well supported by the East German government; and this allowed them to spend long periods in rehearsal.) Generous funding enabled these companies to experiment and explore the boundaries of theatre. Many of these companies saw themselves as schools, or training institutions, where actors, as well as sharpening their performance skills, could engage in philosophical and

Brecht in discussion with actors, Berlin 1953

scientific debate and discussion about the relationship of theatre to the wider social, political and cultural landscape.

**The *Berliner Ensemble***

The *Berliner Ensemble* first visited England in 1956 and immediately captured the attention of the theatre-going public. For many years, British theatre had been trapped within the confines of *realism* and *representational* forms. *Brecht's* style of *presentational* theatre, with its sparse mode of production and tightly-worked *ensemble* performances, profoundly impacted both theatre-goers, and a new generation of British theatre artists, including Joan *Littlewood*, William **Gaskill** (the artistic director of London's *Royal Court Theatre*) and Peter *Brook* (who would later go on to found the *International Centre for Theatre Research* in Paris).

**Joan *Littlewood* and Ewan *MacColl***

*Littlewood* and her partner, the folk singer Ewan **MacColl**, were already committed socialists, whose early work had been influenced by the Russian **Blue Blouse** workers' theatre movement and by the German **agit-prop** theatre of Erwin *Piscator*. They formed a radical, touring collective, **Theatre Union**, which combined sketches, songs and *satire* in devised performances for ordinary working people. Subsequently, *Littlewood* developed her collaborative and *ensemble* style at the *Theatre Royal* in the East End of London. The 1963 production of *Oh! What a Lovely War*, influenced by *Commedia*, was performed in *Pierrot* costumes. The play, a savage *satire* on World War I, was devised, using material from Alan Clark's book *The Donkeys*, a history of British involvement in the war, and scenes from Jaroslav Hasek's play, *The Good Soldier Schweik*. Projections of horrific images of war and shocking statistics were juxtaposed with the broad comic action sequences to create an uncompromising, disturbing and powerful indictment of war. *Oh! What a Lovely War* is remembered as a landmark in socialist and popular devised theatre.

## A New Political Climate

In the 1960s, as the bleak and austere post-war years began to recede in the memory, a new political climate began to transform the face of Britain. Described by some traditionalists as an era of 'permissiveness', it was a time of: relative economic prosperity (neatly encapsulated by Harold Macmillan, then Prime Minister, who told the Conservative Party Conference in 1957, 'We've never had it so good'); greater educational opportunities, with more young people finding their way into an expanded university system; a cultural renaissance, summed up in the phrase 'the Swinging Sixties'; and a shift towards greater egalitarianism, manifest in the growing women's liberation movement.

The same tendencies were also observable in the United States. In keeping with the spirit of the times, Judith *Malina* and Julian *Beck* founded *The Living Theatre*, a theatre collective committed to political and aesthetic radicalism. Initially, *The Living Theatre* brought the work of influential European playwrights to the US; but, by the 1960s, they had begun to devise plays that advocated anarchist-pacifist ideas. They adapted versions of *Antigone* and *Frankenstein* before creating their best-known work, *Paradise Now*, a semi-improvisational play involving audience participation. In a scene that quickly achieved notoriety, the actors recited a list of social taboos, including nudity, while they undressed. This led to the company's arrest in London for indecent exposure. Between 1964 and 1968, the company toured throughout Europe, providing a model for the establishment of similar theatre collectives based on radical political and artistic ideals, and committed to group devising.

*Beck and The Living Theatre*

Joseph *Chaikin* worked with *Beck* and *Malina* on *The Living Theatre's* production of *The Connection* before co-founding **The Open Theater** in 1963. A theatre collective, *The Open Theater* began life as a closed experimental theatre laboratory but went on to create collaborative works based on the improvisational techniques of the acting teachers, Nola *Chilton* and Viola *Spolin*. Much of their work was performed in maximum-security prisons. In 1974, three members of *The Open Theater* formed a new company, **The Talking Band**. Originally the company worked with contemporary poets, but subsequent collaborations have also involved designers and musicians. Their theatre blends gesture, movement, visual imagery and text to create interdisciplinary, highly-charged and energetic works that can be considered important forerunners of the *physical theatre* movement in the UK (see page 170). Attached to the company is The Talking Band Performance Lab, which provides a forum for artists to exchange ideas, create new works and experiment with new performance techniques.

*Guerrilla Theatre*

'*Guerrilla Theatre*' is the term used by Ron Davis, the founder of *The San Francisco Mime Troupe*, to describe the popular political theatre of his own company, and the work of **Bread and Puppet Theater**, whose name comes from the company's practice of offering fresh bread to the audience as a way of creating a sense of shared community (and based on their conviction that

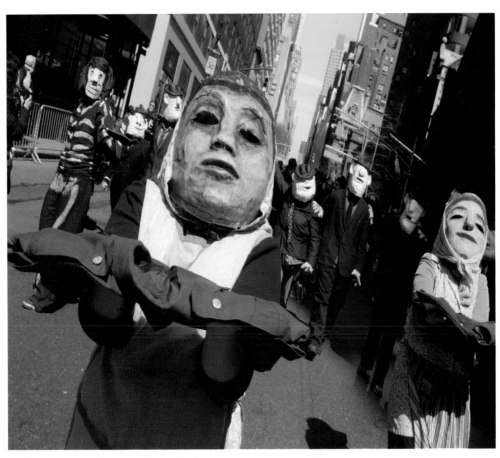

Members of the *Bread and Puppet Theater* march in an anti-war protest, New York, 2004

art should be as essential to life as bread). Founded in the early 1960s by Peter **Schumann**, *Bread and Puppet Theater* devised large-scale political spectacles (using giant-sized puppets), which were often performed as part of larger political demonstrations and protests against the Vietnam War. Both of these companies used carnival and *Commedia dell'Arte* conventions to create large-scale, innovative and politically-driven performance pieces.

## New Funding Initiatives

New writers, new funding, new theatres

As a consequence of the post-war economic boom in Britain, the Arts Council provided increased funding, particularly to those theatre companies who set out to encourage new writing. More generous levels of subsidy allowed for longer periods of rehearsal, and this meant that new plays could be commissioned, developed and produced. A new collaborative approach between writers and other kinds of theatre artists was an important aspect of the work of the **English Stage Company**, founded by George **Devine**, to promote new writing. This company, which took over the *Royal Court Theatre*, was largely responsible for the renaissance in British theatre that began in 1956 with John *Osborne*'s play *Look Back in Anger*. Following hard on the heels of *Osborne*'s success, other writers (including Arnold **Wesker**, John **Arden** and Edward **Bond**) were able to take advantage of the new collaborative ethos

167

fostered by the creation of the *Royal Court*'s writers' group. During the 1970s and 1980s, the *Royal Court* became an important centre both for new writing and for new styles of collaborative rehearsal and performance.

In Britain, during the 1960s, the Arts Council, as well as funding the more established building-based companies, also offered support to small-scale organisations, which came to be known as the **alternative theatre companies**. One of the first was *Portable Theatre*, formed in 1968. *Portable Theatre* is best known for its two group-written plays, *Lab-By* and *England's Ireland*. The first, based on a newspaper story about a wrongful conviction for rape, was collaboratively written by seven writers: Howard *Brenton*, David *Hare*, Trevor *Griffiths*, Brian *Clark*, Snoo *Wilson*, Hugh *Stoddart* and Stephen *Poliakoff*; the second dealt with the history of British political involvement in Northern Ireland, and was co-written by *Brenton*, *Hare*, *Clark*, *Wilson*, Tony *Bicât*, David *Edgar* and Francis *Fuchs*. The writers associated with the work of *Portable Theatre* reads like a veritable 'who's who' of Britain's most significant political playwrights.

In addition to *Portable Theatre*, other alternative theatre companies involved in the creation of collaborative works include *CAST* (*Cartoon Archetypical Slogan Theatre*), *AgitProp Street Players*, *Dogg's Troupe* and the *Pip Simmons Theatre Group*.

## The Influence of Joint Stock Theatre Company and the Work of Mike Leigh

Formed in 1974 by the directors William *Gaskill*, Max *Stafford-Clark* (both of whom had been artistic directors of the *Royal Court*) and David *Aukin*, and the playwright David *Hare*, the collaborative approach taken by **Joint Stock Theatre Company** is readily discernible in the name that was chosen. The company was run along the lines of a joint stock company, which means that the company's initial funds were raised from contributions from each member and any profits (measured by the success of its productions) were divided between these contributing members. In effect, the company was cooperatively owned by its members.

The *Joint Stock* method

The animating idea was to create a new form of collaborative and *ensemble* theatre, in which the final product would be devised through workshops and other forms of theatrical, social and political research. *Joint Stock* developed an approach to producing plays that has had a significant impact on the working methods of a number of alternative and *avant-garde* theatre companies. The method was based on a ten-week rehearsal period in which the first six weeks were taken up with identifying themes and content through research, physical activities and improvisation involving the whole company, including the writer, director and designer. There would then be a break in the company's work to allow the writer to prepare a script based on the content that had emerged during the devising process. A four-week rehearsal process followed, where the script could undergo revision and modification as a result of further input from the whole company; thus the final play was a reflection of the collaboration between the actors, writers, directors and designers involved. The *Joint Stock* 'style' consisted of tightly-directed and highly-detailed *ensemble* acting, minimalist sets and a predominantly *Brechtian* (i.e. *presentational*) mode of performance.

Among the many important plays produced using the *Joint Stock* method are Caryl **Churchill**'s *Light Shining in Buckinghamshire*, *Fen* and *Cloud Nine*; David **Hare**'s *Fanshen*; Howard **Brenton**'s *Epsom Downs*; and Hanif **Kureishi**'s *Borderline*.

**The workshop period involved the company in activities that are now the familiar approach in most forms of devised theatre.** Exercises, improvisations and physical activities were interspersed with: lectures from outside experts; reading, research and study periods; group discussion and political analysis. (In devising *Fen*, company members spent a short period of time actually living and working among the people of the fenlands.) An important aspect of the company's working method was the 'truth quiz', in which company members had to answer direct questions from other company members, not just about their characters, but also about their particular personal politics and their relationships with other members of the collective. This was intended to ensure that there was no separation between the actor as social being and as performer. The company demanded total commitment from its members!

In 1975, *Joint Stock* began work on an adaptation of William **Hinton**'s history of the Chinese 'cultural revolution', *Fanshen*. The book chronicled the changes that occurred in the lives of the peasants, during the years of the revolution as the old system of feudalism was swept away by the rising tide of socialism. This particular production would have a profound effect on the company, who decided that, from that point on, the collective should be organised on the same egalitarian principles as the village peasants who were depicted in their production. Equal status, equal pay and an equal say in company policy all came to be enshrined in *Joint Stock*'s philosophy, practices and procedures.

Joint Stock's production of *Fanshen*, 1975

Joint Stock's operating policy subsequently became a model for many of the left-wing theatre companies that followed.

## Task 2: Collective approaches

- What are the benefits of the ways in which Joint Stock decided to organise themselves as a collective, particularly following their experience of creating Fanshen?

- Are there any disadvantages?

- How do you think these organisational methods impacted on their approach to devising?

Mike *Leigh* was developing a different form of devising in his 'improvised plays'

During this same period, Mike **Leigh** was developing his own unique approach to devising, in his 'improvised plays'. *Leigh*'s work, based on improvisation and painstaking character research, is in the *realist* and *representational* tradition of *Stanislavski. Leigh* was impressed by the authenticity and detail of character that came from the case-study research done by Joan *Littlewood*'s actors during their preparations for performing Brendan *Behan*'s play *The Quare Fellow*, which was based on real-life interviews with Borstal boys.

**Leigh developed a method of devising highly *realist* representations of the extraordinariness of ordinary lives.** *Abigail's Party*, a biting *satire* on the aspirations and tastes of the new middle class, was devised in 1977. It was first performed at the *Hampstead Theatre Club*, a company that specialises in commissioning and producing new plays, and was then adapted for television. The detailed realism of *Leigh*'s work makes it especially suitable for the small screen, although, more recently, he has worked extensively in film, where his best-known works are arguably *High Hopes* (1988), *Secrets and Lies* (1996) and *Vera Drake* (2004).

*Leigh*'s devising method begins with the careful selection of a group of actors who are chosen, after lengthy interviews, for their potential for interesting *ensemble* work. *Leigh* has said that he looks for four qualities in his actors: a sense of humour; a keen eye for habits and physical mannerisms; a good ear for dialects; and an ability to transform their ideas into microscopically-defined and unique characters. Through an extended workshop process, the actors are asked to identify characters based on people they know, or have met. The character development and scenarios that follow are based on highly-detailed research. *Leigh* divides the process of devising into **narrative work** and **behaviour work**. In the former, the biography of the character is established through improvisation and discussion; and, in the latter, the character's ideas, culture and consciousness are developed together with the accompanying physical mannerisms.

## Devising and Physical Theatre

We have already encountered the work of *The Talking Band* in this chapter, and noted their high-energy form of *physical theatre*. In the late 1970s and early 1980s a new form of theatre emerged that was tailor-made for devising. *Physical theatre* can be defined as any kind of performance that presents its content primarily through physical means. Clearly, this is a broad definition that encompasses a whole range of different performance styles, but, in general terms, it is a highly-visual form of theatre in which the emphasis is on the physical dexterity of the performers. Text is often used, but is usually subordinate to the means of physical expression.

The diversity of the genre derives from the different traditions in which its roots can be found. These may be summarised thus:

1   the work of Vsevolod *Meyerhold*, Antonin *Artaud* and Jerzy *Grotowski*;
2   *mime*, particularly the work growing out of the **Jacques Lecoq School** in Paris;
3   European and North American contemporary dance practice;
4   *clowning*, mask and other forms of physical comedy;
5   some forms of large-scale puppetry.

### Task 3: Physical approaches to theatre

- Think about some of the theatrical performances that you have seen recently, and try to identify any examples of the approaches listed above. How effective were they theatrically?

- Can you think of any occasions, in your own work, when you have tried out physical approaches?

- What were the particular challenges? How successful do you think you were?

# Theatrical Antecedents

We have already seen in Chapter 5 that *Meyerhold* wanted to break from the limitations of a *realism* that was the stock-in-trade of the *Moscow Art Theatre*. This involved a totally new approach to the training of actors, which he called *biomechanics*, and which was designed to provide his performers with a thorough training in stage movement. *Biomechanics* was a highly-systematic method. The work began with simple exercises and progressed through a series of *études*, intended to provide actors with a comprehensive movement vocabulary that would equip them to perform any physical action that might be required. Many of *Meyerhold*'s most innovative and audacious productions contained a strong element of physicality.

*Artaud*'s advocacy for a *Theatre of Cruelty* began with a demand for actors to strip away the everyday life mask that conceals the inner core of their being which is the true self. (We have already encountered this idea in our discussion of *Grotowski*'s work in Chapter 5). According to *Artaud*, it was necessary for theatre practitioners to break away from the written word and to invent a unique, new 'language' of theatre, a *physical language* which he described as being 'halfway between thought and gesture'. As we have seen, *Artaud* was never to realise his *Theatre of Cruelty*; this work was left to others, principal amongst them, Jerzy *Grotowski* (see pages 97–99).

Many of *Grotowski*'s productions were devised adaptations of pre-existing texts; for example, *Shakuntala* (by the Sanskrit poet and playwright Kalidasa, and augmented with scenes from other Indian texts, including the *Kama Sutra*), *Akropolis* (based on a text by the Polish playwright Stanislaw

*Wyspianski* incorporating techniques from ancient Indian *Kathakali* theatre and *Meyerhold's biomechanics*), *The Tragical History of Doctor Faustus* ('a textual montage' based on the play by Christopher *Marlowe*) and *The Constant Prince* (by the seventeenth-century Spanish playwright, *Calderón de la Barca*, in three different versions). Arguably, the most famous of *Grotowski's* works was the *Apocalypsis Cum Figuris*, which began life as an adaptation of the gospels but, following an open rehearsal, the original production was abandoned. Many of the scenes, depicting the life of Christ, found their way into the final version, which also incorporated material from Dostoevsky's *The Brothers Karamazov*, and were supplemented by passages from the poetry of T.S. *Eliot* and Simone *Weil*.

*Grotowski* and the actor–audience relationship

    *Grotowski* was always intrigued by the nature of the relationship between the stage and the audience and, consequently, between the actor and the audience. In his major productions, he sought different ways to explore the nature of these relationships. In *Shakuntala*, commentators were seated behind the audience on either side of the room, interpreting the action. The action of *Akropolis* took place on a central platform and in the passageways between a number of surrounding platforms containing seating for the audience. In *Doctor Faustus*, the spectators were invited by the *protagonist* to sit at two long tables on either side of the room as guests at his 'last supper' before being consigned to hell and eternal damnation. In *The Constant Prince*, the setting suggested a surgical operating theatre, in which the audience viewed proceedings from an elevated space. In the *Apocalypsis*, the spectators were enveloped by, and included in, the action.

*Akropolis*, Maja Komorowska, Rena Mirecka, Zbigniew Cynkutis, Andrzej Bielski, Zygmunt Molik, The Laboratory Theatre of 13 Rows, October 1962

*Grotowski's* influence across the western world has been immeasurable. In the United States, Richard **Schechner**, also formed **The Performance Group** in 1967, which, from its inception, followed in *Grotowski's* footsteps. *Schechner* continued as its director until 1980, when the company became **The Wooster Group**, which continues under the direction of Elizabeth **LeCompte**. In 2005, the company created a work entitled *Poor Theater, A Series of Simulacra*, which was a re-creation and adaptation of *Grotowski's Akropolis*. Andre **Gregory** directed a number of collaborative, experimental *Grotowski*-inspired productions during the 1960s and 1970s, the most famous of which was a devised version of *Alice in Wonderland* (1970).

In Europe, *Grotowski's* influence was widespread. Eugenio *Barba*, an Italian director, worked with *Grotowski* from 1961 to 1964, after which he created **Odin Teatret** in Denmark. Since then, he has directed over sixty new works, some of which took up to two years' preparation. Among his best-known works are *Ferai* (1969), *Brecht's Ashes* (1980), *The Gospel According to Oxyrhincus* (1985) and *Mythos* (1998). In the UK, *Grotowski's* influence has been felt in the work of such diverse companies as *Impact Theatre Collective*, the *Northern Stage Company* (particularly in the work of the *Northern Stage Ensemble*, which was created by Alan *Lyddiard*) and the Birmingham-based *Geese Theatre Company*, which creates interactive theatre specifically for offenders and young people at risk. Needless to say, in his native Poland, *Grotowski's* legacy has resulted in the creation of a whole host of companies who continue to follow, and develop, the precepts established by his *Theatre Laboratory*.

## Mime

*Lecoq's impact on physical theatre*

The impact of Jacques *Lecoq* on *physical theatre* practitioners and companies in the UK has been enormous. During an eight-year stay in Italy, he became familiar with the techniques of *Commedia*, before returning to Paris in 1956 to open the *Jacques Lecoq School*. The essence of the *Lecoq* approach is the control of movement and gesture through the major theatrical genres such as *melodrama, comedy, tragedy* and *clowning*.

In 1975, Carlo **Mazzone-Clementi** (*Lecoq's* assistant) and Jane **Hill** founded the **Dell'Arte School of Mime and Comedy** in California. Its mission was to bring the European tradition of physical training to the United States and to provide actor-creators with a thorough grounding in *mime*, mask, movement and *ensemble* creation. In 1976, *Mazzone-Clementi* was instrumental, along with actors Joan *Schirle* and Jon'Paul *Cook*, in creating the **Dell'Arte Players Company**.

In the UK, Steven **Berkoff** (who, interestingly, also cites *Grotowski* as an important influence in his work) trained with *Lecoq*. During the 1970s and 1980s, *Berkoff* developed a highly physical form of theatre in which word, action and sound are all accorded equal status. *Berkoff's* style, often referred to as **total theatre**, is perhaps most clearly discernible in his adaptations of the prose stories and novels of Franz **Kafka**, and in works like *Decadence* (1980) and *West* (1983). In the written text of *Metamorphosis*, *Berkoff* provides a complete physical performance text. It was the dynamic, high-energy work of *Berkoff* that paved the way for many of the *physical theatre* companies that took centre stage in the 1980s, most prominent of which were *Théâtre de Complicité*.

173

The company, founded in 1983 by Simon *McBurney*, Annabel **Arden** and Marcello **Magni** (all graduates of the *Lecoq School*), shortened their name to *Complicité* in 2000. Widely-acknowledged influences include (naturally) *Lecoq* himself and *Meyerhold*. *Complicité*'s early satirical pieces, based on movement, *mime* and *clowning*, shared a cartoon-like quality. As their work evolved, they began to devise works that combined realistic and stylised acting with text, dance, music and visual art. These tendencies are evident in their best-known works: *The Street of Crocodiles*, based on the life and stories of the Polish writer and artist Bruno Schulz (1992); *The Three Lives of Lucie Cabrol*, adapted from a short story by John Berger (1994); and *Mnemonic* (1999), developed around the central image of a corpse preserved from the Ice Age. More recent productions have made increasing use of technology to supplement the sparse staging; video backdrops are used to create multiple narratives that are juxtaposed with the live movement sequences.

David **Glass**, another graduate of the *Lecoq School*, formed **The David Glass Ensemble** in 1992. Since its existence, the company has developed a distinctive style of *physical theatre* – fusing *mime*, text and soundscape. Depending on the demands of the show, the performers are required to move effortlessly from playing a leading role to becoming an abstract part of the scenery. The company has developed an approach to *ensemble* performance in which acting, *mime*, movement and theatrical effects are woven together seamlessly.

One fascinating aspect of the work of the company has been its development of *The Lost Child Project*. This work came about as a result of an initiative at the first *International Centre for Theatre in Education* (*ICTIE*) conference in Bradford. Members of the UK's *Standing Conference of Young People's Theatre* (*SCYPT*) established links with two theatre practitioners from Vietnam. Geoff *Gilham*, Roger *Chamberlain*, three members of *Big Brum Theatre in Education Company* (all members of

*The Lost Child Project* in Vietnam

SCYPT) and ten members of the *David Glass Ensemble* subsequently visited Vietnam. The members of the *Ensemble* worked with young people from the *Hanoi Youth Theatre* and members of the local community to devise a play that explored the themes of lost children and lost childhood. The result of this collaboration was *The Hansel and Gretel Machine*, the first part of what came to be known as *The Lost Children Trilogy*. The second play was called *The Lost Child* and brought together the stories of *Hansel and Gretel* and *Alice Through the Looking Glass*; and the third, *The Red Thread*, once again combines elements from *Hansel and Gretel* and *Alice*. *The Lost Child Project* which began in Southeast Asia, subsequently moved to South America and, eventually, to Europe; its stated objective was to use creativity as a process for affirming human values and rights.

# Dance

The first half of the twentieth century saw the development of what came to be known as **modern dance**, a label that encompassed a divergent range of theatrical movement styles in Europe and North America. Early modern dance choreographers rejected traditional ballet techniques, viewing modern dance as an art capable of manifesting emotional, psychological and spiritual states.

Modern dance as an art form

Pioneers in the field included Isadora *Duncan*, who is mentioned in Chapter 2. Her seemingly spontaneous and 'natural' movements unfettered by rigid technical training, her flowing classical Grecian tunics and her reverence for the sanctity of the body all contributed to the establishment of modern dance as an accepted art form.

At approximately the same time, in Germany, dance innovators like Rudolf *van Laban*, Mary Wigman and Kurt *Jooss* developed **expressionist dance** (*Ausdruckstanz*), a movement which, amongst other things, pioneered community dance and the use of improvisation in teaching. *Van Laban* was most interested in large-scale group choreographies and movement choirs that, he believed, could counter the alienating effects of industrialisation and urbanisation. In works like *Hexentanz* (or *Witch Dance*), *Wigman* rejected pictorial harmony and dainty movements in favour of a wider and more complex range of emotional expression. The direct influence of *Jooss* is seen most powerfully in the work of his best-known protégée, Pina *Bausch* (see page 176). *Ausdruckstanz* was primarily concerned with the development of each dancer's individuality; consequently, structured improvisation was not only used for choreographic inspiration, but was also considered to be essential for training performers to develop physical strength, flexibility and personal creativity.

In the United States, modern dance choreography, as developed by Ruth *St Denis*, Ted *Shawn* and, later, Martha **Graham**, Doris *Humphrey* and Charles **Weidman**, was usually set and polished. Technical virtuosity was greatly prized and, unlike *Ausdruckstanz*, US modern dance techniques were strictly codified and associated with specific teachers/choreographers.

In the 1930s, modern dance in both Europe and North America, in an attempt to address important contemporary concerns, became much more politically oriented. Most notably, Kurt *Jooss's* iconic, anti-war piece, *The*

*Green Table*, won the International Choreographer's Competition in Paris in 1932. In the United States, leftist dancers, including those associated with the *Workers' Dance League*, created choreography in support of labour unions and humanitarian values.

After World War II, New York became the centre for modern dance innovation. In the 1950s, the turn from emotional expression to formalist experiments with space and movement dynamics, and the deliberate use of **chance** in the choreography of Merce **Cunningham** marked a new direction for the art form. The variety of styles associated with the *Judson Dance Theater* collective gave rise to what is now commonly known as **postmodern dance**. The choreographers associated with this company defiantly challenged established performance conventions and values; they began to question the fundamentals of the art form: What is dance? Is dance defined by a set sequence of movements anchored to rhythm? Can everyday movements, like walking, be considered dance? Who can be a dancer? Is specialised training needed? Is any person, or body type, suited to be a dancer? What are the appropriate venues for dance?

**Dance embraces diversity and lack of boundaries**

Dance since the 1960s has been defined by its increasing embrace of diversity. The boundaries between different styles appear to be increasingly fluid as choreographers seek inspiration from a wide variety of sources, from urban street dance through performance art to interdisciplinary and non-Western approaches. While dance forms like **contact improvisation** have gained acceptance and status within the dance community, many dance artists continue to incorporate *ballet*, as well as older modern dance techniques, into their training and choreographic practices.

It is probably true to say that a number of postmodern/contemporary dance choreographers have been influential in the development of *physical theatre*, but, given the limitations of space, we will confine our comments to two prominent choreographers: Pina *Bausch* and Bill T. **Jones**.

Pina *Bausch* trained in her native Germany during the 1950s with Kurt *Jooss*, after which she spent two years in New York. She returned to Germany to work with *Jooss*, and subsequently became director of the Wuppertal Opera Ballet in 1973 and, not long after taking up this post, the name of the company was changed to the *Tanztheater Wuppertal Pina Bausch*. She continues as artistic director and choreographer, where she has created more than thirty full-length works, most of which have been toured worldwide.

During the creation of *Die Sieben Todsunden* (*The Seven Deadly Sins*) in 1976, *Bausch* developed her famous question-and-answer technique as part of the devising process. This technique requires company members to give honest answers to probing questions about their personal lives. In 1977, *Bausch* began working on *Blaubart* (*Bluebeard*), an important milestone in the development of her work. Bringing together elements from *opera*, *mime* and traditional theatre, *Blaubart* was the first piece in which she made a decisive break away from the classical 'balletic' style of her early work. *Bausch* says that her work in the early 1980 focused on humankind's fear of violence and disaster; and, in the 1982 piece *Nelken* (*Carnations*), the performers play increasingly vicious childhood games while being watched by armed guards with dogs.

*Bausch*'s pieces are built around brief episodes of dialogue and action, often with a surreal quality (in *Viktor*, a female dancer pounds a steak, stuffs it – along with her foot – into a shoe, and then proceeds to dance); actions are often multilayered and performed simultaneously; direct address to the audience is often used in an attempt to involve them; repetition is an important structuring device, often as a means of viewing the same action from multiple viewpoints. During the past twenty or so years, *Bausch*'s work has grown steadily more joyous and celebratory: *Viktor*, in 1986, was conceived as an ode to the city of Rome, and *Danzon*, devised in 1995, was built around a Cuban dance.

Acknowledged as one of the most innovative and important performance figures of the twentieth century, *Bausch* is a choreographer who has significantly influenced the new generation of *physical theatre* practitioners.

Like Pina *Bausch*, Bill T. *Jones* studied classical *ballet* and modern dance. He choreographed and performed worldwide as a soloist and duet company with his late partner, Arnie **Zane**, before forming the **Bill T. Jones/Arnie Zane Dance Company** in 1982. The company's work, described as a fusion of dance and theatre, has confronted such divisive issues as racism, sexuality, HIV/AIDS and war. *Jones* is sometimes described as a 'creative activist'. In his 2005 work *Blind Date*, he explores the concept of patriotism. In this multimedia piece, he borrows *Bausch*'s question-and-answer technique and combines company members' memories of learning *The Star-Spangled Banner* with dance sequences set to music by artists as diverse as Bach, Otis Redding and R. Kelly. Increasingly, Bill T. *Jones* has found his way into the theatrical mainstream.

Many of these influences can be detected in the work of Lloyd **Newson**, founder of *DV8 Physical Theatre* in 1986. *Newson* won a scholarship to the **London Contemporary Dance School**, which teaches a variety of modern and contemporary dance techniques. Upon graduation, *Newson* joined **Extemporary Dance Theatre**, where he worked as a dancer and choreographer. An important aspect of *Newson*'s approach is his rejection of abstraction in dance, ensuring that his work addresses current social issues.

In 1990, *DV8* achieved notoriety when the *Sunday Mirror*'s sensationalist headline 'Gay Sex Orgy on TV' gave a huge boost to *The South Bank Show*'s screening of *Dead Dreams of Monochrome Men*, a piece inspired by the serial killer Dennis Nilsen. Set in a pub, *Enter Achilles* (1995) was an exploration of masculinity and its underlying current of insecurity. In 2003, *The Cost of Living* examined questions about how society assesses individuals and, consequently, how we value ourselves. All of these works were subsequently adapted for television.

*DV8* breaking down barriers

*DV8*'s artistic policy asserts that their work is about 'breaking down the barriers between dance, theatre and personal politics and, above all, communicating ideas and feelings clearly and unpretentiously'. Although the work of the company deals with complex contemporary issues, it remains accessible to a broad constituency. The company has fought successfully for funding to cover lengthy research and development periods and, although the devising of the pieces is a collaborative venture, *Newson* retains a rigorous measure of artistic control.

*Forced Entertainment* and *Goat Island*

*Forced Entertainment* was formed in 1984 by a group of six graduates from the University of Exeter who have, remarkably, stayed together for more than twenty years. Like *DV8*, their work is a blend of theatre, dance and digital media that explores contemporary issues. Recent work includes *Exquisite Pain* (2005), a project that explores love, loss and the stories we tell ourselves when things have gone wrong, and *The World in Pictures*

DV8's *Enter Achilles*

(2006), which claims to tell 'the story of mankind'. Their artistic policy affirms their commitment to a collective devising approach, maintaining a shared 'history, skills and an equal involvement in the creative process'.

*Goat Island*, founded in 1987, is a Chicago-based collaborative performance group whose work is developed for local, national and international audiences. Members of the group are involved in the conception, research, devising, writing, choreography, documentation and educational demands of their work. The performances consist of a highly distinctive style of movement – sometimes dance-like, sometimes prosaic and routine – that often makes extreme physical demands on the performers, and sometimes serious attention demands on the audience. Historical and contemporary issues are explored through a combination of text and movement. Somewhat after the fashion of *Grotowski*, the group is constantly experimenting with different configurations of the performer–spectator relationship; many of their pieces are performed in non-theatre venues, such as sporting arenas or parade grounds.

## Clowning, Mask and Other Forms of Physical Comedy

*Commedia* as main root of *clowning*

Most forms of *clowning*, at least in the Western tradition, have their roots in *Commedia dell'Arte*, devising and improvisatory forms. But certain forms of *clowning* pre-date the *Commedia* troupes. In most cultures, the clown is a ritual character who often appears in festivals and carnivals. A popular early form was the **fool** (who was, of course, a *stock character* in many of *Shakespeare*'s plays). Often the butt of jokes, the fool was nevertheless licensed to make comments and observations that would run the risk of censure, and even punishment, if they had been uttered by more 'sensible' people. Ironically, the 'wise Fool' in *King Lear* talks much more sense than the king himself.

*Clowning* is common to many cultures and, it has been said, is popular because it meets a fundamental human need – the need to comment irreverently on subjects that are sometimes considered unmentionable, or not quite proper, in polite circles. The unique status of clowns enables them to: violate social conventions and traditions; mock authority; and engage in forms of offensive and obscene behaviour. In other words, they are permitted to operate, with impunity, on the margins of society, beyond the rules that regulate 'normal' everyday behaviour. The role of the clown therefore is to subvert the accepted order and, often, to expose social absurdities.

Essentially, in contemporary terms, clowns are comic performers who are usually instantly recognisable by virtue of their stylised makeup and outlandish costumes. *Clowning* is a highly visual presentational form, often addressed directly to the audience, which contains physical comedy and slapstick humour. Perhaps the best-known clown figures of the early twentieth century are to be found in the era of the 'silent movie'. We can still enjoy the unforgettable comic performances of Charlie *Chaplin*, Buster *Keaton*, Harold *Lloyd* and the *Keystone Kops* on film, but the usual contemporary setting for a clown character is the circus.

**Circus/theatre crossover**

One of the first companies to explore the crossover between circus and theatre was the Australian troupe, **Circus Oz**. Formed in 1978, they pre-date many of the more recent **Cirque Nouveau** (*New Circus*) troupes, including the internationally-acclaimed Canadian company **Cirque du Soleil**, creating their work (which contains acrobatics, *clowning* to music, and spectacular aerial work) with a company of a dozen multi-skilled performers. Their style is bold, anarchic and subversive; and the company retains a strong commitment to issues of social justice, including support for women's rights and land rights for aboriginal Australians, and opposition to the Australian government's measures for indefinite detention of asylum seekers.

**The Right Size**, formed in 1989, is a company that consists of Hamish *McColl* and Sean *Foley*, occasionally augmented by distinguished performers like Kenneth *Branagh*, Freddie *Jones* and Sir Richard *Wilson* (*One Foot in the Grave's* Victor Meldrew). *McColl* and *Foley* occupy the middle ground between being serious stage actors and clowns. *The Play What I Wrote* (2001), a homage to the TV comedians Morecambe and Wise, is a slapstick comedy in the best circus tradition.

Caroline Simonds trained at *The Big Apple Circus Clown Care Unit* in New York, and moved to Paris in 1991, where she founded *Le Rire Médecin* (*Laughing Doctors*), a large company of 'clown doctors' who work alongside health professionals to create theatrical programmes in hospital settings for children and their families. The individual clown characters are initially created through a process of devising. The company uses *clowning* to enhance the quality of life and mental wellbeing for hospitalised children, and to help make the hospital environment seem less intimidating.

Trestle Theatre production of *Adventures of the Stoneheads*, 2002

We began this section by acknowledging the importance of the *Commedia* tradition in contemporary *clowning*. The use of mask was an important part of classic commedia, and *Trestle Theatre* have been instrumental in bringing masks back into popular theatre in the UK. From its beginnings in 1981, *Trestle* have devised almost thirty productions which have toured extensively. Operating on the borderline between *mime* and *clowning*, they use very little dialogue in their works; meaning is largely transmitted by means of gesture and action.

## Puppetry

Worldwide puppetry traditions

Puppetry is an ancient art form in many cultures and takes a variety of different forms, all of which involve the animation of inanimate performing figures. Like *clowning*, puppetry is often a feature of festivals and carnivals.

Venerable and vibrant traditions of puppetry can be found across the world. In Asia, the best-known form is probably Japanese *bunraku*, while shadow puppetry is thought to have originated in the Middle East, in Central America the people of Teotihuacán included puppets as part of their funeral rites, Australian aboriginal culture has strong traditions of ritualistic carnival puppetry and, of course, in Europe marionette (string) puppetry has been popular from about the sixteenth century. In Britain, the familiar

*Punch and Judy* hand puppet show, with its central character based on the Pulcinella (from *Commedia*), developed in the late eighteenth century.

In the twentieth century, puppetry developed in a variety of different ways. There was a belief among some influential theatre practitioners that, in spite of its roots in popular and folk traditions, puppets could speak eloquently to adult audiences and be harnessed in the service of experimental theatre forms. As we saw in Chapter 2, Edward Gordon *Craig* wanted to do away with live actors altogether, and replace them with the *uber-marionette* (super-puppet). Playwrights of the stature of Maurice *Maeterlinck*, Federico García *Lorca* and George Bernard *Shaw* all wrote puppet plays. But, of course, puppetry has always had a special appeal for children.

Some of the examples above, of course, indicate that puppet plays can take the form of carefully-crafted scripts by serious playwrights, but we end this section with two companies whose puppetry work is devised especially for children.

*The Wee Giant Puppet Company* is a touring company for young people based in Glasgow. The work of the company brings together giant puppets and actors to create innovative, imaginative and educational programmes which are performed in primary schools, youth clubs and community centres. *Meta4 Theatre Company*, a cooperative based in Plymouth, creates plays which are not only intended to be performed *for* children in outdoor settings, but are also devised in order to enable them to *participate*. They do this by means of 'Backpack Giants', lightweight puppets supported on the performer's back using a backpack or rucksack.

## Applied Theatre and Devising

In Chapter 2, we drew an important distinction between *representational* and *presentational* kinds of performance; and we have noted that theatre, at the beginning of the twentieth century, was largely dominated by *realist* and *representational* forms. The audience for this kind of theatre was largely well-to-do, wealthy and **middle class** (essentially, people who could afford the high price of a ticket). Gradually, however, a number of politically-committed practitioners set out to create a theatre that was capable of reaching a much broader audience. The audience they had in mind was the **working class**, and they began to seek out forms that were capable of doing this. The inspiration driving this search for a new audience came, in large part, from the 1917 Revolution in Russia. With the victory of the Bolshevik Party, a new generation of theatre artists, directors and playwrights (both within and beyond the borders of the new Soviet Union) anticipated a transformation from the old, outworn economic relations of capitalism to a progressive, socialist future in which class divisions would disappear. They sought to harness the power of theatre to educate the members of the working class to understand why this social revolution was necessary and how it was to be achieved. Theatre provided one way of preparing them for the part they would be called upon to play in the construction of a new socialist future.

Theatre as educational forum

Practitioners like *Meyerhold*, *Piscator* and *Brecht* understood that the new situation required a new kind of theatre, and they began the task of creating it. Both *Piscator* and *Brecht* knew that, for the new theatre to be effective, it had to make an immediate, direct and powerful impact on its intended audience. In this context, *presentational* forms made considerable appeal. As we have already seen, *Piscator*'s early work took the form of *agit-prop* theatre performed in non-theatre venues where workers would ordinarily be gathered together. As well as having the obvious agitational and propagandist functions implicit in the name, *Piscator*'s theatre was also avowedly **educational** (e.g. the **living newspaper** was developed principally as a means of keeping illiterate workers abreast of current events). From 1924, *Piscator*'s work became more sophisticated and, as a result of his collaboration with *Piscator* in the early 1920s, *Brecht* began to formulate the principles of *epic theatre*. As part of this process, *Brecht* conducted a number of theatrical experiments. Amongst the most interesting of them were the *Lehrstücke* (or 'learning/teaching plays'), a new form of theatre designed to exploit the overt educational potential of theatre. Written in 1929 and 1930, the best known of the *Lehrstücke* are *The Measures Taken*, *The Exception and the Rule* and *He Who Says Yes/He Who Says No*.

Mostly performed in schools, the *Lehrstücke* had a dual purpose: one for the performers, and one for the audience. In keeping with *Brecht*'s evolving theory, the actors were encouraged to look critically at the roles they were required to perform, and to adopt (and demonstrate) their attitudes towards these roles. This new approach was intended to politically educate the actor, to find (in *Brecht*'s own words) 'the new man in himself', i.e. the new, politically committed 'man'. The spectators, in discussions following the presentation, were encouraged to consider the implications of the action they had witnessed. *He Who Says Yes/He Who Says No* presents them with a dilemma. A young student, who has become ill on a journey, must decide whether he will consent to act in accordance with a custom that states that he should agree to sacrifice himself rather than ask his fellow travellers to turn back, or whether he does not consent to act in accordance with the custom. In *He Who Says Yes*, he agrees; in *He Who Says No*, he refuses. He argues that customs that have outlived their usefulness should be discarded, and that a new 'Great Custom' should be inaugurated, in which no action should be taken until the specific circumstances have been carefully examined, considered and evaluated. It is possible to argue that the play represents a form of 'illustrated Marxism', intended to help performers and spectators alike come to a better understanding of the fundamentals of historical and dialectical materialism.

**Twentieth-century children's theatre**

There were other attempts to use theatre in the service of education during the twentieth century. A number of educational projects for children were developed under the auspices of the **Federal Theatre Project**, which was set up in the United States during the Great Depression. Many of these plays can be found in the archives of the *Federal Theatre Project*. Amongst them are a documentary detailing the history of aviation in the style of the living newspaper, a *vaudeville* adaptation of *Pinocchio* and an anti-war Christmas *pantomime*. But, without doubt, the most infamous of the children's plays was *The Revolt of the Beavers*. Described as a 'fantastic *comedy*', it was investigated by a US Senate committee for being 'Mother Goose Marxism'. *The Revolt of the Beavers* was withdrawn after only twelve performances. It was the furore surrounding this production that ultimately led to the cutting of funds for the entire *Federal Theatre Project*. In the wake of the *Federal Theatre Project*'s initiative, a vibrant tradition of children's theatre in the US continues right up to the present day in the work of writers like Coleman A. *Jennings*, Aurand *Harris*, Lowell *Swortzell* and Susan *Zeder*.

Children's theatre also developed across Europe. As early as 1918, in the Soviet Union Natalia **Sats** was instrumental in the development of musical theatre for children. In the 1960s and 1970s, more radical plays for young people were written and performed by companies dedicated to producing work for young audiences. The **Unga Klara** is an independent children's theatre company attached to the *Stockholm City Theatre* and presents plays dealing with issues which are of particular interest to young people and, in Berlin, **Grips-Theater** seeks to create an 'emancipatory theatre' for young people.

*Theatre in Education*

It should be clear from the above that, beginning with *Brecht's Lehrstücke* and continuing through to the work of *Unga Klara*, plays for children have been predominantly, but not exclusively, crafted by playwrights. But they are detailed here in the belief that understanding the significance of these developments is essential in order to understand the growth of the **Theatre in Education** (**TiE**) movement, which began in the UK in the 1960s. The **Belgrade Theatre**, a repertory company based in Coventry, set up the first *TiE* team in 1966 and, in the fifteen years that followed, there was a veritable explosion of *Theatre in Education* work across the whole country – some companies were attached to regional repertory theatres like the *Belgrade*, while others, like *M6*, were freestanding, independent organisations dedicated to producing work for young people.

Although many of the plays associated with the *TiE* movement were especially commissioned from writers with an interest in producing work for young people, one of the problems associated with scripted plays on contemporary themes is that they have a tendency to quickly become outdated; another is that commission fees are costly for companies with limited financial resources. Many *TiE* teams saw devising as one way of alleviating some of these difficulties. Using the existing resources of the company members, the team could generate their work in much more cost-effective ways, and material that dated quickly could be reshaped relatively easily. Another advantage of devising plays is that company members involved in the process have a more thorough understanding of the content and feel a greater sense of ownership.

The much more overtly **educational** purpose of *Theatre in Education* distinguishes it from children's theatre in a number of ways. Firstly, because the performers in *TiE* companies are expected to combine the skills of facilitation with those of acting, they are called **actor/teachers**. This is because a *Theatre in Education* **programme** will have three important components: a performance; a participatory workshop; and supporting teaching materials. Some programmes are wholly participatory, but where this is the case the actor/teachers will be working in role alongside the young people, so are still providing a performance element – but within the context of the participation. **Greenwich Young People's Theatre Company**'s programme, The School on the Green, is a good example of this particular genre. A final important feature that differentiates *TiE* from children's theatre relates to the size of the **audience**. The only limit to the size of the audience for children's theatre is the size of the auditorium in which it is to be performed, but, because of the participatory element within *TiE*, most programmes are designed to be played for one class group at a time. Specific age groups are targeted – programmes have been devised for children right across the school-age spectrum. Half-day programmes may be more appropriate for younger children, whereas full-day ones have been designed for older students.

A number of companies who produced *Theatre in Education* programmes, also saw themselves as a community resource with a broader remit. Companies like the *Half Moon Theatre* in the East End of London built a new theatre (which opened in 1985) specifically designed to provide a meeting place where all members of the local community could come together; *Bruvvers*, in Newcastle-upon-Tyne, take their own brand of community theatre to youth clubs, day centres, care homes and hospitals; and *New Perspectives*, based in Nottingham, devise participatory arts projects and tour to community and rural venues across the whole of the East Midlands.

From the 1970s onwards, some college and university drama departments designed courses specifically for students who wanted to work in these kinds of community contexts. Among the first to offer such courses were Newcastle Polytechnic (now Northumbria University) and the Rose Bruford Training College of Speech and Drama (now Rose Bruford College). Many universities subsequently followed suit and offered similar courses in **community theatre**.

## Applied theatre

During the past fifteen years or so, the use of the label 'community theatre' has fallen out of favour. In part this is because, in North America, the term 'community theatre' refers to what we would call in the UK amateur dramatics and, as similar courses began to appear in North American universities, there was clearly a need to find a term that did not confuse or mislead. Subsequently, the term '**applied theatre**' has been used

New Perspectives adaptation of *Saturday Night and Sunday Morning*, Nottingham, 2006 to designate courses which cover a wide range of community applications of drama and theatre (in the United States, the term 'community-based theatre' is commonly used). It is becoming an increasingly broad area of study as new 'applications' are being developed, and a number of definitions have emerged. For our purposes, we will define 'applied theatre' as **the use of theatre for extra-theatrical purposes**, where 'extra-theatrical' can refer to **education**, **social change** and **community-building**.

Some members of the applied theatre community insist on separating out applied **theatre** (where the emphasis is on performance) and applied **drama** (where the activity is participatory). We do not intend to dwell on this distinction, or discuss the different arguments – for our purposes the term 'applied theatre' will be used to describe both performance and participatory approaches. Because it is a rapidly-growing and ever-expanding field, applied theatre practitioners are still in the process of discussing and debating what kinds of drama and theatre activity might legitimately be included under the heading. Some disagreements remain to be resolved, but the following practices seem to be relatively unproblematic: educational uses of drama and theatre (including youth theatre), prison theatre and theatre in criminal justice settings, reminiscence theatre with the elderly, the uses of drama and theatre approaches in health-care settings, theatre for development, large- and small-scale community-based theatre, drama and theatre work with vulnerable and marginalised populations, and site-specific theatre and museum education. Doubtless, the list will grow as new applications are developed.

## Three Case Studies

In the next section, three brief case studies are offered in an attempt to exemplify different kinds of applied theatre projects. The first provides an example of theatre being used for educational purposes, the second was conceived as a project intended to bring about social change and the third was a community-building initiative. The projects included here have an international dimension, and demonstrate how applied theatre techniques are being used in places as diverse as a northern city in the UK, the remote south Asian country of Nepal, and a rural community in the northwest of the USA.

It is important to emphasise that these case studies are not included as blueprints to be followed slavishly, or even as recommended ways of working. Our aim is simply to provide insight into three contrasting projects that were originally designed for widely differing purposes.

## *Not the Last Supper*, devised by Bottleshop Youth Theatre, Lancaster

Behind the *Dukes Theatre* in Lancaster, for many years, there was an old building that had become home to the youth theatre company that was part of the Dukes' community programme. The *Bottleshop*, once a brewery storehouse, subsequently gave its name to the group of young people who regularly met there to create their own brand of vibrant, innovative and provocative theatre. *Not the Last Supper* was devised during the second half of 1990 and the early part of 1991, and was performed at a Youth Arts Festival, Lancaster's Royal Albert Hospital, as part of a weekend event designed to raise funds for Kurdish refugees (who were fleeing their homes after having been attacked with chemical weapons by the government of Iraq) and, finally, at the Bradford Standing Conference for Young People's Theatre (SCYPT).

The devising process began with facilitators Helen *Clugston* and Kate *Grey* inviting members of the youth theatre to record their feelings about the physical environment that served as their meeting place and rehearsal room. One long-standing member wrote:

> *The room . . . holds the secrets of many people – mainly the young . . . Inside this room you are in another world. Anything could happen outside and the inside would remain unchanged.*

From this evocative beginning, and triggered by the feelings and sensations produced in response to the first task, the group began to create and explore other rooms and locations: the room of solitude, the room of separation, the room of chains, the cathedral and the labyrinth. Through the early stages of the devising work, characters began to inhabit the rooms; events and conflicts that had taken place there were revealed, examined and investigated.

It was as a result of the exploration of the room of chains that one of the play's central characters emerged: Susana sitting alone in her cell (Susana was named after the *protagonist* in a novel by Omar Rivabella, which was to take on central significance later in the process). The cathedral yielded a desolate Madonna asking God to grant her rebirth. Following the building of the labyrinth, members of the group were conducted by candlelight on a journey through a maze of objects and obstacles, and in a corner sat a mother beside a tiny altar. In the reflection period following this journey, one member remarked, 'She was a grieving widow. It reminded me of the disappeared.'

During the devising period, the Gulf War began. Disturbed by events in the Middle East, one young woman offered the group Rivabella's novel, *Requiem for a Woman's Soul*, which tells the story of a woman who had been imprisoned in Argentina and tortured. Pages from her diary are smuggled out of the prison in a box, which is given to a priest who, recognising the tacit complicity of the Church in the detention of political prisoners, becomes ill and is unable to carry out his official duties. This incident provided the group with a question that formed the next part of their exploration: What is in the box that comes from the place where people are tortured? Depictions of life in the prison were created under the title of 'Paradise' (the ironic name by which the prison was known). Members of the group were then asked to record, on tiny pieces of paper, their experiences during the course of one particular week (a week in which the bombing of Baghdad was particularly intense). These 'diary pages' were pinned to the wall and juxtaposed with the depictions of 'Paradise'. The facilitators described this process as 'devising a visual background for the play'.

A chance occurrence provided the impetus for the next stage of devising. One of the group members was unable to attend the next meeting because her mother felt that she had been impudent by refusing to set the table for the family's evening meal. On her return, the facilitators took the decision to explore the girl's profound disturbance at this turn of events. A series of scenes was created, in which family tensions surfaced around the table during mealtimes. This led to further explorations around events that took place at supper tables and an investigation of different kinds of suppers. The supper table began to take on central significance in the emerging play – but not just the supper table, also the altar table in the cathedral and the table upon which unspeakable tortures were carried out.

Three significant elements from the devising process were coming together: group members' reflections on the *Bottleshop* as an environment, the theme of 'the disappeared' arising from the novel *Requiem for a Woman's Soul*, and the significance of the supper table as a site for family tensions. In this coming together, the play's content began to emerge, and the *narrative* of *Not the Last Supper* was not far behind.

The play begins with the arrival, in a small South American town, of a box that has been smuggled out of the nearby prison. It falls into the hands of Anna, the daughter of a local doctor, who sets out to make sense of the contents of the box. In so doing, she seeks the help of the local priest. Anna's request falls on deaf ears, as do the pleas for help of another woman (the mother of Susana), who complains that her daughter has disappeared. The priest remains unmoved and impassive.

Later in the play, Anna's father reveals to his wife that his work at the prison involves him in the torture of political prisoners. The consequence of this revelation is to fracture the family, but the play does more than explore the impact of the arrival of the box on one family, for it exposes the complacency and self-interest of a whole community that has chosen to turn a blind eye to events that are happening on its own doorstep. At the end of the play, powerful images of barbarism culminate in the preparations for a supper to which the doctor has invited a group of his supporters. Once everyone is seated around the table, the doctor proposes 'a toast to the future', after which he looks down at the table, saying, 'The knives! Where are the knives?' The play ends with the sound of knives falling to the ground, then a group of women (led by Anna and Susana's mother) pick up the knives and slowly advance to the table.

We have already seen how *Brecht* created the *Lehrstücke* principally as a means of political education for his actors. In devising *Not the Last Supper*, members of the *Bottleshop Youth Theatre* used their work as a way of coming to an understanding some of the major political issues of the day. Through their devising process they found a language that enabled them to articulate that knowledge and express their feelings about world events that seemed to be careering out of control. The last word is best left to a member of the devising company, who wrote:

'We wanted to make connections with our own experience to help us understand.'

> Theatre can make connections. We wanted to make connections with our own experience to help us understand. We needed to explore the processes at work in a system that allows thousands of people to be kidnapped and tortured by the state because they posed a threat to a political system.
>
> We recognise that we are part of the same world and that those processes will be at work on us as young people in Britain today. We needed to try to understand that, in order to enable us to begin to recognise our own 'cultural chains'.

What is truly remarkable about this piece of work is its maturity, its gravity and its courageous and unflinching attempt to address themes and questions of such magnitude, complexity and broad significance. Much youth theatre work is, understandably enough, designed to explore issues that are of immediate contemporary concern to young people – for example, bullying, teen pregnancy or substance abuse – and, while we would not wish to dismiss this important work, we have included this particular example to illustrate the breathtaking results that can be achieved when young people dare to take on such bold, ambitious and disturbing subject matter.

# Puppets Against Caste, a Save the Children (UK) Theatre for Development Project

Nepal is a small country bordering China to the north and India to the south, west and east. In common with most other Hindu societies, Nepal has a rigid caste system in which every individual is assigned to one of four social groups. Family background is the determining factor: members of the highest caste are referred to as *brahmins* and, in Nepal, individuals in the lowest caste are called *dalits* (or, more commonly in Western parlance, 'untouchables'). Historically, *dalits* have been permitted to do only the most menial of jobs, and they were often isolated and ignored in their own communities. Traditionally, access to educational opportunities has been denied to *dalits*. Despite a declaration by the Nepal government in 1959 that ended caste inequality, the situation for *dalit* girls remains relatively unchanged to this day. During the past fifteen years, a number of NGOs (non-governmental organisations, such as Save the Children and UNESCO) have developed initiatives to address the plight of Nepalese girls in general, and *dalit* girls in particular.

One such initiative took place in 2001 under the auspices of Save the Children (UK). Save the Children is an international organisation dedicated to helping children in need around the world. Their stated aim is to improve the lives of children through education, health care and economic opportunities, and they also seek to promote greater public awareness of the needs and rights of children worldwide.

In 1997, Michael **Etherton**, a long-standing *Theatre for Development* (*TfD*) practitioner, was appointed by Save the Children (UK) as Head of the Regional Office for South and Central Asia, and Regional Education Adviser. Boasting an impressive track record of work in Africa and Asia, he was instrumental in developing the initiative in Nepal.

*Theatre for Development* is a branch of applied theatre that is mostly used in developing countries. It seeks to foster community participation, stimulate discussion, encourage artistic expression, explore alternative options for action and build a collective commitment to social change. Much of *Etherton*'s work at this time was concerned with addressing questions relating to children's rights, as enshrined in the United Nations Convention on the Rights of the Child, adopted by the United Nations in 1989. The Convention spells out the fundamental human rights to which children everywhere are entitled.

Traditionally, NGOs and development agencies concentrated their efforts on needs-based approaches. In such approaches the agency makes an

Applied theatre as agent of social change

assessment of the needs of the marginalised group under consideration, and makes suggestions as to how these particular needs can best be met.

However, once the focus shifted from needs-based approaches to rights-based initiatives, new *TfD* possibilities began to open up. Rights-based approaches began by taking into account the reality of the group's lived experience. It invites the participants to bring stories from their own lives, and provides them with the means to give these experiences and stories dramatic expression. In this form of *TfD*, control of the agenda passes from the agency into the hands of the participants themselves. For children and young people, this is particularly appropriate, since it allows them to speak for themselves, rather than have adults speak on their behalf. This is the approach that was taken in Nepal – the project was set up to enable *dalit* girls to understand their fundamental human rights and to participate more fully in civil society.

The project took place over an eight-day period with a group of eighteen children aged between 12 and 14. There were ten boys and eight girls, half of them *dalits* and half *Brahmin*. Ten adults were also involved (the secondary-school principal, members of the community development committee, youth club leaders, two 'role-model' *dalit* girls who were succeeding in the educational system against all the odds, and two Save the Children staff). In addition to *Etherton* himself, the other members of the team who created Puppets Against Caste were *TfD* facilitators, Rajendra *Tuladhar*, Irauda *Gautam*, Jasmine *Rajbhandhary* and puppeteer Ram *Lal*.

The facilitators began the project by asking the participants to draw pictures collectively. The pictures depicted their ideas of the issues and challenges that face them. From this initial drawing activity, a number of issues were identified: alcoholism, discrimination, caste, the right to education, the problems faced by women while their husbands are working away, and poverty. From the original list, three key issues were selected: alcoholism and quarrels within the family, education rights and the problems faced by the woman while the husband is away. Eventually, these key issues formed the content of three plays, which were presented by the children on the last day of the project. A fourth play devised by the participating adults was also performed. An audience of two hundred villagers watched the plays.

The creative team felt that one of the desirable outcomes of the project should be to find a way to involve the whole community. One of the principal concerns of *TfD* work is to help individuals from disadvantaged communities regain some of their self-esteem, but the team felt that it was equally important for the community to discover more about its collective history, and to make public this shared knowledge of the past. As a way of doing this, the participants were encouraged to collect life stories and memories from the older members of the community.

It is important here to explain the role played by the puppets. They were integrally involved in all elements of the project – from the initial collective drawing exercise, through most aspects of the training programme, to their appearance in the final performances.

Following the collective drawing activity, the puppets were used to encourage the children to take part in the discussions that followed, helping them to explain their drawings. They also functioned as an intermediary, drawing out what it was that the children and the adults were saying to each other. This was one of the principal means by which discussion was opened up on the issue of caste discrimination and on the specific question of why *dalit* girls do not attend school.

It was always intended that discussions with the wider community would follow the performances, and the team were convinced that these discussions could best be facilitated by the children themselves. This conviction, in part, arose from a feeling that the *performances alone* would not bring about change – but wide-ranging community discussions, facilitated by the children around the performances, possibly would. It should be pointed out that some of the children involved in the project had been in school for less than two years, and two of the girls had never been in school. Formerly, *TfD* projects had usually focused just on the creation of a public performance, using improvisation and devising techniques. This added dimension presented a new challenge for the team: how to equip the children to take on the role of facilitators. Clearly, there was an urgent need to incorporate a training programme into the project. Once again, the puppets had a crucial role to play. They modelled the skills of the facilitator, demonstrating how to encourage discussion, communicate and negotiate, question and, where appropriate, challenge.

There are a number of noteworthy aspects of the Puppets Against Caste project that are worth highlighting. Within the space of eight short days the children, who had no previous experience of working in drama or theatre, were able to devise compelling plays on issues that were of real significance to themselves and to their community. That they were able to command the attention of their audience – to communicate with, to delight and to challenge them – constitutes a magnificent achievement. The project successfully brought together adults, young people and children in a genuine community endeavour. They shared stories, ideas, experiences and each other's perspectives, and differences in age, gender, status and caste

Puppets Against Caste project

were subordinate to the requirements of the collective process of creation. But perhaps most important of all was the effect of the community discussions facilitated by the children in the aftermath of the performances – in particular, discussions surrounding the vital topic of caste discrimination and its attendant injustices. The impact of the whole project was particularly profound for the children who, as a result of their experiences, felt a real sense of purpose and a growing sense of value within the village community.

## *Common Wealth*, a community-based theatre project

Darrington is a small town that sits at the foot of the Cascade Mountain Range in Washington State, United States. Primarily it is a logging community, but the area is also home to the Sauk-Suiattle Native American community, who live on a reservation a few kilometres north of Darrington. The population of the town is fewer than 1,200, and approximately 200 live on the reservation. For eight months, beginning in the autumn of 2004, Will *Weigler*, a playwright, director and applied theatre practitioner, worked with the residents of the town and the Sauk-Suiattle community. The outcome of this work was the creation of a play called *Common Wealth* that was performed in the spring of 2005.

The project's origins date back to the spring of 2004 when *Weigler*, part of the **Earthwatch Institute's** Community Fellowship Programme, first travelled to Darrington. The Earthwatch Institute is an international organisation that works to alter public perceptions about environmental sustainability. The aim of the Community Fellowship Programme in Washington State was to field a team of artists who would use artistic expression as a means of reinforcing the importance of environmental conservation.

Theatre as intercultural exchange

Following this first contact with the area, and as a result of a discussion with the county historian, *Weigler* learned that there was a feeling of unease about examining and confronting the past. He began to think about how it might be possible to create a theatrical event that would help revitalise a sense of connection to their past among people in both communities. They would achieve this by relying on their own stories about the best parts of their historic relationships with each other and their mutual connections to the natural environment. The aim of the project was to use theatre as a way of enlivening public discourse and fostering intercultural exchange, and, ultimately, to build a bridge between the communities.

Realising that the success of the venture would depend on his ability to make an authentic, living connection with the people in the area, *Weigler* moved to Darrington. Throughout the autumn of 2004 and the winter of 2005, he attended local events and created opportunities for people to get to know him. He invited elders, adults and children from the town and the reservation to relate stories and share local songs that they felt expressed their sense of identity and defined who they were. *Weigler* used what he learned to try to understand the strengths of each of the communities and the challenges that they faced. The stories and songs were subsequently augmented by interviews, community discussions and book-based historical research.

Using his skills as a playwright, *Weigler* began to shape this material into scenes that might (or might not) find their way into the finished play. He described his approach as 'an inclusive, collaborative process that involved bringing drafts of scenes and lyrics in progress back to community members for validation and further input'. These consultations with the community were a vitally important aspect of the whole project; by continually returning to those who had originally provided the material, the playwright ensured that community members retained a sense of ownership of the play as it was evolving. Gradually, an original theatre script, with music and song, began to take shape. Weaving together the interconnected lives and histories of the people of both communities over the course of 150 years, a number of key figures from the past appeared in *Common Wealth*, each of whom had played a significant part in forming and preserving Darrington and Sauk-Suiattle history.

Following an eight-month devising (and writing) period, the performances took place in the spring of 2005 in a large festival tent in a local park, a neutral space where both the townsfolk and the Native Americans could come together.

In a local press release, *Weigler*, who also produced and directed the play, wrote:

> *The play opens with the salmon beginning their journey down the rivers. It then follows the seasons through spring, summer, autumn, winter, and back to spring again. In each season, the time frame shifts back and forth revealing the lives of the people who have lived in this corner of the world ... Fictional characters are interspersed with portrayals of real people, and the whole show is staged in a dynamic, physical theatre style.*

The making of *Common Wealth* was a genuine community endeavour. Over sixty individuals, children as well as adults, from both communities were involved as cast and crew. Donations from a wide range of local organisations and individuals provided a $7,000 production budget. All four performances were sold out, and it is estimated that 40 per cent of the local population saw the play. The show was performed as a benefit for the local low-income service agency in Darrington.

The theme of connection is clearly perceptible in the play's desire to link the present-day Darrington and Sauk-Suiattle communities, to provide a forum for elders, adults and children to speak to each other and to understand how the seeds of the present are to be found in the past. Unlike the other examples above, *Common Wealth* had a tangible product in the form of a finished playscript. This can be viewed as a legacy of the project – it functions as a kind of collective memory for the community and, for future generations, can serve as a storehouse of creative potential and provide an impetus for further community initiatives. The script of *Common Wealth* (a copy of which is housed in the local library) is an impressive testament to the Darrington project; but community-based theatre events are much more concerned with the nature of the artistic process than with the finished product. Because of the dialogic character of the devising process, these kinds of theatre events have the power to transform social relationships within the community.

A report on the project acknowledged that there was evidence of success in two major areas: community building, and historical and cultural preservation. But specific outcomes are often difficult to quantify. Research suggests that collaborative artistic production helps in the identification of common goals, promotes cooperation and fosters the effective communication of complex ideas.

It is clear that *Weigler's* ability to mobilise local support for the event, and encourage wide community participation, was a key factor in the success of the venture. His relentless drive and inexhaustible commitment to the whole project should not be underestimated, and nor should his versatility. Throughout the eight months, *Weigler* functioned as initiator, chief researcher, facilitator, deviser, playwright, director, producer, publicist and cultural diplomat. And, in the odd idle moment, he even turned his hand to set-building and lighting design. Vital though he was in conceiving and realising *Common Wealth*, *Weigler* would be the first to acknowledge the industry, dedication and creativity of all of those who participated.

Clearly, it is extremely rare to find all of these talents combined in one individual. The best advice to those wishing to embark on similar large-scale, community-based performance projects would be to trust to the collective strengths and wisdom of the community, set up a number of committees with specific responsibilities (for example, fundraising, publicity, community liaison) to manage the logistics, assemble a creative team capable of bringing the project to fruition and be realistic about what the project can legitimately achieve.

## Two Approaches to Devising

Having gained some insight into three contrasting applied theatre projects, we would like to suggest that there are essentially two different approaches to the process of devising.

Goals, achievements, aims

In the first, the group sets out with a strong sense of direction, a well-developed idea of what the content of the play should be – even a sense, perhaps, of what the finished product will look like. Some theatre in education companies, for example, will begin their devising process by formulating and clearly articulating the educational goals that the programme is designed to achieve. Having satisfactorily defined what these goals are, they will then begin to search for the artistic vehicle that will best serve their purposes. This could be a myth or a fairy tale, a historical event, a series of photographs, a newspaper article, or an issue that is of particular concern to the devisers. This approach begins *consciously*, relies heavily on the analytic, research and creative abilities of the group, and culminates in an end product that will, by and large, conform to the initial impulse that originally set the process in motion.

Sensations, feelings, fluidity, surprises

The second approach is much more *intuitive*; it begins with a sensation, or a feeling, or a level of disturbance that is sometimes elusive, or hard to pin down. Because there are no predetermined outcomes, no clear-cut sense of direction and no discernible ends in view (other than, of course, the conviction that something worthwhile and performable will take shape), this way of working often feels tentative, risky and fraught with difficulties – like setting out on a journey through an inhospitable landscape without a map or a compass. But, on the positive side, the very uncertainty can give rise to unanticipated surprises, unexpected detours and exciting new discoveries. This is an approach for the adventurous, the ambitious and the fearless, and, with commitment and determination, it can yield bold, impressive and powerful results.

It is not our intention to suggest that one approach is better than the other. Both have their advantages, and much will depend on the experience of the group. Before moving on to present a set of guidelines designed to help in your own devising work, we think it is probably worth elaborating, in a little more detail, some of the characteristics of the second of the approaches outlined above, since it is perhaps not quite so easy to grasp as the first. We used the term 'intuitive' in connection with this way of working, because a necessary prerequisite is a willingness to allow free rein to the **unconscious**.

We are aware that, for most of the time, we are consciously in control as we go about our everyday business, but there are times when we are surprised by our own behaviour. In these moments, we have all had the experience of thinking, 'Why did I do that?' This is when our unconscious has taken over and we have acted in ways that are 'strange', 'weird' or 'out of character'. 'Slips of the tongue' are often the result of the workings of our unconscious mind. But it is probably through dreams that we are most aware of the unconscious at work. A jumble of images can sometimes produce bizarre and, sometimes disturbing, dream visions that can puzzle us for hours or days.

Jerome *Bruner*'s 'disciplined intuition'

The unconscious plays a vitally important part in the intuitive approach to devising. In describing the first approach, we laid emphasis on the importance of analysis, but it is an oversimplification to characterise that approach as analytic and the second as intuitive. In outlining the characteristics of intuitive thinking, Jerome **Bruner**, the American educationalist, coined the phrase '**a disciplined intuition**'. By this, he means that analysis (the 'discipline') and the unconscious (the 'intuition') must proceed hand in hand in any creative or artistic endeavour. He makes the point that analysis and intuition are not mutually-exclusive opposites, and that it is a mistake to think that intuition is always vague and that analysis is always rigorous. So, in the first approach, analysis may lead the way, but the intuitive aspect should not be neglected. Similarly, in the second, intuition may predominate, but it is an invitation, and a spur, to further exploration, which must always be subject to careful analysis.

*Bruner* is at pains to point out that the analytic and the intuitive cannot be artificially separated, or reduced to a formula to produce a recipe for good work. He stresses that the starting point for all creative work is **practice**, and this is a theme that we will have cause to return to over and over again in the final section of this chapter, which provides a set of practical guidelines for your own devising work.

# The Ten-stage Devising Process

At the beginning of this chapter, we promised to offer a step-by-step process that could be used in devising your own work. Before moving on to the practicalities, we want to reiterate that a devised theatre product is work that has emerged from and been generated by a group of people **working in collaboration**. Being the social art par excellence theatre is always a collective achievement; and this is as true of traditional, text-based work as it is of a devised production.

**Working as an *ensemble***

You will have noticed that in the earlier part of this chapter the idea of *ensemble* came up time and time again. Contained within this notion of *ensemble* is the idea that it is the sum of the parts rather than the individual elements that create the *ensemble* effect. **In performance terms, this means that the end product is dependent upon the whole group working together, rather than on 'star' performances by individuals in the group.** If you look at some of the play texts produced by the *Joint Stock* method, you will see that they are *ensemble* pieces in the sense that there tend not to be major and subsidiary roles: David *Hare's Fanshen* is a particularly good example. In short, it is a very democratic method, which doesn't suit those individuals who like to think of themselves as star players; equally, it is not an approach that is likely to appeal to loners.

**In order to play as an effective *ensemble*, you first have to become one!** Interestingly, many *ensemble* companies rely on a stable group of actors who come to know each other and each other's work very well. This knowledge creates trust and allows a group to work off each other's strengths. It also allows a group to develop a shared vision of the the kind of work they wish to create together.

In order to become an effective devising group, you must begin by becoming a cohesive, functioning unit. This may involve discussion, being playful and working on games, activities and physical exercises together. But it will almost certainly also involve working out some ground rules for your work, prior to beginning the devising process.

**Warm-ups and physical work**

Many groups like to begin every session with some physical work or warm-up activity. Inevitably, much time (especially in the early stages of a devising process) will be spent sitting, talking and thrashing out ideas. Physical work helps to energise the group and can also be a good way to get to know each other and bring the group together. It's often a good idea to have individuals take turns to lead the warm-up session, so that responsibility for the work is shared amongst the group members. Agree before each session who will plan the next session's warm-up, and if it's your responsibility to lead don't let the others off the hook, however tired or 'not in the mood' they might be.

**You may find it useful to keep a list of all the games, activities and exercises that you know as a group**. Some may be from your previous drama experience, while others may stem from childhood or other kinds of group activities you have been involved in. **You should keep adding to this list as you go.**

You may already be familiar with the idea of a contract. Drama teachers often negotiate contracts that contain ground rules for their classes. These ground rules can govern behaviour, provide guidance on how the space is used, suggest appropriate ways of working together, but (most important of all) offer protection to individuals within the class. Try to remember the kinds of ground rules that were laid down in your previous drama classes. How well did the contract work?

It will certainly help you later on in the process if you begin by establishing a contract that guides your work together. Once the ground rules have been established, and agreed on by everyone, they will often take the heat out of any disagreements that might emerge. They will also help to make any conflicts less personal. You should view the rules as belonging to the group, not to individuals. This way, if you need to refer back to them or question whether they are being properly observed, you are doing so on behalf of the group who decided on them in the first place!

**Ground rules**

The following ground rules are taken from a selection used by three devising groups working on *Theatre in Education* projects. Look closely at the list below. **Discuss and then place the ground rules in order of importance.** What kind of situation or problem is each of the ground rules designed to cover or prevent? Which ground rules will be the hardest to keep?

We collectively agree to:

- Be prepared for each session and complete agreed tasks.
- Attend regularly and be punctual.
- Make an active contribution during sessions.
- Compromise, be flexible and listen to others.
- Sustain responsibility for the production in chosen areas.
- Take an appropriate share of responsibilities for the work.
- Offer and receive constructive criticism.
- Be willing to commit to tasks and explore possibilities.
- Make an equal input/take equal responsibility for the devising process.

**Discuss and decide on your own ground rules for this devising project.** This is a chance to voice any concerns, fears, hopes and desires that you have for the project and to listen to others. Try to work out a set of ground rules that will help you all feel safe, committed and focused on the work to come. Keep the ground rules to hand, so that you can return to them when the need arises.

It can sometimes be useful to use a 'neutral chair' or an 'outside eye' in your work. This means that one member of the group observes how the work is progressing. The neutral chair can point out when people have been ignored, or not listened to; when someone's enthusiasm gets out of hand; and when someone seems to be blocking or taking the group off task.

**Decide what kind of 'blocks' get in the way of creative work** – being tired, fed up, having no ideas, being too worried about other things – and think of what strategies you will use to get past these 'blocks', should they get in the way of the work.

Although devised theatre is a collective and democratic form of work, it is still important to make sure that all the roles needed for the production of theatre will be covered. It is worth allocating responsibility for these roles early on in the devising process; then people can be thinking about their responsibilities as the devising develops. Allocating the roles will also avoid discovering too late that some aspect of the production has not been considered. The allocation of roles should reflect the strengths and interests of the group members. Taking responsibility for a role doesn't mean taking over. It means that you are responsible and answerable to the group for that particular aspect of the work. You may well call on others to help you, and part of your responsibility is to listen to, and include, other people's ideas.

# 1 Identify

**Identify the strengths in your group**. First and foremost, these will, of course, be associated with drama – for instance, acting, directing and design. But you should also take into account related strengths like singing, dancing, creative writing, visual art, sewing and technical or computer skills. Because the devised work emerges from the group, it makes sense to try and use as many of the individual strengths and skills as possible.

Be sure to allocate responsibility for:

- design
- technical aspects including lighting, sound and video
- recording the process, keeping the notes from one session to the next
- directing
- writing
- props and costumes.

You may have the freedom to choose your own area of content or you may have been offered a stimulus to work with in the form of a picture, poem or idea. **In either case, you need to identify the theme that you are going to work on. By 'themes', we mean broad areas of human experience – for example, war, childhood or poverty**.

If you are offered a starting point, it will be because it provides a particular example of a broader theme. The stimulus will have been chosen for its potential to open up themes for dramatic enquiry. In the same way, the plays that you have studied provide 'particular' examples of a theme. On the surface, *King Lear* is a story about the lives of a king and his daughters, but it is told in order to reveal broader themes of family ties, kingship, age and madness. The devising process usually begins with the identification of a human theme of some substance, and by developing concrete situations, lives and dilemmas you will be revealing the theme to your audience.

We are going to use a particular example of a starting point, and the themes it generates, in order to illustrate how you move from stimulus to drama. If you have the time, you may want to follow our example as a training exercise. If you have already begun work on your own theme, you can follow the instructions, using your own ideas rather than ours.

*The Migrant Mother 5* by Dorothea Lange, 1936

**Working from a stimulus – an example in practice**

Look at the picture above. It is of a particular woman and three children. The title of the picture is *The Migrant Mother 5*. The photographer, Dorothea Lange, took it in a camp for migrant farm workers in the US during the 1930s. Lange wrote:

> *She told me her age, that she was 32. She said that they had been living on frozen vegetables from the surrounding fields, and birds that the children killed. She had just sold the tyres from her car to buy food...*

We know, then, that this woman is a mother, that she is poor, and that she is alone with three children. These are the particular circumstances of the picture. But as you look carefully at the mother and her three children, try to decide what broader human themes are suggested by the picture. Motherhood? Poverty, perhaps? Begin by making a list of all the broad areas of experience that might be suggested by this picture.

- Which theme interests your group the most?
- Which theme could you commit yourself to exploring further?
- Which theme do you, yourself, care most about?

It is always important to use drama conventions to help you get a feeling for the stimulus, so that you can begin to **explore the material from the inside and discover its potential themes through dramatic exploration**.

The logical starting point for your exploration would be the character of the mother. You could begin by asking questions about the **human experience and the relationships** that are represented in the picture. Use the following ideas to help you explore these questions:

- Physically model the characters. Pay attention to the exact physical position of the figure/s.
- What does the character think at this moment?
- What does the character feel at this moment?

- Are there any clues in the stimulus about the given circumstances?
- What lies *beyond* the picture? What is the landscape? Are there other people present? Are there any significant 'props' that relate to the character? What can you hear, as well as see? Try to physically represent these ideas by adding figures, or props, or **soundscapes**, to the sculpted figures.
- What might have happened immediately after or before the picture was taken?
- Make a series of images that show what might be happening. If you are interested in the results, try to improvise the scenes, focusing your attention on how the central character acts and reacts.

This initial exploration of the particulars (the characters, settings, possible dramatic tensions or conflicts) should help you identify some of the broader themes. **It will be these broader themes that you will seek to develop in devising, rather than the narrow particulars in the stimulus.** This process of selecting the theme is vital – you must **care about** the theme yourself, because if it interests and inspires you, then it stands a good chance of interesting and inspiring others.

**Managing the theme: perspective and focus**

The selection of a theme will tend to suggest a perspective or angle for the devising process. **Themes can be organised under different headings**, which will prompt different approach to the rest of the devising process. In terms of *The Migrant Mother 5*, these headings might include:

- **Sociological theme** (emphasises social roles and relationships), e.g. the role of women in society, or relationships between mothers and children.
- **Cultural theme** (emphasises attitudes, values and morality), e.g. what is our responsibility to the poor, unemployed and homeless?
- **Psychological theme** (emphasises the effects on the individual), e.g. the stresses and strains of motherhood and poverty, or the life of this particular woman.
- **Historical theme** (emphasises the events in a particular period), e.g. the years of the Great Depression in North America and the experiences of those who lived through this time, or how the lived experience of poverty has changed.
- **Artistic theme** (emphasises the role of the artist, and styles and techniques used), e.g. the role of the artist in times of social hardship, or images of women in photography.

Listing themes under these kinds of headings helps you begin to focus your work. A broad theme like 'the experience of poverty' will need to be focused more precisely so that it can be adequately explored during the devising process. You can't cover every possible element of a broad theme. This focusing will also help members of the group find commitment and clarify their own interests in the devising.

Either choose one of *The Migrant Mother 5* themes you listed earlier (or, if you are working with your own stimulus, one of the themes you have identified). Draw a large circle and divide it into segments like the slices of a cake. The circle represents the whole theme; each 'slice' represents a narrower aspect of the theme. If the circle represents the theme we've chosen – the experience of poverty – we might now subdivide the theme into the following segments: causes of poverty, the effects on relationships and family life, society's responsibility to the poor, the relationship between poverty and crime. Fill in the 'slices', or segments, and, through discussion, decide which segment your group will now focus on.

**The devising process is always an exploration of the human experiences suggested by the theme.** Think of it as a journey towards understanding the experiences, through to organising your discoveries and ideas into a communicable form for others. **It usually helps to have a key question that will guide the exploration.** This question will help to remind you that you are not presenting an audience with answers. One question leads to another, and each question raises new possibilities, or prompts further thinking about, and exploration of, the theme.

For our chosen segment, or aspect, of the broad theme of 'poverty', we might select 'the relationship between crime and poverty'. For our key question for the devising process, we might borrow the question *Brecht* posed when writing *Mother Courage*: 'Is it possible to be both poor and good?' This question opens up the possibility of exploring the extent to which 'being honest' and 'doing the right thing' may be easier if you have money than if you and your children are starving. Did the migrant mother have the right to steal the vegetables from the field? Should her children have killed the birds? What else were she and her family driven to do by poverty?

**Choose a key question for your segment. Brainstorm the possibilities in a spider diagram spreading out from the key question.** Our own brainstorming began with the subsidiary questions first raised by our key question.

## Style and genre

Any initial ideas about the style and genre that you may use in the devised performance do not have to follow the selection of theme. In some cases you might be given a style or genre that you must use in your devising, and the theme may be suggested by the style or genre you have been given.

It is possible that when you were offered a free choice in your devising, you were first drawn to a particular style or genre rather than to a theme. You may begin the devising process wanting to produce a piece of hard *realism* in a *representational* style similar to the work of Mike *Leigh*. Alternatively, you may decide to work in a *Brechtian* manner on a *presentational* piece that with direct address to the audience, the use of songs, slides and video inserts in a *non-realist* setting.

Think about what *The Migrant Mother 5* photograph (or your chosen stimulus) suggests in terms of style? Which practitioners or playwrights are associated with these styles?

## Means and meanings

If your devising is led by a choice of genre and/or style, you will need to research its important features. The choice of style and genre will influence the treatment of the theme. Remember that the 'means' (form) and the 'meanings' (interpretations of theme) of a performance are inseparable. The 'means' used will become part of the 'meanings' produced and received in performance. **The 'means' will tend to emphasise certain kinds of 'meanings' rather than others** – for example, a *comedy* will produce different meanings and effects on the audience from those of a *tragedy*, even if the content and theme are the same.

*The Migrant Mother 5* might be a useful resource for exploring a wide range of different styles and genres.

## Key questions to guide the devising

*Naturalism* developed as a 'means' of describing the relationship between environment and character. A devised piece in the genre of *naturalism* might focus on the struggle of the mother to keep her family together, and to protect her children from the appalling poverty and potential violence in her environment. It may emphasise that a woman in this situation has no choice but to suffer the consequences of the circumstances in which she finds herself. The structure of the piece will probably focus on the chain of 'cause and effect' in a series of events presented chronologically.

**If you have chosen a theme under the psychological heading, then a *realist* and *representational* style may be the most suitable 'means' for developing the theme.**

We already know that *Brecht* developed *epic theatre* as a 'means' of describing the relationships between historical circumstance and class relations. A *Brechtian* piece might focus on the mother as a representative of her class rather than as an individual. The migrant mother represents the dispossessed who roamed America looking for work in the 1930s as the result of the failure of capitalism and the greed of banks. Her encounters, probably presented in the form of episodes (involving rich farmers and other migrant workers), would not necessarily lead the audience to empathise with her, but would encourage them to try to understand the underlying causes of her poverty and decide who is really to blame. The episodic structure will not tell the complete story; rather, it will juxtapose scenes linked by what *Brecht* called 'knots'. Members of the audience will have to make the links for themselves in order to arrive at the meaning.

**If you have chosen a theme under the sociological or historical headings, then *Brecht*'s style of political and *presentational* theatre may be the most suitable 'means' for developing the theme.**

It is also possible to imagine the mother as the main character in a Greek tragedy, with a chorus that comments on her plight. The chorus may move between the *representational* (questioning the mother and the moral choices and actions she takes) and the *presentational* (reminding the audience of their moral responsibility for the poor, or urging them not to make the same mistakes).

**If you have chosen a theme under the cultural heading, then using the style, or adapting the genre, of Greek *tragedy* may be the most suitable 'means' for developing the theme.**

Consider your chosen theme, or the theme you chose in relation to *The Migrant Mother 5*, and its thematic heading. **Which styles and genres do you think will be the most appropriate 'means' for exploring the chosen theme?** Discuss the possibilities.

As the work develops, your ideas about style and genre may well change. You may also need to use a wider range of 'means' during the devising and rehearsal process, but it helps to have some idea about which 'means' you think will prove to be the most appropriate to the 'meanings' that you are interested in exploring.

## Audience

It is important to consider who your audience will be. It may be that you will have very little control over choosing an audience for your work. The audience may have to be your classmates or another drama/theatre class. It may also include a teacher or examiner, who will grade your work. Even so, **thinking about your target audience is an**

Vision

important part of the devising process. What is likely to interest them?

Finally, treat yourself to a daydream! **What vision do you have of the performance itself?** You have a lot of work to do, but it may help you through the hard times if you have a clear sense of what you are trying to achieve in your ideal vision. Imagine how it might all come together in the 'perfect' performance at the end of the devising process.

# 2 Research

Identify sources of information

One of the reasons it is important to feel committed to your chosen theme is because you will need to totally immerse yourself in research. Devising carries the responsibility of seeking out the truth. This means ensuring that the information you use is based on accurate sources. The audience will expect that you have done your homework thoroughly, and that your performance will be based on more than your hunches.

In your text-based work, you are probably already familiar with the idea that the period of the play, and the context in which it was written, need to be researched. You may have researched other plays by the same author or of the same period. You may also have read critical commentaries written about the play.

In devised work you have to go further. The research process is similar to the one that the playwright will undertake before producing a play text. It is important to ensure that the material you use in your devised piece is solidly based on fact, as well as on your own creative impulses. Characters, settings, plot – even the language and gestures used – should be true to the real-life experiences that you are dramatising. In terms of our poverty theme, we owe it to both our audience and those who suffer poverty in their lives to give a true account in our devising.

What kinds of information will you be seeking? Research in theatre draws on a wide range of factual, artistic and literary sources. We will suggest what these sources might be, but before you start there are some important considerations.

**Begin by making a list of all the possible sources of information that you think it would be useful to consult. Then divide the research work between the members of the group.**

Use a critical eye

Always **be alert to bias and distorted information**, particularly when you look at statistics or official reports. Always pose these questions: Who has produced this information? For whom? For what purpose?

- **Does the information given tell the whole story**, or is it carefully selected to give a particular perspective?
- **Look for alternative accounts.** Never rely on a single source for your information – check it out against other sources.
- **Pay particular attention to sources that seem to contradict each other**, or which give very different accounts of the same experience or information. These may well provide you with useful tensions and conflicts of opinion to develop later.
- **Be careful to ensure that your research includes different 'voices'.** How is poverty differently experienced by the old or young? How do men

or women, minority ethnic groups, or the disabled, experience poverty? Again you may find contrasts between the accounts given by different voices, which may be usefully developed later.

- **Challenge your own values and attitudes**. Closely examine your own beliefs and try to think how you learned them. If you want to challenge your audience to take a fresh look at a theme such as poverty, you need to challenge yourself first!

Sources:
WWW and CD-ROM

We live in a world in which there is more information available than ever before. This information is increasingly visual as well as textual, which is very useful when devising theatre. Electronic encyclopedias and the internet are always useful starting points. While we were writing this chapter, we needed to find the Dorothea Lange photograph. You might like to follow our journey for yourself.

1 We opened a search engine and typed in *'The Migrant Mother* 5 Dorothea Lange', because we already knew the title of the picture and the name of the photographer. The results gave us a list which included 'http://www.fotomuseum.ch/ENG/9804SHOW1/Pix_01_Zoom.html', which is a perfect copy of the original migrant mother photograph held in the Library of Congress in America. We copied the picture and pasted it straight into this chapter.

2 We also checked this site – http://www.loc.gov/rr/print/128_ migm.html – and found out more about the series of pictures Lange took of the migrant mother. This is where we found the contextual information about the picture that we gave you.

3 Next we decided to look and see what kind of styles and genres of theatre were popular in America at the time that the photo was taken. We went to a very useful site which gives links to other theatre-related sites: 'http://www.brookes.ac.uk/VL/theatre/images.htm'.

4 There we found a link to an American site which was recommended, and were taken to 'http://rs6.loc.gov/ammem/amtitle.new.html'.

5 In the list of topics, we found a reference to the Federal Theatre Project 1935–39 and, as this was the right period, we clicked the link to discover more and were taken to 'http://memory.loc.gov/ammem/fedtp/ fthome.html', which contained pages of interesting information and images.

6 Finally, we decided to look for social history information about the Great Depression and used the 'Go' menu on our browser to go back to the same site we used in Step 3, and were taken to 'http://memory.loc.gov/ ammem/afctshtml/tshome.html', which again had all the information we might need.

Choose keywords carefully when you do an internet search. If we had just typed in 'poverty', we would have received thousands of sites. Narrow down the search for what you are really looking for: 'poverty, children, pictures', for instance, or 'poverty, statistics, England'.

Media and bibliographic research

**Always keep an eye on the newspapers (which are also available electronically) and TV schedules.** You may well find articles and documentaries that are relevant to your chosen theme. While researching, we came across an article in the *Guardian* titled 'Britain Lagging on Child

Health'. In this article we discovered that low birthweights in England (an indication of poverty) are on a par with Albania, and that by another poverty indicator we have a worse rate of infant mortality than Slovenia. An expert is quoted as saying:

> We should ask ourselves why we are now below countries like Slovenia . . . and why the gap has widened between the health of rich children and poor over the last 20 years.

But remember to think about where this information is coming from – whose opinion does it represent? The *Guardian* is a liberal newspaper that represents the left of centre in politics. You may well read a different story in a right-wing newspaper, such as the *Daily Telegraph*.

Finding books on the subject you're interested in may be a little more difficult. However, many university library catalogues are available online and many of them allow visitors to search for book titles they hold. You could also search a site that sells books, like www.amazon.co.uk, to find book titles which you could then borrow from the library.

**Another important approach is to consider how other artists have dealt with the same theme**. Artworks, photographs, sculptures, prose, poetry and plays all offer different kinds of information.

Artworks attempt to get inside the human dimensions of the experience – how it might feel, the struggles, the hopes and the lost dreams. They may well provoke strong feelings in you, like the feelings that you will want your audience to experience. The artist also demonstrates how the broad experience and theme might be turned into something particular – a story with characters, a symbol or an image.

*The Migrant Mother 5* is a particular image of the misery that affected thousands of people living during the Great Depression. Dorothea Lange selected this particular image to stand for that suffering. Look at the picture again. Why do you think it has become one of the most reproduced photographs in the world?

Two of the most poignant pieces of writing that we found when researching *The Migrant Mother 5* were a poem by W.B. *Yeats*, the Irish poet and playwright, and an extract from John *Steinbeck*'s novel *The Grapes of Wrath*. *Steinbeck* wrote:

> And the dispossessed, the migrants, flowed into California, two hundred and fifty thousand, and three hundred thousand . . . and new waves were on the way, new waves of the dispossessed and homeless, hardened, intent and dangerous. . .
>
> And a homeless hungry man, driving the roads with his wife beside him and his thin children in the back seat, could look at the fallow fields which might produce food but not profit, and that man could know how a fallow field is a sin and the unused land a crime against the thin children. . .
>
> . . .and in the South he saw the golden oranges hanging on the trees, the little golden oranges on the dark green trees; and guards with shotguns patrolling the lines so a man might not pick an orange for a thin child, oranges to be dumped if the price was low.

**Artworks**

In his poem 'He wishes for the cloths of heaven', *Yeats* wrote:

> *Had I the heaven's embroidered cloths,*
> *Enwrought with golden and silver light,*
> *The blue and the dim and the dark cloths*
> *Of night and light and the half-light,*
> *I would spread the cloths under your feet:*
> *But I, being poor, have only my dreams;*
> *I have spread my dreams under your feet;*
> *Tread softly because you tread on my dreams.*

In your search for artworks, don't neglect the popular arts and entertainment. The migrant mother would almost certainly have heard popular songs of the time; songs like 'Brother Can You Spare a Dime' or 'The Good Ship Lollipop'. Popular songs, sayings, jokes and other forms of entertainment provide a good source of information about the attitudes and experiences of people living at the time. They can also be usefully worked into the devised piece.

**Workshop: turning ideas into actions**

As theatre artists, the theme that you have chosen will find its final form as drama and theatre. Always remember that **the medium of drama is action**; and that all of your ideas will need to be **tested in action**. The research stage can become individual and solitary. But, like other parts of the process, the research stage can be **active**, as ideas emerging out of the research are tested **in practice**. Although you are only trying out ideas at this stage, you may well find that these ideas ultimately find their way into the finished piece, or lead you on to new lines of enquiry and new developments.

Whenever the group finds itself stuck in passive mode, always remember the old lady in an anecdote told by the French novelist, André *Gide*. When her younger nieces accused her of being illogical, she claimed to have no idea what they were talking about. When they explained to her what logic was, she replied contemptuously, 'What rubbish! **How can I tell what I think till I see what I say?**' You might consider writing this slogan on a large piece of chart paper and placing it on the wall of your rehearsal room. It will serve as a constant reminder to **try ideas out in practice, rather than endlessly talking about them**.

For example, if you find a statistic or statement, surprising, shocking or disturbing, transpose it into drama – as an image, or as a character who lives the experience, or as scenes which represent given circumstances of the context or situation. Ask yourselves: How is this information actually experienced by people in their lives?

Take the *Guardian* article that we referred to earlier. It claimed that the gap between the poorest and richest children has widened over the last twenty years. Use your drama/theatre skills to find out what this actually means. How do children themselves experience the gap? How are we affected by the consequences of this widening gap?

Make two sets of *still-images* that can be linked together (one for a child born in poverty and one for an economically privileged child), with the following captions as a means of beginning to see how these questions might be explored in drama:

- The baby is born.
- The infant child sees his mother cry.
- The first day of school.

- The family treat.
- The two children meet in the park.

Fictional sources of information can be explored actively. The writer can describe a situation, but it takes drama to bring it to life. Try out the following suggestions for a role-play sequence based on the *Steinbeck* extract:

### Task 5: Bringing it to life

- Make tableaux to represent each of the three paragraphs in the extract. You might use these titles:
  a) dispossessed, homeless, hard, intent and dangerous
  b) a fallow field is a sin and the unused land a crime against the children
  c) so a man might not pick an orange for a thin child.

- Divide the space into two, with a 'fence' dividing the orchard from the road on which the migrants travel. Half the group improvises the guards patrolling the orchard. The rest of the group should help them to find the physical actions by asking questions like: How would they behave? How do they do their jobs? What do they talk about as they work? Why are they necessary? Why was the decision taken to employ them? What are their instructions? Have they ever fired their guns in anger?

- A second group represents a migrant family with hungry children standing on the other side of the fence. Improvise what happens when they ask the guards for oranges for their children.

- Let the family continue to put pressure on the guards. What would happen if one of the children made a run for the orchard? As you improvise this scene, decide on the moment the child makes a sudden dash for the oranges during the improvisation – how will the migrants and the guards react? Don't plan these reactions. Just see what happens. You might want to recreate the improvisation in slow motion, so that the split-second reactions of the other characters can be closely observed.

## 3 Focus

What is important to you and your audience?

Research is likely to continue throughout the devising process. As you develop your work, your interest will lead you to new sources. But you will eventually reach a point where you are confident that you have collected together enough research material to begin the process of deciding what you will keep and what you will discard. It's important to keep things manageable. Keep reminding yourself of the aspect of the theme that the group committed to. Always bear in mind the key question that guides you, and the needs of the target audience. Use these anchors to help you decide what to keep and what to throw away.

When all of the research materials are gathered together, ask the group members to present their most important research findings to the rest of the group. Set out the material in a large space and take some time to look closely at it. Group members should use this time to absorb the material.

When everyone is familiar with the material, you should begin trying to group research items together under appropriate headings. These might include:

- ideas for characters and roles
- ideas for situations and possible dilemmas
- facts and figures
- background information on the theme.

Now take two large sheets of paper and write down the following questions (one on each sheet):

- What is the importance of this theme **for us**?
- Why should our **target audience** care about this theme?

You may want to discuss your responses to these questions, but some individuals may want to push their own viewpoint. You could try having a 'silent argument' (the group has 20 minutes of silence to argue **in writing**). If, for example, someone writes down, 'Because the theme is important to everyone', someone else might add, 'Who says so, because it wouldn't be to X?', etc.

Finally, use a sheet of paper to brainstorm your responses to the question:

- What MUST we see and hear?

This is an important list, which represents your personal stake, or interest, in the devising. In effect, you are saying that these images and these voices must be part of the final piece. When this list is complete, it will give you a clearer sense of the developing piece.

**Focus on the social function**

**Does this process of focusing, and getting a 'feel' for the material you have selected, begin to suggest the social function of your devised piece?** Themes can be focused for an audience in a number of different ways.

In Chapter 2 we noted that performances can have a broad range of social functions – from the didactic, with its emphasis on educating the audience and teaching a particular lesson, through to the stirring up of public debate on issues, through to the purely entertaining and pleasurable.

**What effect do you want to achieve?** There can be a mix of social functions – *Brecht* reminds us that a performance that seeks to bring about a change in the viewpoint of audience members is unlikely to be effective unless it is also entertaining. Similarly, a piece which is lively and pleasurable for the audience can also be a biting social commentary and seek to challenge the audience's attitudes. A good example would be Dario Fo's political *farce, Accidental Death of an Anarchist*.

**You will also need to focus on the styles and genres that you think will be useful to you**, and decide on whether the play is *presentational* or *representational* theatre, or a mixture (but be alert to the possibility of jarring clashes that may confuse your audience).

**Focus on the artistic intention**

Now consider the relationship between the performance and the audience. Will it tend towards a *representational* style that seeks to represent a powerful fictional world for the audience, or will it tend towards a *presentational* style that presents characters and situations to the audience directly? Again, it's possible to use a mix of the two styles, subject to the note of caution sounded above.

Don't forget **the strengths in the group**. If you have singers, choreographers, musicians, videographers, make sure that you consider using these skills in your piece.

**Modify your vision**

Finally, you should go back and look at the vision you described in Stage 1. Modify and redraft the vision on the basis of the work and decisions taken since.

# 4 Develop

## The bits not the whole

Your vision is of the final performance, but you must begin with the individual parts that will make up that performance. **It's usually wise not to start with the plot.** You may choose to begin by creating the characters, situations and scenes that may find their way into the final product. Starting with the plot and then dramatising it can have the effect of closing your mind to the exploration and discovery of dramatic ideas. Drama is not the same as storytelling.

Think of this stage of the process as being like making a collage, or montage. Before you can begin, you have to gather together all the scraps of material or images that you might want to use. Then you experiment with them, looking for shapes, patterns and textures that might work together to create the effect you want. Only then do you begin to stitch or paste the bits together to make your collage or montage.

## Characters

As we have suggested, **characters are living examples of the chosen theme.** The migrant mother was a real woman who lived through the experience of poverty. Character figures at the heart of this stage of the process. Sometimes the idea for a character, or characters, will be suggested by the stimulus, like the migrant mother. But, if you are building characters from scratch:

- Remember that a dramatic theme is always rooted in human experience. How can the theme be embodied in a character? Identify the kind of person, or people, that you want to base your characters on.
- Are there any useful ideas for character from your research?
- Use the work on given circumstances in Chapters 3 and 8 to flesh out your characters.
- Use the 'Circle of Life' exercise below to develop character.
- Keep a record of the characters' given circumstances and circle of life. Refer back to this information, particularly if you are creating realist characters, who are expected to behave in ways that are consistent with their given circumstances.

## The 'Circle-of-Life exercise

Divide a large sheet of paper into five sections, with a circle in the centre of the page, where the name and age of a character are written. The surrounding paper is then divided into four sections that will represent areas of that character's life and the people they interact with. These sections are labelled 'Home', 'Family', 'Play', and 'Day'. The heading '**Home**' indicates where the central character normally lives, while '**Family**' indicates any immediate or extended family and may include estranged family members we might otherwise expect to find at home. '**Play**' indicates any type of social life and '**Day**' indicates the character's workplace, if appropriate, or otherwise encompasses their daily routine – for example, if they are too young to work or are unemployed.

Now brainstorm ideas about the character and enter these into the appropriate section. Divide into four groups, take a different section each and create a short dialogue between the central character and one other character selected from the chosen section of the diagram.

## Scenes and settings

This should have given you ideas for scenes and settings that might be usefully developed. But keep your mind open to new possibilities. Remember that what you are trying to do is to identify events, times and places involving your characters, which will illuminate the theme and your key question.

Remember that our key question for the migrant mother work was: Is it possible to be poor and good? Two scenes suggest themselves. In the first, a farmer who has plenty of food threatens to throw the mother off his land if he catches the children stealing vegetables again. How will she react? In the second scene, a moneylender offers the woman cash for her wedding ring. Will she sell it, and what will she tell her husband?

**Use separate pieces of paper or card to brainstorm other possibilities for scenes.** Write down the essential information for each scene under these headings:

- the ACT (what happens)
- the SETTING (where and when it happens)
- the AGENTS (who makes it happen)
- the AGENCY (how the action is carried out)
- the PURPOSE (why it happens).

Once you have a selection to choose from, discuss the dramatic possibilities of each. Select two or three scenes to work on, keep the others for future reference and make a note of your choices. Improvise the scenes, but designate a group member to be an observer, who should note:

- moments of real tension
- significant gestures or movements
- that which is 'true' and not 'true' to the given circumstances
- 'what if?' developments to the scene.

The observer might also 'hot-seat' the actors in character about their motives, feelings and reactions to what is going on.

If appropriate, the improvisations can be interspersed with other dramatic conventions like **sculpting, thought-tracking, alter ego, shape-shifting** and **flashbacks**. The purpose here is to step back from the realism of improvisation and work on finding depth in the characterisation. **Using these conventions can also avoid endless discussions**. If there are differences of opinion in the group, try to find ways for these differences to be tried out or dramatically explained rather than argued about ('How can I tell what I think till I see what I say?').

### Scenarios and scripting

The previous exercise may have given you anchor scenes – not the whole plot, but some key moments that may provide the basis for a plot summary. Do you have ideas about the ordering of these anchor scenes? Remember that you can move backwards and forwards in time, using the most appropriate scene as your starting point.

**Try placing your anchor scenes in order.** How close together are these scenes in terms of time and setting? Arrange the scenes to show the gaps in between the anchor scenes. Do the gaps need filling in with additional scenes? Use additional sheets of paper with your ideas on to fill in these gaps.

Remember that the links between the anchor scenes don't have to be more scenes in a *realist* style. You could use songs, *monologues*, images, dance, storytelling or video as links, which would emphasise the theme, mood or context rather than the storyline. If your anchor scenes are *representational*, then these kinds of link can add a *presentational* dimension to your work.

The anchor scenes are crucial to establishing your piece. You may want to script the anchor scenes to help fix them for the actors.

Use any notes made during the improvisation and during discussion to **prepare a draft script for the anchor scenes** at least. Refer back to the advice we gave on language and character in Chapter 8.

You should now have a series of anchor scenes and some ideas about links between them. The next stage of the work moves from exploration to the important question of how you communicate your intentions to an audience. The anchor scenes and links need to be carefully rehearsed so that characters have a chance to develop and the playing of the scenes can be shaped and focused towards performance.

**Rehearsal strategies**

Throughout this book there are examples of rehearsal strategies that you might use at this stage:

- Use the textual analysis questionnaire in Chapter 8 to identify the **wants, will, moral stance, physical appearance** and **summary adjectives** for characters.
- Use the exercises for playing **objectives**, **strategies** and **obstacles** in Chapter 3.
- Identify the units in each scene using the exercises in Chapter 8.
- Use the *Brechtian* rehearsal techniques described in Chapter 4.
- Identify and fix a rehearsal schedule based on the example given in Chapter 6.

# 5 Building the Performance Text

**The *montage* of attractions**

The performance text includes everything that will be seen, heard and experienced in the performance itself. It is a weaving together of all of the elements of performance into a coherent and well-crafted text. The performance text is not the same as the plot or the *mise en scène*, although it includes both. Because it includes all aspects of the performance, the performance text is a composition like a play text, musical score or novel, and it is constructed according to artistic principles and intentions. In the previous section you began the process of gathering and developing the materials for the performance text, rather like collecting together the scraps of material for a collage or *montage*. It is in the creation of the performance text that these pieces will be woven together in preparation for performance.

'*Montage*' is a term that was first used to describe the principles of *non-realist* composition. An important feature is the juxtaposition of different elements (in a collage, the scraps of material) to create a pattern or shape that **brings together the diverse parts into a new, meaningful whole** – the performance text.

You can use *montage* after the first stages of rehearsal, which (we have suggested) are principally used to develop the characters and scenes. **Now the earlier work must be pieced together so that it becomes a complex, layered, textured and coherent whole for the audience.**

It is the director's responsibility to orchestrate the building of the *montage*. All of the theatrical elements needed to create a performance text need to be combined to create a clear, fluid, stylistically coherent whole designed to hold the attention of the audience.

The aim of the montage is to attract the audience's attention – their senses, intelligence and feeling. *Meyerhold* realised that effective moments in the theatre are not always driven by the twists and turns of the plot. Changes in light, a dramatic use of space, intelligent design, a striking physical image, a dramatic change of tempo or mood, colours and textures in costume and setting – all of these may provide strong moments of 'attraction' for an audience. But they must be planned for!

**Decide where the moments of attraction are going to be in your performance text** and how they will be achieved. What will the audience need to see and hear in order for each moment of attraction to be effective?

How will the sign system of theatre be used? In Chapter 10 we identify the multiple systems that theatre uses to communicate its meanings to an audience, and in the Performance Analysis Questionnaire we list the sign systems. Whoever is taking directorial responsibility for your work should familiarise themselves with these sections and the ideas within them.

**Is the whole performance based on one style of acting, or is there a mix of styles?** In other words, do you find that you have a mix of *representational* scenes, in which the characters are totally locked in their world, and *presentational* scenes, in which the actors are directly showing the audience what happens, or happened? If so, it is vitally important that the audience finds the mix acceptable. It is often the case that the design, the lighting or the creative use of space will help your audience understand that the different acting styles are being used for a clear purpose.

**Consider how the 'look of the play' can be established and enhanced through design.** What settings and props will be used, and how will an appropriate theme be established through the choice of colours, textures and patterns? The design should offer a commentary on the dramatic action rather than merely provide a realistic landscape. Your ideas about the relationship between the theme that you have chosen and the particulars of your plot and characters (the overall intention) can be expressed through your choices concerning the design of the performance.

**How will technical effects be used?** Remember that lighting, sound, video images and other technical devices can be used to offer an interpretation or commentary on the plot and characters. These effects are rarely used to faithfully recreate realistic settings. Lighting and sound can be used to describe moods, feelings and portents of what will happen next, as well as to signal night/day and the sounds of birds! But, once again, remember that if you are using technical effects to express ideas and the theme, you need to be sure that the audience will accept your combination of *realist* and *non-realist* elements in performance. If some of the *realist* scenes are lit using strong colours to express the mood but others are not, the audience will question why this is and look for the logic of your choices – why are certain scenes lit in this way and others not? Aim for consistency.

The relationship between the world of the performance and the audience's world is partly established through your choice between a *representational* style which creates a distance between the performance and the audience, and a *presentational* style which seeks to involve the audience more directly. **But it is the use of space that does most to establish the actor–audience relationship** (think of *Grotowski*'s experiments outlined earlier in this chapter). Remember that the use of space, the delineation of the areas reserved for the performers and the spectators, creates a different actor–audience relationship.

**Make a ground plan for your performance, showing the division between audience and performance space.** Carefully locate the scenes in the performance space. It is important to consider the following:

- How physically close to the audience do you want your actors to be?
- Will the audience stay in a fixed position, or might they be asked to move, as in a **promenade** performance?
- How will the audience be arranged? End-on? In the round? On three sides? In some other configuration?
- How can exits and entrances be managed? Might the actors move through the audience, for instance?
- Will there be a consistent use of space for particular locations? Will family scenes always be played in one place and street scenes in another? How will the logic of your choice be made clear to an audience?
- How can the stage architecture and lighting be used to clearly guide the audience's awareness of how space is being used in your performance – use of levels, staging, colour codes, etc.?

Finally, remember that the use of space will need to be signalled to the audience. How might these signals be used creatively – to lead the audience in, or to blur the boundaries between audience and performance space, for instance?

**Rhythm and pace**

The rhythm and pace of individual scenes should have been established during the rehearsal process. The use of linking material between anchor scenes should also have produced a rhythm and pace in the structure of your piece. Now the **overall** rhythm and pace needs to be established.

**Make a list of the scenes.** Connect this list to a second list of the attractions. Are they evenly distributed, or **does a rhythm need establishing that builds up and down from the core attractions of the piece?**

You might like to draw a flow diagram based on the example given in the Performance Analysis Questionnaire. Divide the performance up into units and make a simple flow chart to show the rhythms and pace of the performance – the bottom of the chart to represent 'slow/quiet', and the top to show 'fast/loud'.

# 6 Refocus

**Fixing the overall intention**

By now you will have spent a good deal of your time as a group developing your ideas. If you have done this with an open mind, it is possible that you may have drifted from your original intentions and focus. **When devising, it is possible to become so absorbed in the drama work that you forget that the audience will be coming to this material much as you did in the beginning.** Now might be a good time to check to see what it was that you first decided was important to communicate to an audience.

Now the *montage* is nearing completion, you might want to go back and reconsider the choices you made in Stages 1 and 3 ('Identify' and 'Focus'). Are they still relevant? Do they now need to be modified? Does the montage need further development to bring it back into line with your intentions?

# 7 First Sharing

It is not uncommon in a devising process for the work to become obscure to anyone who has not been a part of the devising. You have been working intensely in your group, and you will probably have had hours and hours of discussion about your ideas and the emerging montage. While the *montage* may make perfect sense to you, it may not communicate as clearly to an audience.

**Critical feedback**

That is why it is important at this stage to share all or some of the work under performance conditions. It's a good idea to choose your audience carefully. If you have a particular target audience (children, for instance), it would make sense to ensure that they are represented. You need an audience that can offer honest, critical feedback on your work. It doesn't help to just invite your friends, because they may say what they think you want to hear.

**Check intentions and effects**

Before the first sharing, list the questions that you want to put to your audience. Don't prepare the audience by giving a full account of your intentions; only tell them as much as they need to know in order to follow the performance. When the performance is finished, give the audience a few moments to share their responses with each other before putting your questions to them. Someone should take responsibility for recording everything the audience offers.

If the audience is critical of your work, if the gap between your intention and the effect it produces on your audience is wider than you had hoped for or if they didn't understand some aspects, **try hard not to be defensive.** Resist the temptation to argue and justify your work. And don't blame the audience. Instead, **listen and record the comments for later analysis.**

As *Brecht* constantly reminded his actors, 'the proof of the pudding is in the eating'. Think of yourself as makers of the pudding, and your audience as the ones who taste it. **If you find that it isn't working in performance, you need to go back and fix it.**

# 8 Rework

**Mind the gap!**

It's important to leave some rehearsal time between the first sharing and the assessed performance. There are several considerations:

- How can the gap between your intentions and the effects experienced by your trial audience be bridged?
- How can the performance be made tighter and more coherent?
- What additional work needs to be done to clarify the intentions?
- What changes of rhythm and pace need to be made (did the audience comment on the work being a 'little slow' or talk about 'too much happening')?

**It will help to go through the Performance Analysis Questionnaire and apply it to your own work.** The questionnaire sets out what a critical member of the audience might be looking for in your performance. Using the questionnaire will help you to see the work from a critical perspective, as well as from your own angle as deviser/performer.

# 9 Perform

**Where does it begin and end?**

The performance begins at different times for the actors and for the spectators. For the actors it begins in the period of preparation in the run-up to the show's opening. During this pre-performance period, you/the actor needs to prepare both physically and mentally: focusing on your character and the relationships with others in the piece, going through speeches or difficult moments and reminding yourselves of your intentions. Familiar warm-ups and exercises can help to prepare the body and voice, and to calm nerves.

For the spectator, the performance usually begins when the lights go down. But first contact with the piece may begin before that. Posters, flyers and other marketing strategies are an important aspect of setting the expectations of your audience. The lobby, foyer or entrance way can be dressed to create the right mood for the performance. Important pre-performance information can be included in programme notes and publicity images. You might even consider starting your performance in the lobby by orchestrating encounters between characters and audience, or through song and visual images as the audience arrives.

**How will you measure your success?**

**Before the first performance, establish the criteria you will use to judge the success of your work.** Having identified the effects you want to achieve, what do you anticipate from your audience at the various key moments of the play: laughter, or silence, or pity? If so, what signs from the audience will you be looking out for? Laughter is fairly obvious, but in quieter moments how will you distinguish between, for example, engagement and lack of interest in the audience?

**Between idea and act: were your intentions realised?**

Poet and playwright T.S. *Eliot* reminds us of the gap that often exists in creative work between the idea and the execution of the idea. He said that 'Between the idea and the act falls the shadow.' In the case of devising, the 'shadow' can take many forms. Return to your vision in Stage 3. What aspects of this vision were you able to realise? How would you account for any differences between the vision and the actual performance?

# 10 Evaluate

**The process**

- Collect.
- Summarise.
- Select and emphasise.
- Headings and paragraphs.

We have encouraged you to keep an archive of all of your research materials, together with a record of developments during the devising process. This material now serves as the basis for your written account of the process you have been through.

In writing your evaluation, you will need to describe how you moved from Stage 1, in which you first identified your theme, styles and genres, and target audience. You will then need to describe how you focused the theme and identified the social and artistic intentions. The middle section of the evaluation will describe the working methods you used to devise a piece of theatre that helped you realise your intentions. Finally, you will need to make an assessment of the effectiveness of your performance.

A good way to begin is by making summary notes of what happened at each stage in the process, under the appropriate headings. These notes can then form the basis for your written evaluation. The way in which you now assemble your notes will depend on the assessment focus for the evaluation.

There are ten stages in this devising process. It is not a simple question of giving equal weight to all ten stages. If you are asked to comment on the research that you did, or to describe your intentions, or to comment on your role as an actor, you will give more weight to certain stages of the devising process than others.

When you know the focus for the evaluation, go through your summary notes and highlight the relevant information. You can then decide which stages should be given emphasis and add any additional information that you might have overlooked or which needs to be amplified.

Draft a series of headings. These headings might be based on the headings used for the stages of the devising process or they might simply reflect the focus of the evaluation.

Remember that you should keep description – telling the story of your devising process – to a minimum. **You should ensure that your account contains both analysis and evaluation**.

Once you are confident that your headings provide a solid structure for the evaluation, assemble the relevant notes into paragraphs and prepare your first draft.

## Devising Process Questionnaire

This Devising Process Questionnaire is designed to provide you with a set of key questions to guide your work in each of the ten stages of the devising process. The questions suggest what you might look for and do in each stage, and they also provide a checklist of what you should have done in order to complete the stage successfully. Remember that any devising process is much messier and more complicated than our simple framework suggests. While we believe that all of these stages form part of an effective devising process, it is important to remember that some stages may well overlap, or even that the order of the stages may be different. The questions included here are intended to provide you with a framework, but not all of them may turn out to be relevant to your particular project.

| | |
|---|---|
| **1 Identify** | Have you agreed and established the ground rules for your work together?<br>Have you decided on the 'blocks' that might get in your way as you devise together?<br>What strategies will you use when you get 'blocked'?<br>Have you allocated production roles and responsibilities?<br><br>What stimulates you about the 'stimulus'? What questions and curiosities does it raise?<br>Would using drama conventions like *still-images*, thought-tracking and hot-seating help you to make an initial exploration?<br>What human themes and experiences are touched on by the stimulus?<br>Have you narrowed down a theme so that it is focused clearly?<br>Have you agreed on a key question that will guide your devising decisions?<br><br>Does the stimulus suggest a particular performance style or genre?<br>Does the chosen theme and/or key question suggest a style or genre?<br>Have you identified the mix of genres and styles that you will use?<br><br>Who will be your audience?<br>Who would be most interested in this theme?<br>How much experience will the audience have of the styles and genres you are thinking of using – will they recognise the conventions?<br>What effect are you hoping to have on the audience: what do you want them to think and feel?<br>How inclusive do you want to be – how broad an age and cultural background do you want to appeal to?<br>Why would this audience be interested in your product?<br>How will the audience's interests and expectations be remembered and included in the shaping of the work?<br><br>Have you dreamt a vision of the performance that excites and encourages you? |
| **2 Research** | Which sources of information are you going to use?<br>Who is going to collect the information?<br>Have you included a balance of views and voices?<br>Are you making full use of the WWW?<br>Can you find inspiration in other artworks that relate to the stimulus or theme?<br>Have you used a full range of drama conventions and workshop strategies to explore the research materials?<br>Have you identified and researched the work of other practitioners associated with the styles and genres of your own work? |

| | |
|---|---|
| **3 Focus** | What will you choose to keep from your research and what will you now put on one side?<br>What is the logic behind your selection?<br>Have you considered the audience in making this selection?<br>What should the social function of the performance be: should it educate and/or should it entertain?<br>Will the performance include both *realist* and *non-realist* styles?<br>Will it include *presentational* and *representational* theatre?<br>What is the logic of your choices? |
| **4 Collect and Develop** | Will you use any of the characters from the stimulus or research?<br>What are their given circumstances?<br>What other characters might you develop to bring the themes alive?<br>Which methods and styles of characterisation will you use (e.g. *Stanislavskian*, *Brechtian*, *physical*)?<br>Have you explored characters practically by using improvisation and other conventions?<br><br>What are the key scenes that will best illustrate and develop your chosen theme and key question?<br>Have you established your framework of anchor scenes?<br>What is important about each of these scenes from the point of view of the chosen theme?<br>How will the anchor scenes be sequenced?<br>Is this sequence: cause and effect (*narrative*); episodic; thematic development?<br>What links between the anchor scenes are needed and what form will these links take: scenes, songs, storytelling, video clips or other images?<br><br>Which rehearsal strategies will best suit your work?<br>Will the ideas and methods of particular practitioners be used?<br><br>Is too much discussion and too little action beginning to bog you down?<br>Have you used drama conventions rather than discussion to resolve differences of opinion or problems with character development and structure? |
| **5 Building the Performance Test** | What will be the key 'attractions' in the performance?<br>How will these 'attractions' be realised?<br>How will space, design, light, contrasts of style and other theatrical elements be used to add power to your scenes?<br><br>Who will take responsibility for coordinating and directing the performance text?<br>Which type of director will best suit the performers and the need to ensure that the performance text is effective and completed on time?<br><br>What conventions will you need to establish so that the audience will understand the mix of styles and genres in the work?<br><br>How can the 'look', or the 'world', of the play be established through design?<br>How can technical effects be used to create 'attractions', moods and atmosphere for the audience?<br>How will the space be divided between performance and audience?<br><br>Have you established the rhythm and pace of the performance?<br>How will the audience's attention be held for the duration of the performance?<br>Is the balance between highly active scenes and more moody and quiet scenes right?<br>Is there enough variation in pace, mood and style to keep an audience engaged or might there be flat spots that need attention?<br>Have you checked that the logic of the performance will be clear for an audience in terms of everything that happens, that is seen and that is heard during the performance? |

| | |
|---|---|
| **6 Refocus I** | How far have you drifted from your original intentions identified in Stages 1 and 3? Do you need to modify, or correct, the performance text so that the relationship with your chosen theme and key question is restrengthened? Do you need to modify, or correct, your original intentions in the light of the new discoveries made during the devising process? Will the relationship between your intentions and the performance text be clear for an audience? |
| **7 First sharing** | Which audience will offer you the most useful feedback? How will this feedback be collected? Does the characterisation work? Does the plot, if there is one, seem credible and logical? Is the progression and rhythm of the performance effective? Are the setting and other design features clear enough for the audience? Are the performers' skills good enough – is further-targeted rehearsal needed? What range of effects does the audience describe? |
| **8 Refocus II** | What is the 'gap' between your intentions and the effects the audience experienced? How can this 'gap' be closed? Does the performance text need editing or adding to? What additional work will need to be done on characters, scenes and technical effects? What changes in rhythm and pace might need to be further explored and tested before the next performance? |
| **9 Performing** | How will the performance space be prepared? Where, when and how does the performance begin and end for both performers and audience? What criteria will you use to judge the success and effectiveness of your performance? Have you realised the initial vision that you had for the performance? Were some of your initial ideas unrealisable? Were some ideas technically too difficult to realise? Were there problems with people, time, space, technical support? Might the performance have worked better with a different audience in a different space? Would you want to repeat or continue to develop the ideas and themes in your performance? |
| **10 Evaluation and Writing up** | Have you collected together all the evidence from the first nine stages? Have you summarised the main points from each stage? Which stages will you emphasise in your evaluation? Have you drafted a series of headings which will keep you focused on the main point of the evaluation? Does your evaluation make sense to an 'outsider'? Someone who has not been intimately involved in the process? Which text types will you use in your evaluation? Is the balance between recounting, explaining, persuading and discussing ideas appropriate? |

# 10 Reading the Signs of Performance

## Evaluating Performance

In earlier chapters, we have taken you through the processes of staging a play text and devising your own dramatic sequences and performances. In both cases the process began with the initial ideas and vision that you started the process of production with and then worked through all the stages of production to the final stage of performing for an audience. This process assumed that you, yourself, were part of the production; that you were involved in all the decision-taking. From this perspective, your task was to transform your ideas about the play or devised work into a product – the finished piece of work. Your evaluation of the final product – the performance itself – was based on the extent to which you were able to successfully and clearly translate your ideas and vision into an experience for the audience – an experience which was effectively communicated through theatre.

The evaluation of your own performance, the product of the rehearsal/devising processes, rests on the extent to which the performance was able to 'speak for itself'. In other words, the extent to which all your intentions and ideas were successfully translated into what the audience actually *saw*, *heard* and *experienced* during the performance. In this sense, however hard and long you may have worked, it is the performance itself that counts. The audience were not there during rehearsals, they did not hear all the discussions or know about all the choices you made. The only part of the work that they share with you is the product of all your work – the performance.

Although one of the unique characteristics of theatre, as opposed to sculpture or poetry, is that the artists (performers) and the audience both need to be present in the same place and time, it is not usual for the artists to speak to the audience beyond the performance itself. It is not usual, for instance, for artists to hold a discussion with the audience where they explain all their intentions or tell the audience what they *should* have seen, heard or experienced. Either the performance speaks for itself or it doesn't!

Your evaluation of a performance by another group places you firmly in the position of the audience. In a sense, what you have to do is to reverse the process of evaluation. Instead of starting with the initial ideas and tracking them through to the performance, you now need to start with the effect of the performance itself and try to track backwards to discover what kinds of ideas, visions, rehearsal processes and interpretations might have been made and used during the invisible processes of production that led to the performance.

In evaluating your own work, you move from *production* to *reception* – how the work is received by an audience. **In evaluating the work of others, you move from *reception* – the effect the performance had on you – to *production* – how this effect might have been constructed during the process of production.** What you see and hear and experience during the performance forms the basis for this detective work.

## Task 1: What the critics say

The most commonly available form of performance evaluation or criticism is to be found in the **reviews** of recent performances in the media. These *reviews* are based on how a performance was experienced by a specialist member of the audience - a critic. The critic's job is to give an accurate account of the performance - what was seen and heard - and to offer an opinion on the performance based on their prior experiences and knowledge.

1 Find two or more *reviews* of the same performance in the newspapers.

2 Make copies of the *reviews*.

3 Use different colour highlighters to mark: information that appears in both *reviews*; any differences of opinion or differences in factual information.

- Do the *reviews* include any additional information about the actors or director, other performances of the same play or the venue?

- What are the reviewers' opinions, or judgements, based on? What aspects or moments of the performance do the reviewers use as examples to justify their opinion of the play (these might include acting, directing, design or interpretation of a play text).

If possible, try to see the performance yourself. Is your experience different? In what ways? Can you understand the performance from the reviewer's point of view? Write your own *review* based on what was the same or different in your experience of the performance.

# The Role and Power of the Critic

You may have had the experience of having a 'critic in the house': someone who was sent to review your performance for a local newspaper for instance. Often, a great deal of attention will be paid to the critic – to where they sit, how they seem to be responding during the performance, anything they might have said before they left. **The critic is powerful!**

You as the critic

Part of this power is based on the critic publishing a *review* that may well influence whether people come to see the show or not. But, part of this power is also based on the *knowledge* that a critic has and the *value* that is placed on the critic's taste and preferences. In many ways your own study of theatre has begun to give you the same power. You no longer experience a performance in quite the same way as you once did. You know something of the history and traditions of theatre. You know what to look for in a performance. You have some sense of the difference between 'good' and 'bad' acting. You may have studied and worked with the play that you are going to see and that will have given you certain expectations. You have devised and rehearsed and produced your own work. You know what it is like to be a performer in performance.

For these reasons, you are becoming a 'special' member of the audience too. You will experience the performance differently from other members of the audience who have not studied theatre, or taken the same interest as you have. **Your experience of the performance will be coloured by your prior learning and experiences in drama.**

# Between Intention and Effect

Different individuals are affected differently

The prior experience and learning that we bring to a performance goes beyond our specialised knowledge of theatre and drama. All forms of theatre offer a commentary on the human condition. So, **who you are and what you have already learnt about the human condition will also influence your experience of the performance** and the effect that the performance has on you. Each of us experiences the world in different ways – we have our own stories, our own journeys, our own bodies and our own place in the world. For this reason, no two members of the audience will have quite the same human experience of the performance.

The differences between individual responses to a performance might be based on:

- gender
- age or generation
- physical appearance (or how we imagine others see us!)
- culture
- ethnicity
- class or social and economic status
- beliefs
- political views
- key life experiences similar to those represented in the performance
- prior knowledge and experience of performance.

---

### Task 2: Different audiences, different effects

Go back to the scene from *The Crucible* that was used in Chapter 3.

Imagine and describe the different ways that this scene might be experienced by:

- a middle-aged woman whose husband has had an affair with a younger woman;

- a middle-aged man who has strong religious beliefs but who also feels trapped in a 'loveless' marriage;

- a young girl who has been harassed at work by a male employer;

- a young man or woman whose parents divorced because of infidelity.

---

Because there will be so many different responses to a performance, it is important to be aware that what you experience during a performance and what you have to say about a particular performance will depend on where you are coming from as a person. **Any *review* of a performance is, therefore, a mixture of the *subjective* – your particular and personal response – and the *objective* – factual information based on what was actually seen and heard by everyone who was there.**

Test out your opinions in discussion

The trick is to establish a relationship between the two: to understand and explain your own response by referring to what it was that you actually saw and heard during the performance, and in the same way to look and listen carefully during a performance and try to work out what the playwright, performers and directors *intend* you to experience. It is also important to try and talk with other members of the audience after a show. How are their responses the same or different from your own? What did they see and hear? If they saw and heard things differently from you, try to understand why that might be – *where* are *they* coming from?

**Producers have intentions that affect the audience**

**It is always important for you to bear in mind, both as a performer and as a critic, that** *intention* **and** *effect* **are not the same.** Sometimes performers and directors will speak of their work having a certain kind of effect for an audience. But for the reasons we have given, they cannot know what effect the work will have on the individuals who make up an audience. They can only have the intention that the work should effect the audience in a certain way. One important job for the critic is to make this distinction between intention and effect. The director may intend a certain line to be funny, for instance, but the effect may be to make you cringe! You can work out the intention, to be funny, and then work out why it failed to have that effect on you.

There is, if you like, a triangular relationship between:

What was seen and heard?

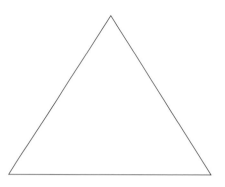

What was intended?                    What was the effect on you?

**Task 3: Testing the subjective within the objective**

Try and remember a performance that you were part of, or watched with others in your class, which either didn't 'work' (the audience didn't respond as you expected) or which aroused very different responses from your classmates in the audience. Use the triangle above to try to work out why.

- Begin with the facts – the words spoken, the number of actors, the set, the images created on stage.

- Then consider what your intentions were, or what you imagine the intentions might have been in a performance you watched.

- Then consider the responses of the audience, or the effect on you.

Because there will be so many different subjective responses to a performance, it is very difficult to write or talk about a particular performance in general terms, without making the false assumption that everyone was affected by what they saw and heard in the same way. In the past, it was often assumed that what was seen and heard on stage would be the same for everyone. People still sometimes talk about the play's *effect* as if there could only be one effect.

# A Short History of Signs and Meanings

*Semiotics*: a science of signs and their meanings

There have been many attempts to try and produce a stable, reliable and completely objective method for analysing performances. Many of these attempts belong to a form of literary criticism known as **semiotics**. The first *semiotician* was Ferdinand **de Saussure** who proposed *semiotics* to be **the science of the life of signs in a society**. *Saussure*'s theory was that meanings in society are tied to the signs that are commonly used or understood. This is how we communicate – the words that we use in speech and writing are 'signs' for certain meanings. Words as speech and as writing are the most obvious signs. Languages are made up of sounds and symbols (writing) that have particular meanings, or significance, for those who use the language. A sign, in language, is made of two elements, the word itself, which is known as a *signifier*, and the idea or concept that it is a signpost for, which is known as the *signified*.

$$\text{Sign} = \frac{\textit{Signifier} \text{ (the word 'cat' for instance)}}{\textit{Signified} \text{ (the idea, or image, of a cat)}}$$

Language is a system based on the difference between signs used

In *Saussure*'s theory, a language is always a system based on *difference*. In other words, different sounds and written words mean different things. If a language user makes the sign 'dog' in speech or writing it is intended to *mean* something different from 'cat'. People communicate by building up signs to indicate what they mean by establishing 'differences' between their intended meaning and other possible meanings – a *fat* cat establishes that the cat is different from a *thin* cat! But I might respond by asking, 'What do you mean 'fat?' or, 'How fat?' I am asking for more signs to help me understand what is *different*, or particular, about this cat.

*Saussure* made a distinction between language as a system and language as speech. Language as a system refers to the conventions of language use – the grammar if you like – of sentence construction, paragraphs etc. Language as speech refers to how the language is actually used to communicate meanings. What *Saussure* hoped was that it would be possible to develop a science of meanings in which we could accurately and certainly know what is meant by looking at how the system of signs is used and the relationship between *signifiers* and *signifieds*.

This assumes that everyone means the same thing when they use a common *signifier* such as 'cat'. But of course, life isn't like that! We may have quite different pictures in our heads even when we hear a simple *signifier* like 'cat'. The idea that comes into your head will depend, as we have suggested, on where you are coming from! If you have a dread fear of cats, you will have a different idea from someone who loves them!

People don't always *mean* what they *say*

And of course, people don't always mean what they say! In Chapter 7, there is an exercise based on the opening dialogue of *A Doll's House*, on page 128. In that exercise we discover that there are different ways of understanding the meaning of the words spoken by the characters. This is particularly important. Artists often play with the relationship between the *signifier* (what is seen or heard) and the *signified* (what is actually meant) in order to be ironic, or to create ambiguity and uncertainty, or to create *sub-text*, or to disturb and challenge the audience. A famous example of a playwright using words to mean the opposite of their usual meaning is to be found in the closing lines of *Waiting for Godot* by Samuel *Beckett*:

Vladimir:       Well? Shall we go?
Estragon:       Yes, Let's go.
                (*They do not move*)

CURTAIN

## Theatre is Physical, Visual and Aural

Signs, of course, come in all shapes and sizes. *Saussure* was concerned with language but we use all kinds of other visual and gestural signs in our daily lives. Traffic lights, for example: the red light is the *signifier* which signifies 'stop!' In some cultures, shaking hands is a *signifier* that signifies a welcome or introduction. As we will find out in this chapter, **theatre also communicates its meanings through sign systems based on difference**. If the stage is bathed in blood-red light it will mean something different from if it is lit by natural light or by purple light.

*Saussure*'s mistake was to try and isolate language from the other systems that might be used together with language. A simple *signifier* in language like 'hello' becomes more complicated when it combines with the physical signs of body language! Rather than simply meaning a welcome it might be a threat, an insult or a put-down according to the body language of the speaker. Unlike written forms of communication, theatre uses a combination of physical, visual and aural (what is heard) signs as well as the signs of spoken language.

The full meaning of the dialogue in a play may come from the other physical and visual signs at work. In other words, in order to understand the dialogue it has to be put into the *context* of the actor's physical signs and any other visual or aural signs that are being made. In theatre then, as in life, we respond to the ways in which the physical, visual and aural signs *combine* to make a meaning for us.

*Signs in theatre are physical, visual and aural*

---

### Task 4: How close is drama to living?

The drama in education practitioner, Dorothy Heathcote, claims that:

'Actual living and theatre, which is the depiction of living conditions, both use the same network of signs as their medium of communication; namely the human being signalling across space, in immediate time, to and with others, each reading and signalling simultaneously within the action of each passing moment...'

- From your experience of both actual living, and drama and theatre, how true would you say this claim is?

- Is 'signing' in life the same as 'signing' in the theatre?

- If there are differences what are they?

- Is this claim more true of certain styles of theatre than others?

---

*Iconic signs are pictures of the real thing.*
*Symbolic signs are symbols of the real thing*

The physical, visual and aural signs used in theatre tend to fall into two categories, the **iconic** and the **symbolic**. In an *iconic* sign the *signifier* is literally a 'picture' of the idea, or concept, that is *signified*. For example, the male and female signs on toilet doors are *iconic* signs. The sign is made up of a literal picture (*signifier*) which directly represents 'man' or 'woman' (the *signified* meaning). In most forms of Western theatre, the actor is often an *iconic* sign because the actor literally 'signifies' a character: one human being (the actor) *signifies* another (the character). In the same way, set designs in a *realist* style are often *iconic* – the real furniture that is used *signifies* the imaginary room or place that is represented in the play. If a director and designer decide to use real, useable objects on stage to represent the playwright's directions then they are using *iconic*, or literal signs. *Brecht*, for instance, insisted that the tools, clothing and other props should look as if they had really been used in life.

In a *symbolic* sign there is no obvious or direct connection between the appearance or sound of the *signifier* and the idea or concept that is *signified*. Spoken language is made up of *symbolic* signs – there is, usually, no obvious connection between the meaning and the sound, or look, of a word. A change in lighting that *signifies* a change in mood in the play rather than a change of time or place is a *symbolic signifier*. The music in *melodrama* that accompanies the entry of the villain is a *symbolic signifier*. The use of a rose to *signify* love or romance is also a *symbolic signifier*.

**Signs only communicate among people who share the same understanding of their meanings.** The signs used to communicate in English are only understood by those who speak the language. Both *iconic* and *symbolic* signs often depend on a shared cultural understanding of the sign and its intended meaning. A rose *signifying* love is recognisable in those cultures that make an association between the *signifier* 'rose' and the *signified* 'romantic love'. The same is true in a performance – the signs that are used will only make sense to an audience if they are familiar from either their own cultural experience or from their knowledge and understanding of the Western theatre tradition. If I go to watch *Kathakali* and *Kabuki* performances, I often fail to understand many of the signs used because I don't have enough knowledge or experience to understand them.

## All Signs in Theatre have a Symbolic Intention

Modern performances mix *iconic* and *symbolic* signs

It is useful to make a distinction between the *iconic* and *symbolic* signs used in performance. *Iconic* signs are often used to create a *realist* style and *symbolic* signs are often used to create a *non-realist* style.

It is also likely that you will find a mix of *iconic* and *symbolic* signs in a modern performance which reflects the trend in theatre towards mixing *realist* and *non-realist* styles. Part of *Brecht's Verfremdungseffekt*, for instance, was achieved by combining *iconic* signs for tools and other useable props with *symbolic* signs such as distorted or oversized furniture and doorways or two-dimensional sets in order to emphasise the true social relationships between the characters.

Every sign in performance has a *symbolic* intention and a *symbolic* effect

But always remember that every sign in performance has a *symbolic* intention and a *symbolic* effect. It is part of the magic of theatre that every sign, whether it is *iconic* or *symbolic* in form, is taken to have a *symbolic* value; is taken to mean something important. Anything that is seen, heard or experienced in the performance is taken to have a special value far in excess of its value outside the performance. Imagine an empty stage with a single chair on it. The chair may be an *iconic* sign (a real useable chair) but its value will be *symbolic*. In other words, we don't just think 'Oh, there's a chair'. We will look and wonder what it represents – absence perhaps, or loneliness, or a particular period of history, or the character of the chair's owner or maker.

Imagine that your own bedroom, or the mantelpiece in your front room, was a 'set' for a performance. How would each of the objects be 'read' by an audience? What clues of character would they find in the selection and arrangement of the objects? What *symbolic* value would be given to that old teddy, the bits and pieces on your shelves? Once your bedroom, or front room, is treated as if it was the setting for a character, then everything that is placed in it becomes a potential symbol of that character in the same way that *Ibsen's* long list of furniture and other objects in the opening stage directions for *A Doll's House* were intended to be read as symbols of Nora and Torvald's character and class (see page 231).

The Italian *semiotician* Umberto *Eco* made a distinction between 'involuntary' and 'intended' signs. Involuntary signs are natural signs over which we have no control – smoke signifying fire, clouds signifying stormy weather – but also sneezing, or other 'involuntary' human signs that are not intended to have meaning for others. Intended signs are made with the intention of communicating a meaning. **It is an important principle in theatre that every sign, everything that is seen and heard as part of the performance, is intentional.** There is no such thing as an involuntary use of sign in performance – everything that is seen and heard will be 'read' by the audience as an intentional sign which is meaningful.

We once saw a production of *Macbeth* in which some electrical work needed doing on stage during the first interval. When the audience returned there was a ladder and screwdriver on the set that had not been there before. Our first reaction was not to dismiss these objects as 'unintentional' but instead to think about their *symbolism* in the play – is the ladder a *symbol* of the Macbeth's ambition? Does the screwdriver *symbolise* Macbeth's and Lady Macbeth's intentions towards Duncan? In other words, we assumed these objects had been **deliberately placed with meaningful intentions.** This is why in your own work you need to be very disciplined in your signing – everything, even the accidents, will be read as being intended by you.

---

### Task 5: Space of intentionality exercise

In most performance traditions, the performance space is divided in some way so that some section of the space is reserved as a 'stage' or the place in which the fiction will be created. The audience understands that whatever happens in this space is *intended* to be read as part of the performance rather than as part of the everyday world. In the Chinese tradition, the performers would draw a circle with chalk to mark the performance space, or what we shall call the '*space of intentionality*'.

1 Draw a chalk circle on the floor and agree with the rest of the group that anything that is placed or done inside the circle is to be read as an intentional *signifier* which will *signify* something to the audience.

2 Collect together the following objects and place them outside the chalk circle:

- wooden chair
- religious book
- candle
- flower
- baby's shoe
- family photo torn in two.

3   Take it in turns to place the chair in the circle. How do you read the chair each time it is placed? If the chair is turned on its side in the middle, what does it suggest? If the chair is turned away from the audience, what does it suggest? The game is to play with the 'suggestiveness' of the sign in the space. Play with the group's imagination by choosing unusual, or 'loaded' ways of placing the chair in the space and see what the audience make of it.

4   Now begin to add in the other objects, one at a time. What is suggested when you begin to combine the signs - when you place the religious book next to, or further away from, the overturned chair, for instance? Gradually introduce more and more of the objects and notice how much we tend to read in to their arrangement in the *space of intentionality*. You may find that you are developing a whole story and imagined world around the objects in the circle! What role does the 'space' itself play? As you move objects around and change the distance between the objects, how much of what is suggested is a result of the use of the space? The space between; the space surrounding; the space between the audience and the chalk circle? In the *space of intentionality*, the space marked out in chalk becomes one of the 'objects' that you work with.

5   Finally, you can add an actor in whatever position you choose. You may also use a single spotlight with a choice of blue, red or gold gels - how can you light the objects to make further suggestions to the audience?

## The Sign Systems of Theatre

*Semiotics* has had a considerable influence on literary criticism. The idea is that we can understand what a text such as a novel or poem 'means' by analysing the 'signs' used in the text. We can refer to the 'words on the page' and what they *signify* as a way of explaining our responses to the text and discussing the writer's intentions. But of course a performance is not like a book or a poem.

The differences between analysing performance and literature

The words on the page are printed and permanent. We can close the book, put it under the pillow and go to sleep. When we wake, the words are still in the same place. A performance, however, leaves no permanent record that can be referred back to or looked at over and over again. **The morning after a performance there is nothing left save our memories of what we saw and heard the night before.** Even if we go to the next performance of the same play, it will no longer be the same as the first. This difference helps to explain why the records of performances, in the Western theatre tradition, tend to be in the form of literature – the play text. The play text is a permanent record of what was said and the stage directions, but the text of the performance is more than the words and the directions – it is literally everything that is seen and heard during the performance itself.

Theatre uses multiple sign systems simultaneously

In literature, there is only one sign system at work – language. In theatre, there are not only many different sign systems used (language, physical gesture, costume, lighting, etc.) but they are also used simultaneously. The French semiotician Roland *Barthes* in his *Critical Essays* described the performance text as a 'cybernetic machine' rather than as a passive text like a novel:

*What is theatre? A sort of cybernetic machine. When not working, this machine is hidden behind a curtain; but as soon as it is revealed it begins to transmit a certain number of messages in your direction. These messages are distinctive in that they are simultaneous and yet have different rhythms. At every point in a performance you are receiving (at the same second) six or seven items of information (from the scenery, the costuming, the lighting, the position of the actors, their gestures, their mode of playing, etc.), but some of these items remain fixed (this is true of scenery) while others change (speech and gestures) . . . We have therefore a density of signs.*

So, there are two further problems when it comes to making a *semiotic* analysis of a performance. First, there are **multiple sign systems at work** and as we have seen, our response in performance may be the result of several signs (physical, visual and aural) combining together. Second, we cannot sequence, or order, the signs in performance like we can when we read a sentence in a book. You can't read all the words on a page simultaneously – you have to read the words (the signs) in the order that they appear on the page. But in performance, when several signs may occur in the same moment, different members of the audience will 'read' the signs in a different order. Was the sense of gloom generated from the lighting? From the change in costume? From the change in the tone of the actor's voice? Which did I notice first? Peter *Brook* suggests that:

*What's the difference between a poor play and a good one? I think there's a very simple way of comparing them. A play in performance is a series of impressions; little dabs, one after another, fragments of information or feeling in a sequence, which stirs the audience's perceptions. A good play sends many such messages, often several at a time, often crowding, jostling, overlapping one another . . . in a poor play the impressions are well spaced out, they lope along in single file, and in the gaps the heart can sleep while the mind wanders to the day's annoyances and thoughts of dinner.*

### Task 6: Identifying the sign systems of theatre

What are the different sign systems used in theatre?

1 Make a list using slips of paper with one system on each slip. Use the sign systems mentioned in the *Barthes* quotation and add any that you think are missing. Indicate whether the system is visual, physical or aural (including language). When you are sure you have thought of every sign system that might be used, lay the slips in front of you.

2 Try and place the systems in a vertical order so that the most important, or significant, sign system is at the top and the least at the bottom. It is the process that is important here – what decisions did you take? What issues did the process raise? How can you decide whether lighting is more significant than make-up for instance?

3 Is there another way of grouping the systems? *Technical* (sound and lighting effects)?; *Physical* (movement and gesture, for instance)? Or in terms of the *elements* of *drama* (space, time, physical action)?

## Performance Text: the Sum Total of the Signs Used

**Signs in theatre are always actions**

In literature, the text refers to all the signs of language which taken together make a complete or coherent intended message. **In performance the *text* refers to all the signs of 'action' that take place during the performance** – every sign in theatre is an action in the sense that it makes something happen. Theatre's mode of language is speech, which is language as it is used in the world, language in action. When a character says that he is leaving, he does, and even if he doesn't it's still an action! Lighting changes are signs of action too – dimming the lights makes evening happen, makes the mood change. Even objects are actions in performance, in the sense that every object on the stage changes the stage, making it a different place.

When we produce theatre we often ask the question 'How do we make that happen?' meaning how do we turn the idea we have into something that happens (takes place) on stage. In the same way, the critic asks: 'How did they make that happen?' meaning what signs were used to make a response happen – what took place, or is taking place, that effects the critic in this way?

**Text = *textus* + *texere***

The origin of the word 'text' is derived from the Latin words *textus* meaning tissue and *texere* meaning weaving. The text in both literature and performance refers to the 'tissue' or 'fabric' of signs/actions, which together make a complete or coherent message. It also refers to the 'weave' – how the actions/signs are woven together into one piece; how all the signs in the performance are organised. This is the job of the critic and the reviewer – to try and see and comment on the effectiveness of the weave; to see how and why the actions that make up the performance are being used and interlinked. To see, for instance, the relationships between costume, lighting, colour theming, gesture, acting style and the theme or interpretation of the play.

**Kowzan's sign systems of theatre**

## The Framework of Sign Systems

The first detailed attempt to analyse the sign systems used in performance was made by the Czech, Tadeuz **Kowzan**, in the 1940s. Although *Kowzan's* original ideas about the sign systems of theatre are now outdated, his work still has an influence on how we understand the use of signs in a performance and the relationship between the signs of a performance and the sense that an audience makes of it.

*Kowzan* identified 13 sign systems in use. Of these, the first eight belong to the actor and the remaining five to the set and technical effects. *Kowzan* also distinguished between 'auditive signs' (what we hear) and 'visual signs' (what we see). Finally he identified which signs happen in space and time (the actor's gesture, for instance) which signs happen in time only (sound effects, for instance) and which happen in space only (props, for instance).

*Kowzan* believed that his framework would allow scenes or moments in the performance to be *deconstructed*; that the weave of the text could be unpicked into its separate strands. The framework provides a series of headings for critics to use in understanding how the performance has been made – what was actually seen and heard.

*Kowzan's* 13 sign systems:

| | | | | | | |
|---|---|---|---|---|---|---|
| 1 WORD<br>2 TONE | SPOKEN TEXT | ACTOR | | AUDITIVE SIGNS | TIME | AUDITIVE SIGNS – ACTOR |
| 3 MIME<br>4 GESTURE<br>5 MOVEMENT | EXPRESSION OF THE BODY | | VISUAL SIGNS | | **SPACE** and TIME | VISUAL SIGNS – ACTOR |
| 6 MAKE-UP<br>7 HAIRSTYLE<br>8 COSTUME | ACTOR'S EXTERNAL APPEARANCE | | | | **SPACE** | VISUAL SIGNS – ACTOR |
| 9 PROPS<br>10 DECOR | APPEARANCE OF THE THE STAGE | OUTSIDE THE ACTOR | | | **SPACE** and TIME | VISUAL SIGNS – OUTSIDE THE ACTOR |
| 11 LIGHTING<br>12 MUSIC<br>13 SOUND EFFECTS | INARTICULATE SOUNDS | | | AUDITIVE SIGNS | TIME | AUDITIVE SIGNS – OUTSIDE THE ACTOR |

### Task 7: Using *Kowzan's* system

You will need to have access to a video extract of a live performance, filmed as theatre, for this task. Ideally, the production should be traditional and based on a *realist* play, or a classical play staged in a *realist* style – *Shakespeare*, *Ibsen*, *Chekhov* or *Miller*, for instance. For the purposes of this exercise you do not need to know the whole story of the play or to see the whole play first.

1 Choose a one-minute extract to study.

2 Divide the sign systems up among the members of your group so that you have no more than three each to concentrate on.

3 Watch the extract very closely and only make a note of the signs that belong to your chosen group of sign systems.

4 After the extract has finished complete your notes and try to work out what was intended by these signs. If there were differences in the quality of the costumes worn by different characters what might this indicate? If there were differences in the way that characters moved, what might this be showing about the characters?

5 Now go around the group and listen to each other's findings. You may be surprised by how much information has been gathered and by the different interpretations in the group.

6 Finally, discuss the overall effect of the signs used in your chosen extract. Is there a theme running through them? What is the effect of the weave, as a whole?

Despite the detail of *Kowzan's* framework, it still does not take into account all of the sign systems used in performance today, and it also assumes a certain tradition in theatre which is less popular today than it was in *Kowzan's* time.

*Kowzan*'s list works best with *realist* performances

The framework works best when it is applied to productions of *realist* plays, in the *Stanislavskian* directing tradition, which are intended to be a faithful interpretation of a playwright's work. In this tradition, all the sign systems tend to be used to support the written text; to tell the playwright's story. In other words, the signs are organised to reinforce the words and directions in the play text. In this tradition of *realism*, the playwright is often very specific about the signs required. The job of the production team (actors, directors, designers and technical staff) is to follow the playwright's instructions.

Here, for instance, is the opening stage direction from *Ibsen's A Doll's House*:

*A comfortably and tastefully, but not expensively furnished room. Backstage right a door leads to the hall; backstage left, another door to Helmer's study. Between these two doors stands a piano. In the middle of the left-hand wall is a door, with a window downstage of it. Near the window, a round table with armchairs and a small sofa. In the right-hand wall, slightly upstage, is a door; downstage of this, against the same wall, a stove lined with porcelain tiles, with a couple of armchairs and a rocking chair in front of it. Between the stove and the side door is a small table. Engravings on the wall. A what-not with china and other bric-a-brac; a small bookcase with leather bound books. A carpet on the floor; a fire in the stove. A winter day.*

*(A bell rings in the hall outside, and a moment later the door is heard to open. NORA comes into the room, humming happily. She is in outdoor clothes, and is carrying an armful of parcels)*

### Task 8:  Working with *Kowzan*'s framework

1   Use *Kowzan*'s list to identify the 'signs' that will be needed to realise *Ibsen*'s stage directions. You can also add any other 'signs' that you think will assist. You may want to think of additional sound effects, lighting, etc.

2   Make a diagram, or drawing, of the stage with all that *Ibsen* required in exactly the positions he describes.

3   Use the diagram and your list as the basis for the following role-play with two partners. Decide on your roles and get started!

A = the director
B = the designer
C = the actor cast as Nora

The director is holding a design meeting with the designer; they have to decide on the set, props and costumes that will be used. The designer is anxious to get enough detail from the director to be able to start looking for the props and building the set. The designer might want to discuss, for instance, how to design the room so that it is comfortable and tasteful but not expensively furnished. The actor is also taking part in the discussion because they think that talking about the details of Nora's apartment will help them to understand the character. The actor is is also thinking about how their costume will look and hoping that the director will give them some advice on how to play their entrance – how will their first 'signs' be chosen to complement the work of the designer?

In the role-play you may have discovered that there was not much room for the director, designer and actor to talk about their own ideas and vision for the play; to make their own creative choices. The meeting is about how to understand and then realise *Ibsen*'s own intentions for the play in performance. Playwrights in the *realist* tradition aim to offer a 'slice of life' or the 'illusion of reality'. One level of the evaluation of a *realist* play is to do with the extent to which the performance is 'real', 'lifelike' or 'true to life'.

Signs can be used to create the illusion of reality

**In this form of theatre, the sign systems are often organised by the director to tell the story and to create a consistent and realistic setting for it.** The first eight of *Kowzan*'s systems, those that belong to the actor, are used to create a 'living example' of the playwright's character. The actor playing Nora will use all eight to play a 'convincing' performance of *Ibsen*'s imaginary character. The remaining five systems are all then used to create the 'living illusion' of Nora and her husband Helmer's apartment.

The review of a conventional production of *A Doll's House* will tend to dwell on the play text in performance, rather than on the performance text. A judgement may be made about how effectively the sign systems have been used and woven together to present the play text: whether characters were 'convincing', whether the set is 'true' to the period and the social setting of the play.

## New Directions in Twentieth-Century Theatre

Although many performances are still based on this conventional model of theatre, there were important changes in theatre during the twentieth century which often make the task of analysing a performance more complex and which require a more sophisticated model for analysis than that offered by *Kowzan*.

The status of directors, actors and designers has changed since *Kowzan*

The status of directors, actors and designers has changed so that **this group of artists are now seen as being responsible for doing more than merely 'telling' the playwright's story.** They are now seen as artists in their own right rather than as servants to the playwright. There is an expectation that these artists will offer their own 'interpretation' of the playwright's work. Directors and designers may play with the sign systems in order to offer their own idea of the play or to introduce themes that may not have been suggested by the playwright. *Meyerhold, Artaud, Grotowski, Brook, Lepage* and **Mnouchkine** are all examples of twentieth-century directors, or *auteurs*, who have tended to adapt and transform original works into quite new pieces that are as much an expression of the director's imagination as the writer's. A good example is *Brook*'s production of *A Midsummer Night's Dream*.

This form of interpretation is often evident in 'revivals' and in productions of classic plays like those of *Shakespeare*. We discussed the whole issue of creative interpretations of play texts in Chapter 8. If a director chooses to set *Macbeth* in present-day Bosnia, for instance, there would be two kinds of information flowing through the sign systems: *Shakespeare*'s original story and characters and the director's own commentary on the play's theme. The director, not *Shakespeare*, is suggesting that new meanings can be found in the play by setting it among the conflicts in Bosnia. If Macbeth is costumed as a Bosnian warlord, we will have the experience of some signs (the words) belonging to the playwright and some signs (the costume) belonging to the director's interpretation. Now the audience has a more complex task: to

Patrick Stewart and Kate Fleetwood in *Macbeth*, Gielgud Theatre, London, 2007

make sense of the 'difference' between the original play of *Macbeth* and why and how the director has chosen to *add* an additional layer of information through changing the settings, costumes and maybe even the physical style of acting.

Richard Loncraine's film adaptation of *Richard III*, 1995

The status of actors has changed

The status of actors has also changed, so that **we think of actors as artists in their own right rather than as 'mouthpieces' for the playwright's words.** Part of our interest in the modern theatre is in the actor as a performer as well as in the actor's performance of a classic role. The director Eugenio *Barba* puts it this way: 'Why is it that when I watch two actors playing the same character, only one of them interests me?' In *Kowzan*'s framework, there is no mention of the distinctive contribution that the actor as performer makes to the 'meaning' of the performance. In modern theatre the performer is recognised to be the principle *signifier*.

A skilled performer, or a performer with a very strong stage presence, will bring 'life' to a character in ways that an amateur, or less skilled actor, cannot. It is not simply a question of *which* signs the actor makes; it is how the actor makes a sign which affects us in performance. So, **part of the analysis of the performance will be the analysis of the performer** – the way in which the performer works on stage and the extent to which your response to what happens in the performance comes from the personality and skill of the performer, rather than from the character and what happens to the character in the story. When this happens we become as interested in the *signifier* (the actor) as we are in the *signified* (the character). In *Kowzan*'s framework the identity of the performers and the director is made invisible; it could be anyone making the signs rather than someone who signs in their own particular way.

Certain performers are able to bring something so special and different to a role that we speak of the role 'belonging' to the performer; *Olivier*'s Othello, *McKellen*'s Richard III. Certain performances become legendary or are referred to as the benchmark for other performers to match. Helene *Weigel*'s performances of *Brecht*'s female characters are a benchmark for all actors taking on these roles now. In the same way, certain TV and film actors are expected to bring something extra special to a performance – can you imagine anyone else playing Inspector Morse or Del boy? Or think of the problems when a new actor takes on an established role in a long-running soap or drama series. We can never quite forget the original performer. We are also conscious, sometimes, of the other roles that certain actors have played before and this affects our response to how the same performer creates the character in the performance we are experiencing now.

**Task 9: Same character, different actors**

Have you seen the same character played by two different performers?

- If so, what were the *differences* in the performance?

- Which differences were of style, of intention, or from different direction?

- Which differences do you think were because of the different ways in which the performers played their character?

If you have difficulty finding an example from your own experience, look at different video versions of a *Shakespeare* play such as *Macbeth* or *Romeo and Juliet*. You could also visit the *King Lear* website where different performers talk about how they approached the role of King Lear:
http://www.bbc.co.uk/education/archive/lear/

**There is no mention of the audience in *Kowzan*'s framework**

There is no mention of audiences in *Kowzan*'s framework; no mention of the interaction between actors and audiences; how the space between the performers and the audience is arranged; the 'signs' made by the audience – laughing, crying, applauding; no mention of how the performance 'signs' to the audience how to respond.

The audience as a part of the performance, and the nature of the spatial relationship between the actors and the audience, became an increasingly important consideration in twentieth-century theatre. In the *realist* tradition of *representational* theatre, there is very little contact between the actors and the audience. The high *proscenium* stage which was introduced in the nineteenth century – brightly lit, with all of its 'tricks' like lighting, music and other effects hidden away – isolated the performance from the dark auditorium and the silent faces of the audience. The advent of film and TV has increased the theatre's interest in involving the audience more, ensuring that there is something special in the **live and shared experience** of performance.

From a commercial point of view, the theatre needs to offer an experience which is different from the experience of watching drama on film and TV. There is often an emphasis on making the audience feel included in the performance in some way rather than having the performers totally ignore the audience as they did at the end of the nineteenth century.

**The use and division of space is important**

The way in which the performance space is organised will have an important effect on our response to the performance and the performers. Since *Brecht* it has become usual to reveal all the 'tricks' in the performance: the lights are visible, entrances are not hidden from us, the musicians can be seen, props and scenery are often moved before us. The *cybernetic machine* is no longer hidden from us, and the experience of a performance – the effect of the signs – will include both the proximity of the actors and any other signs which are not a part of the performance itself but which contribute to it. If an actor is in a state of great distress only a few feet from you in the audience, it will have a powerfully different effect to your being further away. In some cases the 'performance' may include events in the foyer before entering the auditorium: actors sitting or walking among the audience, specially chosen music, the pictures and posters of the show, or maybe from the period of the play to set the context.

### Task 10: What does an audience *contribute* to the performance?

- Make a list of the different ways in which an audience's contributions might affect the performance and the performers: applause, silence, laughter, etc.

- How would the following methods of staging affect the audience? Consider the differences between:
  - a proscenium stage
  - a thrust stage
  - theatre in the round
  - promenade (where the audience moves around the space with the actors)
  - street theatre
  - environmental space (outdoor, or in museums and old buildings).

**The mix of styles and genres**

There is no consideration of style and genre in *Kowzan*'s framework. The way in which the actor signs, for instance, may be in a certain style or in a mixture of styles (e.g. *representational/Stanislavskian*, or *presentational/*

*Brechtian*). The signs in the performance may be organised in order to reflect or correspond to a particular genre of theatre (e.g. *tragedy* or *comedy*). During the twentieth century it became quite common to mix genres and styles so that a single performance might include elements of *tragedy* and *comedy*; a broad range of acting styles; dance, *mime* and realistic acting; elements of storytelling, ritual, games, *clowning* or stand-up comedy. In performances that mix styles and genres **it is important to comment on the effect of this mix** as well as to recognise what is *signified* by the individual signs themselves.

During the twentieth century, directors used new media to add to the performance. *Meyerhold*, *Piscator* and *Brecht* are examples of directors who were quick to use new technologies in their work to reflect the increasing importance of technological progress in society. They used slides, captions, film and mechanical constructions in their work. **A modern performance may include technological media such as slides, film strips or video.** It may also 'borrow' from other art forms such as sculpture, puppets and electronic music soundtracks. The boundaries between art forms and different styles and genres of theatre are not as clear-cut as they might have been in *Kowzan*'s time.

**Technical theatre and other media influences**

---

### Task 11: Adding to Kowzan's framework

What criticisms would you now make of *Kowzan*'s framework?

- In what ways is it perhaps no longer a useful tool for analysing contemporary performance?

- Use the list of sign systems that you made in Task 6 and *Kowzan*'s original list to create a new framework of sign systems that you could use to analyse the next performance that you see. Ideally, you should try your framework out several times with different kinds of performance and keep modifying it with experience.

## Signing in the Twentieth Century: Economy of Presentation

These developments in theatre during the twentieth century resulted in important changes in the way that the sign systems of theatre are used and understood. In the example from *A Doll's House* we noticed how all 13 of *Kowzan*'s sign systems were used to do the same job – to faithfully tell the playwright's story in a realistic setting.

The English stage designer Gordon *Craig* asked a question early in the twentieth century that brought about profound changes in the way that sign systems are used. The question was: 'How much is it essential to put on the stage to convey a forest?'

*Craig* was challenging the myth that every tree, branch and leaf needed to be represented – why not a single piece of wood on a bare stage? There were two important consequences of *Craig*'s question that would lead to innovative uses of sign systems in the new *post-realist* (i.e. *non-realist*) theatres of the twentieth century.

*Craig* led other practitioners to value economy of presentation in their use of signs; to only use that which is essential to presenting a forest or any other setting; to use a single *signifier* to signify forest rather than multiple *signifiers*. Later, *Grotowski* would refer to the economy of presentation as a 'poverty of means' in defining his idea of a *poor theatre*.

**Using less to do more!**

**Task 12: Re-designing**

Go back to the opening stage directions from *A Doll's House* on page 231.

1 Look at the list of signs that you made in Task 6. How many are *essential* rather than merely duplicating or reinforcing what is already there? Reduce the list as far as you can to a few essential signs - no more than three or four, which will *symbolise* the room and its relationship to the characters and themes of the play rather than literally representing every detail of a 'real' room.

2 Now that you have cleared the stage and freed up some of the sign systems that were all used just to represent the room, what might you *add*? Add signs of mood, theme, period or portents of events to come.

---

The difference between *iconic* and *symbolic* signs

This paring down of the signs on stage to a few essentials has had two important effects. First, it increases the *symbolic* value of the sign used. A hundred 'trees' on stage is an *iconic* or literal sign – a picture of a forest standing for a real forest. One dead branch hanging, or even lying, in the empty space becomes a *symbolic* sign in the sense that the immediate connection between the *signifier* (the dead branch) and the *signified* (a real forest) may not be obvious. The audience has to work harder to make the connection. They are forced to see the branch as *symbolising* the forest rather than imitating the forest. Because there is only one sign for the audience to consider they can spend longer dwelling on what is suggested. The difference between using a dead branch as opposed to a living one will suggest something, or *symbolise* some aspect, of the forest that is being represented. Is the 'fallen' branch a *symbol* of the main character's situation in the play? Is a 'dead' branch a *symbol* of that character giving up, or failing to take action? The imagination is triggered; the audience is made conscious that this is an *interpretation* of reality, not the *illusion* of reality that we associate with the *realist* tradition of *Ibsen*.

The effect will be to make the audience think about the *signifier* as much as the forest that is *signified*; to make them conscious of the artistic interpretation offered on stage. In the same way that we suggested that the actor (the *signifier*) is of interest to us as well as the character that the actor is playing (the *signified*), now all the *signifiers* (objects, set and space, for instance) become of interest in and of themselves.

When signs are used sparingly and with the intention of increasing the *symbolic* value, or resonances, of the signs, we become conscious of the image that is made in the *space of intentionality*. We dwell on the signs and their arrangement in the space just as you did in Task 5 and we consider the 'stage picture' as we might a painted picture or sculpture. **The signs are more than a mere 'setting' for the other actions – they become important symbols, or artistic statements in their own right.**

Samuel *Beckett* took this idea furthest in plays like *Breath* and *Act Without Words II*, which presented the audience with *signifiers* but no *signifieds*. *Beckett* argued that life was, in reality, meaningless and chaotic and that we *impose* meanings on the world. By stripping his *signifiers* of any intended meaning he hoped to force the audience to realise that it was making its own meanings – creating its own *signifieds* for the *signifiers* present on stage; imposing meanings on the stage *signifiers* that were not intended by the playwright, but suggested by the audience's imagination.

### Task 13: *Waiting for Godot* exercise

Compare the opening stage directions of *A Doll's House* with the opening directions to *Beckett's Waiting for Godot*. Is there any 'meaning' to *Beckett's* directions? In addition to the opening directions, we have also added the directions from the beginning of Act 2.

| Waiting for Godot | |
|---|---|
| Act 1<br>*A country road. A tree. Evening.* | Act 2<br>*Next day. Same Time. Same Place.* |
| *Estragon, sitting on a low mound, is trying to take off his boot. He pulls at it with both hands, panting. He gives up, exhausted, rests, and tries again.*<br>*As before.*<br>*Enter Vladimir.* | *Estragon's boots front centre, heels together, toes splayed... The tree has four or five leaves.*<br>*Enter Vladimir agitatedly. He halts and looks long at the tree, then suddenly begins to move feverishly about the stage. He halts before the boots, picks one up, examines it, sniffs it, manifests disgust, puts it back carefully. Comes and goes. Halts extreme right and gazes into the distance off, shading his eyes with his hands. Comes and goes. Halts extreme left, as before. Comes and goes. Halts suddenly and begins to sing loudly.* |

1   Try to enact Estragon and Vladimir's actions as they appear in the text. As you rehearse these actions, and watch each other, what is suggested? The two roles are often performed using a *clowning* style and *clowning* techniques – does this help you to understand *Beckett's* intentions?

2   Now work both sets of actions simultaneously with one of you as Estragon and the other Vladimir. Focus on the directions that indicate the pace and rhythm of the actions - fast/slow, stop/start. Exaggerate these contrasts as you work. When you are ready, show the two sequences simultaneously, repeating the actions three times - what is the effect?

As we saw in Chapter 4, *Brecht* went further and suggested that economy of presentation was also the key to characterisation and the signs made by the actor. The basis of *gestic* acting lies in the same principle – if a character is old, does it really take all eight of the actor's sign systems to make the same point? Isn't one simple sign sufficient? *Brecht's* rehearsal techniques were about stripping away everything that proved to be inessential to the characterisation, reducing the character to a bare outline of simple *gestes*, or physical actions. In the *Couragemodell* he writes:

> *Positions should be retained as long as there is no compelling reason for changing them; and a desire for variety is not a compelling reason. If one gives in to a desire for variety, the consequence is a devaluation of all movement on the stage; the spectator ceases to look for a specific meaning behind each movement, he stops taking movement seriously.*

Simple means can produce complex meanings

The idea of using signs sparingly and with *symbolic* rather than *iconic* intention also allowed for the development of *epic* theatrical presentations, or large-scale productions spanning many locations and spread over a wide timescale. The use of a few simple signs to indicate places or times was a feature of *Shakespeare*'s theatre as well. *Shakespeare* could move the action very rapidly from one time and place to another because the stage was not crowded with visual signs that would need changing every time he shifted scene. His words described the fictional place and he saw no reason why the other sign systems were needed to repeat the effect of the words.

In *Henry V* (Act 5, Scene 1) there is a good example of *Shakespeare* explaining, via the words of an actor, directly to the audience the conventions that will be used in the performance:

> Vouchsafe to those that have not read the story,
> That I may prompt them: and of such as have,
> I humbly pray them to admit th' excuse
> Of time, of numbers, and due course of things,
> Which cannot in their huge and proper life
> Be here presented. Now bear we the king
> Towards Calais: grant him there; there seen
> Heave him away upon your winged thoughts
> Athwart the sea. . .

*Brecht* would reclaim this tradition of large-scale *epic* historical plays in the twentieth century, which spanned across time and space in a single performance, without using elaborate settings. But it is Peter *Brook* who has gone furthest in using very simple but very carefully chosen *symbolic* signs to create *epic* performances. Colin Counsell writes:

> *In* The Mahabharata *simple bamboo sticks represented bows and arrows, and a chariot by two warehouse pallets laid end to end. Forest undergrowth was figured with coils of wire in a* Midsummer Night's Dream *and in Brooks' . . .* Ubu aux Bouffes *an industrial cable spool became a war machine on which Ubu rode crushing his enemies before him . . . In* Ubu *three bricks arranged in a hearth-shape successfully implied an entire dwelling whilst in* The Mahabharata *a (second) chariot was suggested with a single wheel held up by an actor . . . Locations may be indicated very succinctly, a carpet and some cushions representing the luxury of a king's court . . . In* The Conference of the Birds *the hawk was evoked by two bent fingers forming a beak like hook, the parrot with head movements and a wicker grid held before the actor's face as a cage . . .*

*Brook*'s skill lies in his ability to use *symbolic* rather than *iconic* signs to represent both the setting and the ideas in the performance. But the success of his *symbolic* signs rests on there being a sufficient resemblance to the real objects that are depicted for the audience to understand the connection that is being made.

Signs *combine* to make meaning

For instance, in *Brook*'s *A Midsummer Night's Dream* the magic flowers referred to in the text of the play were *symbolised* by spinning plates on top of long sticks. There is no obvious connection between the *signifier* (the spinning plates and sticks) and the *signified* (the magic flowers). But on reflection there are sufficient connections between the *signifier* and the

239

*signified* to make sense. There is a **physical resemblance** between a stick and a plate and the flower-head and stem of a flower. There is also a **functional resemblance** between the *magic* flower and the *magic* trick of spinning plates. However, the audience has to think more about the connection than if *Brook* had used an *iconic* sign – a prop flower.

---

**Task 14: Symbolic signing exercise**

Look at the extracts from Angela *Carter*'s writing that we used in the story theatre exercise in Chapter 2. In that exercise, you focused on creating physical and vocal signs for the extracts. Now we are going to use the examples from *Brook* to create the stage design and props.

**1** Divide the extracts up among the group; refresh your memories of the work by recalling the mood and atmosphere that you tried to create in your physical and vocal work.

**2** As a whole class discuss what will be **fixed** and present for every extract and what will be **changed** (added and taken away) either between or during each extract. Draw (or make if you have the time and resources) the fixed stage design - the set and the props that will be constant.

**3** Each group should now work out ideas for *symbolic* signs, in the form of objects, props and costume, for use in their extract. Begin by highlighting the text to identify the things and ideas that you want to provide signs for: the leg of a pig; a hard life; the ominous if brilliant look of blood on snow; the red shawl; the forest; the starving wolves; the scabby coat. Now, let your imaginations loose and begin to sketch and think about how you would use your ideas in performance.

---

## Signing in the Twentieth Century: Multiple Signs, Multiple Messages

**Using signs to comment on the story that is being told**

In Task 12 you discovered that the second effect of economy of presentation in performance is to free up the sign systems for other purposes and intentions. If, instead of using all 13 of *Kowzan*'s suggested sign systems to recreate the playwright's character, to re-tell the story and to represent the setting, a director only uses the simplest and fewest of signs, then there are still systems and space available that can do other kinds of work. We have already noticed examples of directors using signs to provide a simultaneous commentary on the story or central action on the stage. *Meyerhold* began the tradition of including headlines from the newspapers as backdrops to his stage story so that audiences were made to think about the relationship between events in the world and events on the stage. *Brecht* then developed the theory and practice of a form of *epic* theatrical presentation in which the purpose of the sign systems was to tell both the story and also *comment* on it; to *create* and also *destroy* the illusion of his characters and settings being real or consistent.

**Remixing the original**

Some of the sign systems can be used to offer interpretations or themes in the performance text that may not be present in the original play text. Alternatively, a performance can be built up out of fragments, images and physical ideas, rather like what happens in dance music and hip-hop. The DJ or producer may take an old song or sample an existing track and then add break-beats, raps, and other samples in order to make a new 'mix' which is based on fragments – samples of the old rearranged in order to make a new product which reflects the recording artist's own identity and vision.

The recording artist has multiple channels of sound to play with and use. Some channels will carry the original material and some will be used to carry the recording artist's interpretation, which may be a style such as trance or techno, or a rap. The original material is like the play text to which the artist adds his own performance text.

## Task 15: The same new song

1 Bring in some current examples of 'remixes' of old R&B or soul songs or special remixes of current tunes. Try and get hold of copies of the originals as well.

2 Play the old and new versions and consider what the new remix adds to the original and how this in turn has changed the effect of the original.

**Performance: text and sub-text**

**In many modern performances**, particularly those in the *auteur* directing tradition, **some of the sign systems will communicate the original play text**, if there is one, **while others will communicate a *sub-text* of the director's artistic intentions or ideas about the play text**. The weaving together of the play text strand and the *auteur*'s own *sub-text* into a coherent performance text for the audience is often referred to as **inter-textuality**. 'Inter' reminds us that a new understanding is made in between the original play text and the *auteur*'s *sub-text* in performance: It is neither the playwright nor the *auteur*'s, but a combination of old and new perspectives.

**Social criticism**

In *Brecht*'s case, the *sub-text* is always political; but there other kinds of intentions for creating a *sub-text* in performance, and some examples follow.

There may be signs that indicate a feminist, or post-colonialist perspective. Here, the *sub-text* is provided in order to make the audience think about the play from a new or challenging perspective. In 1997, the *physical theatre* actor Kathryn **Hunter** played *King Lear*, directed by Helena **Kaut-Howson**, although both rejected the idea that it was a feminist perspective. However, a woman playing Lear is bound to cause us to question the extent to which Lear's character and plight are particular to old men rather than universal for both men and women. *Hunter* claimed that 'there's a Lear in all of us' and *Kaut-Howson* spoke of 'the meeting between the character of Lear and Kathryn'. (You can read about this production and the views of the director and actor at: http://www.bbc.co.uk/education/archive/lear (page 212)).

**Inter-culturalism**

There may be a deliberate 'borrowing' from different cultures in terms of performance styles or setting in order to draw attention to, or *defamiliarise* the cultural context of the original play. The intention in using a diverse range of cultural traditions may also be to draw attention to the effect of mixing different kinds of performance.

During the 1980s Jatinder **Verma** and his company **Tara Arts** produced a number of classic plays from the Western tradition using a variety of Asian forms of performance such as *Kathakali*, masks and Asian settings. *Molière*'s *Tartuffe* was staged in the context of an eighteenth-century Mogul emperor's court in India.

Peter *Brook* frequently refers to and uses a variety of non-European performance traditions in his work. The 'tricks' in his famous production of *A Midsummer Night's Dream* (the spinning plates on sticks to represent the magic flowers, the trapezes from which Oberon and Titania swung, and the stilt-walking

241

of Puck) were all borrowed from the Chinese State Circus. In the *Mahabharata* he used a number of techniques from different Asian theatre traditions.

*Beckett*, as we have seen, often referred to clowns and *clowning* in his work. Joan *Littlewood*'s *Oh! What a Lovely War* borrowed from *music hall*, *vaudeville* and end-of-the-pier performances as a setting for her dramatic exploration of the First World War.

A theatrical language

There may be an emphasis in the performance text on movement, non-human sound and visual images in order to increase the live experience of the performance for the audience and/or to try and suggest a language of the theatre in addition to words. Many twentieth-century practitioners were fascinated by *Artaud*'s quest for an alternative 'language' of gestures, movement and strong visceral images.

The sources of these attempts to define such a language often 'borrow' from Asian performance with its highly-stylised gestures which are 'read' by the audience like a language system. *Artaud* was drawn to Balinese and Cambodian performances; *Grotowski* to *Kathakali*; *Brook* and *Brecht* to Chinese circus and *opera* techniques.

Other practitioners have been interested in the actor–audience interaction as the heart of performance and have deliberately blurred the boundaries between the signs of performance and those of non-performance; between the performance and audience spaces; between different kinds of performance (dance, carnival, ritual). Again, both *Artaud* and *Grotowski* were interested in this dimension of performance, and more recently both *Brook* and *Barba*'s *Odin Teatret* have experimented with space and performer–actor interactions beyond the conventional.

The American director Robert *Wilson* has influenced a new generation of *performance artists* with his idea of a *theatre of visions* which offers the audience a series of apparently random and unconnected visual and physical images as a means of trying to capture the randomness and free associations of the unconscious mind. His *Einstein on the Beach* was a collaboration with the composer Phillip Glass, which lasted five hours and used giant TV and film projections, carefully integrated into the musical score.

## Conventions are *still* the Key!

In the first chapter we included a section entitled 'Conventions are the Key!' in which we stressed that communication in theatre is made possible through its conventions. The conventions of the performance are a kind of agreement between the performers and the audience about the possibilities of dramatic representation.

Complex conventions make the audience work harder to understand

**In the twentieth century, practitioners constantly sought to stretch the boundaries of theatre**; to invent new conventions as the 'means' for representing increasingly complex 'meanings' about the human condition. This led, as we have seen, to increasingly complex uses of the sign systems of theatre. For a performance to communicate to its audience there has to be some logic or key that helps and guides the audience to understand everything that is seen and heard. The conventions (the agreements between performers and audiences about how the 'means' of theatrical communication are being used) have become increasingly complex and demanding for the audience.

One of the attractions of the nineteenth- and early twentieth-century *realist* tradition in theatre (which is still dominant in popular theatre, film and TV) is to do with the simplicity of its logic. It tells a story in a realistic setting; it is often based on ordinary, recognisable characters, who use everyday language to communicate. Performances in this style of theatre are easy for an audience to follow. Everything on the stage, including the characters, has the comforting familiarity of 'everyday life'. *Stanislavski* famously said:

> these characters become your real friends. 'Let's go see the Prozorov's' or 'Let's go see Uncle Vanya'. You are not going to see the Three Sisters or Uncle Vanya as plays, you are really going to call on old friends.

Stories, of any kind, often have the simple logic of a beginning, middle and end. When there is a strong story, simply told, the logic of a play's performance is clear to the audience from their own familiarity with the structure of stories. If the characters on stage behave 'realistically' and their behaviour is based on the given circumstances of the situations in the story, again it is easy for the audience to understand the logic of what's happening on stage. It is a cultural logic, based on an understanding of how humans are likely to behave in certain social situations. Plays in the *realist* tradition seek to be 'truthful' to life and to establish their 'truth' through the lifelike nature of the acting and setting and the credibility of the story being told. The signs that are used tend to be *iconic*; 'pictures' of the real thing.

Since the beginning of the twentieth century, however, practitioners have questioned both the comfortable familiarity of *realism* and also its claim to be 'truthful'. Many of the signing practices we have described in the previous section have been attempts to go beyond *realism*; to break the familiarity and comfort of *realism*; to question how truthful lifelike representations are by emphasising *symbolic* rather than *iconic* signs.

**Linear and non-linear structures**

These modern forms of *non-realist* theatre have sought, as *Brecht* described it, to 'make strange' rather than make familiar; to break the cosy intimacy of story and plot. This has often meant abandoning the logic of story and replacing it with other kinds of structure – *Brecht's episodic* theatre, for instance. In some cases the performance may not have any story at all, or the happenings on stage may not occur in the order that they would in a story. A story is a **linear** structure; the events are connected together across a timeline; one event causes the next. Performances which are not based on a story structure are often termed as having a **non-linear** (or *alinear*) structure. These performances can be much more difficult and unsettling for an audience to follow.

The difference between a *linear realist* piece with a strong story, lifelike representations of character and *iconic* signs, and a *non-linear* performance with no story, stylised characterisations (if there are characters at all) and *symbolic* signs is like the difference between a landscape or portrait and a conceptual or abstract painting. When we see a realistic painting we know how to understand it – we consider the relationship between the painting and the object or person that it represents. When we look at conceptual or abstract painting we are presented with a greater puzzle. The lifelike likeness isn't there to guide us, so instead we have to look at colour, tone, shape, and pattern to try and make our sense of the picture.

The same effect is true in a *non-linear* performance. Instead of following the story and recognising the characters and situations, we are forced to consider how the *signifiers* of theatre are being used – if they're not being used to tell a story, what are they being used for?

243

*Non-linear* performances often make us more aware of the 'live experience' – we can't follow or get lost and absorbed in a story, or comfortably recognise what's going on, so our attention is focused on 'what's happening to me/us'. There may be nothing to 'follow' in such a performance; there may be no distinction between performance and audience space, or any clues as to how to understand what's going on.

In such circumstances, we often become more self-conscious. More aware of our discomfort at not knowing what's going on, we may feel the heat of embarrassment, the physical disturbance of frustration, the shock of something unexpected happening. We become intensely aware of experiencing something. In the 1960s and 1970s, many practitioners deliberately sought to create this discomfort and sense of experience for

*A Cornfield with Cypresses*, Vincent van Gogh, 1889

*The White Horse*, John Constable, 1819

their audiences. Sometimes these performances would be called 'happenings' or 'events' rather than performances. Julian *Beck* and the *Living Theatre*, Allan **Kaprow**, the painter Claes **Oldenburg**, Tadeusz **Kantor**, Richard *Schechner* and *The Performance Group* were all active in creating 'happenings'. More recently, practitioners such as Pina *Bausch, Welfare State International*, Elizabeth *LeCompte* and *The Wooster Group*, and Yvonne **Rainer** have continued the tradition of experimental, *non-linear* performance in all kinds of spaces for radical and challenging purposes.

There are certain guidelines which might help you to understand a *non-linear* performance:

**Making sense of *non-linear* performance**

- The less the performance emphasises time (the events of the plot), the less important the question 'What will happen next?' becomes. Instead, space, how it is used and what is in it becomes more important. The question becomes 'What is happening here?' or 'What is happening to me?' (physically and emotionally).
- If there is no clear story or characterisation to follow, we begin to pay more attention to concepts like the *rhythm* and *contrasts* between stillness and movement, sound and silence, light and dark.
- If we are not sure what the *signifiers* are *signifying* we become more aware of the *signifiers* themselves – the performers' physicality, the use of space and time, sounds, lights, objects. There may be connotative associations for us – we may be reminded of a resemblance to something in our lives or experience, or we may respond to the technique, or sensory effect, or the aesthetics of the *signifiers*. The performance becomes more like a dance or a piece of sculpture in which there are *non-realist* ideas and forms of representation at work.

## Conclusion

Between the two extremes of *linear realist* performances and *non-linear* stylised happenings there lies the possibility of combining elements of *realism* and *non-realism* in one piece. Most contemporary performances will be of this kind. It is unusual to find a strictly *realist* performance even when it is based on a classic of *realism* such as *A Doll's House*. The tendency for directors and performers to make their own mark on a performance is likely to lead, as we have seen in this chapter, to some stylising in order to offer an interpretation – stylised costume or lighting perhaps.

Increasingly, the conventions used in performance require an educated audience, which is aware of the history and contemporary use of the sign systems of theatre. This is one purpose for your own study of theatre, so that you can make and enjoy theatre as a subtle, effective and powerful means of communicating ideas about the human condition. As you complete your course of study, you are now prepared to enter into the infinite variety of theatre with which we introduced this book.

## Performance Analysis Questionnaire

In the pages that follow, we have created a detailed questionnaire to help you collect your impressions, responses and understandings of a live performance. The analysis of performance is an increasingly complex activity for the reasons that we have outlined in Chapter 10.

H. Ibsen's play *A Doll's House*, 1997

This complexity requires great detail in the questionnaire. There is so much that one might respond to both before, during and after a performance, and performance in today's theatre takes many different forms and has many social functions. The questionnaire is designed to include every sign of performance and to include both the analysis of devised performances and performances based on an existing play text.

The questionnaire is in six sections, as follows:

1 **Expectations.** We seldom go to a performance cold. More usually we have a set of expectations of the play, of the director and the venue, among other sources of information that create a certain expectation of the performance itself.
2 **Summarise expectations.** In this section you are asked to gather together your expectations prior to the performance itself.
3 **Pre-performance.** Once you arrive at the venue, you encounter other sources of information about the performance from the venue itself and from the visual and spatial arrangements in the auditorium prior to the opening of the show.
4 **Text in performance.** If the performance is based on an existing play text, you will need to consider how effectively the play text has been translated into performance. This section will be particularly important when you watch the performance of one of your set texts or of a play text you are studying or know well.
5 **Performance text.** In this section you make an analysis of the actors' technical and interpretative skills in performance. You also consider the use of technical theatre and the dynamics, or flow, of the performance.
6 **Post-performance.** Finally, we help you to collect together your first impressions into a framework for group discussion so that you can share your responses and gain from the views of others in your group.

Each section makes use of some of the terms that we have introduced in this book and asks a number of key questions about the performance.

At some point in your studies it would be valuable to try and complete the entire questionnaire for a live performance so that you can become aware of all that is involved in making, performing and responding to performance. If you experience the performance in a group, then you could divide up the various sections of the questionnaire so that individuals take responsibility for making a complete response to one section only.

In other situations, you may want to select from the questionnaire according to the type of performance that you are going to see and your own purposes for making an analysis. There are parts of the questionnaire which will be irrelevant if you go to see a devised performance rather than a performance of a play text, for instance. You may want to focus on a particular aspect of the performance such as the acting or the use of technical theatre, in which case you would focus on those sections rather than trying to keep a record of all the sections.

The questionnaire will also be useful to you in the final stages of your own performance work. It provides you with a checklist of all that you will need to consider in polishing your work for public performance.

## 1 Expectations

| | | |
|---|---|---|
| Play text | Play text | Title?<br>Is it: a new play, revival, classic, translation, adaptation? |
| | Author<br>(if applicable) | Is this a new or established author?<br>What else has she or he written?<br>Is the author's cultural background relevant in terms of gender, culture/ethnicity, social class? |
| | Period<br>(if applicable) | In what historical period was the play written?<br>What historical period is the play set in?<br>What do you know about these periods? |
| | Genre | Is the play in a particular genre?<br>What other plays have you seen and studied that are in the same genre?<br>What do you expect from plays in this genre? |
| Style | Director | Does the director have a reputation? If so, for what kind of work (e.g. playwright's director/*auteur*)? |
| | Company | Is it a permanent company (e.g. *RSC*/Rep/nationally known)?<br>Are there any 'stars'? If so, what previous work have they done? |
| | Venue | What type of venue is it?<br>What else have you seen there?<br>What do you expect from shows at this venue? |
| Extra | Reviews | Has this performance been reviewed? If so, what were the opinions and points raised in the *reviews*? |
| | Publicity | How and where has the show been marketed?<br>What images and text are used in the marketing?<br>Does the publicity target a particular audience? |
| | Friends | Do you know anyone who has already seen the show?<br>What's the word? |

## 2 Summarise Expectations

Based on your pre-performance research:
- What do you expect the performance to be like, in terms of style and effect?
- What problems might there be in the staging of this play?
- If you have already studied the play, what will you be looking for in the performance?
- Are there any interesting differences in the *reviews* to note?
- What do you expect to enjoy/not enjoy in this performance?

## 3 Pre-performance

| | | |
|---|---|---|
| Venue | Ambience at venue | What is the 'feel' of the venue?<br>What is the age/economic/cultural profile of the audience?<br>How welcoming is the venue? |
| | Visuals/graphics | Are there any posters?<br>Are there any images from the production? Scenes, costumes, set?<br>Are there any photos of the actors as themselves/in character?<br>Are there posters and photos from previous shows? |
| | Programme notes | What information is given:<br>- About the play?<br>- About the interpretation?<br>- About the producers (bioraphies, etc.)? |

| | | |
|---|---|---|
| **Venue** | Pre-performance events<br><br><br>Music/sound | Does the performance extend into the lobby, in terms of:<br>• Displays or material directly related to the performance?<br>• Actors mingling or calling the audience into the theatre?<br>• Sound or music to signal the performance is starting? |
| **Staging** | Performance space | When you enter the theatre/performance space, how is it organised?<br>Sketch the space, paying careful attention to how it is divided into acting/audience space and any fixed objects or scenery present.<br>How do you expect the space to be used?<br>Will there be a close relationship between performers and audience for instance? |
| | Audience space | How will the seating affect the audience's response? |
| | Set | Are there any ambient sounds/lights? |
| **Use of acting/audience space** | (Sketch of the space) | |

## 4 Text in Performance

| | |
|---|---|
| Consider and comment on: | • casting<br>• spoken text<br>• characterisation<br>• genre and/or style<br>• period<br>• setting. |
| Is it a literal presentation of the play, with few changes to the original text and directions?<br>Is it an interpretation of the original play text based on the director's ideas and themes? If so, what changes have been made to the original text?<br>Are the signs used to tell the story in its period and setting mainly *realist* or *non-realist*?<br>Did this performance teach you anything new about the plot, language, characters, setting or themes of the play text?<br>Did you have a problem with, or not like/understand, any aspect of the staging of this play? | |

## 5 Performance Text

Actors use of:

| | Literal | Interpretative | *Realist* | *Non-Realist* |
|---|---|---|---|---|
| Space | | | | |
| Voice | | | | |
| Body | | | | |
| Movement | | | | |
| Timing | | | | |
| Interactions | | | | |

249

Use the tick boxes to decide whether the actors' signing is: literal (according to the original directions) or interpretative (commenting on or 'making strange' the original directions); mainly *realist* (iconic or 'lifelike') or mainly *non-realist* (symbolic).

Was there a dominant acting style: *'representational'* actors 'being' characters (*Stanislavskian*) or *'presentational'* actors 'showing' characters (*Brechtian*)?

Were there any significant changes, or contrasts, in the acting style during the performance? If so, what was the intention and effect do you think?

How conscious were you of the actors as actors rather than as characters?

What effect did the performance of the actors have on your understanding of the play and/or your experience during the performance?

How did the actors use each other and how much direct notice did they take of the audience?

Were there any outstanding/weak performances? If so, what distinguished these actors from others in terms of their signing?

## Technical Theatre

| | Fixed | Change | *Realist* | *Non-realist* | On | Off |
|---|---|---|---|---|---|---|
| Props | | | | | | |
| Costumes | | | | | | |
| Scenery | | | | | | |
| Music | | | | | | |
| Sound | | | | | | |
| Other technical | | | | | | |

Use the tick boxes to decide which technical theatre effects were: fixed throughout or changed during the performance; *realist* or stylised in their appearance or effect; mostly 'switched on' (used) or 'switched off' (not used).

Which effects were you most conscious of during performance?

Were there any significant changes in the use of an effects system – e.g. sudden music, or dramatic lighting changes – if so, what was the intention and effect?

Did the effects blend in with the other signs in performance, or were they in contrast with other signs – i.e. *realist* acting with a stylised set or lighting?

Were there any design themes, such as colour, textures, shapes?

## Dynamics

| Contrasts | Effect | | | | | | | |
|---|---|---|---|---|---|---|---|---|
| | 1 | 2 | 3 | 4 | 5 | 6 | 7 | 8 |
| 1 Rhythm and pace of voice and action | Fast/loud <br><br><br><br> Slow/quiet | | | | | | | |
| 2 Sound/silence | | | | | | | | |
| 3 Light/dark | | | | | | | | |
| 4 Solo/Duo *ensemble* | | | | | | | | |

| | Sound | Movement | Participation | Applause |
|---|---|---|---|---|
| 5 Audience response | | | | |

Divide the performance up into units (see diagram above) – possibly the act/scene structure or time elapsed.

Make a simple flow chart to show the rhythms and pace of the performance. The bottom of the chart represents 'slow/quiet' and the top is 'fast/loud'.

Make a note of any significant moments of contrast between sound/silence and light/dark. What was the intention and effect of these moments?

What was the mix of solo/duologue and *ensemble* playing in the performance? Were there any obvious contrasts – e.g. an intimate duologue followed by a busy crowd or *ensemble* scene?

What did the audience contribute to the performance and how conscious were you of other audience members?

## 6 Post-performance

Use the information that you have gathered in Stages 1–5 to prepare the following notes as a basis for group discussion. Refer back to the evidence that you have collected during the discussion.

| | | |
|---|---|---|
| Personal notes for: | Images retained | When you close your eyes and think back to the performance, how many moments can you *clearly* visualise in your head? <br> Why are these the images that *you* have retained? |
| | Strongest moment | What for you was the strongest moment in the performance? A moment of tension, sadness, anger, beauty or truth, perhaps? A particular scene which affected you the most? One of the images that you retained? |
| | Weakest moment | Which moment was the weakest for you? A scene or use of sign that really didn't work for you? <br> How might that moment have been 'rescued' or done differently? |
| | Inconsistencies | Were there any problems with the logic or coherence of the signs in performance? Anything that jarred or seemed out of place with the rest of the performance? |
| | Didn't understand | Were there any points in the performance that confused you, or where you couldn't work out the intentions? |
| | Strong points overall | Did the performance have a particular strength? The acting or design, for instance? |
| | Weak points overall | Did the performance have a particular weakness? The pace or director's interpretation, for instance? |
| | Personal response | Finally, make a list of issues or points that you really would like raised and shared in the discussion. |

# Resources
# Appendix 1: Glossary of practitioners, stylistic, technical and historical terms

**Abbey Theatre**  Founded in 1904 by the Fay brothers, Yeats, Lady Gregory and Synge in order to encourage and introduce the work of new Irish playwrights onto the stage. Such writers have included Sean O'Casey, Lennox Robinson, T.C. Murray and George Shiels. www.abbeytheatre.ie

**Aeschylus** (525/4–456/5BC)  Greek dramatist. Aeschylus wrote over 90 plays, which include Persians (472), Seven against Thebes (467), and Prometheus Bound (exact date unknown). Introduced plays that reduced chorus numbers and also had more than one main actor. This formation is said to have shaped European theatre. www.theatrehistory.com/ancient/aeschylus001.html

**Agitprop**  A political style of theatre in the 20th century that used music, drama, song, and satire to encourage change by depicting the daily struggles of the working classes.

**Albee, Edward Franklin** (1928– )  American playwright. Plays include The American Dream (1961); Who's Afraid of Virginia Woolf? (1962); A Delicate Balance (1966); and The Lady from Dubuque (1977). His most recent play, Three Tall Women (1991) won the Pulitzer Prize in 1994.

**Anouilh, Jean-Marie-Lucien-Pierre** (1910–87)  French dramatist who achieved critical acclaim and popularity in both France and Britain. Among his many achievements, his adaptation of Antigone (1944) acted as a commentary on the decline of fascism. www.kirjasto.sci.fi/anouilh.htm

**Antagonist**  The character who opposes the protagonist. Their clash of objectives is what makes a play dramatic.

**Antoine, Andre** (1858–1943)  French actor, director and theatre manager, who gained much of his inspiration from the Meiningen Theatre Company. As a pioneer of modern naturalistic theatre, he founded the Theatre Libre in 1887. The introduction of a naturalistic style of acting was accompanied by three-dimensional sets, in place of flats. Founded Theatre Antoine in 1890, which was used as a creative centre for young artists. Finally, in 1906, Antoine was appointed director of the Odeon, where he remained until retirement in 1916. www.wayneturney.2om.com/antoineandre.htm

**Appia, Adolphe** (1862–1928)  Swiss artist and director. Considered to be the first stage lighting designer. He abandoned flat sets in order to create a more atmospheric scene, using mood-evoking lighting and music.

**Applied Theatre**  A generic and constantly evolving term used to describe theatre courses that cover 'extra-theatrical' studies in such fields as community theatre, site-specific work, youth theatre and drama targeted towards the disadvantaged.

**Aristophanes** (448?–385BC)  Influential Athenian playwright of satircal comedy. Plays include The Acharnians (425), The Clouds (423), Lysistrata (411), The Frogs (405), and Plutis (388). www.theatrehistory.com/ancient/aristophanes001.html

**Arden, Annabel**  Co-founder of Complicité and producer of work across a range of artistic genres including opera, theatre and broadcasting. Plays she has directed include The Duchess of Malfi and the

Women of Troy. In 2007 she directed Opera North's The Magic Flute. Her theatrical training includes time spent with Jacques Lecoq in Paris at his Labortoire de Movement. www.complicite.org

**Artaud, Antonin** (1896–1948) French actor, director and poet. Began work as an actor employed by Lugne-Poe in Theatre D'Oeuvre. In 1927 formed the Alfred Jarry Theatre in order to explore surrealism, believing that realism was a betrayal of theatre's purpose. Between 1929–35, he formulated his 'Theatre of Cruelty', which was greatly influenced by the Balinese dancers, whose art was structured around very specific gestures. Artaud's only attempt to realise his idea in a production of Shelley's The Cenci in 1935, failed. However, he is now regarded as a highly influential force in the theatre. www.theatrehistory.com/french/artuad001.html

**Artistic Director** A term used for an individual within a theatre company who generally has artistic control over the choice of productions, casting, direction and the overall ethos of the company. Their role could also include having direct input into the staging of performances.

**Aukin, David** (1942– ) Former Head of Film for Channel 4 from 1990-1998, he commissioned a number of award winning films including The Madness of King George (1994) and Trainspotting (1996). Now Creative Executive for Mentorn TV he has produced a number of successful projects for television and film including Mrs Henderson Presents (2005) and The Government Inspector (2005). www.bifa.org.uk/person/283/David_Aukin.html

**Auteur** French word meaning 'author'. Auteur refers to a director who is considered a 'co-author' in the respect that they significantly revise the original play, and produce a final product which is very much their own creation.

**Avant-garde** French term which is associated with the pioneering artistic period of modernism, dating from the late nineteenth century. Avant-garde drama was first produced across Europe at theatres such as Theatre Libre, The Abbey Theatre and the Moscow Art Theatre.

**Barba, Eugenio** (1936– ) Italian director. Time spent at Grotowski's laboratory theatre in 1961 encouraged Barba to found the Odin Teatret in Denmark in 1964 where he developed his idea of 'the third theatre'. In 1979 Barba concentrated his work into a larger centre for research, the International School of Theatre Anthropology. His theatre interests include the Kathakali tradition and he has directed over 20 productions including Brecht's Ashes (1980) and Mythos (1998). www.odinteatret.dk

**Barthes, Roland** (1915–1980) French literary critic, and theorist. Barthes studied the semiotics of different cultures and how they are expressed in written texts. www.textetc.com/theory./barthes.html

**Bausch, Pina** (1940– ) German dancer, choreographer and actor. In 1973 Bausch founded the modern dance company, Tanztheater Wupperatal Pina Bausch in Germany. She has been heavily influenced amongst others by the dance practitioners Kurt Jooss and Mary Wigman and her most recent work includes Ten Chi (2004) and Rough Cut (2005).

**Beck, Julian** (1925–85) Founder of the experimental New York theatre company, Living Theatre. www.livingtheatre.org/history.html

**Beckett, Samuel** (1906–89) Irish playwright. Not recognised as a playwright until 1953 with Blin's production of Waiting for Godot (1947). Further successes include Endgame (1957), Krapp's Last Tape (1958) and Happy Days (1961). Heavily inspired by his Irish upbringing and much of his comedy is based on this. His later work Breath (1969), Not I (1971), and Footfalls (1975) conveys his detachment from conventional theatre. www.themodernword.com/beckett

**Behn, Aphra** (1640–89)  First female English playwright. Behn's satirical comedies and farces include The Emperor of the Moon (1687), The Roundheads (1681), and The Lucky Chance (1686). Her most famous play is The Rover (1677). www.lit-arts.net/Behn

**Belasco, David** (1853–1931)  American director and resident dramatist and manager at several theatres including the Baldwin Theatre in San Francisco, the Madison Square Theatre in New York (1882) and the Lyceum Theatre in London. Worked closely with Henry C. DeMille, collaborating on many celebrated productions such as The Wife (1887). His individual work includes The Darling of the Gods (1902), The Girl of the Golden West (1905) and The Governor's Lady (1912). www.oldandsold.com/articles32n/drama-7.shtml

**Bely, Andrei** (1880–1934)  Russian novelist and dramatist. Of his Russian contemporaries Bely was much in favour of the innovative work of Meyerhold, and rejected the realist work of Stanislavski. Bely's symbolist plays include He Who Has Come (1903), The Jaws of Night (1907), and The Death of a Senator (1925).

**Bennett, Alan** (1934– )  British actor and dramatist. Bennett was a member of the popular theatre group Beyond the Fringe. Satirical in both his acting and writing, Bennett exposed the hypocrisy and corruption in British politics in plays such as Forty Years On (1968). Later plays explored the issue of class in Britain, including Habeas Corpus (1973), and Enjoy (1980). He has enjoyed recent success with both his play and film adaptation of The History Boys (2004/2006) which has won 3 Oliver Awards and has transferred with huge acclaim to Broadway.

**Berkoff, Steven** (1937– )  Actor, director and playwright. Known for the physical theatre style of his work largely influenced by his training at The Webber Douglas Academy of Dramatic Art and time spent with Jacques Lecoq in Paris. His unconventional approach to the adaptation of canonical authors' writing has included Kafka's Metamorphosis (1969), The Penal Colony (1969) and The Trail (1971). Within the theatre Shakespeare's Villains and Requiem for Ground Zero are just a few of the projects he has toured internationally. www.stevenberkoff.com

**Berliner Ensemble**  Established by Bertolt Brecht and his wife Helene Weigel in 1949 this theatre company originally staged political plays by Brecht in Theater am Schiffbauerdamm including The Caucasian Chalk Circle (1949) and The Life of Galileo. Following his death in 1956, the Berliner Ensemble was controlled by a number of practitioners including five directors in 1992 when it was changed from a state owned to a private theatre company. www.germsn.lss.wisc.edu/brecht/ensemble.html

**Bernhardt, Sarah** (1844–1923)  French actress. In 1862 Bernhardt gave her first performance at the Comedie-Franciase. During the early 1880s Bernhardt toured America, Russia and Australia, which gave her international recognition. Bernhardt's greatest performance was given in 1884 in The Lady of the Camellias. The Theatre des Nations was later renamed in her honour as the Theatre Sarah Bernhardt. www.sarah-bernhardt.com

**Black Box**  A popular style of drama studio most commonly associated with the 1960s and 70s but still installed today within theatres, schools and colleges. The black interior of this style of studio provides a flexible space for performers and lent itself well to the experimental theatre that was being practised during the sixties.

**Blok, Aleksander Aleksandrovich** (1880–1921)  Russian poet and dramatist. Blok's Lyrical Dramas (completed in 1908) experimented with Commedia dell'Arte and theatre of the grotesque. His innovative style was greatly admired by Meyerhold, who consequently produced several of his plays. Blok's later works include The Miracle of Theophile (1908) and The Rose and the Cross (1913). www.kirjasto.sci.fi/blok.htm

**Bogdanov, Michael** (1938– ) British director. After his work for various companies, including the Royal Shakespeare Company, he was appointed associate director of the National Theatre in 1980. His productions include Brenton's The Roman in Britain (1980), Calderon's The Mayor of Zalamea (1981), and Kyd's The Spanish Tragedy (1982). In 1986 he co-founded the English Shakespeare Company and in 2003 was involved in establishing the Wales Theatre Company. Received wide spread praise for his direction of Mal Pope's Amazing Grace (2006) at Wales Millennium Centre as it was the first Welsh musical that had ever been staged at a national theatre.

**Bond, Edward** (1935– ) British dramatist. His second play Saved, first performed at the Royal Court Theatre, caused uproar. He wanted to express the cruelty and self-crucifixion of the contemporary age, symbolised by a baby in a pram being stoned to death. His plays staged at the Royal Court, the National Theatre and fringe theatres include Early Morning (1968), Lear (1972) and War Plays (1985). Now more commonly associated with writing theatre for young people and works closely with Big Brum Theatre Company. Within his role as an associate artist for Big Brum Theatre Company has written plays including The Under Room (2005) and The Balancing Art (2006) which have toured to schools and colleges on a national and international level.

**Boyd, Michael** (1955– ) Currently artistic director for the Royal Shakespeare Company, has a wealth of past experience as an assistant director for the Belgrade Theatre in Coventry (1980-82), the Crucible Theatre in Sheffield (1982–84) and as artistic director at Tron Theatre, Glasgow (1985–1996). Has directed a variety of productions for the RSC including Measure for Measure (1996), Troilus and Cressida (1998) and Romeo and Juliet (2000). Beyond the RSC he has directed Miss Julie (1999) in the West End of London and Hedda Gabler. www.shakespeare.org.uk

**Brahm, Otto** (1856–1912) German director and literary critic, who, inspired by Antoine's Theatre Libre, opened the German equivalent, the 'Freie Buhne', in Berlin in 1889. After ten years training actors at the Deutsches Theater, Brahm took over the Lessing Theater in Berlin, where he worked until his death.

**Bread and Puppet Theatre** Established its roots in 1962 in New York with Peter Schumann as the founder of the company. Known for its over-sized puppets used during performances to draw attention to its anti-war beliefs. www.breadandpuppet.org

**Brecht, Bertolt** (1898–1956) German poet, playwright and theorist. His theatre is often referred to as the 'Theatre of Intellect', engaging the audience to form a critical viewpoint. Undoubtedly influenced by Piscator's Agitprop, multi-media theatre, in the creation of his own form of theatre, 'epic', which was founded upon emotional detachment known as Verfremdungseffekt. Brecht had early success particularly with productions such as The Threepenny Opera, written in collaboration with Elisabeth Hauptmann. While Hitler was in power, Brecht went into exile, and here wrote what are considered to be his greatest plays, including Mother Courage and Her Children (1941) and The Good Person of Setzuan (1943).

**Brook, Peter Stephen Paul** (1925– ) English director influenced by the contrasting styles of Artaud and Brecht. Achieved success at the Birmingham Repertory Theatre, the Shakespeare Memorial Theatre and the Stratford Company with productions such as Titus Andronicus (1955) which starred Lawrence Olivier. In 1962 was appointed co-director at the Royal Shakespeare Company. Productions here included Weiss' Marat/Sade (1964), and A Midsummer Night's Dream (1970). During the 1970s he broke away from the confines of traditional theatre and founded the International Centre for Theatre Research in Paris. He invited performers from a variety of cultures and countries to join his company in order to assemble a theatre that could dissolve cultural barriers. The company toured nationally with productions such as The Conference of Birds (1976), The Ik (1975) and The Mahabharata (1985). www.nationaltheatre.org.uk

**Brown, William Henry** (fl. 1820s) African-American theatre manager and playwright. In 1821 founded the first African-American theatre, based in New York. He did much for the emergence of black actors such as James Hewlett and Ira Aldridge in the Western world. www.musicals101.com/1700bway.htm

**Bruvvers** Newcastle-based theatre company established in 1970 that directs its work towards people who would never normally get access to the theatre and aims to provide work that educates and enlightens its audience on a broad range of topics. www.bruvvers.co.uk

**Buchner, Georg** (1813–37) German dramatist who was the leader of an anti-revolutionist group. His first play, Danton's Death (1835), condemns the French Revolution. Due to the strong political statements in his plays, they were not performed until years after his death. Buchner dramatically differed to his romantic contemporaries and is now recognised as a forerunner of naturalism.

**Calderon De La Barca, Pedro** (1600–81) Spanish playwright of the Golden Age. Established himself by 1629 with his plays The Phantom Lady and The House with Two Doors. Wrote hundreds of grand scale plays, both comic and tragic, and is most renowned for his play Life is a Dream (1635). www.theatrehistory.com/spanish/calderon001.html

**Carter, Angela** (1940–1992) Controversial British writer and poet. Her novels include Shadow Dance (1965), The Magic Toy Shop (1967), Several Perceptions (1968), The Infernal Desire Machines of Dr Hoffman (1972) and Nights at the Circus (1984). Her poetry includes the collection Nothing Sacred (1982) and both The Company of Wolves and The Magic Toy Shop have been adapted into films. www.angelacartersite.co.uk

**Cartwright, Jim** (1958– ) British playwright, producer and director. Trained as an actor at the Central School of Speech and Drama and known for his plays Road, Bed, Two and The Rise and Fall of Little Voice. The gritty realism associated with his work has resulted in several of his plays transformed into film. www.jimcartwright.co.uk

**Chaikin, Joseph** (1935–2003) American director, actor and producer. He first performed in New York in 1958 in Dark of the Moon. Established himself as a dramatist by founding The Open Theatre in 1963, a company which performed innovative scripts. Successes that followed included America Hurrah (1966), Terminal and The Serpent (both 1970).

**Chaplin, Charlie** (1889–1977) English actor, director, musician and composer whose formal training began in 1910 where he toured America with the Fred Karno Troupe. Best known for his artistic talents as a comedy mime artist and clowning skills, his career in films began with Making a Living (1914) which he appeared in as part of the Keystone Film Company. His final film was A Countess from King Kong. In the majority of his films he not only acted but often took complete artistic control over the script, production and eventually the musical score. www.charliechaplin.com

**Chekhov, Anton Pavlovich** (1860–1904) Great Russian dramatist. Chekhov's plays did not gain success on a grand scale until they were staged by the Moscow Arts Theatre, directed by Stanislavski and Nemirovich-Danchenko. Although Chekhov did not always agree with Stanislavski's interpretation, his productions such as Three Sisters, The Seagull and The Cherry Orchard were hugely successful. www.theatrehistory.com/russian/chekhvov001.html

**Chilton, Nola** Drama teacher who founded The Open Theatre in 1963 and trained her actors using exercises to assist in their exploration of the Theatre of the Absurd playwrights. She returned to Israel in 1962 leaving Joseph Chaikin to take over the direction of the company.

**Churchill, Caryl** (1938– ) English dramatist, who began her career as a writer of radio plays. Churchill's first stage play Owners made its debut at the Royal Court in 1972. Most famous for her feminist plays during the 1980s including Top Girls (1982), and Fen (1983). www.contemporarywriters.com/authors/?p=auth259&state

**Cirque du Soleil** Originally founded by street performers Guy Laliberte and Gauthier in 1984, this Quebec-based company have a worldwide reputation for their artistic mastery as advanced circus performers. Their international cast has performed in every continent with elaborate shows such as Alegria and Kooza (2007). www.cirquedusoleil.com

**Cocteau, Jean** (1889–1963) Poet, novelist, theatre practitioner and film maker. He was a practitioner during the surrealist movement and wrote his first novel Le Potomak in 1913. This was later followed by a succession of films that were considered to be avant-garde and unconventional in their style and content, including Le Sang d'un Poete (1930), La Belle et la Bête (1945) and Les Parents Terribles (1948). www.jeancocteau.net

**Commedia dell'Arte** Comedy developed in Italy in the sixteenth and seventeenth centuries. Commedia is recognised primarily because of its stock characters, identified by their costume and mask. Often improvised performances were combined with rehearsed comical 'routines' called Lazzi. Famous commedia companies include the I Gelosi, which performed from the 1570s to 1604. Commedia gave equal status to action as to verbal dialogue and narrative, which meant that Italian commedia could be understood in other countries, overcoming language barriers. www.delpiano.com/carnival/html/commedia.html

**Complicité** British theatre group founded by Annabel Arden, Marcello Magni and Simon McBurney in 1983 and known for their highly physical and visual performance style which was influenced by the work of Jacques Lecoq and the Commedia dell'Arte movement. International productions include The Streets of Crocodiles, The Three Lives of Lucie Cabrol, The Caucasian Chalk Circle and Mnemonic. www.complicite.org

**Congreve, William** (1670–1729) English playwright. His plays include The Old Bachelor (1689), Love for Love (1695) and The Way of the World (1700). www.theatrehistory.com/british/congreve001.html

**Contemporary Dance** A term used to describe dance developed during the 20th century which draws upon modern dance techniques to develop its choreography. DV8, Motionhouse Dance Company and Rambert Dance Company are a few of the contemporary dance practitioners that exist today. www.danceweb.co.uk/library/pedia/?item=6.2.16#Contemporary_dance

**Courtyard Theatre** A temporary theatre constructed for the RSC in Stratford-Upon-Avon in 2006 whilst the Royal Shakespeare Theatre underwent a complete transformation. Opened with Michael Boyd's direction of Henry VI and has a thrust stage auditorium. www.rsc.org.uk

**Coward, Noel** (1899–1973) British playwright and actor. Most successful works include his comedies Fallen Angels (1925), Design for Living (1933), Blithe Spirit (1941), and Present Laughter (1942). www.noelcoward.com

**Craig, Edward Gordon** (1872–1966) British director and set designer. His early work includes designing and directing productions such as the opera Masque of Love (1901) and Ibsen's The Vikings (1903). In 1905 Craig published an essay The Art of Theatre which expressed his view that theatre should be a serious art-form equivalent to music. He also believed that theatre should have one controlling force, an Uber-Marionette, which would make redundant the actor, designer and composer. Although this idea was never truly realised it did highlight the importance and raised the profile of the director in place of the actor-manager.

**Daldry, Stephen** (1961– ) Film director and producer. He trained at the East 15 Acting School in London and spent his early career gaining experience of the industry at The Crucible Theatre in Sheffield. As a director he revived An Inspector Calls (1992) at the National Theatre which led to a national tour and as the artistic director of the Royal Court Theatre he produced such plays as Machinal (1994) and Rat in the Skull(1995). His film Billy Elliot (2000) brought his work to the attention of Hollywood and received several Oscars.

**Devine, George** (1910–65) British actor and director. In 1934, he joined Gielgud's company at the New Theatre. During his time at the New Theatre he met the French director Michel Saint-Denis. Together the pair worked for many years as innovators of the theatre, experimenting with new forms. In 1954 he collaborated with the playwright Ronald Duncan, to found the English Stage Company, which was specifically designed to stage new innovative modern plays. www.royalcourttheatre.com/about.asp?ArticleID=14

**Devised Theatre** A term used for theatre created without script and is devised through the creative process by using stimulus and/or improvisation to devise original performance material.

**Dialectics** Term used to describe the clash of opposites, and the resulting conflicts. Brecht particularly strove to achieve dialectical theatre.

**Dorfman, Ariel** (1942– ) Chilean playwright, who now lives and works in the USA. Known for his plays such as Reader (1995), Death and the Maiden (1996) and Widows (1997), which indirectly reflected the fascist regimes of General Pinochet. www.adorfman.duke.edu

**Drury Lane, Theatre Royal** First built in 1663. Famous performances at Drury Lane include those of David Garrick in Otway's The Orphan, Charles Macklin as Shylock, and Robert Elliston as Hamlet. After Garrick's retirement in 1777, Sheridan replaced him as manager. During the 1920s Alfred Butt introduced musicals to Drury Lane, and today it is one of the key musical theatres in London's West End. www.arthurlloyd.co.uk/DruryLane.htm

**Duncan, Isadora** (1877–1927) American dancer. Duncan was influenced by images from ancient Greek theatre. She broke away from the formalism of ballet, creating a new style, which became the foundation of modern dance. www.isadoraduncan.org

**DV8** Contemporary dance and physical theatre company, formed in 1986. Works include My Sex Our Dance, Deep End, Dead Dreams of Monochrome Men and Just for Show. Several of their productions have been turned into well received films particularly The Cost of Living which won the Prix Italia and Rose D'or awards. www.dv8.co.uk

**English Shakespeare Company** Founded by director Michael Boganov in 1986. The English Shakespeare Company was designed as a touring company that would take classic Shakespeare productions to areas relatively untouched by and deprived of drama.

**Ensemble Midtvest** Danish classical chamber music group formed in 2002 consisting of a string quartet, a wind quintet and a pianist. In addition to working with international composers, the company has recently employed the jazz artist Carsten Dahl to broaden their work into film and dance. www.ensemblemidtvest.dk

**Exposition** The exposition of a play usually occurs at the beginning. Gives the audience background information of previous events that are relevant to the play.

**Expressionist Dance** A style of dance that is related to the German expressionist movement in the 20th century. www.artsalive.ca/en/dan/dance101

**Eyre, Richard** (1943– ) British director, known for his pioneering contemporary productions. Eyre's experience at the Royal Lyceum Theatre (1967–72) led to his innovative work at the Nottingham Playhouse. Here he produced plays of fresh, new, talented playwrights such as Brenton and Hare. Later went on to work at the National Theatre, with productions such as The Beggar's Opera and Guys and Dolls. Also directed the musical production of Mary Poppins both in the West End and on Broadway.

**Fo, Dario** (1926– ) Italian actor, director and dramatist. Fo was a satirical writer who ridiculed and exposed the hypocrisy of the Italian government. During the late 1960s Fo formed a touring company, La Nuova Scena, which performed political theatre under the patronage of the Communist Party. Productions included The Worker Knows 300 Words and That's Why He's the Boss (1968). During the 1970s Fo abandoned the orthodox left wing, and formed a new company La Commune, which served in support of the 'New Left Wing'. www.nobelprize.org/nobel_prizes/literature/laureates/1997/fo-bio.html

**Forced Entertainment** Established in Sheffield in 1984, this experimental company create contemporary drama as a six piece ensemble led by their director and writer Tim Etchells. Using multi- media and theatre to engage its audience, Forced Entertainment often go beyond traditional theatre settings to perform in museums and public sites. Previous performances include Quizoola (1996) and The World in Pictures (2006). www.forcedentertainment.com

**Ford, John** (1586–1639) English dramatist. Ford's later plays are considered his finest. They include Love's Sacrifice (1630), 'Tis Pity She's a Whore (1633), Perkin Warbeck (1634), The Lady's Trial (1638) and The Witch of Edmonton (1658).

**Franz, Ellen** (1839–1923) Actress who managed the group of actors at the Meiningen Theatre Company.

**Fuchs, Francis** (Contemporary) Playwright who worked with six other playwrights in 1972 to create the play England's Ireland observing the British in Northern Ireland.

**Garrick, David** (1717–79) English actor, theatre manager and playwright. As well as making regular performances at Drury Lane Theatre, Garrick's first play Lethe made its début there in 1740. In 1747 became the manager at Drury Lane, producing and starring in Shakespearean productions. Gave his final performance in Mrs Centlivre's The Wonder in 1776, after giving way to Sheridan as manager of the theatre. www.peopleplayuk.org.uk/guided_tours/drama_tour/18th_century/garrick.php-40k

**Gaskill, William** (1930– ) Theatre director. Founding director of the National Theatre responsible for such productions as The Recruiting Officer (1963) and Mother Courage and Her Children (1965). In 1965 became artistic director for the Royal Court Theatre and also taught and directed at The Royal Academy of Dramatic Art.

**Gay, John** (1685–1732) English dramatist, who established himself in 1715 with The What D'ye Call It. Gay tasted real success with his ballad-opera The Beggar's Opera in 1728, which was innovative in its style, genre and plot. Later adapted by Brecht as the immensely successful The Threepenny Opera. www.luminarium.org/eight/lit/gay/gaybio.htm

**B Major** Foundation of Bertolt Brecht's epic theatre. Gestus refers to physical actions which expose an underlying main social theme of a play.

**Gilham, Geoff** Playwright and Drama in Education teacher. Theatre Powys performed his play The Partridge Dance in 1994 and Big Brum Theatre based their theatre in education program Of Birth and Death (2002) on his play Semmelweis.

**Glass, David** Former dancer and founder of the David Glass Ensemble. Glass worked with influential practitioners including Etienne Decroux, Jacques Lecoq and the Peter Brook Company. In the 1990s he formed the David Glass New Mime Company which evolved into the David Glass Ensemble. His highly physical and experimental theatre productions have toured internationally and include Mosquito Coast (1994), Unheimlich Spine (2003) and Gormenghast (2006–2007). www.davidglassensemble.com

**Globe Theatre**  Built in London in 1599 by Cuthbert Burbage. Heavily associated with Shakespeare, and the company of the 'Chamberlain's Men', led by Richard Burbage. www.globelink.org

**Goat Island**  Established in Chicago in 1987, this company creates movement-based work that is often performed in unconventional settings. Includes Solider, Child, Tortured Man (1987), The Sea And Poison (1998) and When Will The September Roses Bloom? Last Night Was Only A Comedy (2004). www.goatislandperformance.org

**Goethe, Johann Wolfgang von**  (1749–1832)  German playwright, and director. Goethe worked closely with Schiller from 1791 to 1817 as director of the Court Theatre in Weimar, and conceived the 'Rules for Actors' in his 'Weimar School of Acting'. His most praised works are Faust, Part 1 and Part 2 (1808 and 1832 respectively). Both parts are commended for their depth and range of style and dramatic possibility.

**Gogol, Nikolai Vasilievich**  (1809–52)  Russian playwright. His unique style of grotesque comedy was the product of inspirational sources such as Tolstoi, Turgenev and Chekhov. Perhaps Gogol's most celebrated play is The Inspector General (1836), which was famously produced by Meyerhold in 1926. www.kirjasto.sci.fi/gogol.htm

**Goldsmith, Oliver**  (1728–74)  Irish playwright, who after training in medicine began writing in 1757. Goldsmith wrote two satirical plays mocking the middle class of London. The Good Natured Man (1768) and She Stoops to Conquer (1773) were both performed at Covent Garden. www.theatrehistory.com/british/goldsmith001.html

**Gorki, Maxim**  (1868–1936)  Soviet writer, dramatist and critic. Played an active role as a member of the Bolshevik party, which is conveyed in his plays. In 1902, the Moscow Art Theatre produced Gorki's first play The Petty Bourgeoisie (1902). Further successes include The Lower Depths (1902) which is considered a dangerous yet ingenious pro-revolutionist realist play. Gorki's career concluded with a trilogy of autobiographical plays, My Childhood (1914), In the World (1916) and My Universities (1924).

**Granville Barker, Harley**  (1877–1946)  British actor, director and playwright. In 1900, after several years as an actor, Barker wrote and directed his own play The Marrying of Ann Lette. Most highly acclaimed for his productions of A Winter's Tale, Twelfth Night (both 1912) and A Midsummer Night's Dream (1914).

**Greenwich and Lewisham Young People's Theatre Company**  Youth theatre company that aims to provide opportunities for young people through the arts. Their project Voices works with asylum seekers and refugees in South East London and Headstart encourages young people from abroad who do not attend school to get involved in creative tasks. Their touring programme to schools includes Red, White and Blue (2005), Master Juba and SK8 (2008). www.glypt.co.uk

**Griffiths, Trevor**  (1935– )  British dramatist whose plays convey his Marxist viewpoint and empathy for working-class lives. Plays include Occupations (1970), Sam, Sam (1972), The Party (1973) and Comedians (1975). www.trevorgriffiths.co.uk

**Grotowski, Jerzy**  (1933–1998)  Polish director, who studied at the Moscow State Institute of Theatre Arts. Was trained in the methods of Stanislavski, and hence believed that if an actor committed themselves completely both mentally and physically, they could work without unnecessary lighting, scenery and costume. He published his ideas in Towards a Poor Theatre. During the 1960s toured nationally with his Laboratory Theatre Company, achieving success with productions such as Wyspianski's Akropolis.www.owendaly.com/jeff/grotdir.htm#here

**Hare, David**  (1947– )  British dramatist and director. His first plays were written for the Portable Theatre, which he co-founded in 1968. These early productions include Slag (1970) and The Great Exhibition

(1972). Became resident dramatist at the Royal Court in 1970 and at the Nottingham Playhouse in 1973. After several successful plays written for the Royal National Theatre, which included Plenty (1978), A Map of the World (1983) and Pravda (1985), Hare was appointed as associate director. In 1998 he founded Greenpoint Films and received a knighthood for his services to theatre.

**Hauptmann, Elisabeth** (1897–1973)  Brecht's lifelong collaborator. She translated Gay's The Beggar's Opera, to produce the hugely successful The Threepenny Opera. She also kept valuable diaries of Brecht's work.

**Hill, Jane** (Contemporary)  Co-founder of Dell'Arte International in 1971 with her husband Carlo Mazzone-Clementi, Hill assisted in introducing physical theatre training to the United States. This led to a summer Grand Comedy Festival in 1972 and the Dell'Arte School of Mime and Comedy opening in 1975. www.dellarte.com/dellarte.aspx?id=40

**Holcroft, Thomas** (1745–1809)  English playwright. In 1778, his first major work, The Crisis, opened at Drury Lane. This was followed by a series of successes including The Follies of a Day (1784), Seduction (1787) and The School for Arrogance (1791). His most famous play is the comedy The Road to Ruin (1792).

**Hugo, Victor** (1802–85)  French poet, dramatist and novelist. Many of his early plays were forbidden production because of his political opinions. However, in 1828 Hugo's play Amy Robstart made its debut at the Odeon. Many of Hugo's later plays were not performed until years after his death because of censorship. www.victorhugo.gg

**Ibsen, Henrik** (1828–1906)  Norwegian dramatist, appointed as resident dramatist and stage director at the Bergen Theatre. Ibsen's move to Rome in 1864 saw a significant move away from the popular trend of romanticism. The first of these plays were Brand (1865) and Peer Gynt (1867), which both convey a mood of inner turmoil. Ibsen's plays screamed messages of social reform, which emerged in the sub-text of plays such as A Doll's House (1879) and Ghosts (1881). During the 1880s and 1890s Ibsen's plays were symbolist; these include The Wild Duck (1884) and Hedda Gabler (1890).

**Irving, Sir Henry** (1838–1905)  English actor-manager. Joined the Royal Lyceum Theatre in 1856 and worked as a professional actor until 1859. Irving's fresh interpretation of plays led to his appointment as manager at the Lyceum in 1878. www.theirvingsociety.org.uk

**Joint Stock Theatre Company**  Founded in 1974 by David Hare, Max Stafford-Clark and David Aukin. It sort to produce new writing and offered an innovative approach towards British theatre. Gradually evolved into a socialist theatre group under the direction of William Gaskill but in 1989 the company closed due to a lack of funding. www.outofjoint.co.uk

**Jones, Inigo** (1573–1652)  English architect and set designer. Jones worked for King James I, as designer for masques, which were staged at the court. Productions included Jonson's The Masque of Blackness (1605). Jones is also responsible for introducing the proscenium arch onto the English stage. He later developed ideas which would create a sense of perspective and depth on stage, such as backcloths and painted shutters and flats, which moved on turntables and grooves.

**Jonson, Benjamin** (1572–1637)  English playwright. Began his career during the 1590s as both an actor and writer with the Henslowe's men. Gained fame as a writer with Every Man in His Humour (1598). Sejanus, His Fall (1603) was a highly controversial Roman historical play, which angered King James I because of Jonson's overtly Catholic stance. Most praised for his intelligent witty comedies Volpone (1605), The Silent Woman (1609), The Alchemist (1610) and Bartholomew Fair (1614).www.luminarium.org/sevenlit/jonson

**Kabuki** Traditional Japanese drama, evolved during the seventeenth century. Originally regarded as a rowdy prostitutes' entertainment, but eventually developed into a highly skilled melodramatic form. Kabuki actors move with puppet-like gestures and deliver the text in a staccato chant and are known for lavish costumes, make-up and music.www.kabuki21.com

**Kaiser, Georg** (1878–1945) German expressionist playwright. Most famous for his trilogy of plays: Die Koralle (1917), Gas I (1918), and Gas II (1920).

**Kantor, Tadeusz** (1915– ) Polish stage designer and director. During the Second World War he founded the Independent Theatre. In 1956 he created the avant-garde Cricot II company, which was a collaborative company of performers and painters. Kantor developed his 'Theatre of Death' during the 1970s in productions such as The Green Pill (1973) and The Dead Class (1975).

**Kaprow, Allan** (1927–2006) American art theorist responsible for an artistic movement during the 1950s known as 'the happening', which gave rise to the movement of 'performance art'. Within his work he attempted to blur the boundaries between art and reality.

**Kathakali** (Story Play) Hindu dance and drama form dating from the seventeenth century, depicting tales of the Mahabharata and Ramayana. The strong focus on facial, eye and hand gestures suggest that it was inspired by Kuttiyattam. www.cyberkerala.com/kathakali/index.html

**Kazan, Elia** (1909–2003) American director. Kazan was co-founder of The Actor's Studio, which promoted a naturalistic style of acting, based on Stanislavski's system and Lee Strasberg's method. Kazan's stage productions include A Streetcar Named Desire (1947), Death of a Salesman (1949), Cat on a Hot Tin Roof (1955) and Sweet Bird of Youth (1959). His films include Streetcar (1951), On the Waterfront (1954) and East of Eden (1955). In 1999 he received a honorary Oscar for his lifetime achievement and three Toby awards. www.moderntimes.com/palace/kazan

**Kean, Charles** (1811–68) English actor and theatre manager. In 1950 took up management at the Princess's Theatre. His productions were noted for their historical accuracy and the great care and meticulous eye for detail in the lighting of sets. He was the first person to accurately focus limelight. www.peopleplayuk.org.uk/guided_tours/19th_century/pictorial_drama.php

**Kean, Edmund** (1789–1833) English actor who developed his talent as the Shakespearean villain, injecting characters such as Richard III with a volatile, monstrous energy.

**Kemble, John Phillip** (1757–1823) English actor and theatre manager. In 1788 became manager of the Drury Lane Theatre, where he had a series of successes with productions such as Henry VIII and Coriolanus. By 1796 ill health caused Kemble to leave Drury Lane and continue work at the Covent Garden Theatre, which he managed until it was destroyed by fire in1808.

**Komissarzhevskaya, Vera Fedorovna** (1864–1910) Russian actress and theatre manager. Joined the Alexandrinsky Theatre in 1896, and enjoyed success in roles such as Nora in Ibsen's A Doll's House. In 1904 formed her own company that would explore new kinds of theatre, inviting Meyerhold to be artistic director. The company produced symbolist plays by dramatists such as Maxim Gorki. www.teatrvfk.ru/eng/history.php

**Kott, Jan** (1914–2001) Influential Polish theatre critic and Shakespeare expert whose works include Shakespeare, Our Contemporary (1964). www.culture.pl/en/culture/artykuly/os_kott_jan

**Kuttiyattam** Ancient religious Indian art-form. Actors perform in a code of gesture and rhythmic chants in Kuttiyattam theatres, such as the Vatukumnathan Temple of Trichun. Main temples stage about one performance per year, each lasting several days. Costumes are lavish; the brightly coloured headwear symbolises Indian gods and demons.

**Lecoq, Jacques** (1921–1999) French mime artist, who trained at the School of Dramatic Arts in Paris and worked for a period with the Commedia dell'Arte. During his later years became a teacher at the French School of Fine Arts and the highly disciplined Lecoq School in Paris now trains mime artists from all over the world in the relationship between body, movement and space.

**LeCompte, Elizabeth** (1944– ) American director and playwright. In 1979 she became artistic director of the Wooster Group, in which she co-wrote and directed productions such as Sakonnet Point (1975), Rumstick Road (1977) and Nayatt School (1978). In 1984 became Associate Director of the American National Theatre and in 2007 directed Hamlet.

**Leigh, Mike** (1943– ) British director best known for his film work based in realism, including Bleak Moments (1970), Nuts in May (1975), Home Sweet Home (1982), High Hopes (1988), Life is Sweet (1991), and Secrets and Lies (1996). In 2005 experienced stage success with 2000 Years based on religious tensions within a Jewish family. www.alt.flix.co.uk/direcgui/mikeleig.htm

**Lepage, Robert** (1957– ) Leading Canadian director of his generation and is considered an auteur director. Known for his production of Hamlet, which was altered so dramatically it was renamed Elsinore and has directed a number of other Shakespeare plays. Has also explored film and adapted his play The Far Side of the Moon for cinema. Opera has also been an area of experimentation – in 1997 his production of The Caserne opened in Quebec. www.robertlepage.com

**Lillo, George** (1691–1739) English playwright. Lillo is known to have written two major tragedies, The London Merchant (1731) and Fatal Curiosity (1736). www.theatredatabase.com/18th_century/george_lillo.html

**Littlewood, Joan** (1914–2002) English director who studied at the Royal Academy of Dramatic Arts. Founded her own amateur company 'Theatre Union', which after the Second World War reformed as 'Theatre Workshop'. The company, based at the Stratford East Theatre in London, gained huge success with productions including Oh! What A Lovely War (1963). www.stratfordeast.com/history.php

**Lope De Vega** (1562–1635) Spanish dramatist and poet of Spain's Golden Age. Lope's three-act verse commedia plays set a standard style for other Spanish playwrights to follow. His comedies include The Idiot Lady (1613) and The Dog in the Manger (1613–15). Among his greatest works are his plays which focus on the theme of adultery including The Wise Man's Punishment (1598–1601) and the tragic Punishment Without Revenge (1631).

**Lorca, Federico Garcia** (1898–1936) Spanish poet and dramatist. Lorca's early works include the unsuccessful symbolist play The Butterfly's Evil Spell and the more popular revolutionary play Mariana Pineda. In 1932 he founded a student touring theatre group, named La Barraca, which proved a great success in the rural areas of Spain. His final works, Blood Wedding (1933), Yerma (1934) and The House of Bernada Alba (1936) angered Spanish fascists due to their revolutionary sub-text, resulting in Lorca's murder.

**M6 Theatre Company** Founded in 1977 and based in Rochdale, M6 constantly strives to create theatre for young people that is accessible, inclusive and stimulating. They have toured with such plays as Danny, King of the Basement (2007) and One Little Word (2008). Also has a thriving youth theatre which aims to develop the artistic and life skills of its participants. www.m6theatre.co.uk

**Maeterlinck, Maurice** (1862–1949) Belgian symbolist poet and playwright who in 1911 won the Nobel Prize for literature. As a predecessor of the Theatre of Silence, Maeterlinck believed in the use of dramatic pauses, which encourage the audience to use their own imaginations to fill in perhaps verbally inexpressible emotions. His plays include Pelleas and Melisande (1893). www.kirjasto.sci.fi/maeterli.htm

**Malina, Judith** (1926– ) Actress and drama practitioner. Co-founded The Living Theatre in 1947 and continues to have joint artistic control over the company. Has a successful career as an actress appearing in television projects such as ER and The Sopranos. Her film credits include The Addams Family (1991) and Awakenings (1996). www.livingtheatre.org/history.php

**Marlowe, Christopher** (1564–93) English playwright and poet. His first plays, such as Tamburlane the Great (c. 1587) were extremely popular because of their fresh and often controversial approach. His plays, which include The Jew of Malta (c. 1589) The Mascacre at Paris (c. 1589), and Edward II (c. 1592), were most often produced by the Admiral's Men. The last of Marlowe's plays, Dr Faustus, a demonic play about the seven deadly sins, is perhaps his most famous and widely produced play. www.marlowe-society.org/marlowe/life/life.html

**McKellen, Ian (Murray)** (1939– ) British actor. He developed his reputation as a classical and enterprising actor with the Prospect Theatre Company. McKellen's work with the Royal Shakespeare Company from 1974 includes performances as Macbeth (1976), and in touring productions such as The Three Sisters (1978) and Twelfth Night. Has also appeared in films such as Richard III (1995), Gods and Monsters (1998) and The Lord of the Rings trilogy (2001). In 2007 took the title role in Trevor Nunn's production of King Lear at The Swan Theatre in Stratford-Upon-Avon and The New London Theatre. www.mckellen.com

**Meckler, Nancy** (Contemporary) British director of Shared Experience. Productions include Anna Karenina. Meckler's film work tackles taboo social issues such as homosexuality and AIDS, including Sister My Sister, and Alive and Kicking. She has also worked with the Royal Shakespeare Company on productions of The Comedy of Errors (2005) and Romeo and Juliet (2006). www.sharedexperience.org.uk

**Meiningen Theatre Company** The Meiningen Theatre Company at the court of George II was directed by the Duke of Saxe-Meiningen and his wife Ellen Franz. The Meiningen Theatre promoted the idea of an ensemble company who worked closely together. Both Antoine and Stanislavski were inspired by the company when developing their naturalistic styles of acting. www.meiningermuseen.de/mmuseeneng/georg2.html

**Melodrama** Style of drama descended from the medieval morality plays begun in France in 1800 by the writer Guilbert Pixercourt. Melodrama uses stock characters and always portrays a tale of good triumphing over evil and was an extremely popular form of middle-class entertainment throughout the nineteenth century.

**Meyerhold, Vsevold Emilievich** (1874–1940) Pioneering Russian director who dedicated his life and career to revolutionising theatre. Trained as an actor from 1898 but after leaving the Moscow Art Theatre in 1902, his early attempts at introducing symbolist drama to the provinces of Russia were not successful. Innovative work at Stanislavski's experimental studio theatre also proved unpopular. In 1906, he was invited by the Russian actress Vera Komissarzhevskaya to become artistic director for her new exploratory theatre. Productions with Komissarzhevskaya included Ibsen's Hedda Gabler and Maeterlinck's Sister Beatrice. In 1908, he was appointed director of St Petersberg's Imperial Opera and Drama Theatres where he developed his theory of the actor-cabotin, based on Commedia dell'Arte. He also injected political opinion and particularly Bolshevism into his theatre of revolution, which led to his appointment as head of the Theatre Division of the People's Commissariat for Education in 1920. During the 1920s Meyerhold developed his theory of biomechanics, which was a system of movement derived from the circus, with athletic movements working as a 'machine' for acting. His later productions included Sukhovo-Kobylin's Tarelkin's Death, Gogol's The Inspector General and

Mayakovsky's Soviet play Mystery-Bouffe. They introduced a shift from symbolism to Theatre of the Grotesque, in which Meyerhold would use more than one contrasting genre. www.meyerhold.org

**Middleton, Thomas** (c. 1580–1627) English playwright. Middleton's early works, including A Trick to Catch the Old One (c. 1604) and A Mad World, My Masters (c. 1605) were comedies written for the Boys of St Paul's. Middleton also wrote for the Henslowe's Men and the Admirals Men. He collaborated with other writers such as Thomas Dekker to produce plays including The Honest Whore (1604), and with William Rowley to produce A Fair Quarrel (c. 1616) and The Changeling (1633). Middelton's last play, Women Beware Women (c. 1625) is perhaps his finest. www.thomasmiddleton.org/responses.php

**Miller, Arthur** (1915–2005) American playwright. Perhaps Miller's most famous plays are Death of a Salesman (1949) and his tale of witchcraft trials, The Crucible (1953). During his brief marriage to Marilyn Monroe in 1955, Miller retired from writing and did not return until 1964 after their divorce. Miller's marriage to the famous film star was the subject of his comeback play After the Fall (1964). He went on to produce two more successful plays, which were emotional works of modern tragedy: Incident at Vichy (1964) and The Price (1968). He continued to write into the 1990s with plays such as The Last Yankee and Broken Glass and his final contribution to theatre was Finishing the Picture staged in Chicago in 2004 based on his experiences of filming The Misfits in the 1960s. www.ibiblio.org/miller/life.html

**Mime** (or mimus) A style of theatre that relies on the physical rather than the verbal to express meaning. Its origins can be traced back to the 5th century when the Greeks would use mime within their theatre to re-enact scenes of situations instantly recognisable and relevant to their Athenian audiences. www.mime.info/history-lust.html

**Mise-en-scène** French term which refers to what is in the scene. It refers to how the director, designer and performer have interpreted the playwright's original vision.

**Mnouchkine, Ariane** (1934– ) French director. In 1964 Mnouchkine founded her own collective theatre group, Theatre du Soleil, which was successful with productions such as The Golden Age (1975). Breaking away from theatre for a short period, Mnouchkine sought inspiration from her father's experience in film by making a film based on Molière. Returning to theatre in the 1980s Mnouchkine worked mainly on Shakespearean productions, such as Richard II (1981) and Twelfth Night (1982). Mnouchkine has collaborated with the feminist writer Helen Cixous on plays like Norodom Sihanouk (1985). Her work is characterised by the influence of oriental performance traditions.

**Molière, Jean-Baptiste Poquelin** (1622–73) French actor-manager and dramatist. Molière's comic talent was inspired by the Italian commedia. His early plays include The Blunderer (1653) and Lover's Quarrel (1656). The comedy of Molière's plays relied heavily on the skill of the actor, rather than technical and artificial resources. His plays such as The Affected Ladies (1659) School for Wives (1662) and The Magnificent Lovers (1670) were a resounding success with the Parisian audience. However, they were heavily criticised by the church. www.site-Molière.com

**Monologue** A lengthy speech for one person. Often actors are required to prepare a monologue for an audition.

**Moscow Art Theatre Studio** Founded in 1897 by Konstantin Stanislavski and Vladimir Nemirovich-Danchenko. Heavily inspired by the Meiningen Theatre Company, the Moscow Art Theatre was designed to achieve a new style of realist performance. The company premiered in October in 1898 with Tolstoi's Tsar Fyodor Ioannonvich at the Hermitage Theatre. It then went on to produce the opening performances of Chekhov's most successful plays. The Moscow Art Theatre also proved itself to be pioneering in its experimentation, over 30 years, with symbolist plays by writers including Gorki, Ibsen, Hauptmann and Maeterlinck. www.actors-studio.com/history/mat.html

**Naturalism**  A theory of human psychology. A naturalist play requires the actor to identify with the psychology and consequent behaviour of their character. Naturalism was a modernist movement born out of Darwin's Origin of Species by Means of Natural Selection (1859), and the ideas of Zola. The naturalist plays of writers such as Ibsen and Chekhov provided the fundamental building blocks for Stanislavski's system for acting. Today naturalism is most commonly used in television.

**Nemirovich-Danchenko, Vladimir Ivanovich** (1859–1943)  Russian director who worked as an acting teacher at the Moscow Philharmonic Society. However, in 1897 he left and collaborated with Stanislavski to found the Moscow Art Theatre, taking with him some of his best students, including Meyerhold and Olga Knipper. Nemirovich-Danchenko was a close companion of the great Russian writer Chekhov, and consequently the Moscow Art Theatre became the home of Chekhov's plays. www.mhatschool.theatre.ru/en/about/history

**Neo-classicism**  An artistic movement during the Italian Renaissance which recaptured rules from ancient Greek and Roman drama. Neo-classicism in the theatre refers particularly to Aristotle's Poetics.

**Newson, Lloyd** (1957–  )  Dancer and artistic director. Newson's interest in the human psyche arose from his study of psychology and social work at Melbourne University. He went on to win a scholarship to attend London Contemporary Dance School before working with a series of dance companies including Modern Dance Ensemble and Extemporary Dance Theatre. In 1986 he established his own physical theatre company, DV8. www.dv8.co.uk/about.dv8/LN_butterworth.html

**Nietzsche, Friedrich** (1844–1900)  German philosopher. Nietzsche's influential theories of theatre were expressed in his essay The Birth of Tragedy. www.en.wikipedia.org/wiki/Friedrich_Nietzche

**Noble, Adrian** (1950–  )  British director. Noble worked for several prestigious British theatre companies including Bristol Old Vic, the Royal Exchange Theatre and as artistic director and chief executive of the Royal Shakespeare Company. His famous productions include The Duchess of Malfi (1980), A Doll's House (1981), King Lear (1982), Henry V (1982) and As You Like It (1985). Following his departure from the RSC in 2003 his successes include the West End production of Chitty Chitty Bang Bang and Jean Paul's Satre's play Kean (2007). He has recently staged Verdi's version of Macbeth at the Metropolitan Opera House.

**Noh**  Meaning 'talent', Noh is a Japanese form of ritual theatre which heavily focuses on gesture. It evolved in the fourteenth century and was originally performed by priests in Buddhist temples. Noh is made up of a variety of contrasting voices, music and movements, which express the Japanese theory that the world is in a constant state of change, and also the dialectic theory, 'yin and yang'. www.artelino.com/articles/noh_theater.asp

**Nunn, Trevor Robert** (1940–  )  British theatre and film director. Nunn joined the Royal Shakespeare Company in 1965 as artistic director and later became chief executive. Nunn had a series of successes with the company, which have included The Reveger's Tragedy (1966), The Comedy of Errors (1976), Macbeth (1976), and All's Well That Ends Well (1981). More recent successes include King Lear and The Seagull. Outside of the Royal Shakespeare Company Nunn is also responsible for staging the West End hit musicals Cats (1981), Starlight Express (1984), Sunset Boulevard and Les Misérables.

**O'Neill, Eugene Gladstone** (1888–1953)  The earliest successful US playwright. From 1916 O'Neill belonged to a group of writers called the Provincetown Players. He produced his first play, Beyond the Horizon, in 1918. O'Neill was a writer of multiple genres, and his many works include Anna Christie (1920), Lazarus Laughed (1925–6) and The Iceman Cometh (1939). www.eoneil.com

**Oldenburg, Claes Thure** (1929– )  American sculptor known for his public art installations and innovative pop-art work during the 1960s. He regularly collaborates with Coosje Van Bruggen on large scale projects including The Music Room in 2005. www.oldenburgvanbruggen.com

**Oldfield, Anne** (1683–1730)  English actress. Oldfield's first professional performance was in 1692, at Drury Lane. However, she established herself as an actress in 1703, in a performance of The Careless Husband. Oldfield was successful in various roles, which included Silvia in The Recruiting Officer (1706), Anromache in The Distrest Mother (1712) and Lady Townly in The Provoked Husband (1728). www.nndb.com/people/050/000102741

**Olivier, Laurence** (1907–89)  British actor and director. After establishing himself as a great theatrical actor at the Birmingham Rep and the Old Vic theatres, Olivier became an international film star in films such as Wuthering Heights. In 1941 Olivier returned to Britain to direct and star in The Demi-Paradise (1943) and Henry V (1944). In 1944 Olivier became director of the Old Vic Company, and gave what were considered to be his finest performances as Richard III and Oedipus. In 1963 Olivier became director at the newly formed National Theatre, creating highly acclaimed productions such as Othello (1964) and The Dance of Death (1971). The remainder of Olivier's career was devoted to film roles, the most remarkable of which was as King Lear in 1984. www.laurenceolivier.com

**Osborne, John** (1929–94)  British dramatist and actor. His third play Look Back in Anger premièred in 1956 at the Royal Court and was a huge success. Osborne's major plays represent a break away from the conventions of realism. They include The Entertainer (1957), Inadmissible Evidence (1964) and A Patriot for Me (1965).

**Pinter, Harold** (1930– )  British dramatist. Pinter's early plays include The Birthday Party (1958), Slight Ache (1959), The Caretaker (1960) and The Homecoming (1965). His play Landscape and Silence (1969) marked a change in Pinter's style; he began to experiment with the concept of time. His plays that followed (Old Times in 1971, No Man's Land in 1975 and A Kind of Alaska in 1982) were staged by the Royal Shakespeare Company. In 1975 Pinter became associate director of the Royal National Theatre, working extensively with Peter Hall. His contribution to the arts has been marked with several prestigious accolades including the Nobel Peace Prize in Literature in 2005 and the Legion d'Honneur in 2007. The British Library recognise his canonical status as a playwright in their recent purchase of his complete literary archive for over £1,000,000. www.haroldpinter.org

**Poliakoff, Stephen** (1952– )  Playwright, director and screenwriter. Poliakoff trained at King's College in Cambridge before becoming writer in residence for the National Theatre in 1976. His writing for television is extensive and includes Stronger Than the Sun (1977), Soft Targets (1982) and Joe's Palace (2007). His other main career pathways have been film such as Hidden City (1988) and Century (1993) and theatre which began with Granny in 1969.

**Postmodern Dance**  A style of dance that was popularised during the twentieth century in reaction to modern dance. Judson Dance Theatre were at the forefront of this movement. www.artslynx.org/dance/postmodern.htm

**Presentational Theatre**  The terms 'presentational theatre' and 'representational theatre' describe the relationship between the world of the performance and the audience's world. In representational forms of theatre, such as realism and naturalism, there is no direct contact between the performers, the performance and the audience. The performers create a parallel reality on stage and ignore the presence of the audience. In presentational theatre, such as Brecht's epic theatre, there is direct communication between the performers and the audience and the events of the performance are presented directly to the audience as if these events were a part of the audience's 'here-and-now' experience.

**Producing Houses** Theatres that create productions on site with an ensemble of actors and artistic director.

**Proscenium stage** The most common stage used in Western theatres. The audience sit away from the stage and view the action as if looking through a picture frame.

**Protagonist** A Greek term which refers to the main character of a play.

**Psycho-realism** The term that is sometimes used to describe the performance effects of Stanislavski's system of acting which sought to produce 'realism' in characterisation through creating a balance between the actor's 'inner experiencing' of the role and its precisely crafted physical and vocal expression.

**Racine, Jean** (1639–99) French poet and dramatist. Racine gained popularity and success with the Parisian audience with productions such as Andromaque (1667), which were staged by Molière at the Hotel de Bourgogne. He is most famous for his tragedies which include Britannicus (1668), Berenice (1670), Mithridate (1673) and Phedre (1667).

**Rainer, Yvonne** (1934– ) American dancer and film maker. Rainer is known for her innovative pioneering breakthrough in dance during the 1960s. Rebelling against the traditional conventions of dance, Rainer often made use of multi-media resources, such as film clips and projected images. In 1990 she was a recipient of a MacArthur Foundation Fellowship and currently teaches at the Whitney Museum in New York.

**Ravenhill, Mark** (1966– ) British playwright who is known for his shocking contemporary play Shopping and F***ing. Currently he is moving towards creating theatre for a younger audience and has premièred his play Citizenship at the National Theatre and Product at the Edinburgh Festival. In 2006 he collaborated with the physical theatre company Frantic Assembly on a touring production of Pool (No Water). www.inyerface-theatre.com

**Realism** Based on the notion of direct mimesis (art impersonating life). Realist theatre is traditionally performed on a proscenium arch stage.

**Receiving House** A theatre that accommodates for artistic productions that tour around different venues with their work.

**Reinhardt, Max** (1873–1943) Austrian actor and director. Reinhardt began his career as an actor at the Deutsches Theatre in Berlin, where he was tutored and influenced by Otto Brahm. Here Reinhardt gained successful experience directing the plays of Gorki, Strindberg and Wedekind. After his appointment as director of the Deutsches Theatre, Reinhardt opened an intimate attaching theatre called the 'Kammerspiele', which introduced new modern plays. His later achievements include founding the Salzberg Festival, where he directed Hofmannstahl's Jedermann in 1920.

**Restoration drama** A period in English drama, similar to the French neo-classical era, which dated from 1660 to the early 1700s. Plays of the restoration period include Dryden's Indian Queen (1664) and George Villiers The Rehearsal (1617). www.theatrehistory.com/british/restoration_drama_001.html

**Robertson, Thomas William** (1829–71) English playwright. Robertson introduced a style of realist farce onto the English stage. He is most renowned for his plays Caste (1867), Play (1868), School (1869) and M.P. (1870), which show Robertson to be a forerunner of naturalism. www.wayneturney.20m.com/robertsontom.htm

**Romanticism**  The predominant artistic movement of the late eighteenth century and most of the nineteenth century, up to 1875. The movement began in Europe during the Age of Enlightenment with the philosopher Kant, whose ideas were dramatically realised in the plays of writers such as Rousseau, Nietzsche and Schopenhauer.

**Rose Theatre**  Built in London on the south bank of the Thames in 1587. The Rose was owned and managed by Philip Henslowe, and produced plays mainly by Christopher Marlowe. The Rose was the home to companies such as the Strange's Men, and the Admiral's Men. www.rosetheatre.org.uk

**Royal Court Theatre**  From 1904 the Royal Court Theatre was managed by J.E. Vedrenne and Harley Granville Barker. It was during these years that the theatre introduced and established the huge influential talent of Shaw. From 1956, George Devine used the theatre to present plays of the English Stage Company. The company was responsible for introducing talents such as John Osborne, Arnold Wesker and John Arden into British theatre. In the 1970s the Royal Court Theatre introduced the innovative talent of writers such as David Storey and Edward Bond, and the plays of Joint Stock. www.royalcourttheatre.com

**Royal National Theatre**  After the Second World War, £1 million of public funds was given to build a national theatre for Britain on the banks of the Thames. The first appointed Director of the National Theatre was Lawrence Olivier, who enabled the company to perform at the Old Vic Theatre until building was completed. Olivier retired as director in 1973, after success with productions such as Hamlet and Peter Shaffer's The Royal Hunt of the Sun. Today the National Theatre is highly acclaimed as one of Britain's most prestigious companies. www.nationaltheatre.org.uk

**Satyr play**  Developed in ancient Greece, satyr plays were parodies of historical myths and legends. The only remaining original satyr is Euripides' Cyclops. These original satyrs gave rise to a style of drama we now recognise as farce.

**Schiller, Friedrich** (1759–1805)  German playwright. Schiller worked closely with Goethe at the Court Theatre in Weimar. His plays include Robbers (1781), Love and Intrigue (1782–3), Don Carlos (1787) and his trilogy Wallenstein's Camp, The Piccolomini, and Wallenstein's Death (all 1799). Schiller is greatly praised for his final play Wilhelm Tell, written in 1804. www.schillerinstitute.org

**Scribe, Eugène** (1791–1861)  French playwright who created the 'well made play' along with Victorien Sardou. Scribe wrote over 400 plays including Un Verre D'eau (A Glass of Water) (1850).

**Semiotics**  The study of signs. In the theatre semiotics applies to the meanings within a play, which are decoded by the audience. Semiotics in theatre can be present in the actual written text, sub-text, or in costume, setting, lighting or the actions of a character. Codes in different productions of the same play can alter due to individual interpretation.

**Shaffer, Peter** (1926– )  British dramatist. In 1958 Gielgud directed Shaffer's first success, Five Finger Exercise. Perhaps Shaffer's most famous drama is The Royal Hunt of the Sun (1964), which was a great success for the National Theatre and his entertaining farce Black Comedy (1965). He has developed a strong professional partnership with John Dexter who directed many of his plays in the seventies. Two of his later works Equus (1973) and Amadeus (1979), were verbally and visually spectacular and considered contemporary masterpieces which have both since been transformed into film. Equus has proved to have timeless popularity illustrated by its major revival in the West End in 2007 and national tour in 2008.

**Shakespeare Memorial Theatre**  Built in honour of the prolific playwright. The theatre opened on 23 April 1879, on the anniversary of Shakespeare's birth. www.shakespeare.org.uk

**Shakespeare, William** (1564–1616)  Prolific English playwright, born in Stratford-upon-Avon. In 1594 Shakespeare became a member of a company of actors called The Lord Chamberlain's Men. Shakespeare's early works, which include The Comedy of Errors, Two Gentlemen of Verona, The Taming of the Shrew, Titus Andronicus and Richard III, were produced by the Lord Chamberlain's Men, and gave Shakespeare recognition and popularity on the London stage. This led to further successes which include Love's Labour's Lost, A Midsummer Night's Dream, The Merchant of Venice, Romeo and Juliet and Richard II. From 1598 The Lord Chamberlain's Men, renaming themselves as The King's Men, performed at the Globe Theatre. During this time Shakespeare wrote what are considered to be his finest plays: Much Ado About Nothing, As You Like It, Twelfth Night, All's Well That Ends Well, Measure for Measure, The Merry Wives of Windsor, Julius Caesar, Hamlet, Othello, King Lear, Macbeth, Antony and Cleopatra and Coriolanus. Late works include Pericles, Prince of Tyre, Cymbeline, The Winter's Tale and The Tempest. Shakespeare has a timeless quality which appeals to a contemporary audience. His plays are still widely produced today in both the theatre and in film. www.shakespeare.org.uk

**Shared Experience Company**  Theatre Company founded in 1975, which tours fringe theatres in Britain, particularly in London. The company is renowned for their fresh energetic approach and minimalist sets in productions of British classical plays and adaptations of literary classics such as Anna Karenina. www.sharedexperience.org.uk

**Shaw, George Bernard** (1856–1950)  Irish playwright and critic. Shaw's first play Widowers' Houses (1892) conveyed his political opinions on the greed-driven ruling bourgeois and aristocracy. Shaw was also heavily critical of his contemporary British theatre and did much for the promotion of the director in replacement of the actor-manager. Shaw's greatest success, Pygmalion (1914), led critics to hail him as Britain's leading playwright. www.shawsociety.org.uk

**Shchepkin, Mikhail Semenovich** (1788–1863)  Russian actor. In 1822 Shchepkin was invited to join the Maly Theatre Company in Moscow. Shchepkin was a great realist actor in the plays of Gogol, Chekhov and Gorki, and was greatly admired by Russia's creator of naturalistic acting, Konstantin Stanislavski.

**Sheridan, Richard Brinsley** (1751–1816)  Irish playwright and theatre manager. In 1776 Sheridan was appointed manager of the financially struggling Drury Lane Theatre, where he remained until 1809. Sheridan is best known for his satirical comedy The School for Scandal (1777), which is a mocking portrayal of gossip and scandal among the upper class.

**Shirley, James** (1596–1666)  English playwright. Shirley's sharp comedies include The Witty Fair One (1628), Hyde Park (1632), The Lady of Pleasure (1635) and The Sisters (1642). His tragedies include The Traitor (1631), The Politician (c. 1639) and The Cardinal (1641). www.luminarium.org/sevenlit/shirley

**Siddons, Sarah** (1755–1831)  English actress. Siddons' skill developed when she worked with a Manchester-based touring company. Perhaps her greatest performance was at Drury Lane in 1785, as Lady Macbeth. Siddons was a dignified and elegant actress, whose success only grew when she left Drury Lane for Covent Garden in 1801.

**Soliloquy**  A speech delivered by one actor when no other actors are present on stage. A soliloquy is often an intimate speech during which a character expresses his or her true emotions and thoughts.

**Stafford-Clarke, Max** (1941–  )  British director who has worked for several prestigious theatre companies such as Traverse Theatre, Joint Stock Theatre (of which he is founder), and the Royal Court Theatre. In 1993 he established Out of Joint Theatre Company who are dedicated to showcasing new plays and contemporary playwrights such as Mark Ravenhill, David Hare and Timberlake Wertenbaker. One of his most recent and well known projects is his direction of Hare's play The Permanent Way. He

has also written a monograph entitled Letters to George: The Account of a Rehearsal.
www.outofjoint.co.uk/aboutus/biogs.html

**Stanislavski, Konstantin Sergeivich** (1863–1938)  Russian actor, director and acting trainer. In 1898, Stanislavski founded the Moscow Art Theatre with Nemirovich-Danchenko. They addressed the major problems that theatre of that period was facing. Dramatists were increasingly writing realist plays, rather than popular melodramas, and hence demanded a realist style of acting. Influenced by the Meiningen Theatre Company and the great actor Tomarso Salvini, Stanislavski devised a system of acting. This system was broken down into ten elements. Stanislavski is noted for his success in directing and acting in the plays of Chekhov, such as The Seagull and The Cherry Orchard, which relied on the skill of the actor to communicate the subtle sub-text. www.kryingsky.com/stan/Biography/bot.html

**Steele, Richard** (1672–1729)  Irish dramatist. Steele's first play The Christian Hero (1701) was written whilst he was a soldier. The main influence Steele had on the theatre was his promotion of new genres and styles. In 1715 Steele was knighted and was later appointed manager at the Drury Lane Theatre.

**Strasberg, Lee** (1901–82)  American director and acting trainer. Strasberg was a great believer in Stanislavski's system for acting, and from this he created the 'method', which he introduced during the 1950s at the Actor's Studio. Strasberg went on to train many great 'method' actors in both film and stage. These included Marlon Brando, Montgomery Clift, Ann Bancroft, Shelley Winters, Paul Newman and Joanne Woodward. Strasberg's method is still widely used today by many actors whom we see on our screens. Examples include Meryl Streep, Al Pacino, Robert De Niro and Dustin Hoffman.

**Strindberg, August** (1849–1912)  Swedish writer. Strindberg's most famous naturalist play is Miss Julie (1888), however elements of Strindberg's pioneering break to symbolism are also evident in this play. Strindberg's later symbolist plays have received immense praise and include The Great Highway (1909) and The Dream Play (1902). In 1907 Strindberg worked with August Falk, running the Intimate Theatre, which was modelled on Reinhardt's Kammerspielhaus. The chamber plays he wrote for the theatre include Storm Weather (1907), The Burned House (1907), The Ghost Sonata (1907) and The Pelican (1907). These are all related by the theme of death. Strindberg's highly stylised theatre influenced and helped to shape the twentieth century modernist movements such as surrealism, expressionism and absurdism.

**Symbolism**  Modernist movement which began with the French poets during the 1870s. Symbolism was a rejection of realism and naturalism. Ibsen was one of the first symbolist dramatists, with plays such as The Wild Duck. The most famous symbolist dramatist was Maurice Maeterlinck. His plays include The Intruder, The Blind (both 1890) and Pelleas and Melisande (1892).

**Synge, John Millington** (1871–1909)  Irish playwright. Synge produced his most acclaimed works in his final years. These plays include In Shadow of the Glen (1903), Riders to the Sea (1904) and The Well of the Saints (1905). Many of these later plays were controversial in the respect that they questioned Irish morality, and were the cause of some disturbance and rioting in Ireland. From 1905 Synge played an active role in the Abbey Theatre in Dublin, which introduced the plays of new writers onto the stage. www.online-literature.com/synge

**Tableau**  French word, meaning 'living picture'. Actors form a still-image on stage, which is often used to create dramatic impact, and can give the audience an opportunity to reflect. Tableaux were very popular in late eighteenth and nineteenth century drama, observed particularly in plays such as Caste by Tom Robertson.

**Tara Arts Company**  Founded by Jatinder Verma. During the 1980s the company produced a number of Western classic plays, using Asian styles of performance, such as Kathakali. www.tara-arts.com

**Terry, Ellen** (1847–1928)  English actress. Terry performed for 25 years at Irving's Lyceum Theatre in leading roles such as Ophelia (1878), Lady Macbeth (1888), and Volumina (1901). After Irving's death Terry attempted management at the Imperial Theatre, employing her son Edward Gordon Craig as set designer in a production of Ibsen's The Vikings (1903).

**Theatre Royal**  Opened in 1884 by the actor/manager Charles Dillion with their first performance of Richelieu, Theatre Royal is situated in Stratford East in London. In 1953 Joan Littlewood brought Theatre Workshop Company to its doors producing such plays as Twelfth Night(1953) and Volpone (1955). In more recent times the theatre has staged such productions as The Battle of Green Lanes (2004), Sammy and Family Man (2008). www.stratfordeast.com/history.php

**Thespis**  Greek actor whose idea it was to create a main character who was detached from the chorus. The word 'thespian' is still used today to describe actors.

**Thrust Stage**  A style of staging that extends out into the audience on three sides creating a more intimate relationship between the actor and their observers

**Tolstoy, Leo Nikolaivich** (1828–1910)  Great Russian writer who is most renowned for his novels Resurrection, Anna Karenina and War and Peace, all of which were dramatised by the Moscow Art Theatre. However, Tolstoy is also remembered for several successful plays, which include The Power of Darkness (1886) and The Fruits of Enlightenment (1891).

**Tourneur, Cyril** (c. 1575–1626)  Little known writer who is famous for only one play, The Revenger's Tragedy (c. 1606).

**Tragi-comedy**  Throughout history playwrights have tried to synthesise the genres of comedy and tragedy into a new hybrid genre. The Elizabethan dramatists often mixed comic and tragic elements in their plays. Measure for Measure is tragedy with a happy ending. The Fool in King Lear is an example of a comic character in a tragedy. Chekhov was the first modern writer to exploit tragi-comedy in plays like The Cherry Orchard in which a helpless and introverted group of characters are unable to see the comedy and tragedy of their lives. In tragi-comedy it is only the audience who sympathise with characters whilst appreciating their ludicrous behaviour.

**Vakhtangov, Eugene** (1883–1922)  Russian actor and director. Vakhtangov began his career at the Moscow Art Theatre, as an actor in 1911. His symbolist and expressionist work gave momentum to the Moscow Art Theatre's Studio Theatre. Vakhtangov's achievements within the Studio Theatre led to it being renamed the Vakhtangov Theatre after his death. www.direct.vtheatre.net/vakht.html

**Wagner (Wilhelm) Richard** (1813–83)  German composer of musical drama. Wagner is renowned for his operas, which include Rienzi (1838–40), The Flying Dutchman (1841), Siegfried (1856) and The Twilight of the Gods (1869–74). Wagner believed that dramatic art should exist as a unity of expressive elements, in his idea of total artwork (Gesamtkunstwerk). These ideas, as well as others, were expressed in his essays Art and Revolution (1849), The Art Work of the Future (1849) and Opera and Drama (1851). www.wagneroperas.com

**Warner, Deborah** (1959– )  British director, who has worked for prestigious companies such as the Royal Shakespeare Company and founder of the Kick Theatre Company in 1980 which performed plays by practitioners such as Brecht and Buchner. She has also directed film including her production of The Last September (1999), opera and classical music projects. Happy Days (2007) is her most recent production at The National Theatre in London.

**Wedekind, Frank** (1864–1918)  German playwright. Wedekind differed dramatically to his romantic contemporaries. His plays were non-realist, almost symbolic works, and have caused many people to hail Wedekind as a very early forerunner of expressionism. Wedekind shocked audiences by exploring taboo issues in his plays, such as Spring Awakening (1891).

**Weigel, Helene** (1900–71) Austrian actress and theatre manger. Weigel was married to the great theatre practioner and playwright Bertolt Brecht. She led the Berliner Ensemble Company, which produced Brecht's plays.

**Weill, Kurt** (1900–1950) German composer whose work ranged from the music for Brecht's The Threepenny Opera to Broadway musicals. Weill was married to Lotte Lenya, who was a famous Brechtian actress.

**Weimar Court Theatre** Founded in 1784, in Weimar town, Germany. In 1791 Goethe was appointed artistic director. The company performed plays by Goethe, Schiller, Lessing, Shakespeare, Calderon and Voltaire.

**Weiss, Peter** (1916–82) German dramatist, heavily inspired by the two contrasting forces of both Brecht's political theatre and the surrealism of Artaud. Weiss' most famous play is Marat/Sade (1964). Other works include The Investigation (1965), The Song of the Lusitanian Bogey (1967) and Vietnam Discourse (1968), which all portray his revolutionary Marxist stance.

**Welfare State International** British Theatre Company Founded in 1968, recognised for its high energy and bright festival-like atmosphere, which encourages input from the local community. Often grand-scale effects such as fireworks accompany the dramatic action and gigantic puppets are used throughout their performances. www.welfare-state.org

**Wertenbaker, Timberlake** (1956– ) Anglo-American dramatist. Resident writer at the Royal Court Theatre, 1984–5. Her plays include Case to Answer, Abel's Sister, The Grace of Mary Traverse and Our Country's Good.

**Wesker, Arnold** (1932– ) British dramatist, poet and author. Wesker's first plays, Chicken Soup with Barley (1958), Roots (1959) and I'm Talking about Jerusalem (1960), strongly voiced his communist attitude. Wesker's working-class plays The Kitchen (1959) and Chips with Everything (1962) saw a distinct break away from naturalism. His most recent plays have been epic large-scale productions, which centre around major world themes. These include The Wedding Feast (1974), The Journalists (1975) and The Merchant (1976). He has explored opera with his adaptation of his play Caritas in 1991 and The Kitchen which premiered in Tokyo in 2000. www.arnoldwesker.com

**Wigman, Mary** (1886–1973). Dancer, choreographer and teacher. Wigman trained at the School of Rhythmic Gymnastics and later in her career with Rudolf Laban and Jaques Dalcroze. The school that she set up in Dresden in 1920 was at the forefront of the development of modern dance and she played a pivotal role in the birth of expressionist dance.

**Williams, Tennessee** (1911–83) Highly influential American playwright. Williams wrote his first play, The Glass Menagerie, in 1945. His most highly acclaimed play is the classic drama A Streetcar Named Desire (1947). Other well-known works include Cat on a Hot Tin Roof (1955), Orpheus Descending (1957) and Sweet Bird of Youth (1959). www.kirjasto.sci.fi/williams.htm

**Wilson, Robert** (1941– ) American director. Wilson worked extensively with brain-damaged children and by studying the difficulty of perspective in autistic children he created performance pieces such as A Letter to Queen Victoria (1974). Wilson's productions are 'epic' in terms of their grand-scale lighting and scenery and his drawings, furniture designs and installations have been exhibited in museums and galleries. During the 1980s Wilson worked solely in Europe gaining success with productions including The Man in the Raincoat (1981), Great Day in the Morning (1982) and The Civil Wars (1983). More recently he created a new production based on an Indonesian poem entitled I La Galigo at the Lincoln Center Festival in 2005. www.robertwilson.com

**Wycherley, William** (1641–1715)  English playwright. Wycherley had few successes, but is renowned as a satirical genius for his plays The Country Wife (1675) and Plain Dealer (1676).

**Yeats, William Butler** (1865–1939)  Irish playwright and poet. Yeats' verse drama was expressed in the form of music accompanied by dance. Early plays include The Countess Cathleen (1899) and The King's Threshold (1903). In 1904 Yeats part founded and became manager of the Abbey Theatre, which encouraged and introduced new writing talent into the theatre. Yeats' later plays were heavily symbolist. They include At the Hawk's Well (1916) The Dreaming of the Bones (1931) and Purgatory (1938). www.yeats-sligo.com

**Zola, Émile** (1840–1902)  French novelist and playwright. Zola was the leading innovator of naturalism. His plays include Therese Raquin (1873). They contain believable characters which have a personal psychology. This approach broke away from the two-dimensional characters of melodrama. Zola's ideas were the main inspiration for Antoine's Theatre Libre, and later Stanislavski's Method and Moscow Art Theatre. www.kirjasto.sci.fi/ezola.htm

# Appendix 2: Theatre timeline

In the charts that follow we have created a timeline from 600BC to AD1910. This timeline maps out the major developments in Western theatre as well as the intoduction of major non-European performance traditions. The majority of references to non-European traditions are to be found towards the beginning of our timeline. This is because many of these traditions, which are still alive and regularly performed, have changed less radically over time than the European traditions.

The timeline is divided into historical artistic periods from the *Classical* to *Realism* and *Naturalism*. **These period headings are only a very rough guide to the diversity of work to be found in any one period.** In the period of late romanticism (1800–1850), for instance, there were already artists working in ways that would become associated with the later periods of *Realism and Naturalism*. You may want to turn to the discussion of periods, styles and genres in the Chapter 1 to help guide your reading of these charts.

We do not intend you to try and go through all that is in these charts. They are, perhaps, best used when you want to place a play or practitioner in a historical context. If you are studying *Hedda Gabler*, for instance, and know that it was written in 1890, you can look at what else was happening in this period of *Realism* and *Naturalism* from 1850 to 1910. You can also look at the earlier work of *Ibsen, Brand*, written in 1865, in the context of the period of late *Romanticism*, 1800–1850. In each period we have given the titles of key play texts of the time so that you can read other works belonging to the period you are interested in. It is also important to remember that theatre doesn't exist in a vacuum. You can learn about the social and historical context of a play, playwright or practitioner through other artworks of the period – paintings, music, literature – and from reading about social, philosophical and political ideas of the period.

This brief history gives you a 'thumbnail' sketch of different periods in theatre history. You may want to flesh out what is here by doing your own research and sharing it with the rest of the group. You could:

- Take a period and research it more fully by looking at one of the plays that are mentioned as an example of the period and by using history books or a CD-ROM like Encarta to give a presentation on the period to the group. Alternatively, you might do an exchange with the History A level group. They can fill you in on the most important events and ideas of a period and you can give them a presentation on the theatre of the time. You might also do an exchange with groups doing other arts subjects.

- Take a genre and/or performance tradition and research it further. Look at dictionary definitions for example. A powerful way of getting information and illustrations is to use the search engine on your Internet browser. Try typing in 'Kabuki, pictures' for instance, and see what you can find. All of the major practitioners, periods and genres will have web pages out there in cyberspace! We have included a **webliography** in Appendix 3 to get you started. Use this information to do a class presentation including visuals where appropriate.

## NON-EUROPEAN THEATRE

The birth of Sanscrit drama in India based on episodes from the Hindu legends of the *Mahabharata* and the *Ramayana*. The *Natyasastra* (a treatise on theatre) is the first and most detailed account of the theory and practice of performance (rather than playwriting) written in the ancient world.

Classic Sanscrit plays of the period include Sudraka's *The Little Clay Cart* and Kalidasa's *Sakuntala*, which are both love stories borrowed from the *Mahabharata*.

## EUROPEAN THEATRE

### Classical

The 'golden' age of Greek theatre and the development of the classic genres of *comedy* and *tragedy*. The Greeks also developed the *satyr play*, which was performed after a *tragedy*. The *satyr plays* were more informal, often crude, with phallic imagery. The plays satirised, or were parodies of, myths, legends, historical heroes and even the *tragedies* that would have been performed before the *satyr play*. *Satyr plays* combined songs, dances and sketches and laid the basis for the later development of both modern *farce* and *burlesque*.

The Roman theatre was particularly influenced by the *satyr plays* as well as by Greek *tragedy* and literary *comedies*. The Romans developed new forms of theatre which are still popular today. These forms include:

- *Mime*: vulgar, often improvised episodes performed without words by unmasked actors.
- *Farce*: masked clowns in improvised slapstick routines based on simple plots; would later emerge again in the form of *Commedia dell'Arte*.
- *Pantomime*: a single masked dancer miming to a song performed by the chorus. The dancer would change masks as new characters were introduced.
- *Spectacles*: the Romans were very fond of lavish spectacles including gladiatorial contests and mock sea-battles enacted in flooded amphitheatres. In 692 AD the Roman Church forbade any more theatrical performances thus ending the European Classical period.

**600BC–600AD**

## EUROPEAN THEATRE

### Medieval

At first, certain parts of the Catholic mass were enacted in church, particularly in the Easter liturgy. These enactments were developed in the monasteries and later spread to other churches. The 'plays' were performed by the community in Latin.

Three principle forms of drama developed from the liturgical dramas:

- *Mystery plays*: based on episodes from the Bible.
- *Miracle plays*: based on the lives and deaths of saints and martyrs.
- *Morality plays*: in which virtues like goodness and truth and vices like greed and sloth became characters in simple 'good triumphs over evil' stories. The plays became increasingly political and appealed to the socially-oppressed peasant class. The *morality plays* influenced subsequent genres such as *melodrama* and *Brecht's Lehrstücke*, or learning plays.

*Mummers' plays* were also popular. These plays were performed by local groups of amateurs in disguise on special occasions such as Christmas and would include songs, folk and sword dances and a ritual drama often involving St. George. The tradition of *mummers* was revived in Victorian times and can still be seen in some rural areas at Christmas.

Two German nuns, *Hroswitha* and *Hildegard*, revived the art of playwrighting, which had disappeared in the West since the Roman writers *Terence* and *Plautus*. Their plays followed the models of *miracle* and *morality plays*.

**600–1500**

## NON-EUROPEAN THEATRE

The birth of drama in China when music, dance and storytelling became woven into single performances played in a circle marked by chalk.

*Noh* drama develops in Japan. Masked and unmasked male actors used highly-stylised costumes and gestures to tell simple stories of ghosts, greed and revenge. Although the origins of *Noh* are in simple peasant performances, it developed into an aristocratic form of theatre. There was a more comical and satirical form of *Noh* called *Kyogen*, which played to a wider audience. The *non-realist* and *representational* style of both performances would appeal to twentieth-century European practitioners trying to escape the dominance of *realism*.

The 'Golden Age' of *Khmer* dance-dramas in S.E. Asia. These dance-dramas were developed from harvest and thanksgiving rituals into elaborate masked performances. Both male and female dancers wore richly patterned and embroidered costumes. The movements of the dancers and the patterns their feet make on the stage all have special meanings. The movements were based on the movement of puppets in the earlier *shadow plays*. These dance-dramas are still performed today and the performance style hasn't changed over the last 500 years.

The development of *Alarinjo* theatre in the Oyo Yoruba empire in what is now known as Nigeria. This form of travelling, storytelling theatre using elaborate costumes and masks evolved out of the *egungun* masquerades of dancers, masked performers, drummers and large-scale puppets. The *Ozidi* saga is still performed. It takes six years to prepare and three days and nights to perform.

The Balinese *Gumbuh* form develops and becomes the traditional source for subsequent Balinese performance genres, such as *topeng* and *legong*. The plays, based on Japanese legends, were performed in temple courtyards, and a performance would last all day or night. The performance mixed stylised costumes and dance, *clowning* and music. The *Gumbuh* would have a profound effect on Antonin *Artaud's Theatre of Cruelty*.

## NON-EUROPEAN THEATRE

The development of *Kabuki* in Japan as a popular form of romance or *melodrama*. Soon after its introduction women performers were banned. There is much action, costume-changing and elaborate scenery. The highly-stylised movements of the actors are based on a form of puppet theatre called *Banraku* used by Japanese *shamen* for ritual purposes. *Banraku* also continued to flourish as entertainment.

## EUROPEAN THEATRE

### Renaissance

The Golden Age of English drama. Elizabeth I banned the performance of *morality plays*, which had begun to comment on and criticise the monarchy and the unjust laws of the land. The travelling groups of actors who performed the plays were persecuted and executed when caught. The new secular theatre that developed in London mixed new humanist ideas with elements of the old *morality plays* (e.g. Christopher Marlowe's *Dr Faustus*). Ben Jonson wrote his savagely biting comedies during this period, including *Volpone*.

The plays of *Shakespeare* dominate the Renaissance period in England, but *revenge tragedy* was also popularised by writers such as **Tourneur, Webster, Middleton** and **Shirley**. As a genre, the plays were based on the Greek *tragedy* but followed the model for *tragedy* established by the Roman theorist **Seneca**. The plays often began with the appearance of a ghost to the main character who would ask for vengeance. The audience is placed on the side of the avenger, and the ensuing story is often graphically violent. The story of *Hamlet* follows this model.

The Roman's fondness for elaborate spectacles was revived in the English court *masques*. With some of their origins in the *mummers' plays* of medieval times, these were hugely expensive, lavish and elaborate forms of ritual entertainment, or pageants, often performed to observe Twelfth Night, Christmas and Midsummer as well as to impress foreign dignitaries and important guests at court. Writers like Ben Jonson collaborated with architects like Inigo **Jones**. *Masques* were often participatory and combined *mime*, *music*, *dance* and *visual* effects.

The development of *Commedia dell'Arte* in Italy which kept alive the popular travelling theatre tradition in Europe. This improvised form was based on simple scenarios and *stock characters*. The professional actors would specialise in a particular character and develop skilful, physical juggling or slapstick *lazzi* or tricks to amuse the audience. The plays would be built around the same *stock characters* such as *Pantalone, Arlechino* and *Columbino* and be interspersed with the *lazzi*. The hero and heroine characters were unmasked, whilst the middle-class and servant characters (*zanni*) wore caricature masks. The *Commedia dell'Arte* has had an important effect on European *non-realist* theatre, particularly in continental Europe. The Italian writer/performer Dario Fo is a modern exponent of a political form of the *Commedia dell'Arte*.

The 'golden age' of Spanish drama with prolific writers such as *Lope De Vega* and *Pedro Calderón de la Barca*. *Lope De Vega* devised a formula for writing hugely popular, action-orientated plays enjoyed by all classes. His masterpiece, *Fuenteovejuna*, foreshadowed the call for greater social justice in the *naturalist* plays of T.W. Robertson and George Bernard Shaw in the late nineteenth/early twentieth century.

**1500–1650**

| | EUROPEAN THEATRE | NON-EUROPEAN THEATRE |
|---|---|---|
| **1650–1700** | **Baroque**<br><br>French *neo-classical* theatre dominated European performance. This genre revived the strict observation of the classical rules of *tragedy* established by *Aristotle* and *Seneca* (e.g. the unities of time, place and action). *Corneille's Le Cid* is a popular example of the genre and later *Racine*, while observing the classical laws, would begin to allow more flexibility into his play structures (e.g. *Phèdre*). Soon after, the great French playwright *Molière* would further flex the classical rules by introducing elements of *Commedia dell'Arte* into his work as well as new conventions such as indoor settings for his plays. *Neo-classicism* in Italy led to the development of *opera*.<br><br>The Puritans under Oliver Cromwell had banned theatre of any kind. After Charles II was 'restored' to the throne, the brief but important period of *Restoration* drama flourished. This genre was based on the *neo-classical* theatre of the French court at Versailles where Charles had spent his exile, but the English version was less lofty and more decadent! Women were allowed on stage for the first time and this often became an excuse for raunchy and titillating dramas based on the manners of the court, and featuring licentiousness, adultery and cuckoldry. The dramas were based on the highly-developed wit and banter of the aristocratic class. Playwrights of this period included William **Wycherley** and William **Congreve**. This short period marked the end of the dominance of the aristocracy both in society and in the theatre. The aristocratic comedies of this period would be challenged and replaced by the *sentimental comedies* and *domestic tragedies* which were the staple of the middle-class commercial theatre in the next century.<br><br>**Aphra Behn,** the first English woman playwright, wrote satires, farce, operas and spectacles based on the *Commedia dell'Arte. Behn* had a colourful life; she was born in Surinam, the setting for her play *Oroonoko,* employed as a spy and imprisoned for debt. | *Kathakali* developed as a major Hindu drama form in the early part of this period. Actor training is a long and arduous process which takes as long as ten years to complete. Stress is placed on eye and facial exercises and on memorising 600 different hand movements. Like the other Hindu performance traditions, *Kathakali* is still popular today, and had a major influence on twentieth-century practitioners such as *Jerzy Grotowski* and *Eugenio Barba.* |

## NON-EUROPEAN THEATRE

The first theatre in America was built in Williamsburg, Virginia, in 1723, despite the vehement opposition of Puritans like William Penn. The first professional company in America was the *London Company of Comedians*, later renamed the American Company, under the leadership of the Englishman Lewis Hallam.

## EUROPEAN THEATRE

### Late baroque/early romanticism

The Golden Age of English acting for both male and female actors such as David *Garrick*, Sarah **Siddons**, John *Kemble*, Edmund *Kean* and Anne **Oldfield**. Many of these actors' reputations were based on playing Shakespeare's characters. *Garrick* inaugurated the glorification of Stratford-upon-Avon as Shakespeare's birthplace in 1769. Theatre was very popular during this period and some theatres in London, such as *Drury Lane*, had a capacity of 3,000. This period also saw the development of provincial theatres in which touring *stock companies* would perform from their repertory of plays. From this period the English have laid claim to the art of acting. It was during this period that the social status of actors began to rise – *Garrick* died a rich man with a state funeral at Westminster Abbey.

*Ballad-operas* were a popular new genre which had an appeal to all classes. *Ballad-operas*, like John **Gay**'s *The Beggar's Opera*, satirised, or parodied, the Italian operas which were popular at the time. They mixed popular songs and melodies together with action-orientated plots, which often poked fun at the government and the establishment. The popularity and satirical nature of this genre led to new censorship laws in 1743 that gave the Lord Chamberlain sweeping powers to approve and ban plays. These laws existed until 1968. The form and popularity of the *ballad-operas* led to the development of *burlesque* as a popular form of working-class entertainment in America. *Brecht* paid tribute to this early genre of a popular theatre, which offered social comment and criticism, in his reworking of *The Beggar's opera* which he retitled *The Threepenny Opera*. Despite the popularity of the *ballad-operas* and the huge audiences that turned out for the great actors of the period, the theatre became an increasingly middle-class pastime. This audience liked *sentimental comedies* like Sir Richard **Steele**'s *The Funeral* and Richard *Sheridan*'s *The School for Scandal*. In these comedies, evil behaviour was seen as the result of bad examples (friends, family, and environment) but righteousness could be achieved through moral instruction and good examples. The rewards of good behaviour were money, titles, property and social status! *Domestic tragedies* were also popular with the middle-class audience; these *tragedies* also confirmed the middle-class view of the world but George **Lillo** would be the first playwright to base his main characters on non-aristocratic, ordinary people in plays like *The London Merchant*. These two new genres of middle, class theatre laid the ground both for *realism* and *melodrama*. In the foreword to *She Stoops to Conquer*, the Irish playwright, Oliver **Goldsmith** attacked the sentimentality of the audience and established through this play what he called *laughing comedy* which was a harder edged,

**1700–1800**

| EUROPEAN THEATRE | NON-EUROPEAN THEATRE |
|---|---|
| **Late Romanticism**<br><br>The turn of the century saw the heyday of *romanticism*, which was an artistic movement based on the philosophical ideas of *Kant and Rousseau* (and later of *Nietzche* and *Schopenhauer*). The romantic artist was judged according to the uniqueness of their personal vision and personality rather than for their technical craft. The flamboyant and colourful Lord **Byron** was a classic example of the romantic artist. He was famously described as 'mad, bad and dangerous to know'! *Romanticism* in theatre reacted against the constraints of *neo-classicism* and was often based on the representation of the heroic individual's struggle to maintain lofty ideals and virtues in an imperfect and corrupt world. The themes of *romanticism* included nature, the oppression of the poor, liberty and nationalism, the exotic and the heroic rebel. *Shakespeare* was the ideal model for the romantic playwright. The plays often dealt with extreme experiences like suicide, infanticide and incest. The most accomplished romantic playwrights were the Germans *Goethe* and *Schiller* and others in the *Sturm und Drang* (storm and stress) movement. In literature, *Coleridge, Shelley, Keats, William Blake* and *Sir Walter Scott* all shared similar ideas and ideals. The romantic movement would have a great influence on the *post-realist* theatres of the twentieth century (e.g. *Brecht's epic theatre*) and is sometimes credited as the birthplace of the modern *avant-garde* tradition in theatre.<br><br>The most commercially - successful genre of this period was melodrama. *Melodramas* were a contemporary version of the old *morality plays*, which substituted the morality of the new, powerful and affluent middle classes for religious morality. A *melodrama* exploits sensational action at the expense of serious thought and character and often ends in a spectacular conflict between 'good' and 'evil' in which 'good' (or at least the middle class's idea of good) always triumphs. *Melodramas* often used spectacular scenery, songs and 'cliff-hanger' curtain scenes in order to heighten the audience's emotional response. In depicting ordinary bourgeois life and settings, the *melodramas* formed the basis for *realism* in the next period. Famous examples include: Dion **Boucicault**'s *The Corsican Brothers* and Thomas **Holcroft**'s *A Tale of Mystery*. Later popular *melodramas* would include *Maria Marten, Murder in the Barn* and *Sweeney Todd*. A more sophisticated form of *melodrama* is to be found in plays that combine elements of both *melodrama* and *realism* like T.W. *Robertson's Caste*. | The *Peking Opera* was established in the early 1800s. The major emphasis was on the performance of the highly-trained and athletic actors. Males played all parts. Sets and props were minimal, but the costumes were highly elaborate and stylised. The *Peking Opera* would have an influence on *Brecht* and *Brook*. |

**1800–1850**

| | 1800–1850 | 1850–1910 |
|---|---|---|
| **NON-EUROPEAN THEATRE** | William Henry *Brown* founded the first African-American theatre in New York in 1821. The theatre and the company were persecuted by the police but managed to stage *The Drama of King Shotaway* in 1832 which dealt with the slaves' revolution in St Vincent and is an early example of *political theatre*. | |
| **EUROPEAN THEATRE** | Although his plays would not be performed for another three decades, the German playwright and militant revolutionary Georg *Büchner* foreshadowed *naturalism* in a series of plays written in this period including *Danton's Death* and *Woyzeck*. In these plays he expressed his sympathy for the socially downtrodden and explored, as the *naturalists* would also, the relationship between social class and environment. | **Realism and naturalism**<br><br>Henrik *Ibsen* reacted against both *romanticism* and *melodrama* by writing plays that were concerned with ordinary lives in ordinary settings, and which used everyday speech rather than verse. His plays sought to offer the 'illusion of reality', or *realism* on the stage; a 'slice of life' as we would say today. He is often referred to as the 'father of modern drama' because he was the first *realist* playwright of the modern age and his influence still dominates the stage and screen of today. *Ibsen* wrote his plays for a middle-class audience, but he sought to question the constraints and hypocrisy of middle-class morality. Many of his plays were extremely radical and provocative both in terms of their content and structure. *A Doll's House*, for instance, which debated the role of women and women's emancipation, was deeply disturbing to audiences of the day. *Ibsen* also wrote romantic plays like *Peer Gynt* and symbolist plays like *When We Dead Awaken*.<br><br>The new emphasis on realistic settings, characterisation and acting led to major developments in directing, acting and scene design. The *Meiningen Troupe* initiated long rehearsals, actor training and the use of new technologies in stage machinery and lighting. Later, *Antoine* would develop a new intimate, middle-class theatre based on the presentation of *realist* plays in very lifelike settings at the *Théâtre Libre* in Paris. Other 'little theatres' based on *Antoine*'s model would open all over Europe and specialise in offering *realism* to an educated middle-class audience. |

282

| EUROPEAN THEATRE | NON-EUROPEAN THEATRE |
|---|---|
| *Ibsen's realism* was strongly influenced by the behavioural theory of *naturalism*. This theory, popularised by Emile Zola, suggested that your heredity and environment determined everything in life. In this sense it was a theory of human behaviour based on Darwin's theories of evolution – the survival of the fittest. Your family and the environment in which you lived and were brought up predetermined your life. If you were born into poverty and a poor environment you were bound to end up poor and probably criminal! *Zola's Thérèse Raquin* became a model for *naturalism* as a theatrical style. Setting was the key feature of this style – the set was a part of the action, highly detailed and very realistic. The classics of *naturalism* include *Hauptmann's The Weavers, Gorky's The Lower Depths*, the mine-town plays of D.H. **Lawrence** and the sea plays of Eugene **O'Neill**.<br><br>Although this period is best remembered for the birth of modern *realism* and *naturalism*, there were other important movements developing too. The French producer Paul Fort opened the *Théâtre d'Art* to encourage a *non-naturalistic* style of theatre. Later, *Aurélien* **Lugné-Poë** would take over and rename the theatre as *Théâtre de l'Oeuvre* and establish *symbolism* in his direction of plays by *Maeterlinck* and *Hauptmann*. *Symbolist* plays challenged the claims to truth made by both *realism* and *naturalism*. The *symbolists* believed that truth lay beyond mere appearances; they aimed at producing a new drama that would reflect the mental or spiritual life rather than the crude world of the senses represented in *realism*.<br><br>The plays were strong on atmosphere and effects, the influence of supernatural powers and the occult, and often used *non-naturalistic* scenery painted by leading painters of the day such as *Bonnard* and *Toulouse-Lautrec*. The most renowned *symbolist* plays of this period were the Dream plays of *Strindberg*. These early experiments with *symbolism* would have a profound effect on the development of *post-realist* theatres in the twentieth century. Perhaps the biggest shock of this period was the performance of Alfred Jarry's *Ubu Roi*, which was a crude, subversive attack on both *realism* and *symbolism*. Its strong imagery, obscene words and actions and the use of puppet movements and gross make-up would have a profound influence on Antonin Artaud who named his theatre after *Jarry*. In turn both *Brecht* and *Brook* would also be influenced by this remarkable play. | |
| **1850–1910** | |

| NON-EUROPEAN THEATRE | EUROPEAN THEATRE |
|---|---|
| | The century closes with the playwrighting of Anton Chekhov and the establishment of the *Moscow Art Theatre (MAT)* under the leadership of Konstantin *Stanilavski* and Vladimir *Nemirovich-Danchenko*. *Chekhov* developed a new form of *tragi-comedy*, which pictures characters as average and helpless individuals suspended in a web of futile and absurd relationships. He combined the funny with the sad, the absurd and the terrifying, the pathetic and the grotesque. The audience was led to sympathise with the characters' pain whilst laughing at their folly. In order to play *Chekhov, Stanislavski* would develop his system of *psycho-realism* in acting, although later directors at the *MAT*, such as *Meyerhold* and Andrei Bely who directed *Chekhov* in a form of *symbolic-realism* - may have got closer to the complexities in *Chekhov*'s work which combines a highly, complex use of symbols in *realist settings.*<br><br>This was also the 'golden age' of technical theatre. New technological developments in stage machinery and lighting were exploited to both create more realistic illusions on stage and also to create fantastical atmospheric effects in *symbolist* pieces. Amongst the great technical innovators who began their work in this period were the theorist and designer, Gordon *Craig*, the lighting designer Adolphe ***Appia*** and the director Max *Reinhardt*. The development of cinema in the 1880s would both effect and transform the live theatre of the next century. |
| | **1850–1910** |

# Index